The drama of biblical eschatology is often a technical and complex subject that can be bewildering to the uninitiated. Dr. Paul Benware has offered a vital service by providing a compass to navigate the challenging prophetic terrain. Understanding End Times Prophecy *makes accessible an otherwise formidable and confusing subject.*

J. Gregory Behle
Professor of Christian Education
The Master's College, Sun Valley, Calif.

One of the finest works of its kind on the subject. Dr. Benware's revision will bring prophecy students up to speed on new eschatological issues that are now having a negative effect on the doctrines that deal with the return of the Lord.

Mal Couch
President
Tyndale Seminary, Fort Worth, Tex.

Millions have read the Left Behind books and have been inspired at this fictionalized rendering of the End Times. Bible prophecy must be understood from a biblical foundation of God's covenants and His character. Dr. Benware's book is a must for the student of God's Word to gain an understanding of the various views of the end times. Read this book with an open Bible and stand in awe of our God and His plan for mankind.

Brent D. Garrison
President
Southwestern College, Phoenix, Ariz.

Conflict, contradictions, and confusion: All words that describe current perspectives on end-times prophecy. Thankfully, Dr. Paul Benware has provided a map to guide us out of the interpretive chaos and into a sound understanding of what the Bible has to say about the future. Balanced, fair, and easy to understand, Dr. Benware has produced the single best text on eschatology.

Michael Rydelnik
Professor of Jewish Studies, Moody Bible Institute
Author of *Understanding the Arab-Israeli Conflict*

REVISED AND EXPANDED

UNDERSTANDING END TIMES Prophecy

A COMPREHENSIVE APPROACH

PAUL N. BENWARE

MOODY PUBLISHERS
CHICAGO

All Scripture quotations, unless otherwise indicated, are taken from the *New American Standard Bible*®, Copyright © 1960, 1962, 1963, 1968, 1971, 1972, 1973, 1975, 1977 by The Lockman Foundation. Used by permission.

Scripture quotations marked KJV are taken from the King James Version.

Cover Design: Smartt Guys
Cover Image: Corbis
Editor: Jim Vincent

Library of Congress Cataloging-in-Publication Data

Benware, Paul N., 1942-
    Understanding end times prophecy : a comprehensive approach / Paul N. Benware.
        p. cm.
    Includes bibliographical references and indexes.
    ISBN-13: 978-0-8024-9079-7
        1. Eschatology. I. Title.

BT821.3.B46 2006
236--dc22

2006007025

ISBN: 0-8024-9079-4
ISBN-13: 978-0-8024-9079-7

We hope you enjoy this book from Moody Publishers. Our goal is to provide high-quality, thought-provoking books and products that connect truth to your real needs and challenges. For more information on other books and products written and produced from a biblical perspective, go to www.moodypublishers.com or write to:

Moody Publishers
820 N. LaSalle Boulevard
Chicago, IL 60610

10

Printed in the United States of America

To all those who "love His appearing"
regardless of their eschatological position.

Contents

Part 3: Understanding the Coming Prophetic Events

Part 4: Understanding the Future of the Individual

Part 5: Appendices

LIST OF
Illustrations

Foreword

In the last several decades interest in prophecy seems to have been declining (except when some trouble erupts in the Middle East!). This has been detrimental to the well-being of the body of Christ. It has robbed us of an important perspective on life here and now, for the knowledge of the future should affect our actions in the present. To ignore what God says about the future cannot but cloud our insights into the present.

Why has this happened? Possibly because we are so content with our lot in this life that life hereafter has lost its attraction. Perhaps because churches are not offering prophetic teaching, since they perceive that people do not want it (and they have geared their programs to offer what people want, not what they need). Perhaps because our training institutions are devoting less time to it and doing it with less specificity. Perhaps because we do not want to face the reality that it is God who is in control, and He is bringing His plan to His preannounced conclusion in His time and way. Perhaps because we forget that prophecy consists not only of a scheme of future events but also includes teachings on resurrection, judgments, heaven, and eternal punishment, all of which subjects are eminently relevant.

Books that play up the spectacular come and go (and often need to be revised!). Basic books will always be needed, and this is such a one. This book builds on Dr. Benware's many years of teaching and preaching prophecy both at Moody Bible Institute and in churches he has pastored.

He knows from experience what needs to be taught and how to communicate it, and he does so clearly and thoroughly in this book.

Understanding End Times Prophecy will meet the need especially of Christians who want a clearer understanding of Bible prophecy. Hopefully it will be around for a long time to help many see not only what God is doing but also how they can best fit into His grand plan.

CHARLES C. RYRIE

THE CRITICAL IMPORTANCE OF Bible Prophecy

Bible prophecy has suffered badly at the hands of friends and enemies alike. Some have a strong bias against supernaturalism and predictive prophecy. Consequently, they have always viewed Bible prophecy as nothing more than the fanciful expression of a person's creative imagination or, sometimes, as history written under the guise of prophecy. People with such an attitude will never hold the prophetic Word in high esteem.

Yet, ironically, it is those who are strong believers in the prophetic Scriptures who perhaps have hurt it the most.

With newspapers in one hand and Zechariah (or another prophet) in the other, they make sensational declarations about what most likely will take place. And though they deny that they themselves are predicting soon-coming events, their pronouncements definitely leave that impression. After decades of such proclamations through sermons and writings, many believers have become apathetic about the prophecies of the Bible. The attitude exists among many of God's people that, "when Jesus and the end times come, they will come, but in the meantime I have to live my life in the real world." Such an attitude is wrong because Bible prophecy *is* for living in the real world right now.

The Scriptures testify to the critical importance of the doctrine of future things. For example, John prefaced the Revelation with the encouragement that the person who knows prophetic truths and orders his life according to those truths will live better *now*. He is one who is blessed by

God in the present (Rev. 1:3). Prophecy has been given by God to have a positive effect on us in our everyday lives. Consider these five benefits of knowing Bible prophecy.

1. BIBLE PROPHECY REMINDS US THAT GOD IS SOVEREIGN

In a world that seems chaotic and completely in the grip of wickedness, we need to remember that our God sovereignly controls it all. The prophet Isaiah declared that the powerful Creator of this world is not at all impressed with the supposedly great power of men and nations (Isa. 40:12–26). In fact, he asserted that God regards them as dust on the scales, as a drop from a bucket, as nothing and meaningless. Our God is the king of the universe, who reigns both now and in the future (Ps. 2:1–12). And although Satan is called the "god of this world," he does not dictate what happens on this planet but remains unquestionably under the sovereign authority of the Lord God (Matt. 28:18–20; Rev. 1:18).

The prophetic Word proclaims the power and sovereignty of God and reminds us that His sure purposes for the future will indeed come to pass. Neither people nor demons can thwart the plans of God Almighty. This great truth brings insight and comfort to the believer living in this hostile world.

2. BIBLE PROPHECY REMINDS US THAT GOD IS GOOD

Christians often live out their days in personal pain, with unresolved problems and in terribly unfair situations. Prophecy reminds us of the goodness of God by showing that He has written the final chapter on the human condition, which presently includes suffering and pain. If this life and this world were all there was, or the best we had coming, we might rightly challenge the idea that God is good and loving. Prophecy reveals with crystal clarity that the ending of the story is good for the children of God. And it is a kind of good that we really cannot fathom. The apostle Paul, who endured incredible adversity, suffering, and trouble proclaimed without any reservation, "I consider that the sufferings of this present time are not worthy to be compared with the glory that is to be revealed to us" (Rom. 8:18).

Bible prophecy is a precious area of doctrine to the people of God who are suffering. One author correctly observed that

> *what happens in our lives when we live as he directs is up to God. Sometimes the blessings come. Sometimes they don't. Only when we lose hope in formulas that guarantee success will we develop true hope in a God who can be trusted when life makes no sense, because one day he'll take us home.*[1]

Taking us home is the ultimate good. It is in the Father's house that His children will experience full and unhindered fellowship and be free from death, pain, and the other ravages of sin. Prophecy shouts to us that God is good.

3. BIBLE PROPHECY MOTIVATES US TO HOLY LIVING

Without the perspective of prophetic truth, living holy lives is far more difficult. The apostle John once wrote of the Lord Jesus' return for His children and noted that when that sudden, supernatural event takes place it will bring joy to some believers but shame to others (1 John 2:28). He then says that believers who really believe and gladly anticipate the Lord's coming will actively work at personal purity (3:3). Persuaded by these truths, they will simply not allow sin's presence in their lives and will be ready for the Lord's return. Believers who do not anticipate the Lord's return will have a greater tendency to allow sin to take up residence in their lives. That was Jesus' point when He said that it is the evil servant who says that his master's coming is delayed (Matt. 24:48–51). Jesus taught that this attitude, which denies the Lord's soon return, stimulates sinful behavior.

A believer who gets out of bed in the morning thinking *My Lord Jesus could return today* will probably not let sin take root in his life. But Christians who rarely, if ever, reflect on the realities of the future life, the Lord's coming, and the judgment seat of Christ are far more vulnerable to temptation and sin. And perhaps that explains something of the sin and apathy seen in much of the church today. Could it be that many are saying, "My Lord delays His coming"?

4. BIBLE PROPHECY HELPS US ESTABLISH PROPER PRIORITIES

What is really important to us? Many things have importance in our lives, and that is certainly legitimate. But the reality of future things sheds significant light on the great issues of life and helps us to see what is most important. The apostle Peter spoke of the coming end-time judgments in the Day of the Lord and then exhorted Christians to live in light of these ultimate realities (2 Peter 3:10–13).

Many of God's children seem to make decisions about what they will do with their lives with no conscious thought concerning the kingdom to come. Those, however, who do live with an awareness of the coming kingdom of God, with its joys and rewards, think differently regarding the use of their time, money, and resources. The goals and purposes of life are often altered by an understanding of future realities. Prophecy can assist us in making better choices in the present as it reminds us of things that have eternal value.

5. BIBLE PROPHECY GIVES US HOPE

If there is anyone who ought to live with a positive confidence in this world, it is the child of God. If there is anyone who ought not to live constantly under a blanket of defeat, fear, and depression, it is the child of God. Though none of us are exempt from painful, negative, even depressing situations, we ought not live in those conditions. A very real joy, pleasure, and glory are coming, and they are wrapped up in the "blessed hope" of Jesus' appearance (Titus 2:13). "Let us rejoice and be glad" (Rev. 19:7) are words for the future and remind us to have hope because the best is yet to come. Whereas the unbeliever may engage in wishful thinking about the future, the believer can look ahead with a confident expectation that God will accomplish everything that He has promised to do.

Does this doctrinal area of Bible prophecy make a difference? Yes, emphatically yes! God wants us to know many truths about what is going to take place in the future, and He wants those truths to change us right now in the present. He desires that prophetic truth change the way we think, the way we behave, and the way we view Him. And though we will not come to complete understanding of each aspect of this doctrine, we have been given enough information and help in the person of the Holy Spirit who illuminates His truth to accomplish these changes.

PART ONE

Understanding
THE BASICS OF
Bible Prophecy

CHAPTER ONE

INTERPRETING
Bible Prophecy

E very Bible believer would acknowledge that God is the master communicator. Through the creation He has revealed His existence, wisdom, and power. Through the Scriptures He has revealed much of His Person, plans, and purposes. But if He is the master communicator, why do we often not understand what He is saying? Intelligent people regularly disagree on what God is communicating to mankind. They fail to agree on how the universe came into existence, on how the universe will come to an end, and on most points in between those two issues! The fault, of course, does not lie with God the communicator but with man the interpreter of God's messages. And there is probably no part of God's message that is subject to more disagreement and diversity than that of Bible prophecy. Therefore, it is important for us to spend some time discussing how to interpret the prophetic Scriptures before we investigate the specifics of those events yet to come.

AMID THE CONFUSION, SOME CLEAR TRUTHS

Many Christians view Bible prophecy with confusion or cynicism. Some of them are convinced that prophecy is so complicated that only those with special gifts of insight or intellect can make sense of intricate details, such as ten-horned beasts and locusts that resemble horses but have the faces of men. Others have been exposed to enough bizarre interpretations and failed predictions that they have retreated into "eschatological agnosticism," pleading ignorance on prophetic matters.

This is perhaps understandable for the person who once was totally persuaded that a certain prominent politician was the Antichrist or had several times waited for the rapture to take place on specifically announced days. But as we approach the subject of interpreting the prophetic Scriptures, we need to remember several things that the Bible has clearly said.

1. Prophecy Was Given by God to Be Understood.

The apostle John began the book of Revelation with the declaration that this book was "the Revelation of Jesus Christ" (Rev. 1:1); that is, it was an unveiling of truth about the future work of Jesus the King and Judge. The Lord has revealed prophetic truth so that we will be changed by it. This presupposes that truth can be understood. If the prophetic Word is important to the Lord, it ought to be important to us as well.

2. God Has Given Us Help in Understanding the Prophetic Word.

When we were born into the family of God, we were anointed by the Holy Spirit (1 John 2:20, 27), and this anointing gives us the capacity to understand the truth of God. Prior to our conversion we had darkened minds with no real capacity to understand messages from God. Now we not only have a new capacity to understand God's truth, but the Holy Spirit is committed to illuminating the truth of God so that we can understand it. The Spirit, who alone knows the mind of God, takes these matters and opens them to us (1 Cor. 2:11–13). If that is true, then no Christian can legitimately say that Bible prophecy is unintelligible and the exclusive domain of a few scholars.

3. God Has Given to Us His Scriptures.

The Scriptures given by God through writers are verbally inspired (2 Tim. 3:16; 2 Peter 1:19–21). The very words of Scripture are critical. Contrary to the view of some, God did not simply toss out an idea and have a human author develop the thought. The very words of all Scripture, including those prophetic portions, are significant and worthy of our time and attention.

This should motivate us to investigate Bible prophecy and do our best to understand this message that God has communicated to us: a message He clearly wants us to understand. As the apostle Peter put it, "We have the prophetic word made more sure, to which you do well to pay attention" (2 Peter 1:19).

FOUR PRINCIPLES FOR PROPER INTERPRETATION

With those realities in mind, here are four principles for sound interpretation of biblical prophecy.

1. Interpret the Prophetic Passage Literally.

Of all the rules for interpreting prophecy, this is the most important. But, when we speak of interpreting literally, what do we really mean, since it is obvious to everyone that many prophetic portions are loaded with symbols and figures of speech? We interpret literally when we approach the words of a Scripture passage in the same basic way that we would any other literature or any ordinary conversation.

For example, if I told you that I just saw three brown dogs in the alley, you would interpret that statement literally. You would not seek to find hidden meaning in my comment but would assume that I saw three (not five) brown (not black) dogs (not cats) in the alley (not in the park). Not to interpret literally in everyday life would render our communication confusing and fundamentally useless. And our approach to the prophetic Word is very similar.

> *The literal method of interpretation is that method that gives to each word the same exact basic meaning it would have in normal, ordinary, customary usage. . . . It is called the grammatical-historical method to emphasize . . . that the meaning is to be determined by both grammatical and historical considerations.*[1]

"To determine the normal and customary usages of Bible language," wrote Paul Tan, "it is necessary to consider the accepted rules of grammar and rhetoric, as well as the factual historical and cultural data of Bible times."[2]

Literal interpretation assumes that, since God wants His revelation understood by people, He based His revelatory communication on the normal rules of human communication.

Literal interpretation understands that in normal communication and in the Scriptures figures of speech are valuable as communication devices. Again, if I were to say to you, "I was sitting in the backyard the other evening, and there were millions of mosquitoes out there," you would immediately recognize "millions" as a figure of speech (in this case, a hyperbole), realizing that I did not count the mosquitoes but was simply saying that there were a large number of them. You would interpret my statement within the normal use of language. If a person declares, "I'm freezing!" we take that statement normally. We do not assume that their body temperature has dropped to 32 degrees but, rather, that they feel very cold. Literal interpretation is not, therefore, a rigid "letterism" or "mechanical understanding of language" that ignores symbols and figures of speech. In light of the many symbols and figures of speech in Bible prophecy, we need to further define the literal (normal/usual/customary) approach to interpretation.

Literal interpretation is to be the basic, primary way of approaching the texts of Bible prophecies. Generally speaking, literal interpretation is a system based on the grammatical-historical approach of hermeneutics. (*Hermeneutics* is the science of biblical interpretation. It sets forth the laws and principles that lead to the meaning of the Scripture text.) Whenever we come to a prophetic passage, our commitment must be to understand that passage according to the accepted laws of language and not to seek some mystical or figurative interpretation.

One author encourages the interpreter of Scripture to "commit [himself] to a starting point and that starting point is to understand a document the best one can in the context of the normal, usual, customary, traditional range of designation which includes ease of understanding."[3] For example, when God said to Abraham that He would give him and his descendants the land of Canaan for an everlasting possession and that He would be their God (Gen. 17:8), how should we approach that passage? Literal interpretation would see it as a promise of God regarding a relationship and a land area. Literal interpretation would take this statement at face value and not seek a mystical meaning, for there is nothing in the passage that would compel one to do so.

This general approach provides the foundation for true interpretation. However, it is not the whole story, as Elliott Johnson observes:

What we have discovered is that a normative principle must be a general principle, but a general principle cannot legislate a particular sense or senses. Rather a general principle can only specify general limits to a textual sense. Thus our definition of literal would be appropriately designated as a system of limits. This system specifies the general maxim . . . that any sort of text is consistently interpreted in its own context. As an example, "serpent" as a word normally means "animal" and only an animal. But this normal usage and sense does not legislate that "serpent" in Genesis 3:14 must mean merely an animal. On the other hand, a literal system begins with recognizing "serpent" as an animal. Then it looks to the immediate or extended contexts for other clues to the meaning. This serpent speaks (3:1–5), and speaks as the enemy of God. Thus in the literal system, this serpent is more than an animal; it is God's enemy. . . . The value of this literal system is that it specifies a normative role for the textual contexts in interpretation and a normative practice of interpretation. It thereby excludes ideas extrinsic to the text.[4]

It is essential, therefore, to have this literal mind-set as we approach the prophetic Word of God. Without it there is no reliable check on an interpretation, and the interpreter becomes the final authority. If in Genesis 17:8 the land of Canaan does not refer to a specific piece of real estate in the Middle East, to what does it refer? Can it refer to heaven or the church? Such ideas would come from outside the text of Genesis 17:8. But when such spiritualizing or allegorizing takes place, the interpretation is no longer grounded in fact, and the text becomes putty in the hand of the interpreter.

Our basic approach to God's prophetic Word, therefore, must be a literal one. Once inside this literal system, we deal with specific words and phrases. Should we take a particular word literally or symbolically? Sometimes it is easy to make such a choice.

When John 1:28 tells us that John the Baptist was baptizing at the Jordan River, we have no interpretive problem. When the next verse records the statement that Jesus is the "Lamb of God," we have no interpretive problem with that either. We immediately recognize that the word *lamb* is used in a figurative way to communicate truth about the real man Jesus of Nazareth. When Isaiah prophesied that "a shoot will spring from the stem of Jesse, and a branch from his roots will bear fruit" (Isa. 11:1), we are dealing with figurative expressions of a literal person—Jesus Christ. "It will thus be observed that the literalist does not deny the existence of figurative language. The literalist does, however, deny that such figures must be interpreted so as to destroy the literal truth intended through the employment of the figures. Literal truth is to be learned through the symbols."[5]

Symbols are valuable tools of communication. Symbols communicate truth concisely, and they communicate it graphically. In Revelation 11 the apostle John could have spent a great deal of time describing the spiritual and moral condition of Jerusalem. Instead, he called the city "Sodom and Egypt." Quickly and vividly he communicated a volume of truth that remains graphically fixed in our minds.

Symbols and figures of speech, then, represent something literal. It is the task of the interpreter to investigate this figurative language to discover what literal truth is there. But there will not always be agreement on some figures of speech:

> There may be discussion by literalists as to whether a given word or phrase is being used as a figure of speech, based on the context of a given passage. Some passages are quite naturally clearer than others and a consensus among interpreters develops, whereas other passages may find literal interpreters divided as to whether they should be understood as figures of speech. This is more a problem of application than of method.[6]

For example, in Revelation 2:10 the church at Smyrna is warned that they would have "tribulation [for] ten days." Does the "ten days" refer to a week and a half of intense trouble, or does it symbolize a brief period of time or perhaps ten periods of persecution? This church was literally headed for persecution, but whether or not the ten days is to be understood literally is a point of discussion among literalists.

In Revelation 8:8, John says that one-third of the sea became blood as a result of a judgment from God. Does a part of the ocean actually become real blood? Or should the blood be seen as representing some aspect of this judgment that is yet unclear? Bible students differ on the literalness of this verse. But such differences do not indicate some basic inconsistency in a literal approach. Rather, as noted above, the issue is a problem of application, not method. Because we have different backgrounds, training, and experiences, we will have differing viewpoints on specific details, such as whether the blood of Revelation 8:8 is literal or not. But all literalists will likely be in agreement that this verse is telling us of some terrible judgment to come. So even if they did not agree on the literalness of the blood, they would not leave the literal approach and spiritualize this prophecy, seeing it as a picture of religious delusion coming on the world (Lenski) or the invasion of the Roman Empire by the Vandals (Barnes).[7] These allegorical interpretations illustrate that, when the literal interpretation of prophecy is abandoned, there is a lessened accountability to the text itself.

Those (such as amillennialists) who resist this principle of literal interpretation adhere instead to the spiritualization of prophecy. A spiritual (or allegorical or mystical) approach treats the literal sense as secondary to a deeper, more spiritual meaning. Those who spiritualize prophecy work on the principle that these portions of the Bible have a hidden meaning. They assume that the literal approach obscures the real, deep meaning of the passage. However, abandoning the literal as the primary meaning is a terribly arbitrary way to approach the prophetic Scriptures. As Bernard Ramm observes, "The curse of the allegorical method is that it obscures the true meaning of the Word of God."[8] It should be added that most objectivity in biblical interpretation is lost, since one allegorical interpretation is as valid as another. Why should not Barnes's interpretation that the third trumpet judgment (in the Revelation 8 passage) refers to the Vandals' invasion be just as authoritative and valid as Lenski's idea that the third judgment speaks of a coming worldwide religious delusion?

Though conservative amillennialists faithfully use the literal approach of interpretation in most other doctrinal areas, they have chosen to approach prophetic passages with spiritualization. So, for instance, instead of seeing Jesus Christ ruling in the future over the nation of Israel on this present earth, they say His rule is a spiritual one in the hearts of those who belong to His church. This spiritualizing seems especially out of place when it is combined with a literal approach to a passage such as Luke 1:31–33.

In that passage, the angel Gabriel informed Mary that she, a virgin, was to have a son who would rule on David's throne over the nation of Israel. Amillennialists interpret the statement about the birth using the literal approach and arrive at the conclusion that Jesus was physically born of the virgin Mary. But they then spiritualize the second part of Gabriel's statement concerning the rule of Jesus, making Jesus' rule not over the "house of Jacob" on "David's throne" but over redeemed saints in the church of Jesus Christ. A consistent literal approach, letting language be language, will avoid such an inconsistent and somewhat arbitrary approach to the Scriptures. This example highlights the inherent contradiction of using two different systems of interpretation.

The first and great interpretive rule, then, is to interpret prophetic passages literally. "The literal system is necessary because of the nature of Scripture. First, Scripture is *sufficiently clear* in context to express what God promised to do. Second, Scripture is *sufficiently complete* in context to establish valid expectations of the future acts of God."[9] It is the literal approach to the Word of God that provides a solid, reasonable approach to interpreting the prophetic Scriptures.

2. Interpret by Comparing Prophecy with Prophecy.

God did not give all prophetic information to any individual prophet. Rather, through many authors over a period of centuries the prophetic picture developed and became more complete. Therefore, to gain a fuller understanding of a prophetic subject and to avoid erroneous conclusions, it is needful to compare prophecy with prophecy. The apostle Peter said that "no prophecy of Scripture is a matter of one's own interpretation" (2 Peter 1:20). Peter's point includes the idea that no prophecy found in Scripture is to be interpreted by itself but, rather, in reference to everything God has said on the subject.

The future millennial kingdom is spoken about in Revelation 20, where it is said to last for a thousand years. But we would be headed for serious error if we assumed that all God has said about this aspect of the kingdom is found in Revelation 20. The prophets of the Old Testament have spoken volumes on the subject of the millennial kingdom, and, in order to understand Revelation 20 correctly, it is essential to visit Isaiah, Daniel, Jeremiah, and others to learn what they have said.

If all we studied on the subject of the Antichrist was Daniel 7, we would not get a complete picture, for the apostles Paul and John have significant points to contribute. Since God is the author of the entire prophetic Scriptures, we must assume that no prophecy will contradict another. God is not the author of confusion and clearly will not contradict Himself as He sets forth things to come. When faced with difficulties, therefore, we need to remember this inherent unity of meaning in the Bible and keep in mind that difficulties are not contradictions. We must also assume that one passage may contribute to the understanding of the other, since God is the author of both.

Often New Testament authors will refer back to Old Testament prophecies. They do this for a variety of reasons, including to show that a prophecy has been fulfilled and to tie together a previously given prophecy with the one being given to the New Testament writer. Whereas the New Testament message could give a deeper or clearer understanding of the Old Testament passage, that Old Testament portion does explicitly or implicitly include the same message. For example, three times the prophet Daniel speaks of the "abomination of desolation." Daniel's prophecies give information about the timing of the event as well as some characteristics of it. But the Lord Jesus' statement in Matthew 24 is certainly valuable in clarifying a number of issues related to this phrase.

But an interpreter cannot disregard the statements of the Old Testament as if they are inferior to deeper, spiritual New Testament meanings. Passages such as Isaiah 2:2–4, which speak of a marvelous golden age to come on this present earth, must not be disregarded by means of spiritualization. Concerning the amillennial spiritualization of such Scriptures, one postmillennial writer observes that they leave "a whole continent of prophecies unexplained, many of which then become quite meaningless."[10] Old Testament prophecies must be allowed to speak. Their message will be enriched and enhanced by later New Testament prophecies but not negated or changed by them.

So, then, it is imperative that the interpreter of prophecy compare Scripture with Scripture. By so doing, a more complete and accurate picture is seen of what God is going to do and perhaps how and why He is going to do it.

3. Interpret in Light of Possible Time Intervals.

When the prophets proclaimed God's message, they frequently were unaware that there was going to be an interval of time between prophetic fulfillments. "In such passages, the sacred writer, as he foresaw these events in his day, viewed them in the distance of time like peaks of a mountain range, without realizing that valleys of time lay between them. This is true especially concerning events in the first and second advents of

Christ."[11] When a prophet placed several events side by side in his message, that did not necessarily mean that the fulfillment would occur at the same time or that one fulfillment would immediately follow the other.

For example, Zechariah spoke of the first advent of Christ, when He would come "endowed with salvation, humble, and mounted on a donkey" (9:9). This was fulfilled at the triumphal entry into Jerusalem. But without hesitation the prophet went on to say that Messiah would reign over all the earth (v. 10), which will not be fulfilled until His second coming. It is highly unlikely that Zechariah knew that the fulfillment of his two statements would be separated by several thousand years.

The same is true of other prophets. Isaiah spoke of Christ coming "to bring good news to the afflicted . . . to bind up the brokenhearted, to proclaim liberty to captives . . . to proclaim the favorable year of the Lord" (Isa. 61:1–2). Jesus Himself interpreted this passage in Luke 4:16–21, indicating that these words referred to His first-advent ministry. In fact, Jesus stopped His reading in the middle of a sentence and commented that those words were presently being fulfilled. But the Isaiah passage goes on to speak of "the day of vengeance of our God," which speaks of activities at His second advent. Did Isaiah imagine an interval of thousands of years between those two clauses? Probably not.

This telescoping phenomenon is found a number of times in the prophets and reveals gaps in prophetic fulfillment. A key passage that we will investigate later, Daniel 9:24–27, contains a gap that is critical to a proper interpretation of that prophecy. It is, of course, only in the progress of God's revelation that we can see such intervals of time between prophetic fulfillments.

4. Interpret Figurative Language Scripturally.

Communications research shows that we understand and retain far more information when we can *see* it along with hearing it or reading about it. Since the prophets did not include charts and graphs in their prophecies, and since they did not have PowerPoint, they had to rely on the language that they used. Though some did on occasion use props and act out their messages, language was still their primary tool. The use of symbols as a communication device became quite important to the message they were giving. As already mentioned, figures of speech and symbols represent something literal. In attempting to discover the meaning of these symbols, it is helpful to note three different interpretive categories of prophetic symbols: (1) the immediate context, (2) the larger context, and (3) the historical-cultural context.

First, we should consider the immediate context. Some symbols are interpreted in the text by the prophet himself. At other times an interpreting angel appears in the text to explain a particular symbol, or the Lord Himself reveals the meaning to the prophet.

In Revelation 17:1, the apostle John sees a "great harlot who sits on many waters." Some of this imagery is explained later in that chapter, when John is told by an angel that the "waters" represent the many peoples and nations of the earth (v. 15). In Ezekiel's famous vision of the "dry bones," the Lord reveals that the dry bones represent the entire nation of Israel (Ezek. 37:11). The explanation of this symbol has undoubtedly saved us from hours of endless debate and discussion on the subject.

Second, we should consider the larger context. A second category of prophetic symbols involves those whose meaning is suggested by other Scriptures outside of the immediate text. A large number of symbols and figures of speech have been used in one place in the Bible, then used in another place by another writer. It is no surprise to find Daniel, for example, using a symbol found in Isaiah, who wrote more than a century earlier. New Testament writers had the symbolic wealth of the Old Testament to draw on, and under the guidance of the Holy Spirit, the final author of the Old Testament, they employed many of these symbols. This is especially true of those symbols found in the New Testament book of Revelation where

> *a count of the significant allusions which are traceable both by verbal resemblance and by contextual connection to the Hebrew canon number three hundred and forty-eight. Of these approximately ninety-five are repeated, so that the actual number of different Old Testament passages that are mentioned are nearly two hundred and fifty, or an average of more than ten for each chapter in Revelation.*[12]

With statistics like that it becomes pretty clear that a knowledge of the Old Testament is essential to an understanding of the book of Revelation and crucial in keeping an interpreter from getting involved in prophetic speculation and excesses.

In Revelation 12:14, for example, the woman is given two wings of the great eagle to escape from the serpent. The chapter itself points to the woman representing the nation of Israel and the serpent being Satan. But what are the wings of the eagle? Does it mean that in the last days Israel will be rescued by an airlift? Probably not. The imagery of the eagle's wings is found in Exodus 19:4 and in Isaiah 40:28–31 and speaks of the care and deliverance of our powerful and loving God. Revelation 12:14 teaches that God will rescue His people in those last days just as He did at the time of the exodus out of Egypt. The passage reveals *what* God is going to do but not *how* He is going to do it.

Another example can be found in Revelation 11:3–4, where the text speaks of God's two witnesses who are "the two olive trees and the two lampstands that stand before the Lord of the earth." No interpretation of Revelation 11:4 can hope to be valid if it does not carefully investigate Zechariah 4, where that symbolism is found. Prophetic symbols, then, are not an invitation to let one's imagination run wild. The symbols found in Scripture and then used by other writers of Scripture do set parameters for interpretation. Symbols do not give an interpreter freedom to apply any meaning he wants to a text.

Third, we should consider the historical-cultural context. Some symbols are related to the historical-cultural times of the writer. Those symbols do not find meaning in other sections of Scripture but, rather, in the days of the writer himself. For example, the "white stone" found in Revelation 2:17 and the "pillar" in 3:12 come from the cultural context of John's day. To understand in a clearer way the message of the Lord in those sections, it would be helpful to learn the meaning of those symbols as they were understood in John's day.

SOUND PROPHETIC INTERPRETATION

Hopefully this brief discussion of some of the rules of prophetic interpretation has highlighted the importance of our hermeneutical principles. Without clear interpretive principles guiding us we will not arrive at clear interpretations. The prophetic Scriptures can be difficult because they deal with events that have not happened as yet. Prophecies that have been fulfilled completely have been fulfilled literally, and that gives us confidence to expect that those prophetic utterances that are not yet fulfilled (or completely fulfilled) will also end up being fulfilled literally. We believe that Jesus Christ will literally return to this earth and reign at His second coming because He literally came to this earth the first time, being born of the virgin Mary at Bethlehem.

As we study the prophetic word we must do so with personal diligence and with a conscious dependence on the Holy Spirit, the author and illuminator of the truth of God. When we do this we may well develop some strong convictions about Bible prophecy. It is not wrong to have firmly held beliefs about prophecy, even though some might suggest that strong convictions reveal narrowness of thinking. Strong convictions may well reveal clarity of thinking. But holding firmly to our own eschatological position does not give us license to personally and caustically attack fellow believers who adhere to differing positions. Unfortunately, anger and arrogance have accompanied eschatological discussions in the past and in the present. To question a position in light of Scripture is certainly legitimate. But to attack the one who holds that position, questioning his or her intelligence and character, is clearly a different matter. As we hold to our viewpoint, we need to reflect the Lord Jesus, who was full of grace *and* truth.

CHAPTER TWO

THE ABRAHAMIC

Covenant

Anyone who has put together a thousand-piece picture puzzle knows that you do not grab the nearest pieces and try to figure out where they belong. Even using the picture on the lid of the box, this approach would soon become overwhelming, not to mention frustrating. The most unskilled picture puzzle assembler knows that the fundamental law of picture puzzles is "Thou shalt put the edge pieces together first." When the edge pieces are all in place, a framework is established. At this point it is possible for all the other pieces to be put in their proper places, even though it may still be difficult to figure out where some of the individual pieces fit.

The same holds true for our "eschatological puzzle." There are many pieces, and they are scattered all over the Scriptures. Sometimes it is hard to figure out where any one piece fits. It is imperative that we do our best to put together the "edge pieces"—the framework—before we try to figure out where each piece goes. That framework for biblical prophecy is the biblical covenants.

When our understanding of the biblical covenants is in place, we are better able to put the other pieces together without "forcing them to fit." When we speak of the biblical covenants as being important to our understanding of prophecy, we are referring to the Abrahamic covenant, the Davidic covenant, the new covenant, and the Palestinian (or land) covenant. Other covenants are found in Scripture, but these are particularly important to end-times prophecy.

THE CONCEPT OF A COVENANT

In Old Testament times a covenant was an agreement between two parties that bound them together with common interests and responsibilities. Generally, these covenants were bilateral agreements where both parties were responsible for the fulfilling of the covenant. In the Old Testament, the Mosaic covenant given at Mount Sinai is an example of a bilateral, or conditional, covenant.

In contrast, an unconditional, or unilateral, covenant involved two parties, but the fulfillment of the covenant rested on only one party. God's covenant with Abraham fits into this category.

Covenants were very much a part of life in the culture of the ancient Near East, and this is reflected in the Scriptures. Covenants were made between individuals, as in the case of Abraham and Abimelech when they came to an agreement concerning the well at Beersheba (Gen. 21:22–34). Covenants were also commonly made between nations, and because of this fact the Lord expressly prohibited Israel from making covenant agreements with certain nations (Ex. 23:23–33). Covenants were serious and sacred matters, and the reputation of the covenant maker was at stake.

Covenants usually included blessings for the one who fulfilled his part of the agreement and curses upon the one who broke his oath. When God made a covenant with Abraham, therefore, it was not a strange or unusual event. It is true, of course, that one did not usually enter into a covenant with God Almighty. But Abraham and his descendants were thoroughly familiar with the idea of a covenant.

It should be noted here that we are not discussing what is known as "covenant theology." Covenant theology is a system that attempts to cover all of Scripture with the theological covenants of works, redemption, and grace. This viewpoint will be discussed later.

THE BASIC PROVISIONS OF THE ABRAHAMIC COVENANT

The record of the making of the covenant and the provisions of the covenant with Abraham are found in a number of places in the book of

Genesis (see 12:1–7; 13:14–17; 15:1–21; 17:1–27; 18:17–19; 22:15–18). This covenant was established between God and Abraham and his descendants Isaac and Jacob. In Genesis 17 the Lord declared to Abraham,

> *I will establish My covenant between Me and you and your descendants after you throughout their generations for an everlasting covenant, to be God to you and to your descendants after you. And I will give to you and to your descendants after you, the land of your sojournings, all the land of Canaan, for an everlasting possession; and I will be their God. . . . Sarah your wife shall bear you a son, and you shall call his name Isaac; and I will establish My covenant with him for an everlasting covenant for his descendants after him. (vv. 7–8, 19)*

There were three basic areas of provision made in the Abrahamic covenant. First, there were *personal* blessings for Abraham; second, there were blessings for Abraham's descendants, or *national* blessings; and third, there was *universal* blessing, which would include all people. In these ways, God promised to bless Abraham and to make his name great.

The *personal* blessings included the fact that not only would a great nation come from him but many nations would come from him and kings would come from his line. He was told that God would prosper him and give him the land of Canaan for an everlasting possession. The blessings given to Abraham's descendants (the *national* blessings) would come through Isaac and Jacob. Those blessings included the guarantee of national existence as well as the greatness of the nation, the land area of Canaan as an everlasting possession, and the continuation of the Abrahamic covenant as an everlasting covenant. The *universal* nature of the covenant focused on the reality that all nations would receive blessing through the physical descendants of Abraham.

Though the Abrahamic covenant was made with Abraham and his physical descendants, that did not mean that God was abandoning the Gentile nations. Great spiritual blessings have come through the Jewish people. God revealed Himself through the leaders and prophets of Israel. It is through Moses, the prophets, and others in Israel that the inspired Scriptures have come to us. But, of course, the greatest blessing of all has come through Jesus Christ, who in His death on the cross has made salvation available to people of all nations.

In all three of these areas of provision in the Abrahamic covenant there has been some fulfillment. And in all three areas there are unfulfilled promises. The fulfilled promises have been fulfilled in a literal way, and that leads to the conclusion that all the promises will have a literal fulfillment.

> *Those parts of the Abrahamic Covenant which have been fulfilled thus far have been fulfilled literally (in accordance with the historical-grammatical method of interpreting the Bible, not in accordance with the allegorical or spiritualizing method). This would seem to indicate that God intends every promise of that covenant to be fulfilled in that manner.*[1]

It would seem that God's method of fulfilling His promises would not change from literal to spiritual while the process of fulfillment is going on, and if such a change did take place it would be clearly revealed to those who were the participants in the covenant. This matter of fulfillment will be dealt with later.

THE NATURE OF THE ABRAHAMIC COVENANT

Probably the most significant issue related to the Abrahamic covenant has to do with its nature. Is it a conditional (bilateral) covenant or an unconditional (unilateral) covenant? How one answers that question determines the framework of one's prophetic studies.

If the Abrahamic covenant is conditional (its fulfillment dependent on Israel's continuing obedience to God), then a case can be made that national Israel has been set aside by her failures and disobedience and no longer can anticipate receiving the promises of the covenant. The blessings of the covenant are then shifted to the church of Jesus Christ for final and complete fulfillment. If, however, the Abrahamic covenant is an unconditional covenant (depending totally on God for fulfillment), then national Israel does have a future, since not all the promises of the covenant have been completely fulfilled.

Most all interpreters agree that the provisions of the Abrahamic covenant were not completely fulfilled when the Old Testament came to an end. Therefore, the issue is how God will fulfill them—literally to Israel or spiritually to the church.

A Conditional Covenant?

Some believe the covenant is conditional. One postmillennial writer, Loraine Boettner, clearly argues:

> *The mass of those who then called themselves Israelites ceased to be such for prophetic and covenant purposes, having forfeited their citizenship in the commonwealth of Israel by refusing to accept the Messiah, and that after this event all the privileges of the Abrahamic Covenant and all the promises of God belonged to the believing remnant, and to them only; which remnant was therefore and thereafter the true Israel and Judah, the Seed of Abraham, the Christian Church.... It may seem harsh to say that, "God is through with the Jews." But the fact of the matter is that He is through with them as a unified national group.*[2]

Because Boettner sees the covenant as conditional, he believes that national Israel has forfeited all claims to the covenant.

Those who see this covenant as conditional point to certain statements made in the Genesis passages that record the giving of the Abrahamic covenant:

> *Contrary to what some would have us believe, the Abrahamic covenant was not unconditional. Otherwise, why would God have said to Abraham, "As for you, you must keep my covenant, you and your descendants after you" (Gen. 17:9)? First God says what he will do ("As for me . . ." vv. 1–8); then he outlines what Abraham must do ("As for you . . ." vv. 9–14) to keep the covenant. . . . God demanded obedience of Abraham and his offspring in receiving and keeping his gracious offer. Elsewhere, it was also made clear that the promise of the land was conditional, based on continuing obedience.*[3]

This author, Joel Green, follows up his statement concerning the land with the observation that Leviticus 26:27–33 indicates that Israel's disobedience would remove them from the land and would lead to a denial of the blessings of the Abrahamic covenant.

Amillennial theologian Oswald T. Allis also believes that Israel's disobedience brought about the withdrawing of covenant promises from Israel:

It is true that, in the express terms of the covenant with Abraham, obedience is not stated as a condition. But that obedience was presupposed is clearly indicated by two facts. The one is that obedience is the precondition of blessing under all circumstances. . . . The second fact is that in the case of Abraham the duty of obedience is particularly stressed.[4]

Thus, Allis believes that the covenant with Abraham was clearly conditional.

He then refers to Genesis 22:18, where God said to Abraham, "And in your seed all the nations of the earth shall be blessed, because you have obeyed My voice." He also mentions God's words to Isaac in Genesis 26:4-5: "By your descendants all the nations of the earth shall be blessed; because Abraham obeyed Me and kept My charge."

Some have also seen a conditional element in two other passages: God's words in Genesis 17:1-2—"Walk before Me, and be blameless. I will establish My covenant between Me and you, and I will multiply you exceedingly"—and even an initial condition in the very first giving of the covenant in Genesis 12:1-3. These verses in Genesis 12 are seen as teaching that the receiving of the covenant blessings was conditioned on Abraham leaving his country and journeying to Canaan.

An Unconditional Covenant?

Do these statements teach that the Abrahamic covenant is a conditional covenant whose fulfillment depended on the faithful obedience of Abraham and his descendants? Initially it might appear that some conditions are being given by God in His various encounters with Abraham. However, an analysis of these and other passages of Scripture establishes the *unconditional* nature of this important covenant.

Genesis 12:1-3. These verses deal with the initial giving of the Abrahamic covenant. Is an implicit condition found in these verses? Some who believe in the unconditional nature of the Abrahamic covenant do think that Abraham had to leave his homeland in Ur of the Chaldees and go to the land of Canaan for the covenant to be fulfilled. But once he did that the covenant had no further conditions.

It is important to observe the relation of obedience to this covenant program. Whether God would institute a covenant program with Abraham or not depended upon Abraham's act of obedience in leaving the land [of Ur]. When once this act was accomplished, and Abraham did obey God, God instituted an irrevocable, unconditional program.[5]

Except for the original condition of leaving his homeland and going to the promised land, the covenant is made with no conditions whatever. It is rather a prophetic declaration of God of what will certainly come to pass.[6]

This viewpoint properly emphasizes the unconditional nature of this covenant and puts the interpreter on solid ground as the rest of the prophetic Scriptures are approached.

Another view that also correctly emphasizes the unconditional character of the Abrahamic covenant holds that God's statement to Abraham to "go forth from your country" (Gen. 12:1) is not a condition but an invitation.

This imperative is followed by two imperfects and then a series of cohortative imperfects in verses 2–3. But does a command amount to a formal condition on the divine intention to bless? . . . The accent of the passage was on the cohortatives which emphasize intentionality rather than obligation. . . . The summons to "go," then, was an invitation to receive the gift of promise by faith.[7]

A third view is that Genesis 12:1–3 contains only the first of several conditions given to Abraham. It is said that during his lifetime Abraham did, in fact, fulfill all the conditions given by God, so God ratified the covenant by divine oath (in Genesis 15 and 22), thus making it unconditional from that point onward: "Thus by the conclusion of the Abraham narrative God's covenant promises to Abraham achieve the level of an oath and are therefore unconditional in nature and certain of fulfillment. Subsequent OT references to the oath assume its unconditionality."[8]

The first giving of the Abrahamic covenant in Genesis 12 may have had an implicit condition in it, which Abraham met by going to Canaan. We, of course, do not know what God would have done if Abraham had chosen to stay in Ur of the Chaldees. It is possible that our creative God could have worked in such a way that the covenant would still have been fulfilled by God Himself. But it did not happen that way, so we simply do not know what might have been. After Abraham did obediently arrive in Canaan, however, and over the next few years as the covenant was repeated and enlarged, no conditions were attached to it.

Genesis 17:1–2; 22:16–18; 26:3–5. In establishing the unconditional nature of this covenant, we must address the issue of the statements found in Genesis 17, 22, and 26, for these passages seem to add conditions to the covenant. Renald Showers makes an important observation about these three portions of Scripture:

> *These statements were made years after God formally established the covenant with Abraham in Genesis 15. When the covenant was formally established, God stated no conditions. According to Galatians 3:15, once a covenant has been established no conditions are added to it. Thus, to say that the statements of Genesis 17:1–2, 22:16–18, and 26:3–5 indicate that the Abrahamic Covenant is conditional is to say that God added conditions after the covenant was established and that God thereby violated the principle of Galatians 3:15.*[9]

Walter Kaiser notes that the grammar of Genesis 17:1–2 and 12:2–3 are very similar and should be handled the same way. In other words, the emphasis of Genesis 17 is on God's intention to bless (as it was in chapter 12), not on some obligation being required of Abraham.[10] Regarding the Genesis 22 and 26 passages, he concludes that the issue in these chapters focuses not on new conditions but on the potential for greater personal blessing to Abraham.

> *In our judgment, the conditionality was not attached to the promise but only to the participants who would benefit from these abiding promises. If the condition of faith was not evident, then the patriarch would become a mere transmitter of the blessing without personally inheriting any of its gifts directly. . . . Certainly the promise was not initiated in either chapter 22 or 26; that had long ago been settled. But each chapter did have a sensitive moment of testing or transition.*[11]

Some have seen a condition in Genesis 17, where the rite of circumcision was given to Abraham. However, circumcision was not given as a condition to the covenant (which had been in existence for years) but as a sign of the covenant. Those who refused to be circumcised would lose out on the blessings of the covenant, but they would not terminate the nation's covenant relationship with God.

Because there simply are no conditions added to this covenant, some might conclude that, since God was guaranteeing the fulfillment of the Abrahamic covenant, it did not make any difference what Abraham, Isaac, Jacob, or any of their descendants did. But that would not be accurate. If any involved in the covenant relationship chose not to "walk before the Lord," they would lose out on the benefits and blessings of the covenant. That is a critical distinction to keep in mind. Sin and disobedience would cause the loss of the covenant blessings but would never cancel the covenant. The blessings of the covenant were indeed conditioned on the obedience of an individual. But the complete and final fulfillment of the Abrahamic covenant depends on God alone. He intends to fulfill this covenant even if His people Israel are not faithful and obedient.

Those of us who believe in the eternal security of the believer see a parallel between ourselves and God's covenant relationship with Israel. As saved people, we look forward to the day when we will be glorified and our salvation is finalized. God has promised to bring His children to glory—that is His stated intention (Romans 8). Can my disobedience negate God's stated intention? The answer is no. Does it make any difference if I am obedient or disobedient? All of us would insist that it makes a great difference. Present blessing, usefulness in service, and future reward depend on obedience, but the final completion of our salvation does not.

The same holds true for the nation of Israel under the Abrahamic covenant. Although their failure would never negate the covenant, it would affect their own blessing and could even temporarily hinder the program of God. For example, through their willful disobedience at Kadesh-barnea (Numbers 14), the purpose of God to bring them into the land of Canaan was delayed some forty years. But the fact is that Israel did eventually enter the land of Canaan. God's purposes were not set aside by Israel's disobedience and unbelief. In summary it can be said that

> *under the covenant an individual Israelite would qualify for personal bless-*
> *ings by obedience which he would not receive if he were disobedient. For*
> *instance, when Israel was obedient they were blessed in the land. When they*
> *were disobedient they were removed and taken away into captivity. The ulti-*
> *mate fulfillment of the covenant with Abraham, however, was never in*

jeopardy as even in the midst of their apostasy they were given strongest assurances of being brought back into the land in subsequent generations and of their continuance as a nation.[12]

More Evidence of an Unconditional Covenant

The Ratifying of the Covenant (Gen. 15:7–21)

Genesis 15:7–21. A third Scripture passage demonstrating the unconditional nature of the Abrahamic covenant describes the ratifying of that covenant in Genesis 15. Abraham expressed concerns about a future heir, since up to this point no son had been born to him. God assures Abraham that he would indeed have a son, and Abraham believed God's word on the matter. God honored the faith of Abraham and encouraged him by ratifying their covenant in a manner that would have been familiar to Abraham.

In those times, people entered into a binding covenant by slaughtering animals and dividing them in two pieces. The pieces were laid opposite one another, and those making the covenantal agreement walked between the pieces, thus solemnly ratifying the covenant by blood. Being familiar with such a procedure, Abraham undoubtedly expected that God would require him to pass between the sacrifices as a participant of the covenant. But He did not. God alone moved between the pieces of the animal sacrifice. This action by God clearly declared that He alone was responsible for the fulfilling of this covenant. Charles Ryrie calls that action "striking," and notes:

> *It means that God swore fidelity to His promises and placed the obligation of their fulfillment on Himself alone. Abraham made no such oath; he was in a deep sleep, yet aware of what God promised. . . . Clearly the Abrahamic Covenant was not conditioned on anything Abraham would or would not do; its fulfillment in all its parts depends only on God's doings.*[13]

S. Lewis Johnson points to God's actions in concluding that "the promises were unconditional promises, that is, dependent ultimately on God's sovereign determination, as the striking ratification of the covenant indicated (Gen. 15:7–21). . . . God symbolically walked between the pieces, and Abraham was not invited to follow." He adds that God undertook "to fulfill the conditions Himself, thus guaranteeing by the divine fidelity to His Word and by His power the accomplishment of the covenantal promises." [14]

Unlike typical covenants that depended on bilateral commitments being met, the fulfillment of the Abrahamic covenant depended totally on the faithfulness of God. This is a very strong statement of the unconditional nature of the Abrahamic covenant.

Other Passages

In addition to the above three Scripture passages, many other passages make clear that the covenant remained in effect even though Israel failed badly. A few examples, which represent a much larger number of similar statements found throughout the Scriptures, are quoted:

Genesis 50:24   "And Joseph said to his brothers, 'I am about to die, but God will surely take care of you, and bring you up from this land to the land which He promised on oath to Abraham, to Isaac and to Jacob.'"

In spite of the many failures and sins of the patriarchs, which are faithfully recorded in Genesis, Joseph declares that the covenant is still in effect.

Exodus 2:24   "So God heard their groaning; and God remembered His covenant with Abraham, Isaac, and Jacob."

Some three hundred years after Joseph, God made it quite clear that the covenant was still in force, even though Israel had not remained faithful to the Lord but had been involved in significant idolatry.

Deuteronomy 9:5–6 "It is not for your righteousness or for the uprightness of your heart that you are going to possess their land, but it is because of the wickedness of these nations . . . in order to confirm the oath which the Lord swore to your fathers, to Abraham, Isaac and Jacob. . . . You are a stubborn people."

This declaration given by God immediately before the Israelites entered the land of Canaan points out with great clarity that it is not the faithful obedience of Israel that is the reason for God's blessing. The blessings of the covenant will come about because God is faithful.

Deuteronomy 4:31   "For the Lord your God is a compassionate God; He will not fail you nor destroy you nor forget the covenant with your fathers which He swore to them."

Earlier in his message, Moses spoke of the day when Israel would plunge into idolatry and forsake the Lord. This faithless behavior would bring the strong discipline of God, including their being dispersed among the nations. But because of the Abrahamic covenant, which would remain in effect in the midst of such disobedience, God would not destroy them and would bring them back both to the land and to Himself.

2 Kings 13:23   "But the Lord was gracious to them and had compassion on them and turned to them because of His covenant with Abraham, Isaac, and Jacob, and would not destroy them."

All through the period of the monarchy, Israel and Judah had periods of idolatry and disobedience. Before the days when kings ruled in Israel, the judges governed a people who periodically sank into the depths of moral degeneracy and spiritual decay. After some six hundred years, peppered with times of terrible failure, 2 Kings 13:23 was written to the same people with whom the covenant was made originally. Numerous times during these centuries God would have been justified to cancel the covenant, except for one thing—He had sworn to fulfill the covenant. It depended on Him alone.

Micah 7:18, 20   "Who is a God like Thee, who pardons iniquity and passes over the rebellious acts of the remnant of His possession? He does not retain His anger forever, because He delights in unchanging love. . . . Thou wilt give truth to Jacob and unchanging love to Abraham, which Thou didst swear to our forefathers from the days of old."

God's prophet Micah had already underscored the many corrupt sins of the nation of Israel, but he was completely convinced that it was impossible to frustrate the covenant commitment of God. Judgment would come on Israel, but Micah was confident that Israel had a future because of the promises given to the patriarchs.

Luke 1:67–73 "[Zacharias exclaimed,] 'Blessed be the Lord God of Israel, for He has visited us and accomplished redemption for His people, . . . and to remember His holy covenant, the oath which He swore to Abraham our father.'"

As the aged priest Zacharias reflected on the centuries gone by, he proclaimed under the direction of the Holy Spirit that God was still intent on fulfilling His covenant commitments.

Acts 3:25–26 "It is you who are the sons of the prophets, and of the covenant which God made with your fathers, saying to Abraham, 'And in your seed all the families of the earth shall be blessed.'"

This portion of the apostle Peter's message was given several months after the nation of Israel had rejected Jesus Christ, yet he maintains that the covenant was still in effect. Renald Showers emphasized the importance of the verb tense in this passage: "Peter's use of the present tense ('are the sons') indicates his conviction that these Jews were still sons of the covenant and that the covenant was still in effect with them. The only way the Abrahamic Covenant could still be in effect with the nation of Israel after its rejection of Christ was if that covenant were unconditional."[15]

Hebrews 6:13, 17–18 "When God made the promise to Abraham, since He could swear by no one greater, He swore by Himself. . . . In the same way God, desiring even more to show to the heirs of the promise the

> unchangeableness of His purpose, interposed with an oath, in order that . . . we may have strong encouragement, we who have fled for refuge in laying hold of the hope set before us.

The author of Hebrews finds his confident hope of salvation based on God's covenant with Abraham. "The Abrahamic Covenant was still to be a source of encouragement to Jews who were living when Hebrews was written (during the AD 60s), in spite of the fact that Israel had rejected Christ several decades earlier."[16] In the mind of the writer of Hebrews, the Abrahamic covenant was still in force and was not set aside by Israel's failure, even their terrible sin in rejecting their own Messiah.

The failure and disobedience of Israel did not set aside the covenant promises. Of course, individuals and groups could lose out on the benefits and blessings of the covenant, but those failures did not annul the covenant. In a time of terrible apostasy, God spoke through the prophet Jeremiah and guaranteed that as long as the sun, moon, and stars existed, the nation would continue in a relationship with Him ("a nation before Me forever"; Jer. 31:35-37). The prophet Ezekiel also spoke of Israel's history of failure and rebellion, yet ended with the promise of restoration (Ezekiel 20). The fulfillment of this covenant rests squarely on the faithfulness of God.

Compelling Evidence

Compelling reasons exist that the Abrahamic covenant was an unconditional covenant, dependent on God alone for its fulfillment. First, the covenant was given without conditions attached to it. If there was an implied condition in the initial giving of the covenant (that Abraham leave his land and go to Canaan), that was clearly fulfilled. When the covenant was reaffirmed later to Isaac and Jacob (Genesis 26 and 28), no conditions were attached to it. Second, the statements of Genesis 17, 22, and 26, which seem to add conditions to the covenant, do not really do so. These statements were given long after the ratification of the covenant and focus on God's intention to bless Abraham in a greater way. Third, the gracious formal ratification of the covenant in Genesis 15 unmistakably validates it as an unconditional covenant. And fourth, dozens and dozens of passages throughout Scripture demonstrate that the Abrahamic covenant was still in effect in spite of the many great failures on the part of the nation Israel.

THE DURATION OF THE ABRAHAMIC COVENANT

How long does the Abrahamic covenant remain in effect? Several times God declared that this covenant was an everlasting covenant. And several times He stated that the land of Canaan would be an everlasting possession of Israel. No time limit was placed on this covenant relationship, which indicates that Israel was to remain a nation forever, sustaining a relationship with the Lord their God. Thus John Walvoord writes:

> *The Hebrew expression for "everlasting" is olam, meaning "in perpetuity." While it might not quite be the equivalent of the infinite term "everlasting," it would certainly mean continuance as long as this present earth should last. It is the strongest expression for eternity of which the Hebrew language is capable. Inasmuch as these promises are reiterated to Isaac and to Jacob and are constantly referred to throughout the Old Testament, the nature of these promises confirms the continuance of Israel as a nation.*[17]

The Abrahamic covenant is referred to as "forever" or "everlasting" several times in Scripture, including Genesis 13:15; 17:7, 13, 19; 1 Chronicles 16:16–17; and Psalm 105:9–10. The prophet Jeremiah inseparably links the existence of the universe with the existence of God's covenant relationship with the nation of Israel. As long as the sun, moon and stars exist, Israel's covenant relationship with God remains in force:

> *Thus says the Lord, who gives the sun for light by day and the fixed order of the moon and the stars for light by night, . . . "If this fixed order departs from before Me," declares the Lord, "then the offspring of Israel also shall cease from being a nation before Me forever."* (31:35–36)

These Scriptures clearly declare the everlasting nature of this covenant. Others focus on the other biblical covenants and reveal the same truth (e.g., 2 Sam. 23:5; Ps. 89:3–4; Jer. 32:40; Ezek. 37:24–28). The everlasting nature of the Abrahamic covenant means that the nation of Israel must exist forever as a nation in relationship with God. "The Scriptures clearly teach that this is an eternal covenant based on the gracious promises of God. There may be delays, postponements, and chastisements, but an eternal covenant cannot, if God cannot deny Himself, be abrogated."[18]

These statements of eternality coupled with the declarations of Scripture that the covenant remains in effect in spite of Israel's disobedience and failure is a firm guarantee that national Israel does have a future in God's program.

THE FULFILLMENT OF THE ABRAHAMIC COVENANT

Opinions differ on this matter of the fulfillment of the covenant with Abraham. It can be a complex issue, but by asking some basic questions we can come to some reasonable conclusions.

Who Were the Parties That Made the Covenant?

Of course, the answer to the above question is God made this covenant with Abraham and the descendants of Abraham. It is right and reasonable to expect, therefore, that the fulfilling of this covenant would involve those same parties. So, as we look at the specific promises of the covenant, we must discover whether they have been fulfilled to Abraham or to his descendants.

Who Are the Descendants (the "Seed") of Abraham?

This becomes a crucial issue in the whole discussion of fulfillment. The position of amillennialism has been that the "seed of Abraham" refers to the spiritual seed of Abraham, that is, to believers of all ages. It is the spiritual seed—people of faith—who receive the blessings of the covenant, since Galatians 3:6-9 states that believers are "sons of Abraham." True believers in the church, both Jew and Gentile, are seen as the ones to whom the covenant blessings come.

However, the issue is clarified when we observe that the "seed of Abraham" is used in three different ways in Scripture.

First, "the seed of Abraham" is used in reference to the physical descendants of Abraham, particularly those who came through Isaac and Jacob. Clearly in the giving of the covenant in the book of Genesis, there was a narrowing of focus to those who were descendants of Abraham through Jacob, thus excluding from the covenant those from Ishmael, the six sons through Keturah, Esau, and others (though they, of course, could find a place in the universal portion of the covenant).

Second, the "seed of Abraham" is used in relation to those Israelites who were genuinely believers, people of faith. In both the Old and New Testaments a distinction within national Israel is seen—some are true believers and others are not. Dr. S. Lewis Johnson's observations on Romans 9 are helpful at this point:

> *Paul writes, "For they are not all Israel who are descended from Israel." It is sometimes thought that Paul in this statement says that believing Gentiles are to be found in the expression "all Israel." Thus, their salvation would justify his statement that the Word of God has not failed, "Israel" being broad enough to include both believing Jews and Gentiles. That cannot be true. The idea is foreign to the text (cf. vv. 1–5). Rather the apostle is making the same point he has made previously in the letter (cf. 2:28–29; 4:12). The division he speaks of is within the nation. They "who are descended from Israel" refers to the physical seed, the natural, ethnic descendants of the patriarchs (from Jacob, or Israel). In the second occurrence of the word in verse 6 Paul refers to the elect within the nation, the Isaacs and the Jacobs. To the total body of ethnic Israel the apostle denies the term "Israel" in its most meaningful sense of the believing ethnic seed. Gentiles are not in view at all. As a matter of fact, the sense of the term "Israel" is clearly established by the meaning of the term "Israelites" in verse 4, and there it can only refer to the ethnic nation's members.*[19]

It is clear that many of the promises will not be fulfilled by the natural seed; Israelites also had to be people of faith—a spiritual seed.

A third use of the term "seed of Abraham" applies to Gentiles who are in Christ because of their personal faith in Him. They are also a spiritual seed of Abraham (cf. Gal. 3:6-9). Gentiles as the spiritual seed of Abraham means that they are heirs of the promise given "to all the families of the earth" (Gen. 12:3). So the idea of a spiritual seed of Abraham includes believing Gentiles. What must be noted, however, is that Gentile believers are not said to fulfill the promises that were given to the physical descendants of Abraham. Concerning the Galatians 3 passage, Walvoord writes,

> *The passage itself . . . makes very clear that Gentiles who are recognized as the children of Abraham come under the promise given to the Gentiles and not under promises given to the physical seed of Abraham. The portion of the Abrahamic covenant which is quoted by Paul refers to the Gentiles in the words: "In thee shall all the nations be blessed." Paul's conclusion therefore*

is: "So then they that are of faith are blessed with the faithful Abraham." This means that they come under the blessing promised the nations, but it does not mean that they come under all the promises given to Abraham personally or to his seed in the physical sense. A Gentile in the present age is Abraham's seed because he is "in Christ Jesus" (Galatians 3:28). [20]

To understand the fulfilling of the Abrahamic covenant, therefore, we must keep these three applications of the "seed of Abraham" in mind. It is incorrect to take the various provisions of the covenant and insist that they are fulfilled to only one aspect of the seed—namely, believing Gentiles who are a spiritual seed of Abraham. There are promises that have to do with national Israel, and there are promises that go beyond national Israel and include all the nations of the earth.

Can the Covenant Be Transferred to Someone Else for Fulfillment?

This third question helps us come to some reasonable conclusions about the fulfillment of the Abrahamic covenant. According to the apostle Paul (Gal. 3:15–19), the answer to this question is a resounding no! He points out that once a contract (or covenant) has been ratified it cannot be changed in any way. That obviously includes the provisions of the covenant as well as the parties involved. The covenant was made with Abraham and his descendants, and it remains that way.

Have All the Promises of the Covenant Been Fulfilled?

The answer again is no. There is no question that portions of this covenant have been fulfilled already. Those promises to Abraham of personal blessing have been literally fulfilled, as the Genesis record testifies. Abraham was prospered by God, his name became great, he did have an heir by his wife Sarah, and he was a channel of blessing to others. But it is also true that key portions have not been fulfilled and, in light of the unconditional nature of this covenant, await their fulfillment. These will be discussed in the next chapter as we look at the Palestinian (land), Davidic, and new covenants. (See also the chart "God's Covenant with Israel" on the next page.)

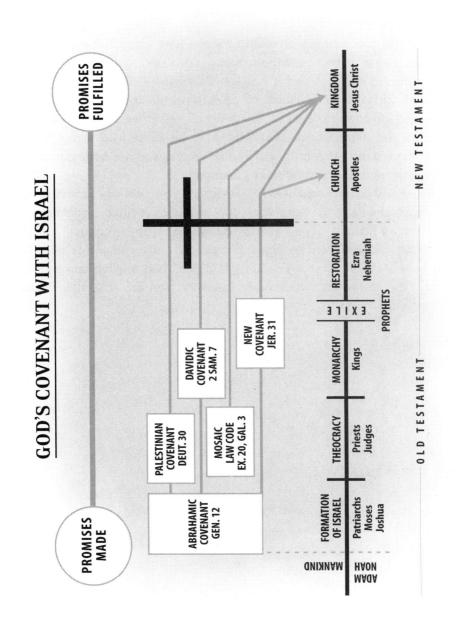

GOD'S COVENANT WITH ISRAEL

PROMISES MADE

PROMISES FULFILLED

ABRAHAMIC COVENANT GEN. 12

PALESTINIAN COVENANT DEUT. 30

MOSAIC LAW CODE EX. 20, GAL. 3

DAVIDIC COVENANT 2 SAM. 7

NEW COVENANT JER. 31

MANKIND

ADAM NOAH

FORMATION OF ISRAEL

Patriarchs Moses Joshua

THEOCRACY

Priests Judges

MONARCHY

Kings

EXILE

PROPHETS

RESTORATION

Ezra Nehemiah

CHURCH

Apostles

KINGDOM

Jesus Christ

OLD TESTAMENT

NEW TESTAMENT

THE ABRAHAMIC COVENANT AND OTHER BIBLICAL COVENANTS

The Mosaic covenant was a conditional covenant made between the Lord and the nation of Israel at Mount Sinai. It was not a covenant agreement that included Gentiles, but it was Israel's constitution, giving them laws and ordinances to guide all aspects of national life. It was never given as a means of salvation for Israel or for anyone else; rather, it was designed to instruct and protect Israel until the Messiah came (Gal. 3:6–4:7). The Mosaic covenant was conditional and temporary and was not a part of the eternal unconditional Abrahamic covenant.

The Palestinian covenant, the Davidic covenant, and the new covenant are enlargements of the Abrahamic covenant and, as such, are also eternal and unconditional. They might be called "sub-covenants" of the Abrahamic because they develop and expand promises made by God in initial ways to Abraham. For example, God promised to Abraham that the land of Canaan would be his. Later, in the Palestinian (or land) covenant, more detail is given.

CHAPTER THREE

THE PALESTINIAN, DAVIDIC, AND *New Covenants*

By many standards the land of Israel is fairly unimpressive. It does not encompass a very large land area. It lacks much of the beauty and grandeur possessed by many other countries, such as Switzerland or Austria, and many lands have far greater natural resources. But no land rivals its importance throughout history up to this present day. And no land is as strategic to Bible prophecy as this one. Its great significance is reflected in the Abrahamic and Palestinian covenants.

THE PALESTINIAN (LAND) COVENANT

The Nature of the Palestinian Covenant

There are four key aspects of the Palestinian covenant that amplify the land aspect of the Abrahamic covenant. From the very beginning of their covenantal relationship, God promised a land area to Abraham (e.g., Gen. 12:1; 13:14–17; 15:7; 17:7–8). The Palestinian covenant reaffirms God's commitment to give the land area to Israel, as well as develops and adds important truths related to the land (e.g., Num. 34:1–12; Deut. 30:1–10).

Second, because the Palestinian covenant is really an elaboration of the land aspect of the Abrahamic covenant, it is also an unconditional covenant. There are no conditions attached to its *ultimate* fulfillment. As with the Abrahamic covenant, disobedience and failure could well bring the loss of blessing but could never annul the covenant. The Old Testament clearly records Israel's sins that caused them to lose the right to live on the land. But, as we shall see, even these failures did not set the covenant aside. Any conditions were related to the receiving or losing of blessing, not to ultimate fulfillment.

It may be argued by some that this covenant is conditional because of the statements of Deuteronomy 30:1–3: "when . . . then." It should be observed that the only conditional element here is the time element. The program is certain; the time when this program will be fulfilled depends upon the conversion of the nation. Conditional time elements do not make the whole program conditional, however.[1]

Third, since the Palestinian covenant is a sub-covenant of the Abrahamic, it too is said to be everlasting. In the original establishing of the covenant with Abraham (e.g., Gen. 13:15; 17:8), as well as later in Israel's history (e.g., Ezek. 16:60), the land is given as an everlasting possession to Abraham's descendants. God is said to be the everlasting God (Gen. 21:33), and the covenant He makes is also said to be everlasting. The word *everlasting* must be taken to underscore the continuance and endurance of this covenant. The fact that the covenant is said to be everlasting is important in understanding its fulfillment. We must keep in mind that an everlasting possession is certainly different than a temporary or partial possession.

Fourth, there is a significant difference between ownership of the land and actually living on the land and enjoying its blessings. The title deed of Canaan was given to Abraham and thus to his descendants. They own the land. Because the covenant is an unconditional one, Israel will eventually live on all the land given under the covenant. That will occur when Messiah comes. In the meantime, however, the Jews can temporarily lose the privilege of actually dwelling in the land through disobedience. But their disobedience, as in the Old Testament, does not permanently set aside the provisions of the covenant.

The Fulfillment of the Palestinian Covenant

The Palestinian covenant was *not* fulfilled at any time in the Old Testament. Some, but not all, who hold to the amillennial position believe that the land promises given to Abraham's physical descendants were literally fulfilled in the Old Testament, and thus there is no future fulfillment. The time of this literal fulfillment is placed either at the time of the conquest under Joshua or in the days of King Solomon.

> *As to the land, the dominion of David and Solomon extended from the Euphrates to the River of Egypt (1 Kgs. 4:21), which also reflects the terms of the covenant. Israel did come into possession of the land promised to the patriarchs. She possessed it, but not "for ever." Her possession of the land was forfeited by disobedience, both before and after the days of David and Solomon. . . . Consequently, we may say that, in the respects in which the Abrahamic covenant particularly concerned Israel, it can be regarded as having been fulfilled centuries before the first advent.*[2]

> *We could summarize these promises concerning the land of Canaan being inherited by Israel as follows: The land was promised through Abraham; the promise was renewed to Isaac, Jacob and Moses. It was fulfilled literally through Joshua. Some Bible scholars find the actual fulfillment in Solomon's day. Compare 1 Kings 4:21 and 5:4 with Genesis 15:18.*[3]

Needless to say, if this position is correct, a large number of prophecies concerning the dispersion, regathering, and conversion of Israel are significantly affected. However, this view is not a strong one, which is probably why not all who hold to the amillennial position espouse it.

A Future Fulfillment

A future fulfillment of the Palestinian covenant is in view based on history and proper interpretation of the Scriptures. Here are three evidences for a future fulfillment.

First, the Scripture passages found in 1 Kings 4:21-24 and Joshua 11:23; 21:43-45, do not teach the fulfillment of the Palestinian covenant. When the statements were written in Joshua, Israel had not come close to possessing the land area. As Walter Kaiser points out,

> *Joshua had conquered thirty-one kings, and now the way was prepared for each individual tribe to conquer the Canaanites in their own designated land areas. Both of these passages are followed by statements that list large areas of the Promised Land that still needed to be taken (cf. Joshua 13:1–7 and*

THE PROMISED LAND

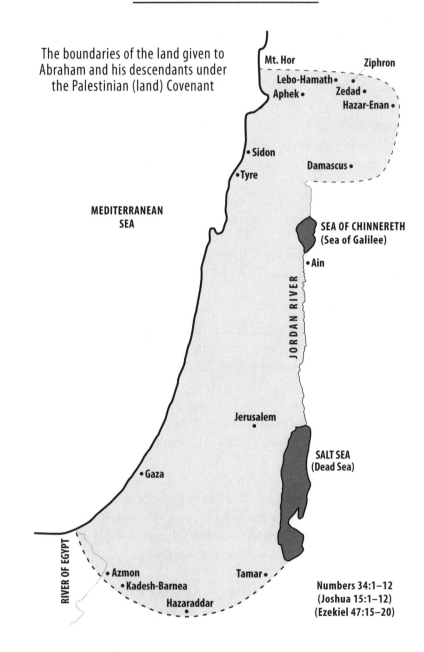

The boundaries of the land given to Abraham and his descendants under the Palestinian (land) Covenant

Mt. Hor

Ziphron

Lebo-Hamath•

Zedad •

Aphek •

Hazar-Enan •

• Sidon

Damascus •

• Tyre

MEDITERRANEAN SEA

SEA OF CHINNERETH (Sea of Galilee)

• Ain

JORDAN RIVER

Jerusalem

SALT SEA (Dead Sea)

• Gaza

RIVER OF EGYPT

• Azmon

Tamar •

• Kadesh-Barnea

Hazaraddar

Numbers 34:1–12
(Joshua 15:1–12)
(Ezekiel 47:15–20)

23:4–7). So the land was not yet conquered and, in fact, would not be conquered by Israel at that time in history (Judg. 1:21–36). The statement in Joshua reflects an Old Testament concept of fulfillment wherein the promise of God was being fulfilled and that generation was getting their share. But it was not the final or ultimate fulfillment of the promise.[4]

The passage in 1 Kings 4 does not teach the fulfillment of the covenant either. In the days of King Solomon, Israel did not actually possess and occupy the entire land area. Other kings still ruled, even though they paid tribute money to Solomon. Even the land that was possessed at that time was not permanently possessed, which is what the Palestinian covenant requires for its fulfillment.

Further, these passages do not teach the final fulfillment of the covenant because long after the days of Joshua and King Solomon, the prophets of God speak of a future possession of the land (e.g., Isa. 11:1–12; 14:1–3; 27:12–13; 43:1–8; 49:8–13; 66:20; Jer. 16:14–16; 23:3–8; 30:1–11; 31:31–40; 32:37–44; Ezek. 20:42; 34:11–16; 39:25–29; Hos. 1:10–11; Joel 3:17–21; Amos 9:11–15; Mic. 4:4–7; Zech. 8:3–8). It is apparent that these prophets did not believe that the land promises had been fulfilled but rather looked ahead to a day when they would be. God, through His prophets, continually held out this great hope of restoration to the nation of Israel.

In addition, the passages in 1 Kings 4, Joshua 11, and Joshua 21 clearly do not teach a final fulfillment of the Palestinian covenant because whatever Israel did possess in those days it clearly was *not an everlasting, permanent possession*. And the covenant requires this for the final fulfillment.

Second, the complete and final fulfillment of this covenant is in the future, and on the earth and not in heaven.

Some amillennialists do believe that there is a future fulfillment of this covenant, since they agree that there is no past fulfillment. However, they spiritualize the many Old Testament passages and say that the fulfillment is in heaven. They see this as an example of God's freedom and creativity, fulfilling prophecy in ways we never would expect:

The promised land was the "inheritance." . . . In the New Testament Abraham's inheritance, the promised land, took the form of "a better country

—a heavenly one" (Heb. 11:8–16). Indeed, the Old Testament concept of the inheritance was recast in the New to designate the all-embracing concept of the kingdom of God. . . . The promise of the land awaits complete fulfillment in a new form, that of the believer's heavenly dwelling with God.[5]

This approach to interpretation sets aside the literal interpretation and employs a spiritualization of prophecy. And, in this case, the interpretation actually changes the provisions of the covenant. Although we agree that God can do anything He wants to do, the real issue is what He said He is going to do!

Again and again, in the plainest of language, God said that He would give Israel a clearly designated land area in spite of their sins. If God did want to tell us that Israel was to possess and occupy the land forever sometime in the future, it is hard to imagine how He could have been any clearer. The spiritualization of these prophecies, as postmillennialist Loraine Boettner observes, leaves "a whole continent of prophecies unexplained, many of which then become quite meaningless."[6] But if the prophecies are approached in a literal way, the evidence is overwhelming that there is a future possessing of the land by the nation of Israel. Thus Walvoord concludes:

The united testimony of the prophets is all to the same point, that Israel will yet be regathered from the nations of the world and reassembled in their ancient land. . . . The promises of regathering linked as they are in Scripture to the original promise of the land as an everlasting possession of Israel, coupled with the fact that no possession of the land in history has approached a complete fulfillment of these Scriptural promises, make it clear that Israel has a future, and in that future will actually possess all the land promised Abraham's seed as long as this present earth continues.[7]

Third, the basic provisions of the Palestinian (or land) covenant as given in Deuteronomy 29 and 30, given to Israel through Moses on the plains of Moab, foretold the worldwide dispersion of Israel, their eventual restoration back to the land that was given to their fathers, and their conversion as a nation. The nation that would be dispersed throughout the world because of their disobedience is the same nation that would be regathered back to the land as a redeemed people. That nation is Israel.

Literal Israel will someday turn in faith to the Lord, and He will save them and fulfill completely and literally His covenant commitments. The promise of the land, which was a key part of the original Abrahamic covenant, was reiterated to Moses in the Palestinian covenant and repeated again and again throughout the centuries by the prophets of God. The fulfillment of this covenant is certainly an important part of the study of future things.

THE DAVIDIC COVENANT

In the world of the Old Testament, there was no great job security in being a king or the son of a king. All too often a king would be assassinated and his entire family wiped out as a rival took the throne by force. Many royal families came to a quick and bloody end as the throne was forcibly taken away. Even the northern kingdom of Israel experienced a number of such bloodbaths. It was no small thing, therefore, when God entered a covenant relationship with David, promising that his physical line would never be cut off.

The Davidic covenant, which was first given in 2 Samuel 7, is an expansion and development of the "seed" promises of the Abrahamic covenant. In the Abrahamic covenant, Abraham was told that he would have a son through Sarah and that a great nation would eventually emerge. He was also told that "nations" and "kings" would come from him (Genesis 17). This covenant commitment by God was narrowed as time went on, focusing on Isaac and then Jacob. Later the promise of a kingdom and a throne was limited to the tribe of Judah when Jacob prophesied that "the scepter shall not depart from Judah" (Gen. 49:10). The Davidic covenant further narrows the focus to one family within the tribe of Judah, namely the family of David.

The Nature of the Davidic Covenant

As with the Palestinian covenant, the Davidic covenant is an amplification of the Abrahamic covenant. This fact assures us that the character of this covenant is the same as that of the Abrahamic—namely, it is eternal and unconditional.

The eternal nature of the Davidic covenant is seen in the Lord's statements to David. For example, He says, "I will establish the throne of his kingdom *forever.* . . . Your house and your kingdom shall endure before Me *forever*; your throne shall be established *forever*" (2 Sam. 7:13, 16; all italics added). Again in Psalm 89:3–4, 35–37, the same emphasis is found:

I have made a covenant with My chosen; I have sworn to David my servant, I will establish your seed forever, and build up your throne to all generations. . . . Once I have sworn by My holiness; I will not lie to David. His descendants shall endure forever and his throne as the sun before Me. It shall be established forever like the moon, and the witness in the sky is faithful.

The covenant is also unconditional. In the numerous passages that speak of this covenant, no conditions are attached to its fulfillment. Like the Abrahamic covenant out of which it flows, God commits Himself to fulfill it. He declares that He will never break this covenant, that He confirms it on His oath, and that His zeal will accomplish it (Ps. 89:3–4, 34–35; Isa. 9:7). Once again it is necessary to emphasize that disobedience could negate the blessings of the covenant to any individual or generation but could not set the unconditional covenant aside. God could (and did) discipline for sin, but His lovingkindness would not depart from David. Fruchtenbaum reminds us of King Saul's disobedience and God's response:

Earlier God did remove His lovingkindness from King Saul because of disobedience. However, the promise is made that although Solomon may disobey and require God's discipline, God's lovingkindness will never depart from him. Because the covenant was unconditional, regardless of Solomon's disobedience and God's chastisement of Solomon, the covenant remained intact and fulfillment is sure. This was true, although the sin of Solomon (idolatry) was a far worse sin than the sin of Saul (improper sacrifice). This is the nature of an unconditional covenant. . . . It was the Davidic Covenant that kept God from tearing away all the tribes from the House of David (1 Kings 11:13).[8]

If God wanted an excuse to cancel the covenant with David, He had many opportunities to do so. But unconditional covenants are not set aside by the failures of the party on whom lay no requirements for the fulfillment.

The Provisions of the Davidic Covenant

There are five basic provisions in the Davidic covenant.

First, David is told that his name would be great. This was fulfilled in David's own lifetime as well as throughout history.

Second, David would have rest from his enemies. This was also one of the realities in the life of King David as God neutralized the power of the surrounding nations.

Third, David was promised that he would have a *house* that would last forever. The word *house* has reference to David's physical line. God guaranteed that the line of David would endure forever and never be cut off.

Fourth, David's *throne* would be established forever. Throne speaks of ruling authority, and this is a guarantee that the right to rule would always belong to the Davidic dynasty and would never pass away permanently, even though there might be times when it might not be exercised. The covenant did not require an unbroken succession of ruling kings in the Davidic dynasty. Again, disobedience could cause the blessings of the covenant to be absent from Israel's experience. The angel Gabriel certainly did not think that the throne promise had been set aside, even though almost six hundred years had passed since a man from David's line had sat on the throne. After informing Mary that she was to be the mother of the long-awaited Messiah, he told her that "the Lord God will give Him the throne of His father David; and He will reign over the house of Jacob forever; and His kingdom will have no end" (Luke 1:32–33).

The fifth provision of the Davidic covenant was the assurance that David's kingdom would never pass away permanently. At times the kingdom would not exist as a kingdom, but "even if historically interrupted for a season, [the Jews] will at last in a *future kingdom* be restored to the nation in perpetuity with no further possibility of interruption."[9]

The Fulfillment of the Davidic Covenant

Conservative Bible scholars agree that the Lord Jesus Christ, the eternal Son of God, is the One who ultimately and completely fulfills this eternal covenant. Jesus is called the "son of David" (Matt. 1:1; Luke 1:32) and the "Root of David" (Rev. 5:5), and in Him the "house," "kingdom," and "throne" find their fulfillment. There is, however, significant disagreement on *when* these promises are fulfilled and *how* they are fulfilled in Jesus Christ.

Premillennialism sees the fulfillment as future, when the Lord Jesus returns at His second coming and rules on this present earth for a thousand years over Israel. This millennial kingdom, which has physical, political, and spiritual aspects, will finally and completely fulfill the Davidic covenant. Furthermore, after the thousand years is completed, this ruler-ship of Christ will continue on into the eternal state on a new earth.

On the other hand, amillennialism and postmillennialism see the ful-fillment of the Davidic covenant as taking place in the present, for Christ is presently ruling on the Davidic throne in heaven over a spiritual king-dom. This spiritual kingdom is the rule of Christ from heaven in the hearts of believers.

But there are those in each millennial camp who differ from the usual viewpoint of that camp. For example, some amillennialists believe that God will fulfill His covenant promises to national Israel sometime in the future, perhaps on a new earth in the eternal state. Also, some premillennialists insist that Christ is ruling on the Davidic throne right now, even though they also believe that the final future fulfillment of the Davidic covenant will be in the future millennial reign of Christ on this present earth.

In arriving at an understanding of *how* and *when* this important covenant is to be fulfilled, certain biblical factors need to be kept in mind. They are: literal fulfillment, unconditional promises, and the existence of two thrones.

Literal fulfillment. First, as with the other covenants, the Davidic covenant needs to be interpreted literally. We noted that the first two pro-visions of this covenant have been literally fulfilled—that of David having a great name and having rest from his enemies. This partial fulfillment points to a literal fulfillment of the yet unfulfilled provisions of the "throne, house, and kingdom." A normal reading of the many Old Testament passages dealing with the Davidic covenant reveals that David, Solomon, the prophets of Israel, and the entire nation expected a literal fulfillment. And in Luke 1, Mary, Zacharias, and many of the godly in Israel anticipated that the Messiah would sit on David's throne and rule the house of Jacob when He came. This was their hope and their convic-tion, and it would seem that the Lord allowed them to live with this expec-tation of a literal, earthly kingdom ruled over by a son of David.

The writers of the Old Testament Scriptures constantly looked forward to a coming Davidic kingdom, which tells us that they did not see any place in the history of Israel where this covenant was fulfilled. They spoke clearly of the sins and failures of Israel but never saw them canceling out the covenant. In fact, the *identical* throne and kingdom that were over-thrown in history were the ones to be restored in the future.

Unconditional promises. Second, the eternal, unconditional nature of this covenant requires that certain things be true. For instance, since the covenant was made with the physical descendants of Abraham, Isaac, and Jacob, the covenant must be fulfilled with them and cannot be transferred to another people. Since God swore on oath, based on His holiness, that His zeal would bring these things to pass, we can be certain that Israel must be preserved as a nation, eventually return to the land of promise, and be ruled over by Jesus Christ, the great son of David.

Two different thrones. Third, the throne of David and the throne of God are not the same thing. That is the critical point for those who see Christ ruling presently in heaven over a spiritual kingdom.

As observed previously, "throne" is not an ornate chair on which a king sat but, rather, the place of ruling authority. Many different thrones are mentioned in Scripture: from the throne of God (Rev. 4:2) to the throne of Satan (2:13); from the throne of the godly elders (4:4) to the ungodly Antichrist (13:2). So a throne can speak of God's sovereign authority, Satan's evil authority, or those who possess a delegated authority.

Since all thrones are not the same, we cannot immediately conclude that David's throne (on which Jesus shall sit) is the same as Jesus' present status of sitting at the Father's right hand. In fact, there is adequate evidence indicating that Jesus is not presently ruling on the Davidic throne and that God's throne and David's throne are not the same at all.

David's throne had its beginning in the lifetime of David, as recorded in the book of 2 Samuel, but God's throne in heaven was established long before David (cf. Ps. 93:2). God's throne is eternal, but David's throne is not, which logically leads to the following observation: "Since God's throne in Heaven was established long before David's throne, and since God's throne certainly was established forever (Lam. 5:19), then it was unnecessary for God to promise to establish David's throne forever (2 Sam. 7:16) if they are the same."[10]

Another contrast between the two thrones lies in the boundaries of each. God's ruling authority is over the entire universe, whereas David's ruling authority is over a specific land area on planet earth. The boundaries of each throne (ruling authority) must be kept distinct from the other, even if the same person happens to be involved with both thrones. Not to keep the sphere of ruling authority in view will result in considerable confusion. For example, suppose that Dr. John Jones occupied the chair of philosophy at the University of Illinois. Later, he was elected governor of Illinois and sat in the governor's chair. The two chairs have two very different spheres of authority, and no one would equate the two just because Dr. Jones happened to occupy both. Jesus may occupy two thrones, but that does not make them the same.

Yet another contrast between the throne of David and the throne of God are their different locations. The throne of God is in heaven (Ps. 11:4; 103:19), but David's throne is located on earth. "There is not the slightest shred of evidence that the throne of David was ever conceived of as anything other than the earthly seat of authority where David reigned and where only his physical descendants could legitimately reign. The term 'throne of David' simply refers to this—nothing else."[11] And there is no explicit statement that the throne of David has somehow been removed from the earthly sphere and transferred to heaven.

Another interesting point is the distinction that Jesus seems to make between His own throne and the throne of the Father:

In Revelation 3:21 Jesus drew a clear distinction between His throne and the throne of God in heaven where He presently sits with His Father. Jesus said, "To him that overcometh will I grant to sit with me in my throne, even as I also overcame, and am set down with my Father in his throne." Since it is the throne of David which God has promised to give to Jesus (Lk. 1:31–32), it would appear that David's throne is Jesus' throne. Since Jesus drew a distinction between His throne and God's throne in heaven, then they must not be the same.[12]

There is good evidence, therefore, that a distinction is to be made between the throne of David and the throne of God and that David's throne is not in heaven but on the earth. However, some premillennialists believe that Jesus is presently ruling in heaven, enthroned as the Davidic king. This present ruling does not negate the future, final fulfillment of the Davidic covenant. According to this view, Jesus entered this aspect of His Davidic kingship at His ascension. This revised form of premillennial dispensational thinking has taken the title "progressive dispensationalism."

Progressive dispensationalism has adopted the "already and not yet" idea of covenant theologian George Ladd. The "already" refers to the partial fulfillment of the Davidic covenant as Jesus presently reigns from heaven on David's throne. The "not yet" looks at the ultimate, future fulfillment in the thousand-year reign of Jesus Christ on the present earth. Peter's sermon in Acts 2 is an important passage for this position.

> *Peter argues in Acts 2:22–36 that David predicted in Psalm 16 that this descendant would be raised up from the dead, incorruptible, and in this way He would be seated upon His throne (Acts 2:30–31). He then argues that this enthronement has taken place upon the entrance of Jesus into heaven, in keeping with the language of Psalm 110:1 that describes the seating of David's son at God's right hand. Peter declares (Acts 2:36) that Jesus has been made Lord over Israel (Ps. 110:1 uses the title "Lord" of the enthroned king) and Christ (the anointed king) by virtue of the fact that He has acted (or been allowed to act) from that heavenly position on behalf of His people to bless them with the gift of the Holy Spirit. . . . Enthronement at the right hand of God, the position promised to the Davidic king in Psalm 110:1, is ascribed to Jesus in many New Testament texts. It is, of course, proclaimed in Acts 2:33–36.*[13]

Is there really a present aspect to the Davidic kingdom with Jesus ruling from heaven on David's throne? Was Jesus enthroned at His ascension? Is the spiritual rule over the church a part of the Davidic covenant? This is a large and complex issue and cannot adequately be analyzed here.[14] However, some key points need to be made in order to arrive at some reasonable conclusion.

First, when all is said, if the position of progressive dispensationalism is correct, then there seems to have been a change in the Davidic covenant. As we have noted already, the revelation of the Davidic covenant in the Old Testament was rulership in the land and over the people of Israel. The viewpoint of progressive dispensationalism does not seem to simply be an addition or an expansion of the covenant with David, but a change. That is something God said He would not do—"My covenant I will not violate, nor will I alter the utterance of My lips" (Ps. 89:34). One Bible scholar has said,

> *It seems difficult not to conclude that this* expanded *kingdom is not a* changed *kingdom. . . . This interpretation includes a change in* throne *(God's personal throne rather than God's delegated throne to David), a* change in realm *(the church with Jews and Gentiles incorporated equally*

rather than Israel in the land with proselyte Gentiles), and a change in reign (spiritual authority only rather than spiritual and political authority).[15]

Second, if such a dramatic addition (change) were to take place, we could rightly expect that there would be clear passages alerting us to such a significant happening. However, no passages exist that give such a declarative proclamation and that are relatively free from significant debate. That is true of the crucial Acts 2 passage just referred to. In that passage, is Peter teaching that the resurrected, ascended Lord Jesus has been enthroned and is presently ruling on the Davidic throne? Progressive dispensationalists have tied Psalm 16 and Psalm 110 together and concluded that the resurrection-ascension placed Jesus on the throne of David. But others have noted that these Psalms have been improperly linked together, resulting in an erroneous conclusion. One author has pointed out that "linking" is not equivalent to "identification"; two things can be linked together without any necessity that they be equated. He then goes on to say,

It is simply incorrect to treat Psalm 16 as linked with Psalm 110 by asserting that both are resurrection proof texts. Psalm 16 is, but Psalm 110 is not. Rather, Peter quoted each Psalm with its own distinct emphasis in support of two different elements in his presentation.[16]

In using these two psalms, the apostle Peter is demonstrating to his Jewish audience on the day of Pentecost that Jesus of Nazareth was Israel's long-awaited Messiah. His resurrection from the dead demonstrated that (Psalm 16), and by His position of authority at the right hand of the Father (as Israel's Messiah) He has sent the Holy Spirit (Psalm 110 with Joel 2). The pouring out of the Holy Spirit is a further testimony that Jesus is their Messiah. These passages simply do not declare that Jesus occupied the Davidic throne as a result of the resurrection-ascension.

Another author has observed that Psalm 110 does *not* link David's throne to the right hand of God, which is a significant point in the position of progressive dispensationalism:

Although Psalm 110 is authored by David, it is by no means necessarily referring to the Davidic throne. Even Peter's use of the Psalm (Acts 2:34–35) only argues for proof of Jesus' ascension and exaltation to God's right hand. The

presence of the same word sit . . . *does not provide a sufficient link to demonstrate that David's throne is God's right hand. So that argument from associated concepts is by no means a necessary or convincing basis for agreement.*[17]

What is clear, then, is that this Scripture does not clearly teach that the Davidic covenant has already begun to be fulfilled. Charles Ryrie has observed that the case presented by proponents of a present rule of Christ is "rather uncertain and unconvincing" because the key texts that are used are admittedly not clear.[18] Again, the point is that, if there was to be such a dramatic change in the fulfillment of the Davidic covenant that is consistently portrayed in the Old Testament, we should expect to find some clear and definitive statements of such a change.

In this regard, a third point should be made concerning the idea that Jesus presently sits on the throne of David. A number of Scriptures found in the New Testament state that Jesus is presently sitting at God's right hand (Acts 7:55–56; Rom. 8:34; Col. 3:1; Heb. 1:13; 8:1; 12:21; 1 Peter 3:22). However, in these passages the only throne mentioned is the throne of God and not David's throne (or Jesus' throne). In these passages Jesus is seen at the Father's right hand, which is the place of authority, and in this place of authority He is presently acting as our intercessor. He is functioning in His priestly role, not as a member of the Davidic dynasty. Jesus' functioning as our authoritative mediator bestows salvation, forgiveness, and the Spirit. These are not elements found in the Davidic covenant, so it is not surprising that the Davidic throne (Jesus' throne) is not said to be present in these passages.

A fourth point on this issue relates to the chronology of the Messiah's rule found in the Old Testament. For instance, in Daniel 2 and 7, the kingdom rule of Messiah (David's great son) is not established until after the kingdoms of man completely come to an end. There is no overlap at all. Once the terrible time of tribulation has run its course and all the kingdoms of man have been destroyed and removed from the earth, then and only then does Messiah rule. There is no hint that His rule partially begins before man's day is over. This consistent testimony of the writers of the Old Testament ought not to be abandoned.

One final point should be made on this subject. Jesus is the anointed King, but being appointed by God as King does not mean that His rule has begun. He awaits the day at His second coming when He will actually reign and fulfill the Davidic covenant. This parallels the reign of David himself, who was anointed by God's prophet-priest Samuel but did not begin to rule until many years later. Unquestionably David was king, but he obviously was not ruling at all.

Jesus was set aside as King at His baptism, then He validated His messianic claims by His authoritative teaching, signs, and miracles. The nation refused to respond in faith and obedience to Jesus' claims and ministry and lost the blessings that could have been theirs. (Remember that blessings can be lost by disobedience without invalidating the promises of the unconditional covenant.) The Davidic kingdom was not inaugurated and Jesus did not begin to rule.

A few days before the leaders of Israel participated in putting Him to death on the cross, Jesus informed His followers that the kingdom was not going to appear immediately (Luke 19:11–27). In the parable of the nobleman, Jesus said that authority to rule was granted in a country far away, but the place of ruling was where they were presently. Jesus is that nobleman, and the country far away is heaven, where the right to rule is granted. But the place of actually ruling is not the country far away but the place where they were presently residing, namely in the Promised Land.

Revelation 5 records a scene in heaven where Jesus receives authority to judge the world in preparation for ruling it. In that Scripture, holy angels and redeemed people give loud praise to the Father and to the Lord Jesus, declaring that honor, power, and dominion belong to them. These are words of rulership. It seems that the judgments that prepare for this rulership immediately begin to fall as the Lord Jesus begins to open the seals of judgment. All these judgments lead up to that moment when it is declared that "the kingdoms of the world have become the kingdom of our Lord and of His Christ; and He will reign forever and ever" (Rev. 11:15). In accordance with the pattern seen in the Old Testament, the Lord rules after the time of tribulation and after man's kingdoms have fallen. Jesus has been established as the king but has not begun to rule.

There are fifty-nine references to David in the New Testament, but none of these references connects the throne of David to the present work of the Lord Jesus in heaven. "Such an inference could be established only by spiritualizing many prophecies both in the Old and New Testaments."[19] There is simply no clear evidence that Jesus is now ruling on the Davidic throne, and there are no compelling reasons to postulate such a rule.

The conclusion is, therefore, that the unconditional Davidic covenant was never fulfilled in the Old Testament, nor is it being fulfilled now. It will be fulfilled in the person of David's great son, the Lord Jesus, at His second coming to this earth. He is the eternal person who will fulfill the eternal covenant. And in following the pattern of the Old Testament, Messiah's rule begins only *after* He returns to this *present* earth and *after* the complete removal of all man's kingdoms (cf. Dan. 2:35, 44; 7:13–14; Zech. 9:10; 14:1–4, 9–11; Matt. 24:27–31; 25:31–33; Rev. 11:15; 19:11–16; 20:1–6). Later on, we will discuss in greater detail the nature and characteristics of Jesus Christ's rule on this earth.

THE NEW COVENANT

There would be a certain sense of emptiness and lack of success if the Messiah came to reign on David's throne and ruled over the designated land area but governed an unregenerate, rebellious people. This would be absolutely unacceptable to the Lord. Since the time sin entered the world through Adam, one of God's great priorities has been to save people from sin. It comes as no surprise at all, therefore, that regeneration and the forgiveness of sins would be very much a part of God's covenant relationship with Israel. It is the new covenant (Jer. 31:31–34; 32:40; Ezek. 16:60–62; 34:25–31; 37:26–28; Rom. 11:25–27; Heb. 8:6–13) that focuses on the spiritual blessings and redemption of Israel. This covenant develops the "blessing" aspect of the original Abrahamic covenant. It also includes material blessings, but the experiencing of these blessings depends on the salvation of the nation of Israel.

The Nature of the New Covenant

The new covenant is like the other covenants that develop the Abrahamic covenant: it is both eternal and unconditional. God declared that this covenant would be everlasting (cf. Jer. 32:40; Ezek. 16:60; 37:26). The unconditional aspect of the new covenant is seen in that no conditions are placed on Israel in any of the Scriptures that deal with this covenant.

On the other hand, there is considerable emphasis on God's efforts in fulfilling this covenant. Numerous times God declares "I will," thus insuring the ultimate fulfillment of the covenant. For example, God says "I will" make a new covenant with Israel, put My law within them, forgive their iniquity, not remember their sin, and not cast off Israel (Jer. 31:31–37). The same emphasis on God's efforts is seen in Ezekiel's message, where literally dozens of times the "I will" of God is declared (cf. Ezek. 34:11–31; 36:22–32; 37:14, 26–28). The great work of salvation in the Scriptures depends completely on God, and there is no question that God intends to fulfill this covenant that focuses on the matter of salvation.

The Parties of the New Covenant

Those involved with the Lord in the new covenant are the people of Israel. In the first mention of the new covenant in Jeremiah 31:31, the Lord says, "I will make a new covenant with the house of Israel and with the house of Judah." He goes on to say that He will make this new covenant with the same people that He made the "old" covenant with. This "old" covenant (the Mosaic covenant) was made with the people whom He brought out of the land of Egypt. The Gentiles were not delivered out of Egypt and were not at Mount Sinai to be a party to the Mosaic covenant (cf. Ex. 20:2; 31:12–17). There is no question, therefore, that the nation of Israel alone is being referred to by Jeremiah.

In discussing the new covenant, the prophet Ezekiel not only speaks specifically to Israel (e.g., 34:14; 36:22) but says that the Lord will save those same people who have profaned His name among the Gentiles. Israel alone is being spoken of by the prophet.

In various passages Israel's restoration back to the land and rebuilding of Jerusalem are connected to the new covenant. These Scriptures point with certainty to the fact that the new covenant will be made between the Lord and the nation of Israel. But a question does arise at this point in light of several New Testament passages. Namely, does the church become a party to the new covenant? This will be discussed under the subject "The Fulfillment of the New Covenant."

The Provisions of the New Covenant

The promises of the new covenant are primarily spiritual in nature, though some material blessings related to the land are also included. In the new covenant God provides for the salvation of Israel. Though not every member of the house of Israel and the house of Judah will be regenerated, the covenant speaks of the national regeneration of Israel. The covenant provides for the regeneration of Israel (Jer. 31:33) and the forgiveness of sins (v. 34). It guarantees the indwelling of the Holy Spirit, which will make it possible for the people to be empowered to obey the Lord with an attitude free of stubbornness and rebellion (v. 33; Ezek. 36:27; Isa. 59:21). The presence of the Holy Spirit will enable people to have an experiential, full knowledge of the Lord (Jer. 31:34).

These marvelous spiritual blessings are closely connected with Israel's restoration back to the land. God says through the prophet Ezekiel, "I will put My Spirit within you and cause you to walk in My statutes, and you will be careful to observe My ordinances. And you will live in the land that I gave to your forefathers" (Ezek. 36:27-28). Under the new covenant, the regenerated people of Israel can and will obey the Lord. Because of their obedience they will be given the material blessings associated with the land. Israel will enjoy wonderful abundance and prosperity, the rebuilding of the temple of God in Jerusalem, freedom from danger of various kinds, and numerous other blessings (Ezek. 34:25-29; 36:24-36; 37:21-28). There is no doubt that the prophets of Israel looked ahead to uniquely wonderful days for the nation of Israel.

The Fulfillment of the New Covenant

Whenever the Old Testament prophets spoke about the new covenant, they viewed it as something yet future. Isaiah (55:3; 59:20-21), Hosea (2:18-20), Jeremiah (31:31-34; 32:40), and Ezekiel (34:11-31; 36:22-29) looked ahead to the time when the Lord would enter into this covenant with Israel and fulfill His promises. The fulfilling of this covenant was inseparably tied to Israel's future restoration back to the land (Jer. 32:36-41; Ezek. 36:24-25; 37:11-14). The nation has never experienced this promised restoration to the land (the Palestinian covenant) and therefore has not experienced their spiritual restoration as a nation.

Of course, neither the spiritual nor physical restoration could take place until the necessary acceptable sacrifice for sins was made. The foundation of the new covenant is the saving work of the Lord Jesus Christ on the cross. But even though the sacrificial death of Christ made all the provisions of the new covenant possible, the new covenant was not fulfilled with Israel in connection with the first coming of Christ. The apostle Paul, some twenty-five years after the cross, still anticipated the fulfillment of the new covenant with the nation of Israel (Rom. 11:1-32). His carefully reasoned discussion of Israel's future in Romans 11 is important to an understanding of the final fulfillment of the new covenant.

In Romans 9–11, the apostle mentions "Israel" eleven times, and each time it refers to ethnic Israel, not to Gentiles or the church. He is talking about his "kinsmen according to the flesh" (9:3). Paul clearly taught that, as a nation, most people in Israel had turned from the Lord, rebelled, and become hardened in self-righteous unbelief. Of course, a believing remnant in Israel had always existed, but the nation as a whole had turned away (chapters 9 and 10).

The passage is clear on this point, that the same people who refused to believe and were temporarily rejected by God would believe and be received back sometime in the future (11:7, 11–12, 15, 23–27). Using an illustration of an olive tree, Paul writes that some of the natural branches of the tree (Israel) were broken off and that wild branches (the Gentiles) were grafted in and received life from the "rich root of the olive tree" (the Abrahamic covenant). He then declares that the day is coming when God will graft the natural branches back into the olive tree, which looks ahead to the day of salvation for national Israel—the final fulfillment of the new covenant. On that day "all Israel will be saved" (11:26).

> *The term, if read without consideration of biblical usage, might be thought to refer to all Israelites without exception, but the usage of the term and the teaching of the Scriptures argue to the contrary. It means in usage* Israel as a whole, *not necessarily every individual Israelite (cf. 1 Sam. 7:2–5; 25:1; 1 Kings 12:1; 2 Chron. 12:1–5; Dan. 9:11). The clues to its force are not only the sense of people (Rom. 11:1), but also the nature of the rejection of the Messiah by the nation, a rejection by the nation as a whole (the leaders and the great mass of the people, but not every Israelite). This usage, as is well-known, is found in rabbinic literature. . . . Thus, Paul affirms that ethnic Israel as a whole will be saved.*[20]

The apostle does not believe that Israel's self-righteousness, unbelief, and sin has removed them from blessing but, rather, is teaching that the day is coming when Israel, as a nation, will be brought into the new covenant, thus fulfilling Jeremiah, Ezekiel, and the other prophets. Some have said that the phrase "all Israel" is looking at the remnant of Jewish believers that has been saved as a part of the church over the centuries. But if that were true, there never was a "breaking off" of the natural branches that Paul discussed. And there was no need to graft them back in, since they have always been part of the olive tree. No, Paul is referring to ethnic Israel and anticipating the day when God will "take away their sins" in light of His "covenant with them" (Rom. 11:27).

In the prophets, the future fulfillment of the new covenant (and the other unconditional covenants) is connected with the coming of Messiah and His kingdom. It will be in the millennial kingdom that this covenant will finally be fulfilled. Israel, as a nation, will be regenerated, experience the forgiveness of sins, be indwelt by the Holy Spirit, and have a full knowledge of the Lord their God, as well as the material blessings associated with their return back to the land.

Immediately prior to the millennial kingdom there will be a seven-year period of great tribulation for Israel. One of the primary purposes of this seven-year period is to bring the nation of Israel back to the Lord, ending their sin and rebellion as a nation (cf. Dan. 9:24). During those seven years the nation will begin to see for the first time that Jesus of Nazareth was, in fact, the long-awaited Messiah and will begin to turn in faith to the Lord. God will graft the nation back into the olive tree, and Israel will be readied for the coming King and His kingdom and the rich blessings of the new covenant. The apostle Paul declared that this must happen because God made a covenant commitment ("for the sake of the fathers"), and God does not change His promises—"the gifts" (the covenant promises) and "the calling" (the national election) of God are irrevocable (Rom. 11:28).

The final and complete fulfillment of the new covenant with Israel will be in the *future* millennial kingdom of the Messiah. What the prophets spoke about will come to pass at that time. But, if that is so, where does the church fit into the new covenant? A number of passages in the New Testament seem to indicate that the church has some relationship to the new covenant (cf. Matt. 26:28; Mark 14:24; Luke 22:20; Rom. 11:27; 1 Cor. 11:25; 2 Cor. 3:6; Heb. 8:8–13; 9:15; 12:24).

In determining the relationship of the church to the new covenant, six points need to be made.

1. The church does not fulfill the new covenant given to Israel in Jeremiah, Ezekiel, and the other prophets. As we have already seen, this is an eternal, unconditional covenant, which God has emphatically

declared He will fulfill. He made the covenant with Israel, and He will fulfill it with Israel. He will fulfill it in connection with the second coming of Christ. In no way can the church fulfill this covenant and cause Israel to be set aside.

2. The silence of the Old Testament prophets on the place of the church in the new covenant does not automatically rule out the church from having some sort of relationship with this covenant. The apostle Paul teaches that the church is a "mystery," and this means that the subject of the church, the body of Christ, is not found in the Old Testament (Eph. 3:3–6). Therefore, it should not overly concern us that the prophets do not mention the church in their discussions of the new covenant.

3. Provision for the blessing of Gentiles was made in the Abrahamic covenant ("in you all the families of the earth shall be blessed," Gen. 12:3). The salvation and blessing of Gentiles was always part of God's plan and concern. In the Old Testament, the book of Jonah reveals much of the heart of God for the Gentiles. It is not surprising that, after the cross, Gentiles in the church are seen as the recipients of salvation and blessing because of the Abrahamic covenant (cf. Gal. 3:14; Rom. 11:11–20). Because the church (now made up primarily of Gentiles) receives some blessings of the new covenant does not mean that Israel will not receive these same blessings, and more, in the future.

A few more comments on this third point regarding Gentile believers. Gentiles in the church are partakers of new-covenant blessings even though the new covenant was made with Israel. Matthew 15:21–28 illuminates this truth. Here the Lord Jesus makes it clear that His miracles are only for Israel; earlier He instructed His disciples regarding the same truth (cf. Matt. 10:1, 5–6). Now a Gentile woman approaches Jesus for the healing of her daughter. He does not do so saying His miracles are for Israel alone (v. 24). But she persists in her request for healing, and finally Jesus does heal her daughter. The truth has not changed that His miracles are only for Israel, yet because of her faith this Gentile woman partook of blessing that was for Israelites.

Suppose that my wife and I have gone to the bank and obtained a mortgage for our home. The two of us and the bank officer representing the bank are the legal parties of the contract (covenant) and once signed and notarized ("ratified") that cannot change. Our children or our friends are not part of our legal obligation. But our children or friends could come live with us and enjoy the blessings of living in that house. They could be "partakers" of the blessings that comes with a house without being parties to the contract.

So it is with the church. We are greatly privileged to be partakers of new covenant blessings, but we have not replaced the parties of the new covenant.

4. The church does partake in the blessings of the new covenant, but not all of them. As members of the body of Christ we, like Israel in the future, are regenerated, indwelt, forgiven, and taught by the Holy Spirit. These blessings, however, are unrelated to the national promises having to do with restoration to the land and the blessings related to that land. Israel alone will receive those.

5. The church is related to the new covenant in the communion service. In the upper room the night before His crucifixion, Jesus instituted the communion with the statement, "This . . . is the new covenant in my blood" (Luke 22:20). Since Jesus spoke of *the* new covenant, we can assume that He was referring to the covenant given in Jeremiah. It is safe to assume that the Jewish disciples would have understood Him to be speaking of that prophesied covenant of salvation found in Jeremiah. Jesus said that it was His death that would institute this covenant.

6. The apostle Paul views himself and others as ministers of the new covenant in 2 Corinthians 3. Paul's ministry focused on the Gentiles, and it was to the Gentiles especially that Paul brought the blessings of the new covenant.

The church, then, is a partaker of the spiritual blessings of the new covenant, enjoying regeneration, the forgiveness of sin, and the presence and ministry of the Holy Spirit. The church is primarily Gentile in its makeup—those who have been graciously grafted in by God *until* their number is complete. Multitudes of Gentiles experience the wonderful blessings of the new covenant. But the church is not national Israel, the people with whom God made this covenant. The church does not and cannot fulfill the new covenant. Its fulfillment awaits the arrival of Jesus the

Messiah. When He returns at the second coming, all the spiritual and material blessings promised Israel will be received.

COMPLETING THE PUZZLE'S EDGE

This first main section on the biblical covenants gives to us most of the "edge pieces" for our eschatological puzzle. Understanding these covenants is critically important to the rest of our prophetic study. Several facts must be kept in mind.

First, these covenants were not made with the Gentiles or with the church, but with the nation of Israel. Once a covenant is ratified it cannot be changed, and that would include changing the *parties* of the covenant.

Second, these four biblical covenants are unconditional and eternal. None of them has been completely fulfilled, which forces us to the conclusion that they will be realized in the future. This is so because God has committed Himself to fulfill them in spite of human weakness and failure.

Third, sin and disobedience can cause, and have caused, the loss of blessing to individuals and to generations, but they cannot annul the covenant.

Fourth, we should expect that the covenants will be fulfilled literally. Our basic approach, as we saw, is to interpret the covenants and all prophetic portions in a literal way. Such an approach recognizes the existence of figures of speech and yet lets language be language. With these things in mind we look next at the major views of Bible prophecy.

PART TWO

Understanding
THE MAJOR
VIEWS OF
Bible Prophecy

CHAPTER FOUR

DISPENSATIONAL THEOLOGY
AND

At the airport two planes are parked at adjoining gates. Superficially it does not seem to make much difference which one you board, since they are only a few feet away from one another. Of course, everyone knows that it makes a tremendous difference which one you take. In this case, one plane is headed for Seattle, and the other is going to Kansas City. The person hoping to do some deep-sea fishing and mountain climbing will probably want to be careful about which flight he gets on—in the end it will make a significant difference.

All too often, Christians view different systems of theology with a certain lack of interest, figuring that it does not make a great deal of difference which one they "board." But each system of theology is going somewhere, and each system has its own eschatological destination. The two main systems are covenant theology and dispensational theology, and the "flight" we choose to get on will lead us to distinctly different places. It is important to examine these two significant systems of theology since they do lead to differing conclusions in the study of Bible prophecy.

COVENANT THEOLOGY

So far we have seen that the way we view the biblical covenants (Abrahamic, Palestinian, Davidic, and new) largely determines our understanding of

God's program for the future. These covenants are foundational to biblical eschatology. It is interesting, however, that covenant theology does not get its name from these biblical covenants. Rather, the covenants of covenant theology are theological ones, postulated by theologians. Some in covenant theology believe that there are three such covenants, whereas others conclude that there are really only two. These theological covenants are known as the covenants of works, redemption, and grace. The reason for the difference in the total number of these covenants is that some covenant theologians believe that the covenant of redemption and the covenant of grace are two phases of one covenant.

Explanation of the System

Covenant theology is a system that interprets all of Scripture on the basis of these two (or three) covenants.

> *Covenant theology teaches that God initially made a covenant of works with Adam, promising eternal life for obedience and death for disobedience. Adam failed, and death entered the human race. God, however, moved to resolve man's dilemma by entering a covenant of grace through which the problem of sin and death would be overcome. Christ is the ultimate mediator of God's covenant of grace.*[1]

Covenant theology as a system was formulated in Europe in the sixteenth and seventeenth centuries. Basically it teaches that, prior to the fall of man, God entered into a covenant relationship with Adam. This *covenant of works* brought with it the promise of eternal life for obedience and death for disobedience. Adam was temporarily put on probation to see what he would do. He failed, and, because he was the head of the human race, he brought spiritual death to himself and to all his descendants. Covenant theologians have differing opinions as to whether or not this covenant has been set aside.[2]

After the failure of Adam, God graciously established the *covenant of grace* in order to bring salvation through Jesus Christ. Louis Berkhof defines the covenant of grace as "that gracious agreement between the offended God and the offending but elect sinner, in which God promises salvation through faith in Jesus Christ, and the sinner accepts this believingly, promising a life of faith and obedience."[3]

The covenant of grace began with Abraham (or perhaps Adam), and this same covenant will continue on until the return of Christ. "According to Covenant Theology, each dispensation or covenant named in the Bible is simply another stage of the progressive revelation of the nature of the Covenant of Grace throughout history."[4] There is a great emphasis on this same covenant of grace continuing throughout history. Those who through faith become a part of this covenant form one, and only one, people of God. This people is the church, or true Israel.

THE THEOLOGICAL COVENANTS

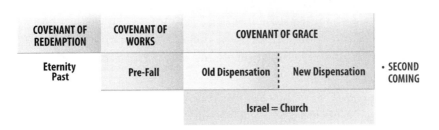

The covenant of grace is actually based on the covenant of *redemption*, which was made in eternity past between the Father and the Son.[5] The Son of God agreed to provide salvation through His death on the cross, and the Father agreed that the Son would be the redeemer and the head of the elect. Operating under the covenant of grace-redemption, the great purpose of God is now the salvation of the elect. Covenant theology views both history and prophecy through the lens of the covenant of grace, and this directs their interpretation of Scripture.

Problems with the System

Our purpose here is not to give a detailed analysis of this theological system but, rather, to observe how it impacts one's approach to Bible prophecy. There are several problems with this system that impact the prophetic Word.

First, covenant theology uses the spiritualizing approach to Scripture.
"In order to make the various covenants of the Old Testament conform to the pattern of the covenant of grace, it is necessary to interpret them in other

than their literal sense," writes John Walvoord. "This is illustrated in the promises given to Abraham and to Israel which are interpreted as promises to the New Testament church. . . . The covenant theory . . . either cancels [Israel's national and racial promises] on the ground that Israel failed to meet the necessary conditions or transfers them to the saints in general."[6]

As we have observed already, those biblical covenants cannot rightly be treated that way. As eternal, unconditional covenants, they require that God fulfill them with the same people that He made the covenant agreement with originally.

Spiritualizing tampers with the promises and provisions of those covenants and casts some doubt on the interpretation that is given. It is interesting to remember that covenant theologians generally approach the Scriptures in a literal way (the historical-grammatical method). But when it comes to some prophetic portions, they employ another hermeneutical approach, that of spiritualization. Using this dual hermeneutic weakens their approach considerably.

Second, covenant theology does not adequately deal with the distinctions found in the Bible.

In putting such great stress on the unifying principle of the covenant of grace, this theological system fails to recognize and deal with some significant differences in the Bible.

Probably the overriding weakness of the idea of this covenant (of grace) is that it is an oversimplification; whereas it observes an abiding similarity in God's relationship to humanity, it fails to account for emphatic differences in that relationship. The covenant of grace is said to cover the time from Adam to the end of the age, with no distinctions being made between the different covenants and covenant people throughout this period. Scriptures related to Israel (e.g., Ezek. 36:25–28) are made to refer to the church. Other such areas of legitimate distinction need to be considered by covenant theologians.[7]

Not to see a distinction between the church and Israel, or similarly neglecting to see any significant difference between the Abrahamic covenant and the Mosaic covenant or between the Mosaic covenant and the new covenant, will lead to unclear and invalid interpretations. Such major distinctions need to be accounted for, and one's prophetic scheme of things will be shaped by acknowledging or denying them.

Third, the biblical covenants (Abrahamic, Palestinian, Davidic, and new) are not simply progressive revelations of the covenant of grace.

The biblical covenants include many elements other than those pertaining to salvation and God's efforts to redeem the elect. The result is that the biblical covenants cannot successfully be squeezed into the mold of the covenant of grace. (This problem with covenant theology is related to the second one.)

> *This mistake becomes apparent, for example, when it deals with the New Covenant. . . . They claim that the New Covenant in the New Testament is essentially the same as the Covenant of Grace in the Old Testament. Covenant Theologians assert that the word* new *does not permit the conclusion that there is an essential contrast between the New Covenant in the New Testament and what existed in the Old Testament. . . . The fact that Covenant Theology is mistaken when it teaches that each biblical covenant is a continuation and new phase of the Covenant of Grace becomes apparent again when it deals with the Mosaic Covenant (the law). It asserts that the Mosaic Covenant was a newer phase of the Covenant of Grace which had been initiated hundreds of years before the Mosaic Covenant. But it is a fact that the Mosaic Covenant instituted required conditions which had not been introduced before. Thus, if the Mosaic Covenant were a newer phase of the Covenant of Grace, it would be adding new conditions to that long-established covenant. Such an addition would violate a principle which Paul taught in Galatians 3:15 when he declared that once a covenant has been ratified, no one adds conditions to it.*[8]

Covenant theology has attempted to force all these biblical covenants into the one mold of the theological covenant of grace. They simply do not fit. To allow the biblical covenants to speak unconfined by the theological covenant of grace brings one to some very different conclusions about things to come—different from those found in covenant theology.

Fourth, the goal of history in covenant theology is not broad enough.

Covenant theology has rightly stressed the concept of God's grace in our salvation and elevated the Lord Jesus to a place of centrality. Some of the best works in the area of soteriology have come from the pens of covenant theologians. However, although the salvation of the elect is an important part of God's purpose for history, it is not the all-inclusive purpose. To neglect the other great areas of revelation dealing with what God is doing is to arrive at inadequate conclusions.

One author has argued that covenant theology "fails to discern the purposes of the ages; the varying relationships to God of the Jews, the Gentiles, and the Church."[9] Another has noted, "Since God has many different programs which He is operating during the course of history, all of them must be contributing something to His ultimate purpose for history. Thus, the ultimate goal of history has to be large enough to incorporate all of God's programs, not just one of them."[10]

God does have varying purposes for the church, Israel, Gentiles, the saved, the unsaved, holy angels, fallen angels, and the universe itself. All these factors cannot be forced into the confines of the theological covenant of grace. Not recognizing the varying purposes of God will often lead to unbiblical eschatological positions, such as that Israel has no future as a national entity.

DISPENSATIONAL THEOLOGY

The second main theological system is that of dispensationalism. *Dispensation* is a word that comes from the Greek word *oikonomia*, which means "economy" or "stewardship." This compound word is based on the two Greek words *oikos*, which means "house," and *nemō*, which means "to manage." The basic concept of a dispensation is that of a stewardship, where one with authority delegates duties to a subordinate, who must carry out those responsibilities. The steward is given adequate information to carry out the stated responsibilities and is held accountable for what he does. If he faithfully discharges his duties, there is reward, but if he fails to do so, there are negative consequences. Failure could very well bring about a change of some sort. The word *oikonomia* is so used in the New Testament Scriptures (Luke 16:1–4; 1 Cor. 9:17; Eph. 1:10; 3:2, 9; Col. 1:25; 1 Tim. 1:4).

Dispensations
As a system of theology, dispensationalism views a dispensation as "a distinguishable economy in the outworking of God's purpose."[11] God is the Authority who reveals His purposes to men and women and delegates responsibilities to them. There have been a number of these divinely

established stewardships (probably six up until the present) with one more yet to come. The apostle Paul uses the word *dispensation* in this theological sense (in Eph. 1:10; 3:9; 1 Tim. 1:4) and refers specifically to the future dispensation when all things will be under Christ's authority (the millennial kingdom dispensation). He refers to the present dispensation of the church as distinct from the dispensation that preceded it (namely the dispensation of the Mosaic Law).

The idea of dispensationalism is summarized by Charles Ryrie:

Dispensationalism views the world as a household run by God. In this household-world God is dispensing or administering its affairs according to His own will and in various stages of revelation in the passage of time. These various stages mark off the distinguishably different economies in the outworking of His total purpose, and these different economies constitute the dispensations. The understanding of God's differing economies is essential to a proper interpretation of His revelation within those various economies.[12]

To understand dispensational theology, certain truths about it need to be noted.

1. A dispensation is not a time period. Although a period of time is involved, a dispensation is a stewardship or administration of God in this world. There are different opinions on the number of dispensations found in the Scriptures, but the issue is not the number of dispensations but the fact that there are differing dispensations. (The majority of dispensationalists recognize seven.)

2. These different dispensations are not different ways of salvation. God's salvation has always been by grace based on the finished work of Christ. Dispensations are not ways of salvation but different ways God administers His rule in this world.

3. Each dispensation does have unique features to it that are clearly revealed by God. The requirements, responsibilities, blessings, and disciplines are spelled out by revelation from God. New responsibilities were introduced by new revelation. That is not to say that everything in a new dispensation is unique. Some operating principles and responsibilities may be discontinued, but some of the principles may be carried over from the previous dispensations. For example,

the right of capital punishment given in the dispensation of human government (at the time of Noah) was carried over into the dispensation of law (at the time of Moses). That is to be expected, since God's truth does not cease to be truth. But each dispensation will have features that are clearly unique to it.

DISPENSATIONAL THEOLOGY

The Distinction Between Israel and the Church

Dispensational theology emphasizes certain differences and distinctions in the outworking of God's purposes in the world. Seeing these distinctions in Scripture leads dispensational theology to conclusions on future things that differ significantly from covenant theology.

There are three indispensable elements (*sine qua non*) of dispensational theology. These three essentials are (1) a consistent literal approach to interpreting the Scriptures, (2) a clear distinction between the church and the nation of Israel in God's dealings, and (3) the glory of God as God's ultimate purpose of history.

Chapter 1 already emphasized the importance of interpreting the Scriptures literally (normally). At this point the focus will be on the second indispensable element of dispensationalism, that of making a clear distinction between the church and Israel. Ryrie calls this distinction "the essence of dispensationalism," adding that the distinction "grows out of the dispensationalist's consistent employment of normal or plain or historical-grammatical interpretation, and it reflects an understanding of the basic purpose of God in all His dealings with mankind as that of glorifying Himself through salvation and other purposes as well."[13]

It is the position of dispensational theology that God has a distinct program for the nation of Israel and one for the church. The church is not Israel and does not take over the covenant promises made to Israel. If that is so, Israel must have a distinct future in the program of God, since many of the promises given to that nation were never fulfilled.

In contrast to the dispensational position, many in covenant theology do not acknowledge any distinction but, rather, equate Israel and the church. They then spiritualize the prophecies given to Israel and relegate them to the church. The spiritual promises encompassed every spiritual descendant of Abraham, "and were not restricted to national Israel. . . . The spiritual promises still are being fulfilled through the church today. Israel's national promises all have been either fulfilled or invalidated because of unbelief."[14]

There is, however, strong evidence in Scripture that the church and Israel are not the same and, therefore, that the church is not fulfilling the unfulfilled promises originally given to the nation of Israel.

Not only do the unconditional, unfulfilled covenant promises made with Israel show that Israel has not been set aside, but the two entities of the church and Israel did not begin at the same time. The church of Jesus Christ began on the day of Pentecost (Acts 2) after the Lord Jesus was given authority as the "head" of the church (Ephesians 1) and the nation of Israel began with Abraham at the giving of the covenant with him (Genesis 12). This would indicate they are not the same entity. Furthermore, the church is said to be a "mystery" and is also said to be one "new" man, terms which point to the church being something new and different. The apostle Paul taught that one enters the church through Holy Spirit baptism (1 Cor. 12:13), which is a ministry of the Spirit that did not commence until the day of Pentecost (Acts 2). It would have been impossible, therefore, for anyone to be in the church of Jesus Christ prior to the day of Pentecost. And finally, the actual usage of the terms "Israel" and "church" reveal that they were not used interchangeably, which again speaks against the view that they are one and the same. In chapter 5 we will address these and other issues in detail.

CHAPTER FIVE

THE VIEW
OF
Premillenialism

A golden age on this earth has long been the dream of mankind. In many different places and at many different times, people have envisioned some sort of paradise. Numerous religions and cultures encourage their people with the thought that there is certainly something better ahead than what is presently being experienced. Of course, there are significant differences of opinion as to how one gets to the hoped-for paradise. Is it human technology and education? Reincarnation? Divine intervention? Or is it a difficult climb into the mountains of Tibet?

Since the loss of Eden, this craving for paradise has resided in the heart of mankind. The biblical reality, of course, is that people will enjoy and experience paradise some day. Indeed, this glory to come was something that gripped the heart of the apostle Paul and clearly was a settled conviction in his mind (Rom. 8:18). The reality of paradise-to-come strengthened him as he dealt with the pain and problems of life.

The Bible does tell us that utopia is coming. The prophets of the Old Testament anticipated a coming golden age for Israel and for all the nations of the earth. In the book of Revelation, the apostle John speaks of a marvelous day when the King of Kings comes, defeats all His enemies, and brings in His kingdom. Kingdom glory will forever be present when Jesus begins to reign. But as believers look at Scripture and look ahead to coming glory, opinions differ as to the exact order of events. All believers, however, who love the Lord and His Word are united in anticipating that great day when we shall see the glorious Lord Jesus Christ. But these same believers are not united on when and how the Lord Jesus will rule and reign.

WHY STUDYING CHRIST'S RETURN IS IMPORTANT

Premillennialism, amillennialism, and postmillennialism look at these events differently and come to very different conclusions. So as we investigate these three positions, we dare not follow the lead of some who would dismiss this matter as too complicated or as having no real importance.

First, it is important because our worldview is significantly colored by the millennial view we embrace. Believers who are quite serious about their Christian lives will discover that their millennial view does affect their approach to life. Is the millennial kingdom present now? Do we bring in the kingdom by advancing the gospel throughout the world? Is the millennial kingdom a future thing? How we answer these and other questions definitely affects our personal worldview.

Second, eschatological study is important because of the great amount of prophetic Scripture that is devoted to this area. The kingdom where the Messiah rules is no minor matter to the writers of Scripture.

Third, it is important because God's purposes on this earth will be fully realized in the millennial kingdom. The issue of the fulfillment of the biblical covenants comes into focus at this point.

We begin by looking first at the view of premillennialism. The views of amillennialism and postmillennialism will be discussed later in part two.

DEFINING THE TERM *MILLENNIUM*

The term *millennium* means a thousand years. It is derived from two Latin words: *mille*, which means "a thousand," and *annus*, which means "year." In the Scriptures, the millennial kingdom is that phase of the kingdom of God where Jesus Christ reigns. The length of this one-thousand-year kingdom is specifically given in Revelation 20:1–6. *Premillennialism* teaches that the second coming of Jesus Christ to the earth takes place before (pre) the millennial reign. Thus, the millennium begins after the return of Christ to this present earth. All dispensationalists are premillennial, but only a small number of covenant theologians are premillennial.

TYPES OF PREMILLENNIALISM

One type of premillennialism is nondispensational. It is known as covenant premillennialism. Its adherents often prefer to be called "historic premillennialists." That is because much of their position was the view that was held by many of the church fathers during the first several centuries of the church. The second type is dispensational premillennialism.

ABOUT COVENANT PREMILLENNIALISM

Covenant premillennialism believes that the millennium is established after the return of the Lord Jesus to this earth as King of Kings and Lord of Lords. Most believe that the millennium is a literal one thousand years, though there is a minority who believes that the millennium is simply an extended period of time. The position of covenant premillennialism is based almost exclusively on Revelation 20:1-6, where the term *a thousand years* is repeatedly used. Unlike dispensational premillennialism, this form of premillennialism does not go to Old Testament Scripture to support the idea of a millennial kingdom.

George Ladd was a covenant premillennialist who did not accept a millennial kingdom in which Israel has a predominant place because he (like other covenant theologians) applied Old Testament prophecies to the church. In this, covenant premillennialism is similar to the position of amillennialism. Ladd says,

> *Dispensationalism forms its eschatology by a literal interpretation of the Old Testament and then fits the New Testament into it. A nondispensational eschatology forms its theology from the explicit teaching of the New Testament. It confesses that it cannot be sure how the Old Testament prophecies are to be fulfilled.*[1]

Covenant ("historic") premillennialism does not make a sharp distinction between the church and Israel, and it regularly spiritualizes the Old Testament. On these major points it is much like amillennialism and significantly differs from dispensational premillennialism. Because of this approach, covenant premillennialism generally believes that the church will remain on the earth during the period of the tribulation, not being raptured out of the world until *after* this seven-year period of trouble.

THE VIEW OF COVENANT PREMILLENNIALISM

The covenant premillennial position has three weaknesses. First, as mentioned, it spiritualizes the prophecies of the Old Testament, applying them to the church, which is viewed as spiritual Israel. Second, it fails to give the nation of Israel its proper place in the program of God. The unconditional, eternal biblical covenants ratified by God require that Israel as a nation be the recipient of certain blessings. Third, there is some inaccuracy in its view of progressive revelation. It is true, of course, that God has revealed more and more truth progressively over the years. And it is true that the New Testament reveals new truth and develops truth previously given in the Old Testament. However, it fails to recognize that many of the Old Testament prophecies should be understood on their own merit because they are clear in their meaning. The idea of progressive revelation does not mean that the Old Testament cannot be understood apart from the New Testament. It does not mean that clear Old Testament prophecies must be reinterpreted, changed, or altered.

ELEMENTS OF DISPENSATIONAL PREMILLENNIALISM

Within the premillennial position, dispensational premillennialism is the majority view. Certain fundamental elements characterize this type of premillennialism.

Return of Christ Before His Kingdom Is Established

The first and most obvious element is the belief that the Lord Jesus Christ returns to this earth before the establishment of His kingdom. This eliminates the idea that any present rule of Christ is to be viewed as the millennium. The millennial kingdom is a future aspect of Christ's rule, which will suddenly come into existence because of the Lord's visible return to this planet. This aspect of the kingdom will not, therefore, come in gradually over an extended period of time. It will be brought in by the Lord Himself and not by human efforts or by the church.

Two Resurrections

Second, dispensational premillennialism points to two resurrections, which are separated by a thousand years. Revelation 20:4–6 speaks of a group who "came to life and reigned with Christ for a thousand years." It then goes on to say that "the rest of the dead did not come to life until the thousand years were completed." Taken normally, these verses state that there is a major resurrection before the millennial kingdom begins and a major resurrection at the end of the millennial kingdom. This text, interpreted in a normal, literal way, is teaching that both of these are physical, bodily resurrections.

THE VIEW OF DISPENSATIONAL PREMILLENNIALISM

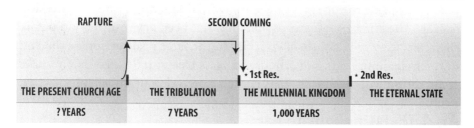

Many, however, insist that the first resurrection mentioned in Revelation 20 refers not to bodily resurrection but to a spiritual one; in other words, it refers to the regeneration of the soul. It was St. Augustine who first held to this position, and he has been followed by those holding to amillennialism and postmillennialism. As we will see later, these two views start the millennial kingdom at the first coming of Christ. But since the Scriptures do not state that any major bodily resurrection took place at Christ's first coming, it is necessary for these positions to allegorize the first resurrection of Revelation 20, making it a spiritual resurrection. But

Revelation 20 is clearly speaking of literal, bodily resurrections for two reasons.

First, those involved in the first resurrection are clearly said to be believers, and their resurrection occurs long after their spiritual regeneration.

The very fact that they were beheaded because of the testimony of Jesus and because of the word of God would indicate that they had been regenerated, and John is stating that death is not the end but that they will be resurrected. Nothing in the text indicates the regeneration of the soul, but everything indicates that it refers to resurrection of the body.[2]

Second, the context of Revelation 20 gives no basis for making a distinction between the two resurrections. The description of the two resurrections is completely parallel, and if verse 5 is speaking of bodily resurrection (which all agree is the case) then verse 4b must be speaking of bodily resurrection also. To allegorize the text and see two entirely different kinds of resurrection here (without any exegetical evidence to do so) is to leave the needed constraints of normal language and depart into a kind of exegesis where few guidelines exist.

The first resurrection refers to the resurrection of believers, which will take place prior to the start of the millennial kingdom. This resurrection is called the "first" not because there has not been any resurrection before this, but because it stands in contrast to the later resurrection at the end of the millennium. After the thousand years have run their course, another resurrection will take place. This is the resurrection of unbelievers.

An Actual Kingdom on Earth

Third, dispensational premillennialism regards the millennial kingdom as a literal kingdom that will exist on this present earth. Jesus Christ will be the supreme ruler over an earth that has had the Edenic curse removed. All His enemies will be removed, including Satan, and all of creation will acknowledge that He is the King. His reign will be characterized by universal peace and righteousness.

A Kingdom Established After All Human Kingdoms End

Fourth, this millennial kingdom will be established only *after* human kingdoms have come to an end. The order of events given in the prophecies of

Daniel establishes this point. According to Daniel 2 and 7, four human kingdoms would exist before the establishing of God's kingdom. The fourth kingdom would have two phases; during the second phase of this fourth kingdom, the kingdom of God would be set up. All agree that this kingdom of God refers to Messiah's rule. But the order of events portrayed by Daniel is specific: when the second phase of the fourth kingdom (which we understand to be the empire of the Antichrist in the end times) is in existence, God will completely and totally destroy that kingdom and all the remaining vestiges of the previous kingdoms. This destruction comes suddenly, not gradually. Only when there is *nothing* left of mankind's kingdoms will God set up His kingdom. No coexistence is allowed between God's kingdom and mankind's kingdoms. There is no gradual, peaceful takeover by the kingdom of God.

These facts, and the clear chronology given by Daniel, do not allow for the establishing of the millennial kingdom at the first coming of Christ. The church is not the millennial kingdom because the church does coexist with human kingdoms. The church did not completely and violently bring human kingdoms to an end. Consequently, according to dispensational premillennialism the millennial kingdom will be established at the second coming, when with great power King Jesus suddenly and completely destroys the kingdoms of this earth and establishes His own kingdom.

Fulfillment of the Abrahamic Covenant
Fifth, the millennial kingdom appears in order to fulfill the covenant promises made to Abraham and his descendants. Premillennialism thus gives a much greater place to the nation of Israel than the other major millennial views.

A Literal Hermeneutic
Sixth, dispensational premillennialism consistently emphasizes a literal hermeneutic. The literal interpretation of both Old and New Testament prophetic passages will always lead a person to the premillennial position. Amillennial writers agree that this is the case. One states that "the Old Testament prophecies if literally interpreted cannot be regarded as having been fulfilled or capable of fulfillment in this present age."[3] Another says that "we must frankly admit that a literal interpretation of the Old Testament prophecies gives us just such a picture of an earthly reign of the

Messiah as the premillennialist pictures."[4] These writers would, of course, subscribe to the idea that spiritualizing some prophecies is acceptable. (For more on the interpretation of prophecy, see chapter 1.) But the premillennial approach of a consistent literal hermeneutic is a strength of this view.

OBJECTIONS TO DISPENSATIONAL PREMILLENNIALISM

Those holding to the amillennial and postmillennial positions have raised objections to premillennialism. Although an extended debate cannot be entered into here, several points are often raised.[5]

1. Only Revelation 20 Supports an Earthly Millennium.

First, opponents contend that there is a sparseness of biblical references to the millennium, with only Revelation 20 explicitly referring to a period of a thousand years. Certainly there would be more in the Scriptures than this one reference if the idea of an earthly millennial kingdom were a clear and important teaching.

It is, of course, true that Revelation 20 is the only passage in the Bible that gives the length of the millennial kingdom as a thousand years. This is unquestionably John's great contribution to the discussion of the kingdom. However, it is incorrect to imply that dispensational premillennialism is built solely on Revelation 20. The fact is that writer after writer and prophet after prophet in the Old Testament detailed what the kingdom of the Messiah would be like. The mural they painted portrays with clarity and detail a king from David's line ruling Israel and all the nations in truth and righteousness. The volume of material on the millennial kingdom is great, and the objection that premillennialism rests on Revelation 20 is incorrect. Without Revelation 20, premillennialism would still be a clear, well-developed theology, lacking only the information on the length of the kingdom of Messiah.

2. A Literal Interpretation Is Too Rigid.

A second objection has to do with the literal way dispensational premillennialism interprets Old Testament prophecies. Critics feel that the interpretive approach is too rigid, failing to recognize that some prophecies have not been fulfilled literally and failing to allow for an allegorical approach. It is sometimes said that dispensational premillennialists are guilty of "hyperliteralism" and "crass materialism."[6]

Premillennialism responds by pointing out that literal interpretation is not a "wooden literalism" and that it does recognize symbols and figures of speech. The point made by dispensational premillennialism is that the Bible (including its prophetic portions) should be interpreted in the ordinary grammatical-historical way. It is inconsistent and unjustified to spiritualize one area of theology. Those passages that deal with the covenants and the millennial kingdom ought to be approached in the same way as passages dealing with the deity of Christ or the inspiration of Scripture. That is not "hyperliteralism." The same hermeneutical principles that govern other areas of theology must also govern the area of eschatology.

3. It Is Not Theologically Necessary.

A third objection raised against the dispensational premillennial view is that an earthly millennium is theologically superfluous. Why should there be an earthly reign of Christ at all? It is pointed out that the establishment of an eternal kingdom on the earth after all the judgments have taken place makes a prior one thousand year reign of Christ on the earth unnecessary.

Some premillennialists have noted that the thousand-year kingdom is needed to demonstrate the greatness and supremacy of Christ to all creatures, whether in heaven, on earth, or under the earth (Phil. 2:10). Although this is undoubtedly true, the main reason for the millennial kingdom is to fulfill completely the covenant promises made to Abraham and his descendants centuries ago. These ratified covenants must be fulfilled, and the time of the fulfillment is in the Millennium. This period of time is not irrelevant at all but is crucial to God's program for the nation of Israel.

4. Jesus' Kingdom Is Not of This World.

Based on John 18:36, a fourth objection is made regarding the premillennial position. In that passage Jesus states that His kingdom is not of this world, for if it were, His servants would fight. Some argue that premillennialism teaches a sudden, violent means of bringing in the kingdom, and this contradicts how Jesus indicated that He would establish His kingdom. It also contradicts Jesus' statement that His kingdom was not of this world.

Premillennialists point out that there is a difference between being "of the world" and "in the world." Jesus Himself made that distinction one chapter earlier (cf. John 17:11–16). Jesus' kingdom would not be "of the world," which means that it will not be of the same nature as the kingdoms of this world. It is a distinctly different order, with such realities as peace, truth, and righteousness reigning supreme. But that is not a denial of Christ's kingdom being present on this earth. As Jesus spoke to Pontius Pilate (in John 18:36), He was simply telling the Roman official that, since His kingdom was different, it would not be established in the ways familiar to him; that is, through insurrections or the military victories of disciplined armies. As described in Revelation 19, the Lord's return does bring a sudden, violent end to the kingdoms of this world. But it is the Lord Himself who executes judgment on mankind. This also is the common testimony of the Old Testament prophets.

5. Israel Displaces the Church

A final objection that is often raised against the premillennial position is that it gives too prominent a place to national Israel. It is felt that the significant place given to Israel in God's program virtually displaces the church as the primary object of God's working.

In premillennialism the church—the bride of Christ—is married to Him immediately before His second coming, and thus it enters a wonderfully prominent and highly visible place (cf. Rev. 19:7–9). The redeemed church certainly maintains an exalted place from that point onward throughout eternity. It is also true, however, that redeemed national Israel has a prominent place. And as was suggested above, the primary purpose of the millennial portion of God's kingdom will be to fulfill the covenant commitments made to Israel in the Abrahamic, Palestinian, Davidic, and new covenants.

The Old Testament Scriptures are clear that national Israel will have a prominent place over the rest of the nations of the earth. But, because the church was not known to the Old Testament prophets, they make no comment on the relationship of redeemed Israel to the church of Jesus Christ during the millennial period. Israel will certainly be prominent among the nations, but that does not mean that the church fades into insignificance during this time.

IN SUMMARY

Premillennialism is the view that Jesus Christ will return to this present earth prior to the establishing of His millennial kingdom. Jesus will reign supreme in power and great glory and will be the object of worship for all mankind. This kingdom will be on an earth where the curse has been removed and where righteousness, peace, and prosperity are universal. Prior to the millennial kingdom there will be a resurrection of believers, and following the kingdom there will be a resurrection of unbelievers. The primary purpose of this period of time is to fulfill completely the covenant promises made to Abraham and his descendants. When this kingdom is over, the next phase of God's kingdom, the eternal state on a new earth, will commence.

The premillennial position is based squarely on a consistent, literal hermeneutic. A literal approach to the prophetic Scriptures leads one to believe that the promises made to Israel have not been fulfilled in the past and are not being fulfilled today. This mandates that they be fulfilled sometime in the future to national Israel, which means that the nation of Israel and the church of Jesus Christ must be kept distinct. This contrast between Israel and the church is a key to the premillennial position, and it is one of the primary ones that sets it apart from other systems of theology.

CHAPTER SIX

THE CHURCH
AND THE
Nation OF Israel

Most realtors will tell you that the three most important factors in selling property are (1) location, (2) location, and (3) location. Most theologians will tell you that the three most important factors in arriving at good theology are (1) definition of terms, (2) definition of terms, and (3) definition of terms.

It is certainly true that the way in which the interpreter of Scripture defines the terms *church* and *Israel* is important, having a profound impact on the theological conclusions of that person. One's definition of these terms will significantly shape that individual's position on many key passages of Scripture. If Israel is seen as a national, ethnic group of people throughout all of Scripture and the church is different from that, then certain theological conclusions will follow. But if the church is viewed as the "new Israel" that has replaced national Israel, then a very different theological position will be held to.

TWO BASIC VIEWS

Theologians hold various views on the relationship of the church to the nation of Israel. But for the purpose of this brief chapter the two main positions will be set forth.

Israel and the Church Are Not the Same.

This view concludes that Israel is a unique nation chosen by God to fulfill His will and work in this world. Israel is a specific ethnic group, descended from Abraham through Isaac and Jacob, which is united by a covenant relationship with the Lord God. This covenant made with Abraham and his descendants is both everlasting and unconditional and largely remains unfulfilled with national Israel. Israel is the only nation on earth that has this relationship and status as is seen by the facts that God calls Israel "My son, My first-born" (Ex. 4:22) and they are seen as an elect people chosen by God Himself. Israel is "a holy people to the Lord your God; the Lord your God has chosen you to be a people for His own possession out of all the peoples who are on the face of the earth" (Deut. 7:6. cf. Deut. 4:37; 10:15–16; 14:2; 26:19).

The election of Israel by God to do His work in the world is a major biblical and theological issue. Two critically important points must be understood regarding this election of the nation of Israel by God. First, Israel's election does not mean that God abandoned the Gentile nations. From the very beginning of God's covenant relationship with Israel, He made it abundantly clear that Gentiles were very much part of His care and concern (cf. Gen. 12:3; 26:4; 28:14). Israel's position as God's elect nation never was intended to isolate the blessings of God to Israel, but rather Israel was to be the channel of God's blessing and salvation to all nations of the earth. Second, Israel's status as an elect nation did not mean that every physical descendant of Abraham would receive spiritual salvation. Jesus and John the Baptist repeatedly warned the Jews of their day that being a physical descendant of Abraham was not a guarantee of entrance into the kingdom of God.

There is an important difference between the election of the individual and the national election of Israel.

> *In dealing with the concept of election, a distinction must be made between individual election and national election. The former is soteriological and results in the salvation of that individual. This type of election extends to both Jewish and Gentile individuals; and any person who has ever believed, either Jew or Gentile, was the object of God's individual election. However, the concern of Israelology is national election because only Israel is called an elect nation. National election does not guarantee the salvation of every individual*

within the nation since only individual election can do that. . . . What national election does guarantee is that God's purpose(s) for choosing the nation will be accomplished and that the elect nation will always survive as a distinct entity.[1]

Therefore, national Israel is unique because they among the nations are in a covenant relationship with God and they alone were elected by God to be the means by which He would restore sinful mankind back to Himself.

The church of Jesus Christ, on the other hand, is distinct from national Israel. Because of Israel's disobedience and unbelief related to the Messiah Jesus, they have been *temporarily* set aside in the plan of God. The church, which is a new and different entity, has been raised up for an undetermined period of time to do God's will and work in this world. The church, which is made up of believing Gentiles and believing Jews, came into existence on the day of Pentecost (Acts 2) and will remain on the earth until removed at the rapture event.

When God's purposes for the church are over, then God will restore Israel to their original place which will bring immense blessing to the Gentile nations. This restoration of national Israel will be the result of God's powerful working during the "Seventieth Week of Daniel" (i.e., the tribulation period), which will take place on this earth after the removal of the church. It must be remembered that the unique place of national Israel and the wonderful purposes of God for all of mankind have coexisted from the beginning. The existence of one does not require the exclusion of the other. Gentile blessing does not require that Israel be set aside.

This view is held by dispensational theology but is not exclusive to it. Long before dispensational theology was formulated there were others (including Puritans, Anglicans, and Catholics) who made a clear distinction between the church and national Israel.[2] Evidences for the position that distinguishes between the church and Israel will be set forth later in this chapter.

The Church Is the New Israel.

The view that has dominated the church since post-apostolic times has been that of *replacement theology*. This view holds that Israel's sin and failure caused God to set aside national Israel completely and permanently and replace it with the church. The promises given to Israel in the Old

Testament have been transferred over to the church. The view is sometimes called "supersessionism," because national Israel is said to be superseded by the person and work of Christ and the community of believers (i.e., the church) that came from His work. This is the position of most in covenant theology. This perspective is advocated by Wayne Grudem. "What further statement could be needed in order for us to say with assurance that the church has now become the true Israel of God and will receive all the blessings promised to Israel in the Old Testament."[3]

Louis Berkhof sees the church as always existing and yet differing from national Israel.

> *After the exodus the people of Israel were not only organized into a nation, but also constituted the church of God . . . the whole nation constituted the church; and the church was limited to the one nation of Israel, though foreigners could enter it by being incorporated into the nation. . . . The New Testament church is essentially one with the church of the old dispensation. As far as their essential nature is concerned, they both consist of true believers, and of true believers only. . . . Yet several important changes resulted from the accomplished work of Jesus Christ. The church was divorced from the national life of Israel and obtained an independent organization.*[4]

William Cox's statement represents the position of replacement theology.

> *The Old Testament records two kinds of promises which God made to national Israel: national promises and spiritual promises. . . . The spiritual promises still are being fulfilled through the church today. Israel's national promises all have been either fulfilled or invalidated because of unbelief.*[5]

While there are some variations within this theological viewpoint, there has been an essential unity on the matter of national Israel being set aside by God and being replaced by the church. The writings of some of the church fathers (such as Origen and Justin Martyr) as well as church councils have fostered an anti-Judaic attitude, which has often been seen in replacement theology. As Ronald Diprose notes, "Some anti-Jewish canons were formulated in the context of Councils, such as the Council of Chalcedon (451), which live in the church's memory as occasions in which orthodoxy was defined." He concludes, "Thus we can speak of a parallel development of Orthodox theology on the one hand and an official anti-Judaic stance on the other."[6]

It should be noted that there has been some modification of the harsher elements of replacement thinking since the reestablishment of Israel as a nation in May 1948. The more extreme and hateful attitude towards Israel has been set aside by many, and some have suggested that blessing may yet come to national Israel in the future. Nonetheless, replacement theology remains firm in its view that Israel has been set aside.

Before presenting evidence for the position that the church and Israel are separate entities in the Scriptures, two observations need to be made about replacement theology. First and foremost, is its relationship to the New Testament. While it is without question found in church history, is this viewpoint found in the New Testament Scriptures? They would argue that such a view can be deduced from a number of Scripture passages. But Diprose offers this important caution: "For *replacement theology* to qualify as a biblical option, passages which *allow* such an interpretation are not enough. There need to be, positively, passages which clearly teach it and, negatively, no passages which actually exclude it."[7]

Diprose's insightful statement is accurate, because the Old Testament clearly sets national Israel apart as a unique nation elected by God Himself. If there is a change in their status or some sort of transference of their status to another, then somewhere in the New Testament it must be clearly and decisively declared. No such statements exist in the New Testament, but actually the opposite is to be found, especially in Romans 9–11.

Second, the perspective of *replacement theology* was shaped by several factors in the early history of the church and did not come about by a careful study of the Scriptures. First, the reality of history is that it was indeed the Jews who rejected their own Messiah Jesus and were the great antagonists of the early church. This fed an anti-Jewish sentiment in the church in the centuries that followed, which influenced some church fathers. A second factor in developing this way of thinking was the embracing of Greek thinking and philosophy by many of the early church fathers. This acceptance of a Greek worldview and the abandonment of a Jewish worldview had a profound effect on their theology. Things physical (such as national Israel and an earthly millennial kingdom) were diminished in importance, while things "spiritual" were elevated. And the allegorical method of interpretation allowed interpreters to take the promises given to national Israel and transfer them to the church. Origen is considered the father of the allegorical method in the church; significantly, he was influenced by the Greeks who employed such methodology.

With these points being stated, it is necessary to look at the Scriptures to see what they do indeed teach about the relationship of the nation of Israel to the church.

EVIDENCE FOR A DISTINCTION BETWEEN THE CHURCH AND THE NATION OF ISRAEL

Those holding to replacement theology put considerable emphasis on the similarities between Israel and the church. They will point to some similar terms that are used for both, that both have a special relationship with God based on election, that both are to bring the truth of God to the world, as well as other matters.[8] Clearly a certain continuity does exist between Israel and the church. But some continuity would be expected since the church is now representing God and His truth in the current age. The church has been commissioned by Christ to carry the good news of His salvation throughout the world as Israel was once commissioned to do. However, this does not mean that Israel's place as God's elect nation has somehow been canceled or His promises transferred to another entity. National Israel maintains her key place in God's plans and purposes for this world.

The following lines of evidence lead to the conclusion that Israel has not been superceded in her place as God's elect and covenant people. These seven evidences argue for the ongoing distinction of Israel and the church of Jesus Christ.

1. The Existence of the Unconditional but Unfulfilled Biblical Covenants

The Old Testament records the indisputable fact that God entered into a covenant relationship with Abraham (Gen. 12:1–3; 13:14–17; 15:1–21; 17:1–27; 18:17–19; 22:15–18) and then personally confirmed it to Abraham's physical descendants Isaac (Gen. 26:24) and Jacob (Gen. 28:13–17). The Gentile nations were not specifically parties to the Abrahamic covenant nor were they parties in the three covenants that expanded on the provisions of the Abrahamic covenant; namely, the land (aka Palestinian), Davidic, and new covenants. These covenants were made with national Israel.

The essential nature of the Abrahamic covenant (and its three "sub covenants") is critical in this discussion (see the discussion on pages 36-44). The covenant is an *everlasting* covenant. No time limit was placed on this covenant relationship, which indicates that Israel was to remain a nation forever in this relationship with the Lord their God.

The everlasting nature of the Abrahamic covenant means that national Israel must remain in their unique relationship with God as long as the earth and the universe exist. And since we can all testify that the universe still exists and has not yet been destroyed, then we can certainly believe that the nation of Israel has not been removed from their unique place either. This covenant continues to exist because of God's graciousness and faithfulness and not because of Israel's fidelity and obedience. "There may be delays, postponements, and chastisements, but an eternal covenant cannot, if God cannot deny Himself, be abrogated."[9] The failure and disobedience of Israel did not set the covenant promises aside.

It is clear that individuals and the nation itself could lose out on the blessings of the covenant (as they did), but those failures did not annul the covenant. In a time of terrible apostasy and judgment of Israel, God spoke through the prophets Jeremiah and Ezekiel. He guaranteed that as long as the sun, moon, and stars existed, Israel would continue as "a nation before me forever" (Jer. 31:35-37); and that in spite of Israel's failure and rebellion God would restore them (Ezek. 20). This was not just a truth found in the prophets of the Old Testament but also with the apostle Paul in the New Testament. "The fact that Paul attributes the status of elect nation to Israelites who are "from the standpoint of the gospel . . . enemies" (Rom. 11:28) shows that the continuing elect status of Israel does not depend on her faithfulness, any more than it did in the times of the Hebrew prophets (see Jer. 31:35-37)."[10]

The Abrahamic covenant is also an *unconditional covenant*; that is, its fulfillment depends on God alone. When God made the covenant with Abraham, it was given without conditions attached.[11] When God later reaffirmed the covenant to Isaac and then to Jacob, no conditions were attached to it. Later statements found in Genesis 17, 22 and 26 which seem to add conditions to the covenant really do not do so (see pages 39-45). These statements were given long after the ratification of the covenant (Genesis 15) and focus on God's intention to bless Abraham in a greater way. This covenant with Abraham, therefore, is both everlasting and unconditional.

Another key part of this discussion is the ratification of the Abrahamic covenant in Genesis 15:7–21 (see discussion on pages 44–45). On this occasion, Abraham expressed concern to God about his lack of a future heir, since up to that point no son had been born to him. The Lord assured Abraham that he would indeed have a son. It is said that Abraham believed the Lord's statement on the matter. And then God graciously honored the faith of this man and encouraged him by ratifying the covenant. The ratification ceremony described in Genesis 15 would have been familiar to Abraham and one that he probably had been involved in many times before when he entered into covenant-type relationships with other men. This ceremony of ratification made the agreement legally binding. Now in this case, God's promise was, of course, sufficient but He nevertheless sought to encourage Abraham through this familiar ceremony.

Normally when a covenant was ratified by blood, the pieces of the animals were separated so that the parties of the covenant would walk between the pieces together. This obligated both parties to fulfill their part of the agreement. However, in this case, God alone passed between the pieces while Abraham experienced a visionary sleep. This unique event reinforced the truth that God was swearing fidelity to His promises and putting the burden of fulfillment on Himself alone.

The apostle Paul makes a highly significant contribution to this discussion in Galatians 3:15–18. His basic point is that once a covenant is ratified (made legally binding) neither the parties or the provisions of the covenant can be changed. He notes that this is true in all human covenants and it is also true in God's covenant with Abraham. (It is worth noting that the unconditional nature of the Abrahamic covenant is emphasized by the apostle by his use of the word "promise" nine times in Galatians 3 in reference to this "covenant.") This covenant is made with national Israel and cannot be transferred to another group or nation. The church, or Gentiles, cannot take over the promises made to national Israel. Paul says that it simply cannot be done! To change the parties of the covenant would violate the commitment made by God, and this is unthinkable.

The covenant remains a covenant with national Israel, and God's integrity is called into question if He, who committed Himself to its fulfillment, does not do so with Abraham's physical descendants. As noted earlier, Gentiles are not abandoned by God, but clearly through national Israel "all the nations would be blessed."

The covenant commitments by God in the Abrahamic covenant and the three covenants, which emerge out it, remain largely unfulfilled except where individual promises to Abraham and David are involved. Because many of the covenant promises remain unfulfilled and because the covenants are both *everlasting* and *unconditional* in nature, they simply must be fulfilled sometime in the future with national Israel.[12] Therefore, the existence of the unfulfilled, unconditional, and everlasting biblical covenants supports a continuing distinction between the church of Jesus Christ and the nation of Israel.

2. The Use of the Term "Israel"

The term "Israel" appears frequently in both Old and New Testaments. The Old Testament records over two thousand usages and the New Testament a little over seventy. The word is used throughout the Scriptures to refer to a specific national group. However, those holding to the replacement-theology position believe that the terms "church" and "Israel" are used interchangeably by the writers of Scripture. Berkhof writes, "We should not close our eyes to the patent fact that the name "church" (Heb. *qahal,* rendered *ekkelsia* in the Septuagint) is applied to Israel in the Old Testament repeatedly."[13] William Cox agrees, noting,

> *God's people were known in the Old Testament as "Israel." The same people, in the New Testament, are known as "the church." As a matter of scriptural fact, these terms are used interchangeably; the church is referred to as "Israel" (Gal. 6:16) while the Old Testament remnant is referred to as "the church" (Acts 7:38).*[14]

The facts of the New Testament simply do not support this assertion, however. The writers of the New Testament consistently make a distinction between "Israel" and "church" and do not use the terms synonymously. The term "Israel" is used seventy-three times in the New Testament, and in each occurrence it refers to ethnic Israel, either the nation as a whole or believing Jews within the nation.[15]

Replacement theology actually uses only three of the "Israel" references to try and establish its case: Romans 9:6; 11:26; Galatians 6:16. The statement in Romans 9:6 is that "they are not all Israel who are descended from Israel." Replacement theologians cite this Scripture to demonstrate a larger use of "Israel" to include Gentile Christians. But Romans 9:1–5 is unquestionably speaking about ethnic Israel, as those to whom belong many spiritual privileges including the covenants. The failure of the Jews to respond positively to Jesus the Messiah, Paul says, did not thwart the purposes of God. While the majority in Israel rejected God's plan, some in Israel did not. As he does elsewhere in Romans (where he uses "Israel" eleven times in chapters 9–11), Paul is simply acknowledging that within the nation of Israel there are believing Jews and unbelieving Jews. He is simply talking about ethnic Israelites who were Abraham's children both naturally and spiritually, and he contrasts them with those in Israel who do not believe. It is not a contrast between unbelieving Jews and the church, and there is not a Gentile anywhere in sight. It should be noted that many replacement theologians agree with this point and, therefore, do not use Romans 9:6 to establish their case.

In Romans 11:26, Paul declares that "all Israel shall be saved." While some holding to the view of replacement theology believe that "all Israel" includes Gentile converts as well as Jewish believers, others in that camp do not. The latter understand that "Israel" in 11:26 is the same as "Israel" in 11:25, where Paul addresses the coming salvation of ethnic Israel. This understanding goes along with the whole context of Romans 9–11, where national Israel is the subject. And it should be noted also that the use of "Jacob" in 11:26 gives further strong support for the interpretation that it is national Israel that is being spoken of.

Therefore, of the seventy-three references to "Israel" in the New Testament, only one, Galatians 6:16, is seen by all replacement theologians as establishing the fact that Israel and the church are interchangeable terms. At issue is the meaning of Paul's statement, "Peace and mercy be upon them, and upon the Israel of God." Replacement theologians base their claim largely on the translation of the word "and" (*kai*); the word that appears before the term "Israel of God." They set aside the primary meaning of "and" in favor of the secondary meaning of "even." All agree that "them" refers to believing Gentiles. So the verse is said to declare that mercy be upon them (believing Gentiles), *even* upon the Israel of God. This translation essentially equates believing Gentiles with the Israel of God. But this interpretation is weak both grammatically as well as contextually.

As S. Lewis Johnson has observed,

> *It is necessary to begin this part of the discussion with a reminder of a basic, but often neglected hermeneutical principle. It is this: in the absence of compelling exegetical and theological considerations, we should avoid the rarer grammatical usages when the common ones make good sense. . . . An extremely rare usage has been made to replace the common usage, even in spite of the fact that the common and frequents usage of and makes perfectly good sense in Galatians 6:16.*[16]

The straightforward rendering of "and" (*kai*) is to be preferred unless there is significant reason within the text itself to go with a secondary rendering. None exists in the text or context of Galatians 6:16.

The position of replacement theology is not only weak grammatically but does not take into consideration the other seventy-two uses of "Israel" in the New Testament. Paul and the other writers use "Israel" to mean ethnic Israel or believing Jews within the nation of Israel. The church is simply not called Israel or spiritual Israel.

Furthermore, the context of the book of Galatians does not support the position of replacement theology. Galatians 6:16 concludes a letter where Paul has been clear that no one is justified by law keeping. Jews and Gentiles alike are saved by faith alone in Jesus Christ. Paul warns them not to be persuaded by Judaizers who were attempting to add the law to faith in Christ. After he establishes that both Jews and Gentiles are justified and sanctified by faith alone, he comes to the end of the Galatian letter. And in 6:15–16, he pronounces a blessing on those believing Jews and those believing Gentiles who have come to and remain in that firm conviction. The two groups in the Galatian church were believing Jews and believing Gentiles, and these are the ones he is referring to. He is not suddenly focusing on just the believing Gentiles and calling them the Israel of God.

An appeal is often made to the idea that Israel equals the church, because believing Gentiles are called "Abraham's seed" (KJV) in Galatians 3:29. And indeed they are given that designation. But this does not mean that Gentiles now fulfill the promises given in the covenants to national Israel. The Scriptures actually use the phrase "seed of Abraham" in several different ways. The phrase is used of the natural, physical descendants of Abraham. This could include all those who descend from Abraham, but in the Scriptures the emphasis is on the physical line of Abraham through Isaac and Jacob. The "seed" is also used of those in Israel who are true believers (cf. Rom. 9:8). And it is used of true believers who are not physically descended from Abraham. Gentiles are, therefore, said to be a spiritual seed of Abraham the believer.

Having observed this, it must also be noted that *the spiritual seed of Abraham is never called "Israel"* or used as a synonym for "Israel." And the spiritual seed of Abraham is never said to fulfill the promises given by God in the covenants to the physical seed of Abraham. "This distinction will explain how the church may be related to the promises of the covenant without being the covenant people in whom the national promises will be fulfilled," Pentecost has noted. "Because we are the seed of Abraham spiritually by the new birth, it does not mean we are the physical seed of the patriarch."[17]

Arnold Fruchtenbaum adds a helpful observation about the matter of "seed":

> *What replacement theologians need to prove their case is a statement in Scripture that all believers are the "seed of Jacob." Such teaching would indicate that the church is spiritual Israel or that Gentile Christians are spiritual Jews. This is exactly what they do not have. Not all physical descendants of Abraham are Jews, but all physical descendants of Jacob are. The very term* Israel *originated with Jacob and not with Abraham. If there were even one verse that showed that the church is the seed of Jacob, replacement theologians could support one of their key contentions. This they cannot do. They only resort to passages that speak of the seed of Abraham, which, by itself, is insufficient to prove their contention, since the use of "Israel" is more restrictive than the use of "Abraham."*[18]

In spite of all attempts to support the idea that it is a "scriptural fact" that Israel and church are used interchangeably, it simply is not so. Therefore, the use of the term "Israel" in the New Testament supports the idea of maintaining a distinction between the church of Jesus Christ and the nation of Israel.

3. The Starting Point of Each Entity

The church and Israel did not begin at the same time and are, therefore, not the same entity. The nation of Israel essentially began when God called Abraham and promised to make a great nation from him. The rest of the Old Testament records the growth, development, and existence of that nation. There is really no significant debate on the matter of the starting point of the nation of Israel. It began with Abraham and was formed over the next seven hundred years into a nation with people, law, and land. The church, however, is not found in the Old Testament because it had its beginning on the day of Pentecost as recorded in Acts 2. The church began centuries after Israel began.

If the church began at Pentecost, then it did not begin or exist in the Old Testament. It is worth noting that in Matthew 16:18 the Lord Jesus used the future tense: "I *will build* My church" (emphasis added). He did not say, "I am building My church" or "I have been building My church." The church was something still future in Christ's ministry, which means that it was not in existence during His ministry or in the Old Testament. His apostles would not have understood what He meant by "His church" being built in the future, but the details about the church would be given to them later. In dealing with the matter of the discipline of an individual (Matt. 18:17), Jesus told them to tell it to the church or assembly. The apostles would have understood that He was speaking of a Jewish assembly. The statement of Matthew 18:17 must be understood in light of the previous statement (Matt. 16:18) of future building of "*My* church."

Certain things had to be true before the church could come into existence. First, according to the apostle Paul, the church is the "body of Christ" (e.g., Colossians 1:18, 24 and Ephesians 2:16; 3:6; 5:23, 30). It is clear that the church (the body) could not exist and function without its Head, the Lord Jesus Christ. Jesus did not assume that role until after He had shed His blood on the cross, had been resurrected, and then ascended back into heaven. It was at that time, after those events, that the Father "put all things in subjection under His feet, and gave Him as head over all things to the church, which is His body" (Eph. 1:22–23).

Furthermore, the church (the body) could not be formed apart from the baptizing work of the Holy Spirit. This is so because a believer enters the church, the body of Christ, only by means of Holy Spirit baptism (cf. 1 Cor. 12:13). But this vital ministry of the Spirit did not begin until the day of Pentecost. Without Spirit baptism no one could enter the body of Christ and, thus, the church could not exist. Not even the apostles were in the body, but they would experience Spirit baptism shortly after Jesus' ascension. On the day He ascended back into heaven, the Lord Jesus informed His apostles that the baptizing work of the Spirit would begin in the near future (Acts 1:5, 8). Ten days later, on the day of Pentecost, this and other ministries of the Spirit began.

When the apostle Peter reflected on the day of Pentecost as the time when this new work of the Spirit began (Acts 11:15), he spoke of it as a time of "beginning." Peter's use of "beginning" (*arche*) speaks of a specific point in time when something new commences.[19] This new thing, the church of Jesus Christ, began on the day of Pentecost.

The apostle Paul also tells us that the church's foundation is the apostles and the prophets of the New Testament, with Christ being the cornerstone (Eph. 2:20). This suggests two things: first, the church must have begun in the time of the apostles if they are the foundation; and second, the church is not seen being built upon the key Old Testament personalities of Abraham, Isaac, Jacob, and David. The church did not begin in the Old Testament and, therefore, it and Israel are distinct.

4. The Unique Character of the Church

The church, unlike Israel, is declared to be a "mystery" (Eph. 3:1–12; Col. 1:26–27). In the New Testament a "mystery" is a truth that was not revealed previously in the Old Testament. The *Expository Dictionary of New Testament Words* indicates the word "denotes . . . that which, being outside the range of unassisted natural apprehension, can be made known only by Divine revelation, and is made known in a manner and at a time appointed by God, and to those only who are illumined by His Spirit."[20]

The apostle Paul is clear that this unknown truth related to the church was something that was hidden from man and was hidden with God until "now" (the time of the apostles and New Testament prophets). The "mystery" included the facts that believing Jews and believing Gentiles would be united as equals in one body and that Christ Himself would indwell them. While Gentile salvation was seen in the Old Testament, this kind of relationship between Jews and Gentiles, and between God and the believer was never true in the Old Testament. The church was something new and significantly different from Israel.

The apostle Paul also declared that the church is "one new man" (Eph. 2:15). He states that based on the death of Christ, reconciliation has taken place between Jews and Gentiles as well as between God and man. The "one new man" is distinct from Israel and it is distinct from the Gentiles. The "one new man" (the church) is *not a continuation of either* but is made up of believing Jews and believing Gentiles. It is something entirely new and points to a very real distinction between the church and Israel.

5. Specific New Testament Scriptures That Support the Distinction

A number of New Testament Scriptures have been mentioned and there are a number that legitimately could be discussed. As was noted earlier (by Diprose), "in order for *replacement theology* to qualify as a biblical option, . . . there need to be, positively, passages which clearly teach it and, negatively, no passages which actually exclude it." Replacement theology does not have any passages that clearly teach that the nation of Israel has been set aside by God and replaced by the church. But it is faced with Paul's powerful presentation concerning Israel in Romans 9–11, which does not allow for replacement theology.

It is beyond the scope of this chapter to deal in detail with the key section in Romans 9–11. Others have done a fine job in demonstrating that the nation of Israel does have a wonderful future and that God fully intends to restore them to a place of prominence as He fulfills His covenant commitments to them.[21]

We simply need to note that the eleven times that Paul uses "Israel" in this section, each time it refers to ethnic Israel, not to Gentiles or the church. He is talking about his "kinsmen according to the flesh" (9:3). Paul knew that most people in Israel had turned from the Lord, rebelled, and become hardened in self-righteous unbelief. Of course, a believing remnant in Israel had always existed, but the nation as a whole had turned away (Romans 9 and 10). But Romans 11 is clear on the point that the same people who refused to believe and were temporarily disciplined by God would believe and be received back in the future when the Messiah would return. Using an illustration of an olive tree, Paul states that some of the natural branches of the tree (Israel) were broken off and wild branches (the Gentiles) were grafted in and received life from the "rich root of the olive tree" (the Abrahamic covenant). He then declares that the day is coming when God will graft the natural branches back into the olive tree, which looks ahead to the day of salvation for national Israel—the final fulfillment of the new covenant. On that day "all Israel will be saved" (Rom. 11:26).

> *It means in usage* Israel as a whole, *not necessarily every individual Israelite (cf. 1 Sam. 7:2–5; 25:1; 1 Kings 12:1; 2 Chron. 12:1–5; Dan. 9:11). The clues to its force are not only the sense of people (Rom. 11:1), but also the nature of the rejection of the Messiah by the nation, a rejection by nation as a whole (the leaders and the great mass of the people, but not every Israelite). This usage, as is well-known, is found in rabbinic literature . . . Thus, Paul affirms that ethnic Israel as a whole will be saved.*[22]

The apostle Paul does not believe that Israel's self-righteousness, unbelief, and sin has removed the people from God's blessings, but rather that the day is coming when Israel, as a nation, will be brought into the new covenant, thus fulfilling the Old Testament prophets. Some have said that the phrase "all Israel" is looking at the remnant of Jewish believers that have been saved as a part of the church over the centuries. But if that were true, then there never was a "breaking off" of the natural branches as the text declares. And there would be no need to graft them back in again, since they have always been part of the olive tree. No, Paul is referring to ethnic Israel and anticipating the day when God will "take away their sins" in light of His "covenant with them" (Rom. 11:27). Can anything be clearer than this in declaring that national Israel does have a future and has not been replaced or set aside by the church?

6. The External Differences

Theologians of all persuasions have a general agreement that there are significant external differences between the church and Israel. They just do not at all look alike. Replacement theologian Louis Berkhof acknowledges the difference: "In essence Israel constituted the church of God in the Old Testament, though its external institution differed vastly from that of the church in the New Testament."[23]

He is, of course correct that there are vast differences, and so, we see the nation of Israel having an army, national boundaries, a system of taxation, a priesthood within the nation, animal sacrifices, and forms of government (judges, priests, and kings) that do not correspond to that which is found in the New Testament church. One wonders, however, how these two entities can be conceived as being the same or one being the continuation of the other. The external differences support the idea that there is a distinction between the church and Israel.

7. The Internal Differences

There are also significance internal differences between the two entities. First, and of great significance, is that the body of Christ is made up of believers only. There has not, nor will there ever be, an unbeliever in the church (the body of Christ), because one can only enter through Spirit baptism. This is in stark contrast to Israel where unbelievers were dominant over much of Old Testament history. So Berkhof's statement is a bit puzzling when he says, "As far as their essential nature is concerned, they both consist of true believers, and of true believers only."[24] It could never be said of Israel, as it can be of the church, that no unbelievers were in it.

Second, the two entities function under two different covenants. Israel functioned under the old covenant, and the church has been privileged to be "partakers" of some of the spiritual blessings of the new covenant. (Note: the new covenant was made with Israel and Judah and must be fulfilled with them.) There is a stark contrast between these two covenants as taught in 2 Corinthians 3 and Hebrews 7-10, and the new covenant is clearly superior to the Old. The new covenant ministry is uniquely a broadened and expanded ministry of the Holy Spirit. The operating principles of the church are significantly different from that of Israel.

Third, the work of God in Israel was especially carried out by the Levitical priesthood, while in the church it is the anointed, spiritually gifted believer priest that carries out the work of God. The New Testament believer has been given "the ministry of reconciliation" (2 Cor. 5:18-20). A believer in the Old Testament, from the tribe of Asher or Gad, could make no such claim.

Other internal differences exist. But these surely show us that internally the church and Israel are quite different. The internal differences point to a legitimate distinction to be made between Israel and the church.

SOME CONCLUDING THOUGHTS

The evidence of the Scriptures is strong and compelling that the church of Jesus Christ and the nation of Israel are distinct entities in the plan and program of God. The church is not Israel, and Israel has not been set aside or replaced. When the biblical covenants made with the nation of Israel are seen as unconditional and unfulfilled, it is essential that the Lord God fulfills them with Israel, the ones who are the original party in the covenant. When the Scriptures are interpreted normally, one comes to the conclusion that Israel means Israel. And the literal (normal) approach of interpretation also leads one to see that the church began at a different time than Israel did; that it was a "mystery" and something "new" built on the New Testament apostles and prophets; and that it is externally and internally different from Israel.

Such evidence, along with Romans 9–11, points to the fact that Israel was not abandoned or replaced by God. The church is important in God's program, but it is not Israel.

This chapter originally appeared in Paul Benware, "Israel Is Not the Church," The Gathering Storm, Mal Couch, ed., (Grand Rapids: Kregel Publishing, 2004). Used by permission.

CHAPTER SEVEN

THE VIEW
OF
Amillenialism

If all Christendom could be gathered together and a vote taken on which of the three millennial views was favored, amillennialism would easily win. Amillennialism is clearly the majority view, since it is held by the Roman Catholic Church, the Greek Church, and a large segment of Protestantism. That, of course, does not make it the correct view, but neither does it mean that it is false. The validity of any view must be determined by a study of the Scriptures.

Amillennialism as a system of theology is usually traced back to St. Augustine (AD 354–430). Before Augustine, for the first three hundred years of the church, the premillennial view was virtually the only view to be found in the church. One notable exception was Origen of Alexandria, Egypt.

Origen (185–254) and other scholars in Alexandria were greatly influenced by Greek philosophy and attempted to integrate that philosophy with Christian theology. Included in Greek philosophy was the idea that those things that were material and physical were inherently evil. Influenced by this thinking, these Alexandrian scholars concluded that an earthly kingdom of Christ with its many physical blessings would be something evil.

THE CHALLENGE TO PREMILLENNIALISM: ORIGEN AND AUGUSTINE

Origen could not accept the position of premillennialism, though he did not really develop an alternative position. He simply believed that a spiritual, nonphysical kingdom would be a better idea.

Origen is also known for developing a new approach to the interpretation of Scripture—that of allegorizing. He seemed to have a consuming desire to find hidden and mystical meanings in the plain words of Scripture, and this led him away from the historical-grammatical method. "Origen's approach to all of Scripture was to spiritualize it. He therefore denied the literal meaning of prophecy. He looked upon its language as highly symbolic and expressive of deep spiritual truths rather than of future historical events."[1]

Although Origen and others began to question the premillennial view, it was Augustine who systematized and developed amillennialism as an alternative to premillennialism. Like Origen, Augustine had been educated in Greek philosophy and could not escape its influence, which is probably why he viewed premillennialism with suspicion, seeing it as a view that promoted a time of carnal enjoyment. Augustine was absolutely convinced that the "chiliasts" (premillennialists) promoted an unspiritual time of fleshly excesses and that no spiritually minded person would follow such a view.

Augustine's attitude, as well as his theology, has since that time dominated much of the church. Furthermore, he found Origen's allegorical method of interpretation a helpful tool in sidestepping the teachings of certain millennial passages. So Augustine came to reject the premillennial idea of an earthly reign of Christ, which had been held in the church for several centuries.

In place of it he developed the idea that the Church is the Kingdom of Messiah foretold in such Scriptures as Daniel 2 and 7 and Revelation 20. In his book, The City of God, *he became the first person to teach the idea that the organized Catholic (universal) Church is the Messianic Kingdom and that the millennium began with the first coming of Christ.*[2]

Augustine, then, was the first to develop a clear amillennial viewpoint. Whereas others have defined and developed the system further, his work is the foundation of it.

DEFINING THE TERM *AMILLENNIALISM*

In the Greek language a word is negated by placing the letter "a" in front of it. Therefore, the word *a*millennial actually means "no millennium." However, this is an unfortunate term because amillennialists do believe in a millennium. But the millennium they believe in is a spiritual one, not an earthly one. The word *amillennial* reflects their denial of a physical, literal reign of Christ on this present earth.

Premillennial author John Walvoord has given a good and complete definition of amillennialism that is considered by amillennialists to be fair.

> *Its most general character is that of denial of a* literal *reign of Christ upon the earth. Satan is conceived as bound at the first coming of Christ. The present age between the first and second comings is the fulfillment of the millennium. Its adherents are divided on whether the millennium is being fulfilled now on the earth (Augustine) or whether it is being fulfilled by the saints in heaven (Kliefoth). It may be summed up in the idea that there will be no more millennium than there is now, and that the eternal state immediately follows the second coming of Christ.*[3]

Amillennialist William Cox agrees with this description and also argues that the term *amillennial* is not really a good one. However, he observes that it is well established, and so far "a more suitable term has not been found to describe amillennialism so as to distinguish it from premillennialism and postmillennialism."[4] Although the term does not represent the view very well, simply remember that amillennialists do believe in a millennium, but not the type of millennium taught by premillennialism or postmillennialism.

TYPES OF AMILLENNIALISM

It has been the contention of many within amillennialism that conservative amillennialists are united in their eschatology. This, however, is not quite accurate. Basically two primary views, which are quite different from each other, exist within amillennialism.

Millennial Rule of Christ in Heaven

According to one view, the millennium is being fulfilled only in heaven as Christ reigns over the glorified saints. The millennium does precede the second coming of Christ, but it has to do with the blessed condition of the saints in heaven. The millennium, therefore, is not something that finds fulfillment on this earth in the present or in the future. Belief in this "heavenly millennium" relies heavily on the spiritualization of those Scriptures that talk about the blessings of a glorious kingdom on this earth. This view is also relatively new, having been developed in the nineteenth century.

Millennial Rule by the Church on Earth

The other view is clearly the majority view within amillennialism. It is basically the amillennialism of Augustine, which teaches that the millennium is being fulfilled in the present age in the church and is on the earth (though Augustine believed that this spiritual millennium would end in AD 650). The basic elements of this majority view within amillennialism will be discussed in a moment.

These two views within amillennialism are quite different, since in one the millennium is on earth in the church and in the other it is in heaven, where Christ reigns over the disembodied believers. The real points of agreement between the two is the denial of a millennial reign of Christ on this earth after the second coming. And, of course, both views allegorize certain kingdom passages.

THE BASIC ELEMENTS OF AMILLENNIALISM

Five basic elements characterize amillennialism. We will consider each in turn.

An Ongoing Millennial Kingdom
That Ends upon Christ's Return

First, and most basic, amillennialism is the belief that the millennial kingdom began at the first coming of Christ and will continue until the second coming. Christ is today reigning in the church in the hearts of believers, as well as over the souls of believers in heaven. Revelation 20 records the length of the kingdom, stating that this kingdom will last for a thousand years. It is the position of amillennialism, however, that the thousand years is to be taken figuratively. The period of time between the two advents of Christ is interpreted as an undetermined length of time. "Amillenarians take Revelation 20:1-6 as a symbolic picture of the interadvent period. They believe the expression 'a thousand years' denotes a complete period of time, the length of which is known only by God."[5]

It is the view of amillennialism that in His death and resurrection Christ was victorious over Satan, sin, and death. And because of this victory the kingdom of God was begun at the first advent and continues as a present reality. "Amillennialists believe that the kingdom of God was founded by Christ at the time of his sojourn on earth, is operative in history now and is destined to be revealed in its fullness in the life to come."[6] In amillennialism, therefore, the Revelation 20 passage does not refer to the future but to the present.

The amillennialist generally sees Revelation as composed of several sections (usually seven), each of which recapitulates the events of the same period rather than describing the events of successive periods. Each deals with the same era—the period between Christ's first and second coming—picking up earlier themes, elaborating and developing them further. Revelation 20, then, does not speak of far-removed, future events, and the meaning of the thousand years is to be found in some past and/or present fact.[7]

Important to the amillennial approach is this view that Revelation 20 (on the millennium) does not follow chronologically from Revelation 19, which describes the second coming of Christ. Instead, Revelation 20 is said to give additional information on the period of time between the two comings of Christ. The statements of Revelation 20 concerning the two resurrections and the binding of Satan must, therefore, be interpreted accordingly.

Satan Already Bound

Second, amillennialism addresses in a significant way the binding of Satan mentioned in Revelation 20:1-3:

And I saw an angel coming down from heaven, having the key of the abyss and a great chain in his hand. And he laid hold of the dragon, the serpent of old, who is the devil and Satan, and bound him for a thousand years, and threw him into the abyss, and shut it and sealed it over him, so that he should not deceive the nations any longer, until the thousand years were completed.

Amillennialists say that this binding took place at the time of Christ's first coming, which is the beginning of the millennium. Satan is, therefore, seen as bound during the entire period between the first and second advents of Christ.

According to amillennialist William Cox, Satan is obviously not bound today if that "means that he cannot move a muscle against God."[8] He believes that the binding of Satan simply refers to the limiting of his power so that "he can no longer deceive the nations by keeping the gospel from them."[9] Hoekema agrees with this viewpoint:

The latter term should rather be thought of as a figurative description of the way in which Satan's activities will be curbed during the thousand-year period. . . . This does not imply that Satan can do no harm whatever while he is bound. It means only what John says here: while Satan is bound he cannot deceive the nations in such a way as to keep them from learning about the truth of God.[10]

So Satan is bound in this present millennial kingdom only in the sense that he is unable to keep people from hearing the gospel.

But what about the "Abyss" that Satan is said to be cast into? That too is interpreted in a figurative way: "The word *Abyss* should . . . be thought of as a figurative description of the way in which Satan's activities will be curbed during the thousand-year period."[11]

The Two Resurrections: One Spiritual, One Physical

Third, the two resurrections found in Revelation 20:4–6 include a spiritual one. These verses speak of those who were martyred for their faith: "They came to life and reigned with Christ for a thousand years. . . . This is the first resurrection." Most amillennialists view this "first" resurrection as a spiritual one. They believe that it refers to the new birth of the believer.

126

THE VIEW OF AMILLENNIALISM

When a person becomes a believer, Christ, in a spiritual sense, rules in their hearts. At death this reign continues in heaven.

Thus, Revelation 20 depicts the "present reign of the souls of deceased believers with Christ in heaven."[12] The second resurrection mentioned in these verses, however, is a physical resurrection, which takes place at the end of the millennial kingdom.

Christ's Literal Return

Fourth, the second coming of Christ will be a literal return of the Lord to the earth. The second coming is a single event; that is, there is no prior return of Christ for the saints at the rapture. The rapture of all believers takes place at the time of the second coming.

Understanding the Present Age

Fifth, amillennialism holds a pessimistic view of the present age. Along with premillennialists, amillennialists believe that "the world is growing increasingly worse, and that it will be at its very worst when Jesus returns."[13] The parable of the wheat and the tares is seen as a description of the growth of good and evil together throughout the present age. The growth of evil will continue until the Antichrist appears and Christ returns.

Further, amillennialists believe that the tribulation (persecution) began when Satan was defeated at the cross and will continue on until the return of Christ. The church has always experienced, and will continue to experience, tribulation. It is, therefore, useless to argue over whether the church will go through tribulation. The church has been through tribulation, is presently experiencing tribulation, and will continue to face tribulation until it reaches heaven. But it may well be that persecution and trouble for the church will get much worse immediately before the Lord Jesus comes again.

Resurrection, Judgment, and the Eternal State

Sixth, amillennialism teaches that at the time of the second coming of Christ there will be one general resurrection and one general judgment. All believers and all unbelievers will be part of these events.

The seventh tenet of amillennialism is that, after this time of resurrection and judgment, the final, eternal state will be brought in. Unbelievers will spend eternity away from God in the lake of fire, whereas believers will enter into glory, spending eternity on a new earth.

Evaluating Amillennialism

The amillennial position has been analyzed extensively by premillennial and postmillennial writers. Several key issues need to be summarized in our evaluation of amillennialism.

1. The Issue of Biblical Interpretation

The first and great issue is the method of interpretation used by amillennialism. Amillennialists, as we have observed already, employ a dual system of hermeneutics. While they approach a great deal of Scripture using literal interpretation (including many prophetic portions), they feel it is legitimate and necessary to interpret other prophetic passages spiritually. The passages that are spiritualized deal with the millennial kingdom, which if interpreted literally would clearly lead one to a premillennial position.

> *Amillennialists . . . believe that though many Old Testament prophecies are indeed to be interpreted literally, many others are to be interpreted in a non-literal way. . . . The difference between an amillennial and a premillennial interpreter comes out when each tries to indicate which prophecies must be interpreted literally and which prophecies are to be interpreted in a nonliteral sense. On this question there would be wide divergence of opinion.*[14]

Premillennialism does not accept the spiritualization of the prophetic word, whereas amillennialism embraces it. As long as there is no agreement on this point, the debate will continue with no resolution. Premillennial theologian John Walvoord says that "a proper study of the millennial issue demands, first, an analysis of the methods of interpretation which have produced amillennialism and premillennialism. This lays bare the problem and opens the way to see the issue in its true light."[15]

He then goes on to observe that once spiritualization of prophecy is allowed it is very difficult to regulate. He is correct, because when an interpreter leaves literal interpretation, he also leaves the guidelines and restraints of history and grammar. There is truth to the idea that when one spiritualizes the Scriptures the interpreter becomes the final authority instead of Scripture itself.

The issue of the interpretation of prophecy was dealt with in chapter 1 and need not be repeated here. But to reiterate one conclusion, if a literal interpretation is consistently applied to the prophetic passages of Scripture, one will arrive at the premillennial position. It is the spiritualization of selected passages that enables an interpreter to arrive at amillennialism.

2. The Issue of the Binding of Satan

A second point in the analysis of amillennial eschatology has to do with the binding of Satan. In Revelation 20:1–3, Satan is said to be bound as the millennial kingdom begins. That fact forces amillennialism to postulate a binding of Satan in connection with the first advent of Christ. It is obvious to everyone that Satan is very active in the world today, so amillennialism spiritualizes the text and defines the "binding" as restricting Satan's ability to deceive the nations of the earth by keeping the gospel from them. But that view does not deal adequately with the text of Revelation 20. Those verses do not look at Satan's present activity but at his future confinement.

The amillennialist is, of course, correct in declaring that Satan was defeated at the cross. But that defeat has not yet removed Satan from his place of authority on this earth (1 John 5:19). When Jesus comes back as the Lord of the earth, Satan will be stripped of his authority and rendered helpless.

The binding of Satan fits well chronologically after the events of Revelation 19:11–21, which tells of Christ's second coming. In Revelation 12–19 the enemies of the Lord are Satan, the beast (the Antichrist), and the false prophet. They will be leading the forces of evil in those last days immediately before the second coming. Revelation 19:19–21 states that "the beast was seized, and with him the false prophet," and they were thrown into the lake of fire. No mention of the fate of Satan is given at this point.

> *Revelation 20:1–10 serves as the final piece of the puzzle in the defeat and ultimate punishment of the utmost enemy of Christ and His saints. Therefore, in order to make sense of the culminating victory of Christ and the conclusive defeat of Satan, Revelation 20:1–10 is a logical and chronological necessity to chapters 12–19.* [16]

Revelation 20:1 ("and I saw") does show a chronological progression in the story of the end times. After seeing Christ descend from heaven to the earth in the mighty conquest of His enemies, the apostle John observes an angel coming from heaven and binding Satan with a chain. This angel had been given the key (which stands for authority) of the Abyss. Satan was then thrown into the Abyss, and it was secured so that Satan could not exit.

At this point amillennialists will often attack the literalism of premillennialists by pointing out that Satan could not be bound with a literal chain. It may be that Satan and angels cannot be tied down with chains purchased at the local hardware store. However, though they are spirit beings, they can be confined and rendered immobile and helpless. For example, in Daniel 10, one powerful angel was able to keep a less powerful angel from carrying out his assignment for some twenty-one days. That angel clearly was unable to operate, and by another angel at that.

In Revelation 12, angels fight against one another, and the evil angels are removed from heaven and confined to the earth. How angels fight and defeat one another is not clear, but it is clear that the demons are "physically" restricted. According to the apostle Peter, some of the evil angels are permanently confined (2 Peter 2:4). The point of Revelation 20:1–3 is that Satan will lose all freedom and power to act on this planet throughout the millennial period. We may not with our limited knowledge of angelic beings be able to do a material analysis of the chains involved, but that does not negate that the picture of the text is Satan being rendered inactive. That is seen not only in the picture of his binding but also in the fact that he will be placed in the Abyss. According to these verses he will be unable to get out of it during the entire thousand years.

It is interesting to observe that a discussion of the Abyss is absent from the teachings of some amillennialists as they deal with Revelation 20:1–3, whereas others present a very weak case exegetically. For example, one writer gives the following few thoughts in a chapter devoted to Revelation 20:

Since the "lake of fire" mentioned in verses 10, 14 and 15 obviously stands for the place of final punishment, the "bottomless pit" or "abyss" mentioned in verses 1 and 3 must not be the place of final punishment. The latter term should rather be thought of as a figurative description of the way in which Satan's activities will be curbed during the thousand-year period.[17]

It is true that the Abyss is not the place of final punishment, but the Abyss *is a place* and should not be spiritualized away as though it had no meaning in the Scriptures. The Abyss as the place of imprisonment for the demons is referenced in Luke 8:31, where the Lord Jesus met a man who was inhabited by many demons. When confronted by Jesus, the demons entreated Him not to order them to the Abyss. They knew full well that their days of living in that man were over and did not bother to debate the matter with Christ. What they feared was confinement in the Abyss, and they begged Jesus not to send them there.

The Abyss is also spoken of in Revelation 9:1–2, 11; there evil spirits are seen leaving the Abyss for a short period at the end of the tribulation. So, when Satan is cast into the Abyss, it is speaking of his total and absolute confinement in a *specific place* for the thousand years. In light of this, it seems somewhat arbitrary to say that the Abyss is figurative of the curbing of Satan's power here on earth.

A final thought on the binding of Satan concerns his inability to "deceive the nations" during the millennial kingdom. We observed earlier that amillennialism teaches that Satan is bound in the sense that he cannot keep the truth of God from the nations. In this sense, of course, Satan has always been restricted. In all of his history he has never been able to do everything he has wanted to do because he is under the authority of his Creator. In this present age he finds himself in the same situation, except that he is now looking forward to a terrible future in the lake of fire.

But Satan does have a measure of success in this present age in hindering the gospel. He still does what he has always done, and that is to resist the plan and purposes of God. Paul clearly states that Satan blinds the minds of the unbelieving so that they will not believe the gospel of Christ (2 Cor. 4:3-4). This successful activity in relationship to the gospel certainly does not support the concept of binding found in amillennialism. Other Scriptures confirm the reality of Satan's present activity (cf. Eph. 2:1-3; 1 Tim. 4:1; 2 Tim. 2:24-26; 1 John 3:8-10). As another example, Paul told the believers at Thessalonica that Satan hindered him from returning to them to preach the Word (1 Thess. 2:18). Satan's activity is also seen in the case of Ananias and Sapphira, when he prompted them to lie (Acts 5:3).

Satan was clearly defeated at the cross, and his ultimate destruction is ensured. But the victory at the cross has not yet been fully manifested in history in all respects—the curse is still in effect, death still reigns, and Satan is still the god of this world. Furthermore, whereas Jesus is the victor, He has not returned and has not exercised His full authority. Thus, "we do not yet see all things subjected to him" (Heb. 2:8). Jesus is not yet reigning, and Satan has not yet been bound in the Abyss.

A normal reading of the text of Revelation 20:1-3 and an exegesis of all the statements in that text does not support a present, partial restriction of Satan. Rather, it points to a future, complete confinement of Christ's adversary, the Devil.

3. The Issue of the Length of the Millennium

A third issue in evaluating amillennialism is the phrase "thousand years" (*chilioi etos*), which occurs six times in Revelation 20. This phrase establishes the point that the length of Christ's reign will be one thousand years. Amillennialism regards this phrase as a figure of speech; that is, *chilioi etos* is speaking of a long period of time, namely this present church age. This view is based on the assumption that numbers in the book of Revelation are often just figurative and, therefore, the "thousand years" of Revelation 20 is best put into the symbolic category. Amillennial scholar Anthony Hoekema clearly states this position:

> *The Book of Revelation is full of symbolic numbers. Obviously the number "thousand" which is used here must not be interpreted in the literal sense. Since the number ten signifies completeness, and since a thousand is ten to the third power, we may think of the expression "a thousand years" as standing for a complete period, a very long period of indeterminate length. . . We*

*may conclude that this thousand-year period extends from Christ's first com-
ing to just before his Second Coming.*[18]

Hoekema's view is commonly held by other amillennialists. And while
we respect the scholarship and the contribution of men like Hoekema, we
need to evaluate his declarative statement on this matter. When we look at
the way in which numbers in Revelation (and in biblical apocalyptic literature) are used, it is not at all "obvious" that the number "thousand" must
be seen as symbolic. Instead, interpreting the phrase "thousand years" in
its literal, normal sense seems the far better approach. The following four
points need to be considered when dealing with the key phrase "thousand
years" in Revelation 20.

First, the most basic function of numbers is to designate the quantity *of something.* Numbering systems have always been devised for the purpose of
expressing quantitative functions such as counting, determining order,
making measurements, performing calculations, and expressing quantity.
A number is, and always has been, by its very nature literal (i.e., 5=5, 23=23,
167=167). Historically, numbers have not been used symbolically. It is true
that some in the course of history have been involved in "number mysticism" where specific meanings are attached to certain numbers. For example, some have said that *5* stands for grace or God's goodness; *12* represents governmental perfection; and *28* equals eternal life. But even the
casual observer is struck by the apparent arbitrary nature of such systems.
In some of these systems it is discovered that some numbers have nearly
the identical meaning as others, while most numbers are used so infre-
quently (or not at all) that it is just impossible to see how they can be symbolic of anything.

Second, the number 7 is used frequently in Revelation. In his book *Biblical
Numerology* John J. Davis presents a convincing case that aside from the
number 7 no number possesses an inherent symbolic meaning.[19] This
number often conveys the idea of "perfection" or "completeness," an idea
which is derived from its usage in the Bible as well as from other ancient
cultures (e.g., Egypt and Ugarit). It could be that oral tradition passed on
since the creation week into many cultures was the catalyst for the number 7 having the special significance of completeness. But even in its use in
the Bible, the number 7 does not lose its normal *quantitative value*, nor does
it always carry the idea of "completeness."

For example, there is probably no symbolic meaning in Paul staying seven days in Troas. And when Revelation speaks of seven seal judgments, seven trumpet judgments, and seven bowl judgments, it could be communicating that the judgment of God is a perfect and complete judgment. But it is also true that there are actually seven seals, seven trumpets, and seven bowls. It should be noted that it is primarily the large usage of the number 7 that makes such an observation possible. But no other number, including the number one thousand, carries symbolic meanings with it.

Third, numbers used in other prophetic literature are used in the usual way. One study of numbers in biblical apocalyptic literature concludes that numbers are used in their normal *quantitative* way about 94 percent of the time.[20] Such a statistic immediately raises doubts about numbers in the book of Revelation being labeled "symbolic" since the normal use of numbers in biblical, apocalyptic literature is according to the basic function of numbers. Does this pattern hold true in Revelation?

Fourth, there are just about 240 occurrences of numbers in the book of Revelation.[21] Eliminating the six occurrences of "thousand years" in Revelation 20 (the meaning of which we are trying to determine), that leaves 234 times where numbers are used. Of these occurrences: 19 times fractions are used (i.e., 1/3 of the earth burned up); 59 times as in numerical sequences (i.e., the fourth angel sounded); and 162 times as full numbers (i.e., 24 elders).

Out of these 234 numbers, it appears that the vast majority are to be interpreted in the way that numbers are normally interpreted; that is as expressing quantities. So when we read that there are seven churches, there are seven actual churches that are in view and we can count them. When we read of 144,000 men carefully selected in groups of 12,000 from twelve specific Israelite tribes, there is no reason not to understand that these are normal quantitative expressions. Why should we not understand that an army of 200,000,000 is actually composed of that number or that forty-two months means forty-two months?

Apparently there are just sixteen times in Revelation where the numbers are symbolic. If this is correct, Revelation pretty much follows other biblical, apocalyptic literature by using numbers in their normal quantitative use about 93 percent of the time. Of the sixteen times when the number is symbolic, fifteen times the symbols are established by previous usage. The one exception is Revelation 13:18 where the "666" mark of the beast is mentioned. The "666" is to be understood as the numerical value of the beast's name, but it clearly has a mystical significance. Since this number is not found anywhere else, its meaning is not clear. But the other fifteen symbolic occurrences have meanings already established by the Old Testament and, therefore, cannot be dealt with in an arbitrary manner.[22]

So when we come to the six uses of "thousand years" in Revelation 20, the evidence is that the one thousand years of Revelation 20 are to be taken in the normal quantitative way and, therefore, an actual one-thousand-year reign of Christ is being proclaimed.[23]

4. The Issue of the Two Resurrections

A fourth issue in our evaluation of amillennialism pertains to the two resurrections found in Revelation 20:4–6. Although not all amillennialists are in agreement, the general consensus is that the first resurrection is spiritual and the second resurrection is physical. (See the chart entitled "The View of Amillennialism" earlier in this chapter.) According to the apostle John, the first resurrection takes place before the millennium begins, and the second occurs at the end of the millennium. A normal reading of the text would dictate that both are physical resurrections. But amillennialists cannot interpret the first resurrection as physical because there was no general physical resurrection of people at the first advent. The conclusion, therefore, is that this must refer to a spiritual resurrection; namely, the new birth of believers. This position has at least two significant difficulties.

On the one hand, the same Greek word is used of both resurrections, so there is no justification for making these two resurrections different in kind. If the second one is a physical resurrection (which nearly all amillennialists agree is the case), the first one must also be a physical resurrection. Nothing in the context of Revelation 20 suggests that these are two different kinds of resurrection. The verb translated "came to life" is used about a dozen times by John in Revelation to refer to physical life, which would suggest that he is speaking of physical life also in Revelation 20.

On the other hand, those who participate in the first resurrection are those who were beheaded because of their identification with Christ and their allegiance to the Word of God. Clearly they were regenerated people before they were put to death. Since it is the physical death of these already-regenerated people that is being spoken of here, it must be their subsequent physical resurrection that is being discussed. Nothing in

Revelation 20:4 indicates that their spiritual birth is being spoken of, but everything indicates that the resurrection of their bodies is the subject of discussion.

5. The Issue of the Loosing of Satan

Just as the amillennial position regarding Satan's binding (issue 2) bears evaluating, so does its position regarding Satan's loosing of Satan after the thousand years. Revelation 20:7–8 states, "And when the thousand years are completed, Satan will be released from his prison, and will come out to deceive the nations." The chronological sequence given by the apostle John is clear: after the completion of the millennial reign, Satan is loosed and can once again deceive the nations for a short period of time. Amillennialists are somewhat vague on this point because it does not align itself very well with their view of the millennium. If this present age is the millennium and if the second coming of Christ ends the millennium, where does this loosing of Satan fit in? A loosing of Satan *during* the millennial kingdom is not allowed by Revelation 20:3 and 7, which indicates his loosing is to take place *after* the kingdom age is over.

Hoekema says that Satan will be released after the millennium and will then deceive the nations. But he does not expound on how this significant period of time is related to the Second Coming.[24] William Cox represents many amillennialists when he says that the loosing of Satan takes place immediately prior to the second coming.[25] But the sequence of events here does not pose a problem for premillennialism. Within this vision that John received (which began at 19:11), there is a clear order of events: at the second coming of Christ to this earth, Satan is bound in the Abyss for the duration of the thousand years, released for a short period of time to instigate a rebellion against Christ, and then is cast forever into the lake of fire. It is, as one author notes, "not only a chronological progression but also a logical one."[26]

SUMMARY AND CONCLUSION

Amillennialism is the belief that the millennial kingdom is being fulfilled in the church during this present age. Most amillennialists believe that the millennial kingdom is on this earth, whereas a minority believe that it is in heaven. The millennium is that indefinite period of time between the first and second advents of Jesus Christ. Christ is said to be ruling in the hearts of believers on the earth, as well as over the souls of the saints in heaven. The millennium will end with the second coming of Christ; then all judgments and resurrections will take place. After this, the eternal state will be ushered in. The term *amillennial* ("no millennium") is not a denial of a millennium but, rather, the denial of a literal, earthy reign of Jesus Christ sometime in the future.

In analyzing amillennialism, the great issue remains the spiritualization of prophecy. There is general agreement that the kingdom prophecies of the Bible, taken literally, lead to a premillennial position. But amillennialists subscribe to a dual system of hermeneutics, believing that it is best to spiritualize numerous kingdom passages. They believe that the Old Testament promises given originally to Israel are to be applied to the church. Amillennialists interpret the key passage of Revelation 20 spiritually and not literally. But peace, prosperity, joy, a full knowledge of the Lord, righteousness, and numerous other things mentioned in the kingdom prophecies are not literally seen in our world today. So, if this present age is the millennium, it is necessary to spiritualize those prophecies. But to the premillennialist (and to many postmillennialists) the amillennial spiritualizing of prophecies renders almost meaningless some of the most wonderful and glorious passages of Scripture.

We have seen that Revelation 20:1–10 is also subject to amillennial spiritualizing. But it becomes quite evident here that amillennialism fails to meet the demands of solid exegesis and is forced to avoid the natural rendering of the text in order to align it with its ideas of the kingdom. As one author says, amillennialism's "effort to get around the natural meaning of the text is completely unconvincing."[27] The spiritualization of prophecy provides a suspect foundation on which to build a system.

CHAPTER EIGHT

THE VIEW

OF Postmillenialism

O f the three major millennial views, postmillennialism has had the most interesting history. It arrived late on the theological scene and grew immensely popular, overshadowing both amillennialism and premillennialism. However, most theologians pronounced the postmillennial system dead when it seemingly was dealt a mortal blow by the events of world history. But postmillennialism is breathing again and finding adherents in various segments of today's church. This revived form of postmillennialism goes by several new names, but it still possesses the basic tenets of classic postmillennialism.

No trace of postmillennialism can be found in the first three centuries of the church. During that time the church held to a premillennial view. The discussion of amillennialism in chapter 6 noted that a change in the millennial view of the church began with Origen (AD 185–254) and was fully developed with Augustine (354–430). In the centuries that followed, a number of theologians pointed out deficiencies in Augustine's system and began to suggest changes. There was a turning away from much of the allegorization of Augustine's amillennialism and a return to a more literal understanding of the Bible.

A BRIEF HISTORY

This return to the literal interpretation led some to the premillennial view, but others developed a third major millennial view, that of postmillennialism.

The credit for developing the postmillennial system is usually given to Daniel Whitby (1638–1726), a Unitarian minister from England. Whitby was viewed by many in his day as both a theological liberal and a heretic. Some of his writings were even publicly burned because they strayed so far from orthodoxy. However, his view of the millennium struck a responsive chord and was embraced by both liberal and conservative theologians. One writer explains this interesting phenomenon in the following way:

> *His views on the millennium would probably have never been perpetuated if they had not been so well keyed to the thinking of the times. The rising tide of intellectual freedom, science, and philosophy, coupled with humanism, had enlarged the concept of human progress and painted a bright picture of the future. Whitby's view of a coming golden age for the church was just what people wanted to hear. . . . It is not strange that theologians scrambling for readjustments in a changing world should find in Whitby just the key they needed. It was attractive to all kinds of theology. It provided for the conservative a seemingly more workable principle of interpreting Scripture. After all, the prophets of the Old Testament knew what they were talking about when they predicted an age of peace and righteousness. Man's increasing knowledge of the world and scientific improvements which were coming could fit into this picture. On the other hand, the concept was pleasing to the liberal and skeptic. If they did not believe the prophets, at least they believed that man was now able to improve himself and his environment. They, too, believed a golden age was ahead.*[1]

The emphasis on man's role of bringing in the kingdom of God on this earth fit well with the prevailing views of the time. People could point to the marvelous advances in science that made life better and the notable benefits of the Industrial Revolution that raised the standard of living for so many. There was a relative peace in the world, and the rise of democracies seemed to be bringing a new kind of freedom to mankind. Thus, postmillennialism gained popularity and quickly became the dominant millennial viewpoint in the church of the eighteenth and nineteenth centuries. But the idea of a steady and inevitable progress toward the golden age of the kingdom was dealt a terrible blow with the outbreak of World War I.

It became clear to most that the world was not progressively getting better and better after all. Postmillennialism staggered badly with the coming of World War I and was pronounced dead with the coming of World War II. Very few still held to this optimistic millennial view. However, several decades after World War II some stirrings indicated that, contrary to the assumption of most theologians, postmillennialism was not dead. Postmillennialism once again is being advocated and is again gaining acceptance within the church.

DEFINING THE TERM: *POSTMILLENNIAL*

The word *postmillennial* conveys the idea that Jesus Christ will return *after* the millennium. Postmillennialists generally agree with amillennialists in holding that the millennium is not to be understood as a literal thousand years. (To see other similarities with the premillenial position, as well as contrasts with historic and dispensational premillennial positions, review the chart "Views Concerning End Times" on page 143.) Some postmillennialists believe that the term *millennium* applies to the entire period of time between the two advents of Christ. Others believe that it applies only to the golden age of peace and righteousness that will be brought in after the preaching of the gospel has gone on for a period of time. They believe that the present age will develop morally and spiritually until the golden age, or millennium, arrives. Boettner, a postmillennialist, defines his view in this way:

> *Postmillennialism is that view of the last things which holds that the kingdom of God is now being extended in the world through the preaching of the gospel and the saving work of the Holy Spirit in the hearts of individuals, that the world eventually is to be Christianized and that the return of Christ is to occur at the close of a long period of righteousness and peace commonly called the millennium. It should be added that on postmillennial principles the Second Coming of Christ will be followed immediately by the general resurrection, the general judgment, and the introduction of heaven and hell in their fullness.*[2]

141

The fundamental point is that Christ returns after the millennium is completely over. It is the church that brings in the millennium. The reign of Christ is not from an earthly throne; rather, His rule is a spiritual one in the hearts of believers.

TYPES OF POSTMILLENNIALISM

Biblical Postmillennialism

Basically there are two types of postmillennialism. The first might be called "biblical postmillennialism" because it takes seriously the doctrines of the Scriptures and the need to spread the gospel throughout the world. The belief is that the church of Jesus Christ, operating in the power of the Holy Spirit, will bring dramatic and transforming changes in the world. This is a work of God according to those theologians of the eighteenth and nineteenth centuries who carefully developed the position of biblical postmillennialism. Of these postmillennial proponents, Stanley Grenz writes:

> *Their outlook differed fundamentally from both secular and liberal Christian utopianism. They were optimistic concerning the future to be sure. But their optimism was born out of a belief in the triumph of the gospel in the world and of the work of the Holy Spirit in bringing in the kingdom, not out of any misconception concerning the innate goodness of humankind or of the ability of the church to convert the world by its own power.*[3]

This classic version of postmillennialism, formulated in those earlier centuries, was continued into the twentieth century by a few theologians. But added to this classic biblical postmillennialism was a newer form known by such titles as "theonomy," "reconstructionism," and "dominion theology." (See the section "The New Millennialism" for a discussion of this newer form.)

Liberal Postmillennialism

A second type of postmillennialism is "liberal postmillennialism." In common with biblical postmillennialism, this type is quite optimistic about the future. It believes in the idea of the ultimate progress of mankind, which will overcome all problems and bring in a golden age. However, very real differences exist between these two types of postmillennialism.

VIEWS CONCERNING THE END TIMES

CATEGORIES	AMILLENNIALISM	POSTMILLENNIALISM	HISTORIC PREMILLENNIALISM	DISPENSATIONAL PREMILLENNIALISM
Second Coming of Christ	Single event; no distinction between Rapture and Second Coming; introduces eternal state.	Single event; no distinction between Rapture and Second Coming; Christ returns after millennium.	Rapture and Second Coming simultaneous; Christ returns to reign on earth.	Second Coming in two phases: Rapture for church; Second Coming to earth seven years later.
Resurrection	General resurrection of believers and unbelievers at second coming of Christ.	General resurrection of believers and unbelievers at second coming of Christ.	Resurrection of believers at beginning of millennium; resurrection of unbelievers at end of millennium.	Distinction in resurrections: • Church at Rapture • Old Testament/tribulation saints at Second Coming • Unbelievers at end of millennium
Judgments	General judgment of all people.	General judgment of all people.	Judgment at Second Coming; judgment at end of tribulation.	Distinction in judgment: • Believers' work at Rapture • Jews/Gentiles at end of tribulation • Unbelievers at end of millennium
Tribulation	Tribulation is experienced in this present age.	Tribulation is experienced in this present age.	Posttrib view: church goes through the future tribulation.	Pretrib view: church is raptured prior to tribulation.
Millennium	No literal millennium on earth after Second Coming; kingdom present in church age.	Present age blends into millennium because of progress of gospel.	Millennium is both present and future, Christ is reigning in heaven; millennium not necessarily 1,000 yrs.	At Second Coming, Christ inaugurates literal 1,000-year millennium on earth.
Israel and the Church	Church is the new Israel; no distinction between Israel and church.	Church is the new Israel; no distinction between Israel and church.	Some distinction between Israel and church; future for Israel, but church is spiritual Israel.	Complete distinction between Israel and church; distinct program for each.
Adherents	L. Berkhof, O.T. Allis, G. C. Berkhouwer	Charles Hodge, B. B. Warfield, W. G. T. Shedd, A. H. Strong	G. E. Ladd, A. Reese, M. J. Erickson	L. S. Chafer, J. D. Pentecost, C. C. Ryrie, J. F. Walvoord

Liberal postmillennialism focuses on societal transformation rather than personal conversion. Their "social gospel" sees the saving of society from social evil as the great purpose of the church. The mission of the church is not to preach the gospel to sinners in need of God's great salvation but, rather, to liberate mankind from poverty, racism, disease, war, and all kinds of injustice. It has the unbiblical view that people are not sinners in need of Christ's redeeming work but are inherently good. It places its confidence in the wisdom and ability of humankind and is convinced that people will achieve positive change through their own efforts. It views the kingdom of God as the product of natural laws at work in an evolutionary process.

It is obvious that liberal postmillennialism does not hold to the high view of Scripture that has characterized biblical postmillennialism. Therefore, in this chapter the analysis will focus on the new and classic forms of *biblical* postmillennialism.

THE BASIC ELEMENTS OF POSTMILLENNIALISM

Eight elements characterize biblical postmillennialism. We will consider each in turn.

The Return of Christ *After* the Millennium
First, as the name "postmillennial" indicates, this view teaches that the return of Christ takes place *after* the millennium. The millennium ends with the personal, bodily return of Jesus Christ.

An Undetermined Length of Time
Second, postmillennialists believe that the "thousand years" of Revelation 20 is not to be taken in a literal way but represents a long period of time:

The "thousand years" is quite clearly not to be understood as an exact measure of time but rather as a symbolic number. Strict arithmetic has no place here. The term [indicates] an indefinitely long period of time, a complete, perfect number of years, probably not less than a literal one thousand years, in all probability very much longer. It is, however, a definitely limited period, during which certain events happen, and after which certain other events are to follow.[4]

Postmillennialism is quite similar to amillennialism on this point. However, although it is the view of amillennialism that the millennium is that period of time between the first and second advents of Christ, not all postmillennialists are in agreement on this matter. Some, to be sure, believe as do the amillennialists, that the entire period of time between the advents is the millennial kingdom. But others believe that during the present church age there will emerge a time of great spiritual blessing (the millennium). The millennium is not seen as the entire period of time between the two advents but, rather, as "a golden age of spiritual prosperity" that flows out of the church age and that will be in existence when Christ returns.[5]

Thus, for some postmillennialists the millennium is in the future. But, since they view the present age as gradually merging into the millennium, it is difficult, if not impossible, to discern an exact starting time for the millennium. Unlike the cataclysmic beginning of the millennium in premillennialism, postmillennialists believe that the millennium will arrive by degrees. It is likened to the ending of one season of the year and the beginning of the next season, so it will probably be impossible to observe an exact starting time of the millennium. This, of course, is not a great issue, since the millennium is simply "a long period of time."

A Spiritual, Earthly Kingdom

Third, the kingdom is spiritual and not the literal, earthly reign of Christ. It is the rule of Christ in the hearts of believers. When an individual believes in Christ and commits to obey Him, the kingdom is present. As the percentage of Christians grows in proportion to the total world population, the kingdom of God expands and the promised blessings of peace and righteousness begin to fill the earth.

Eventually through this expanding kingdom conflict will cease between nations, racial groups, and social classes—and the world will witness the fulfillment of the prediction of the lion and lamb lying down (Isa. 11:6).

A Spreading Gospel, a Better World

Fourth, postmillennialism has an optimistic view of this present age. Postmillennialists believe that the world will get better and better as the gospel of Christ spreads all over the world. The world will never be completely saved, but it will become Christianized and the wonderful blessings of the kingdom—such as peace, joy, righteousness, and prosperity—will come to dominate the entire earth. On the other hand, both premillennialists and amillennialists believe just the opposite: that spiritual and moral conditions in this world will get worse and worse as this present age draws to a close.

In the postmillennial view, however,

> *the world at large will enjoy a state of righteousness which up until now has been seen only in relatively small and isolated groups: for example, some family circles, and some local church groups and kindred organizations. This does not mean that there will be a time on this earth when every person will be a Christian or that all sin will be abolished. But it does mean that evil in all its many forms eventually will be reduced to negligible proportions, that Christian principles will be the rule, not the exception, and that Christ will return to a truly Christianized world.*[6]

It is through the Spirit-empowered preaching of the gospel that the nations of the earth will be converted and begin to practice biblical principles. The gospel is powerful and can bring change as the church proclaims it. Many postmillennialists believe that they take the Lord's Great Commission to go into all the world and preach the gospel (Matt. 28:19–20) far more seriously than do the other two millennial views.

As the gospel goes to the nations, some postmillennialists believe that most people in the nation of Israel will come to Christ, thus literally fulfilling a number of Old Testament prophecies. However, since postmillennialists do not see Israel as being distinct from the church, Israelites enter the church like all other believers and are not a distinct entity in the program of God.

THE VIEW OF POSTMILLENNIALISM

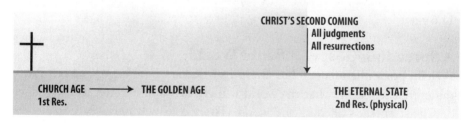

CHRIST'S SECOND COMING
All judgments
All resurrections

CHURCH AGE ———→ THE GOLDEN AGE
1st Res.

THE ETERNAL STATE
2nd Res. (physical)

The Events of Revelation 20

Fifth, postmillennialists share with amillennialists some similar views on the key Revelation 20 passage. As seen already, the "thousand years" is interpreted in a symbolic way. Also, the binding of Satan is spiritualized to mean that Satan is unable to deceive the nations any more, which the postmillennialist sees as evidence that the world is going to be Christianized.[7]

Concerning the two resurrections found in Revelation 20, postmillennialists have taken the same basic view as amillennialists. They too see the second resurrection as a physical resurrection of the body, whereas the first resurrection pertains to something other than a physical resurrection —perhaps to a rebirth of the spirits of the martyrs or symbolically the future restoration and vindication of the martyrs' cause.[8] In any case, the first resurrection is not a physical, bodily resurrection.

It is interesting, however, that postmillennialists agree with premillennialists (and against most amillennialists) that the events of Revelation 20 follow chronologically those found in Revelation 19. Premillennialists, however, view the rider on the white horse in chapter 19 as a reference to the second coming of Christ, whereas postmillennialists believe it to be a picture of Christ being victorious over His enemies through the preaching of the gospel in this present age.

An Explosion of Evil

Sixth, along with premillennialists, postmillennialists believe that an explosion of evil will occur at the end of the millennial age. The purpose of this is that "it may be seen anew and more clearly what an awful thing sin is and how deserving of punishment."[9]

The Use of Allegorical Interpretation

Seventh, in agreement with amillennialism, the position of postmillennialism is that it is permissible to interpret some Scriptures allegorically. As we have seen, this is the bedrock issue in the millennial discussion. Postmillennialists "have no objection on principle against figurative interpretation and readily accept that if the evidence indicates that it is preferable."[10]

However, postmillennialists are careful to point out that they believe in a golden age on this earth and, therefore, take many of the Old Testament prophecies far more literally than amillennialists.[11]

Resurrections, Judgments, and a Renovated Earth

Eighth, following the millennium all of the resurrections and judgments will take place. Postmillennialism is in agreement with amillennialism on the idea of a general resurrection that will involve believers and unbelievers and of a general judgment that involves all mankind as well as angels.

Following the resurrections and judgments, believers will enter their final condition, experiencing the fullness of eternal life in heaven, which will be on a renovated earth. Believers will be rewarded by Christ for their faithfulness. Unbelievers will experience everlasting punishment.

THE NEW POSTMILLENNIALISM

A new variety of postmillennialism has emerged in recent years. It is known by a number of different names, especially "dominion theology," "theonomy," and "reconstructionism." These names reflect most of the key issues found in this form of postmillennialism.

Theonomy

The name *theonomy* comes from two Greek words that mean "God" and "law."

This name emphasizes the belief of theonomists that the entire Mosaic law code is operative today in both its standards and its penalties. The law is not only to be kept by individuals but is to be enforced in society at large. It is through the law of God that the world will become Christianized and prepared for the return of Jesus Christ.

One theonomist author describes the goal this way: "The Christian goal for the world is the universal development of biblical theocratic republics, in which every area of life is redeemed and placed under the Lordship of Jesus Christ and the rule of God's law."[12] Another declares, "Biblical law is our tool of dominion. It enables us to subdue sin in inner places (the moral sphere) and outer places (the dominical sphere)".[13]

Theonomists believe that the death penalty should be applied in accordance with the Mosaic law code, which mandates that murderers, rapists, kidnappers, homosexuals, rebellious children, false prophets, and many other kinds of offenders should be put to death.[14] The law of God, therefore, constitutes the continuing norm for all mankind and must be proclaimed and applied to the lives of individuals and nations.

Reconstructionism

The term reconstructionism emphasizes the way in which the world will eventually become Christianized. Both the church and society at large will be changed by means of God's law and the resulting lordship of Jesus Christ. In *Paradise Restored*, David Chilton writes, "Our goal is world dominion under Christ's Lordship, a 'world takeover' if you will; but our strategy begins with reformation, reconstruction of the church. From that will flow social and political reconstruction, indeed a flowering of Christian civilization."[15] Greg Bahnsen adds:

> *Theonomists are committed to the transformation (reconstruction) of every area of life, including the institutions and affairs of the sociopolitical realm, according to the holy principles of God's revealed word (theonomy). It is toward this end that the human community must strive if it is to enjoy true justice and peace.*[16]

Dominion Theology

The term *dominion theology* focuses on the idea that someday the world will be under the authority of Jesus Christ. He will have dominion over this world, and Christianity will become the dominant principle.

This new form of postmillennialism incorporates into their system the main features of classic postmillennialism. There is great optimism that, since "all power" has been given to the church by Christ, the world will eventually be brought under the truth of God and become Christianized. However, this new postmillennialism goes beyond classic postmillennialism in its program for society. Dominion theologians believe that it is the clear responsibility of the church to move beyond the matter of individual salvation and holiness and actively enter into the realm of public and social responsibility. Christians are to become activists and "promote and enforce obedience to God's law in society."[17] They often chide premillennialists and amillennialists for manifesting in their theology "a desire to escape personal and corporate responsibility in an increasingly complex and threatening world."[18]

In concluding this discussion of new postmillennialism, which has its roots in Calvinism, another new form of postmillennialism found in the charismatic movement should be noted. Sometimes referred to as "kingdom now" theology, it maintains that Christians are "little gods" who can, by the authority of Christ, exercise dominion over the earth. Through faith, what is confessed will come to pass. Needless to say, this view is quite different from both classic postmillennialism and theonomy.

EVALUATING POSTMILLENNIALISM

Much of what has been said earlier about amillennialists applies to postmillennialists and does not need repeating. That is particularly true in reference to their view of Revelation 20 and their acceptance of the spiritualization of some prophetic portions of Scripture. But several other observations need to be made in evaluating the system of postmillennialism.

1. The Issue of an Improving World

The idea that the world is getting better and better does not at all seem to be in line with reality. The evidence points rather to a world that is growing more and more wicked. Technological and scientific advancements have little to do with spiritual and moral progress. It is difficult to see how the facts of current history point to a world that is becoming more righteous and submissive to the law of God.

The reality of evil in this world forces postmillennialists to constantly look ahead to the distant future for a golden age. It has been two thousand years since the first advent of Christ, and still no clear evidence exists for the arrival of a golden age.

2. The Issue of Ignored Scripture Passages

Postmillennialism's view of the end of this age does not reflect the biblical expectation. Numerous passages, such as Matthew 24:4–14 and 2 Timothy 3:1–5, teach that spiritual and moral conditions will worsen as the end of the age approaches. A number of passages, including many in Revelation, speak of great wickedness at the end of this age. Millard Erickson concludes, "Perhaps more damaging to postmillennialism is its apparent neglect of Scripture passages . . . that portray spiritual and moral conditions as worsening in the end times. It appears that postmillennialism has based its doctrine on very carefully selected Scripture passages."[19]

This is a basic problem with the postmillennial system. A large number of passages are really quite pessimistic in their outlook. But they are ignored in the construction of the postmillennial system.

3. The Issue of a Focus on the Church Instead of Christ

Postmillennialism struggles with maintaining a genuine supernaturalism in its view of the kingdom because human beings are so essential to the bringing in of the golden age. Although many postmillennialists (especially theonomists) try to emphasize the power of the gospel and the working of the Spirit, it is nevertheless true that people are essential, since it is the church, not Christ, that brings in the kingdom.

This difficulty in maintaining a genuine supernaturalism is seen in a number of varieties of postmillennialism, particularly that of liberal postmillennialism. But mere humans have not and cannot bring in the millennial kingdom found in Scripture. Only Jesus Christ can bring an end to wickedness and usher in a kingdom characterized by righteousness.

4. The Issue of a Neglected Israel

Because postmillennialism is based on covenant theology, it rejects any distinction between Israel and the church and does not see that Israel has a distinct place in the future program of God. As discussed earlier, dispensationalists believe that Israel does have a future as a nation and that Israel and the church are distinct. This, of course, is a major matter of controversy between the two systems of theology.

5. The Issue of the Prevailing Mosaic Law

New postmillennialism (theonomy) believes that the Mosaic law code is still operative today and must be applied to all men and nations. Although space does not allow a detailed discussion of the Mosaic law and its relation to the world and to the Christian church, certain points need to be made.

The Law was given to the nation of Israel, not to the church or to mankind in general. God entered into this covenant with those He had "brought out . . . of the land of Egypt" (Ex. 20:2). It was Israel's constitution, given to guide that nation in every area of life (31:12–17). Also, the Mosaic law was given as a unit. And, although for the sake of analysis it is often viewed in moral, civil, and ceremonial divisions, this law code was given as an indivisible unit (Gal. 3:10; 5:3; James 2:10). No one can legitimately pick and choose which laws are to be adhered to or which penalties are to be applied, as is done by theonomists.

Furthermore, the law given at Mount Sinai was designed to be temporary.

It would exist as a rule of life for Israel until the Messiah came (Gal. 3:23–4:5). The law was never designed to save anyone but was given to protect Israel from the terrible sins of the Gentiles and to teach them about their God. It was a rule of life for Israel and was not given to govern the nations of the earth. Theonomists contend that we become lawless by not putting ourselves under the Mosaic law. But that is not true.

> *The fact that a person is not under the moral aspect of the Mosaic Law does not mean that he is unrelated to the eternal, unchangeable, moral absolutes of God. Although the Mosaic Law did present the eternal, unchangeable, moral absolutes of God, it was only one way of God's administering His moral absolutes to one group of people (the nation of Israel) during one period of history (from God's meeting with Israel at Mount Sinai to the cross of Jesus Christ). . . . Since God's moral absolutes are eternal, they have been in effect before God instituted the Mosaic Law at Mount Sinai. This means that prior to Mount Sinai God administered His unchangeable, moral absolutes in ways other than through the Mosaic Law. It also means that God's eternal, moral absolutes can be in effect without the Mosaic Law being in effect.*[20]

Theonomists are incorrect when they say that the church is under the Mosaic law and that it is to bring society under the precepts and the penalties of the Mosaic law code (cf. Rom. 6:14–15; 7:4–6; 2 Cor. 3:7–11; Gal. 2:19; 3:19–25; Eph. 2:15–16; Heb. 7:12). This law code (with all its hundreds of laws covering every area of life) was given to Israel as a complete unified constitution. It was not given as such to Gentiles, and because it is an indivisible unit one cannot selectively keep the laws or impose some of the penalties.

The gospel of the grace of God, which is the message of the church of Jesus Christ, does not include the Mosaic law. The apostle Paul's point in his refutation of those who would bring the law into the church was that they are two mutually exclusive systems (Gal. 3:1–4:31). The two cannot be mixed; you must choose which system you want to live under. If you choose the law, then you "fall from grace" (5:4). The law has no role in a person's justification or sanctification. The church has not been given the commission of taking Israel's law code and mixing it with the gospel message of grace and imposing this mixture on the nations of the earth.

6. The Issue of the Return of Christ

Classic, conservative postmillennialism sees the second coming of Christ as a future event, agreeing with premillennialism. However, within the new postmillennialism (theonomy) there is a difference of opinion. Some who are moderate preterists believe that there was a coming Christ in AD 70 in connection with the destruction of Jerusalem by the armies of Rome. This "judgment coming" of Christ, however, does not mean that Christ will not return at *the* second coming at the end of the age. Other preterists ("radical" or "consistent") believe that *the* second coming was in 70 and that there is no future coming of Christ. (See the next chapter, entitled "The View of Preterism," for a full discussion).

In Summary

Biblical postmillennialism promotes a healthy confidence in the power of the gospel to change the lives of people. It rightly sees the very real possibility that God could bring revival now and thus counters an unbiblical form of fatalism. Postmillennialism encourages believers to an activism that can be beneficial to society and, in so doing, challenges the "bunker mentality" that seems to possess many believers. However, the system has some glaring problems.

It is built on the unsteady hermeneutic of spiritualization. It has an unfounded optimism that is not based on a realistic view of what has happened over the last two thousand years or on what is presently going on now. The world is not becoming morally and spiritually better, nor is it being dominated by Christianity. This basic reality forces postmillennialists to place their golden age well in the future, giving the church plenty of time to "shape up" and get on with kingdom business. Furthermore, this optimism cannot be sustained in light of numerous passages of Scripture that speak of growing evil in the end times and the increase in apostasy and false teaching.

The newer form of postmillennialism attempts to make the Mosaic law part of the message of the church. Not only does the law not belong in that message, but the law was not given to the nations of the earth. Israel could not keep the law, and the nations will not do any better. But it is true that there is cause for optimism. Some day, suddenly and dramatically, the Lord Jesus *will* appear and the world will be made better. The kingdom of

Christ is not brought in by the obedient efforts of believers but by the Lord Jesus Himself. He alone can destroy the kingdom of darkness and establish righteousness on this earth (Dan. 2:44; Rev. 19:11–21). Our confidence rests in His powerful intervention.

CHAPTER NINE

THE VIEW
OF
Preterism

Some friends spent the afternoon watching two basketball games on television. The first game was just a replay, having actually been played a month earlier. They all knew that it was a replay and they were also aware of the game's outcome. But the second game they viewed was a live telecast.

The manner in which my friends viewed these two games, of course, was quite different. They watched the first game—which was history—without much passion and without feeling those tense moments that often characterize these devoted sports fans. As they watched the second game, however, loud cheers of excitement and low groans of disappointment filled the room.

The fact that the outcome of one game was history and the other was still future made for a radically different viewing perspective.

What is true for viewing sporting events pales by comparison to the far more significant matter of viewing the Bible. A Scripture passage that is seen as already fulfilled will obviously be approached quite differently than if it is seen as yet to be fulfilled. So there are great differences between preterist interpreters, who declare that most of the prophetic Scriptures have been fulfilled in the past, and the futurist interpreters, who believe these same Scriptures are yet to be fulfilled.

DEFINING AND DESCRIBING PRETERISM

The term *preterism* essentially has the idea of "past," and this word accurately represents the particular eschatological viewpoint that sees most or all of Bible prophecy as being fulfilled sometime in the past. Preterist Kenneth Gentry's definition would agree with this basic thought. "The word 'preterist' is based on the Latin term *praeteritus*, which means 'gone by,' or *past*. Preterism holds that the tribulation prophecies occur in the *first century*, thus in our past."[1]

Preterist R. C. Sproul would agree with Gentry's definition, and he makes the additional point that it is not just any time in the past that is being referred to by preterists but the past event of the destruction of Jerusalem in AD 70 by the army of Rome.

> *The central thesis . . . of all preterists is that the New Testament's time-frame references with respect to the parousia point to a fulfillment within the lifetime of at least some of Jesus' disciples. Some hold to a primary fulfillment in AD 70, with a secondary and final fulfillment in the yet-unknown future.*[2]

But he also notes there are significant differences within the viewpoint of preterism. Not all preterists are the same.

> *We may distinguish between two distinct forms of preterism, which I call radical preterism and moderate preterism. Radical preterism sees all future prophecies of the New Testament as having already taken place, while moderate preterism still looks to the future for crucial events to occur.*[3]

Moderate preterists (e.g., Sproul and Gentry) teach that almost all prophecy was fulfilled in the destruction of Jerusalem in AD 70, but they also believe that a few passages do teach a future second coming of Christ and the bodily resurrection of people at that time. They believe that there was *a* coming of Christ in 70, but not *the* coming of Christ. "Radical" preterists (who prefer the less pejorative term of "full" or "consistent" preterists) believe that all events predicted in the Scriptures including the Second Coming, the resurrection of the dead, and the final judgments have all taken place. They believe that they alone should bear the name "preterist" since they (unlike the moderates who see a few things as still future) see all things fulfilled in the past. Radical (consistent) preterist Edward Stevens states that "only someone who puts all of the eschatological events in the past can rightly be called 'preterist' in the true sense of the term."[4]

Moderate preterists, as well as non-preterists, see radical preterism's denial of any future, bodily resurrection in the Bible as placing them outside the realm of Christian orthodoxy. Since not all preterism's views and ideas can be covered in this brief chapter, the focus will be on the key positions of moderate preterism.

THE BASIC POSITIONS AND PROBLEMS OF PRETERISM: 1. THE OVERALL INTERPRETIVE APPROACH

All who are conservative in their theology will approach the Scriptures in a literal way, that is, in its plain and ordinary sense (see chapter 1). For example, not to approach the person and work of Christ or the doctrine of God in a literal/normal manner would lead one straight into liberal theology. There has always been a great danger in leaving the grammatical-historical method of approaching the Bible because the interpreter who allegorizes the text essentially becomes the final authority on the text's meaning. But as we have observed earlier, those in the conservative amillennial and postmillennial camps believe that it is legitimate to allegorize when it comes to certain aspects of eschatology.

Preterists, who are primarily postmillennial, adhere to these same basic perspectives. But it must be noted that their basic approach to prophetic passages is essentially the same approach that liberal theologians have towards all of the Scriptures.

There may be a difference in the motives of "evangelical preterists" . . . but they still engage in the same interpretive approach or process as the liberal preterists. There is no other approach to interpreting Bible prophecy than the critical approach refined by German liberals from which even evangelical preterists such as Dr. Gentry have gleaned so much. The preterism of today is still naturalistic in its understanding of key biblical passages . . . all preterists argue the same way about Matthew 24 and the Apocalypse, whether they are liberal or conservative. This is clear from the historical development of their interpretive approach—even the conservative preterists constantly refer to critical and liberal scholars as their sources.[5]

This liberal methodology raises significant concerns among many, but some other matters concerning the hermeneutics of preterism are also of concern. Preterism comes to many prophetic passages with an approach that is a combination of literal and allegorical. Speaking of Matthew 24, R. C. Sproul states, "We can interpret the time-frame references literally and the events surrounding the parousia figuratively. In this view, all of Jesus' prophecies in the Olivet Discourse were fulfilled during the period between the discourse itself and the destruction of Jerusalem in AD 70."[6]

This eclectic approach to prophetic interpretation is seen in a positive light by preterists as they believe their interpretive approach is strong. They take some matters in a given passage literally (e.g., Jerusalem means "Jerusalem"), but then switch to an allegorical approach (e.g., Christ's bodily coming means a "judgment coming" in 70). Preterists contend that they are simply abiding by the principle of interpreting Scripture by Scripture (*analogia fide*) and that they are observing the apocalyptic literary genre. But essentially their basic approach, long associated with liberalism, has been avoided by conservative amillennialists and postmillennialists until more recent times.

Inconsistent Interpretations

Here are several observations concerning the hermeneutics of preterism. First, as noted above, there is the regular mixing of the literal and allegorical, and this mixing brings very inconsistent interpretations to a passage. Conservative preterists understand the key place of literal interpretation, but contend that in some areas of eschatology such an approach leads to ridiculous interpretations. Those who generally follow the literal approach of the Reformers (e.g., in soteriology) fail to do so in significant parts of eschatology. The mixing of the literal with the allegorical seems to have given the preterist license to take words, phrases, symbols, and metaphors and assign meaning to them depending on the exegetical need of the moment. The preterist often engages in the illegitimate transfer of a word's meaning from one verse over to another unrelated verse.

For example, preterist Gary DeMar concludes that the cosmic disturbances in Matthew 24:29–30 (the sign of the Son of Man, the darkened

sun and moon and the stars falling from the sky) is symbolic of the passing away of the old covenant world of Judaism in 70.[7] This conclusion is
based on the illegitimate transference of meaning from one verse to another as well as some full-blown allegorization. Concerning Kenneth Gentry's
understanding of the Lord "coming with the clouds" at the fall of
Jerusalem (Rev. 1:7), Robert Thomas has noted Gentry's differing uses of
the "cloud coming":

> *At one point [Gentry] identifies the cloud coming with the judgment against*
> *Judea in 67–70. At another point he sees it as a coming against the church*
> *through the persecution by the Romans from 64–68. Still elsewhere the cloud*
> *coming for Rome was her internal strife in 68–69.*[8]

Referring to another preterist writer, Dr. Norman Geisler observed that
his claim to hold to a literal method of interpretation simply is not correct: "If it (i.e., Revelation 6–18) is taken literally, then it cannot be placed
there since Jesus did not visibly return to earth in AD 70 (Matthew 24:30;
cf. Revelation 1:7 and Acts 1:10–11). Nor did Christ literally execute all the
judgments listed in Revelation 9 and 16 at that time."[9]

These are not isolated examples of preterist hermeneutics, and these
examples do reveal a hybrid hermeneutic whose claims of consistency and
literalness are suspect.

A "Preunderstanding" in the Interpretive Processing

A second interpretive matter relates to the growing idea of "preunderstanding" in the interpretive process. In the spirit of our postmodern
times there is the tendency to leave the expressed meaning of a text and
allow the interpreter to affect the text with what he believes, or "preun-
derstands," that the text ought to be teaching. Instead of searching diligently for the intended meaning of the author, there is the tendency to
substitute personal preferences. But it is through approaching language in
a literal way that this intended meaning of the author is to be discovered.

Walter Kaiser describes this approach as a relatively recent development: "The grammatical-historical method of exegesis has served us all
very well. But in recent decades, the hue and cry has gone up from scholarship at large to allow the reader and the modern situation to have as

much (or in some cases, more) to say about what the text means as has traditionally been given to the original speaker of the text."[10]

The preterist interpretation is often dictated by their theological preunderstanding. Postmillennial preterists, or theonomists, see the world progressing toward that which is good, namely a Christianized world dominated by the law of God. However, Revelation does not paint such a picture, which is why conservative theologians generally (whether amillennialists or premillennialists) have seen Christ returning in judgment to a world that is in terrible shape. But the preunderstanding of preterists that the world will be Christianized requires that they approach the judgment passages in Matthew 24, the book of Revelation and in Zechariah as something in the past and not something in the future.

Thomas Ice writes that Gentry's study of Revelation reflects the typical approach of theonomists to eschatology, noting,

Behind Gentry's exegetical methodology lies a preunderstanding that controls his interpretation of the book. According to the new evangelical hermeneutics, that is a fashionable approach. Gentry's particular preunderstanding is this: a desire for an undiluted rationale to support Christian social and political involvement leading to long-term Christian cultural progress and dominion. Since Revelation's prophecies about a decaying society render impossible long-term cultural progress and dominion, he must find fulfillment of the book's prophecies in the era leading up to and including the fall of Jerusalem in AD 70. How preunderstanding distorts certain hermeneutical principles is a matter for consideration.[11]

The Unclear "Apocalyptic" Genre

A third matter related to the hermeneutics of preterism is that of the unclear genre of "apocalyptic." There is no agreed upon definition of "apocalyptic" genre, but it is nevertheless embraced by preterists in order to give them greater liberty in their interpretations. As Robert Thomas observes,

To justify a nonliteral interpretation, one must assume an apocalyptic genre in which the language only faintly reflects actual events. Specifically, to see the words about Christ's second coming in Revelation 1:7 as fulfilled in AD 70 when the temple was destroyed necessitates allowing a particular genre to override normal rules of interpretation.[12]

Thomas notes differences between that which is apocalyptic and prophetic and concludes that the book of Revelation is prophetic, as it claims (1:3; 22:7, 10, 18, 19), noting that if it is primarily a prophecy, then it can be interpreted like all other prophecies according to grammatical-historical principles.[13]

The standard view of preterism is expressed by preterist R. C. Sproul: "Much of biblical prophecy is cast in an apocalyptic genre that employs graphic imaginative language and often mixes elements of common historical narrative with the figurative language of poetry."[14]

As was noted in chapter 1, figurative language does not give the interpreter license to give any meaning to symbols nor to ignore the immediate contexts in which the figurative language is found. Futurists have responded well to the key issues of the hermeneutics of preterism and have shown that their eclectic interpretive method has strayed from the classical grammatical-historical method.[15] The hermeneutics of preterism will further be illustrated as a number of specific interpretations are now surveyed.

THE BASIC POSITIONS AND PROBLEMS: 2. THE INTERPRETATION OF MATTHEW 24:34

The Key Preterist Text: Matthew 24:34

According to preterists, the key to locating the tribulation sometime in history is the Lord's statement in Matthew 24:34. There Jesus declares, "Truly I say to you, this generation will not pass away until all these things take place." It is safe to say that this verse is foundational to their argument. They believe that if taken literally, "this generation" must of necessity refer to the people who heard the Lord Jesus speak on that Tuesday afternoon on Mount Olivet. In fact, preterism says that it absolutely demands a first-century fulfillment of Matthew 24:4–31.[16] It then follows, in their thinking, that the tribulation must have taken place within a forty-year period of time, which leads them to conclude that AD 70 is the fulfillment of the Lord's prophecies on the Mount of Olives.

Concerning "this generation," all preterists agree that it must be referring to those disciples who actually heard the Lord Jesus speak that day. Preterist Gary DeMar boldly declares that "every time 'this generation' is used in the New Testament, it means, without exception, the generation to whom Jesus was speaking."[17] DeMar's statement begs the question regarding

Matthew 24:34 because the interpreter must not import a meaning from elsewhere before making sure that the immediate context supports, much less "requires," such a contention. The meaning from another portion of Scripture may or may not be the same as the verse under consideration. It is the immediate context that is most critical in revealing the meaning. And incidentally, DeMar's all-inclusive statement is not accurate, since the "this generation" in Hebrews 3:10 refers to the Exodus generation and not the generation that was being instructed by the writer of Hebrews.

The term "this generation" is used in Matthew 23:36 prior to its appearance in 24:34. The phrase "this generation" in Matthew 23:36 does in fact speak of the generation that was alive at the time of the Lord Jesus' discourse as the context indicates. It is a passage that speaks of judgment coming upon that generation of Israel for their rejection of Messiah Jesus. Led by the Scribes and Pharisees, that generation refused to acknowledge that Jesus was the long-awaited Messiah, and their judgment did take place in AD 70. But the meaning of "this generation" in Matthew 23:36 does not automatically mean that the "this generation" in Matthew 24:34 looks at the same people. One usage is prior to the discourse and is speaking of God's judgment, and the other is within the discourse itself where Jesus is speaking of the need for preparedness in light of His coming and their being rescued and rewarded. The "this generation" are the ones who see "all" (24:33) the events spoken of in Matthew 24:4–31, the events of the tribulation. The Lord said earlier in the discourse that the days of the tribulation had been shortened from what they could have been (24:22), and here He is adding that the tribulation events will be so compressed that the ("this") generation that sees the beginning of the judgments will also see the end of them. The events described in great detail in 24:4–31 simply have not taken place and yet the context requires that "all these things" must come to pass.

The Use of Literal *and* Allegorical Interpretation

Preterists, realizing the force of this required fulfillment, leave normal interpretation and go to amazing lengths in their attempts to find fulfillment of these verses in the AD 70 judgment on Israel (see below for this discussion). They try to be very literal on the matter of "this generation" but aggressively allegorize most everything else in the Olivet Discourse. Futurist Thomas Ice nicely summarizes Matthew 24:34:

Now, why does "this generation" in Matthew 24:34 (as well as Mark 13:30 and Luke 21:32), not refer to Christ's contemporaries? Because the governing referent to "this generation" is "all these things." Since Jesus is giving an extended prophetic discourse on future events, one must first determine the nature of "all these things" prophesied in verses 4 through 31 to know what generation Christ is referring to. Since "all these things" did not take place in the first century, then the generation whom Christ speaks of must still be future. It is as simple as that. Christ is saying that the generation that sees "all these things" occur will not cease to exist until all of the events of the future Tribulation are literally fulfilled.[18]

Jesus speaks of "this generation" as "you." Concerning the use of "you" in connection with "this generation" (24:33–34), Randall Price notes that the pronoun does not at all require that the listening audience be in view.

Even though in context Jesus may refer to the future "this generation" as "you," this is a conventional usage of language with respect to reference and does not have to apply to a present audience. In the prophetic passages of the Old Testament, it is common to find such language. For instance, Moses used language similar to Jesus' when he said, "So it will be when all these things have come upon you . . ." (Deut. 30:1). Even though he is speaking to the present generation ("you"), it is evident from the context that his words speak about a future generation that will live thousands of years later and into the eschatological period. The people of this "generation" (verse 1) are those who will have already suffered the judgment of exile (verse 1), captivity (verse 3), been regathered and restored (verses 4-5), and received spiritual regeneration ("circumcision of heart", verse 6).[19]

So it is most likely that Jesus used the word "you" in a variety of ways, including referencing those who represented Israel. Earlier in Matthew 23:35, when speaking to the hypocritical religious leaders of Israel, Jesus said "you" killed Zechariah. Now those who heard Jesus did not do that deed but the present leaders of Israel represented their spiritual ancestors. So the immediate context of Matthew 24:34 and the details of the tribulation in Matthew 24:4–31 neither "demand" nor "require" a first-century fulfillment as preterists contend. In fact, the futurist position on Matthew 24 that emerges out of normal interpretation is far stronger, since it adequately deals with the fact that "all these things" of the tribulation will be seen by "this generation"/ "you."

THE BASIC POSITIONS AND PROBLEMS:
3. THE DATE OF THE BOOK OF REVELATION

Both preterism and futurism believe that when the apostle John wrote the book of Revelation it was prophecy. However, there is significant disagreement on exactly when the book was actually written. Preterists believe that Revelation was written about AD 65, just a few years before it was fulfilled in AD 70. Their teaching requires a very limited time frame from 64 to 67 for the writing of Revelation. Most futurists believe that it was written much later, about 95, and, of course, that it has yet to be fulfilled. Actually it would not be significant to the position of futurism if the book was written in the mid 60s, but preterism would suffer a fatal blow if Revelation were written any time after 70. So the issue is of critical significance to preterism, as is acknowledged by R. C. Sproul.

> *If the book was written in the final decade of the first century (the traditional view), then its prophecies probably do not concern the destruction of Jerusalem, an event that would have already taken place. . . . If the book was written after AD 70, then its contents manifestly do not refer to events surrounding the fall of Jerusalem—unless the book is a wholesale fraud, having been composed after the predicted events had already occurred.*[20]

The External Evidence

In determining the date of Revelation, both external and internal evidences must be evaluated. External evidence, which looks at the facts outside of the book of Revelation, focuses on the writings of individuals early in the history of the church who spoke about the authorship and date of Revelation.

As noted above, the view of the church over the centuries has been that of the late date for the writing of Revelation (about AD 95). The key witness (but not the only one) is Irenaeus (120–202), who was a disciple of Polycarp, a disciple of the apostle John. He provides a nearly direct connection with the apostle John, and his testimony is important and credible. In his work *Against Heresies,* which was written around 180, Irenaeus states that the time when the apostle John wrote Revelation was during the reign of the Roman emperor Domitian.

> *For if it were necessary that the name of him (antichrist) should be distinctly revealed in this present time, it would have been told by him who saw the apocalyptic vision. For it was seen no long time ago, but almost in our generation, toward the end of Domitian's reign.*[21]

This statement of Irenaeus was clearly understood to be referring to the writing of Revelation during Domitian's reign by early writers such as Eusebius, Tertullian, Clement of Alexandria, Jerome, and numerous others. And this has been the understanding of the church generally since those days.

> *Grounds for questioning the accuracy of Irenaeus and other early witnesses are purely subjective. . . . If Irenaeus had been wrong, later witnesses including Clement of Alexandria, Origen, Victorinus, Eusebius, and Jerome would have corrected him. Instead, they confirmed his dating. Most modern scholars concur with the confirmation.*[22]

Preterists, however, cannot allow a late date and instead argue for a 60s date during the reign of Nero. They insist that Irenaeus is only saying the apostle John *lived* into the reign of Domitian, not that he wrote Revelation then. But in dealing with this dubious preterist understanding, Mark Hitchcock observes that the subject of Irenaeus's statement "it was seen" is the apocalyptic vision (the nearest antecedent) and not John himself. In other words, the Revelation was seen in Domitian's reign and not that the man John was seen (that is, "lived") into the reign of Domitian.[23] Furthermore, the verb "was seen" makes sense connected with the "apocalyptic vision" as something John saw but does not make good sense as someone seeing the apostle John.

The forced interpretation of preterism is also muted by the fact that "if John were the intended subject of this statement, Irenaeus, who was trying to bring the matter as near to his own time as possible, would surely have said that John lived into the reign of Trajan, a fact that Irenaeus knew well."[24]

Added to the powerful testimony of Irenaeus is that of Hegesippus (ca. 150), who links the banishment of John to the island of Patmos with

Domitian's reign. And then there are the numerous statements by Eusebius (260-340). For example, in his *History of the Church*, Eusebius speaks of a Domitian date for the banishment of John to the island of Patmos and, therefore, the writing of Revelation.

> *Many were the victims of Domitian's appalling cruelty. At Rome great numbers of men distinguished by birth and attainments were for no reason at all banished from the country and their property confiscated. . . There is ample evidence that at that time the apostle and evangelist John was still alive, and because of his testimony to the word of God was sentenced to confinement on the island of Patmos.*[25]

So Eusebius, often called "the Father of Ecclesiastical History" seems persuaded by the materials available to him that the apostle John was exiled to Patmos where he wrote the book of Revelation. And to Eusebius can be added two declarations by Jerome (340-419) that John saw the Apocalypse while enduring banishment by Domitian, as well as a half a dozen other writers.[26]

On the other hand, the first clear statement to an early date for Revelation (AD 64-67) sometime during the reign of Nero is one line in the Syriac translation (ca. 550) of the New Testament. Preterists have little to work with and so must build their case on vague statements found in a very few writings. For example, Sproul tries to build a case for an early date based on the statement of Clement of Alexandria (150-215), who refers to John's departure from the island of Patmos "after the death of the tyrant." Clement does not identify "the tyrant" in his writings. An unconvincing effort is put forth by the preterist camp to show that Clement is speaking of Nero and not Domitian.[27] In the absence of any early direct references to John's banishment during the rule of Nero, it is this kind of reference that preterism must try and use to build its case in the realm of external evidences.

Preterism's early date position is also hurt by the time when the apostle John arrived in the area of Asia Minor. Thomas has noted,

> *According to the best information, he did not come to Asia from Palestine before the late 60s, at the time of the Jewish revolt of AD 66-70. This was after Paul's final visit to Asia in AD 65. John was part of a migration of Palestinian*

Christians from Palestine to the province of Asia before the outbreak of the
rebellion. A Neronic dating would hardly allow time for him to have settled in
Asia, to have replaced Paul as the respected leader of the Asian churches, and
then to have been exiled to Patmos before Nero's death in AD 68.[28]

If preterism cannot reasonably demonstrate its position then, according to its own testimony, the position is damaged beyond hope. Thus
Hitchcock concludes: "In light of this evidence and testimony, it stretches
the limits of credulity for any preterist to assert that the external evidence
actually favors the early date. To any unbiased mind, the external evidence
overwhelmingly favors the AD 95 date for Revelation."[29]

The Internal Evidence: (1) Reference to the Temple

The internal evidence for the dating of the book of Revelation is not as
definitive since it is prone to be more subjective. But a few points need to
be made regarding the evidence found within Revelation itself. Preterists
advance three points from the text of Revelation in order to demonstrate
a mid-60s date for Revelation. First, they argue that since John was told to
go and measure the temple (Rev. 11:1–2), this means that the temple was
still standing. Therefore, the book must have been written prior to 70
when the temple was destroyed. They also contend that if it was written
after 70, then it is strange that John is silent about this important event.
Sproul admits that their argument is one from silence but declares that
"the silence is deafening."[30]

In response to the preterist assertion, it must be remembered that all
agree that the Revelation 11 passage is prophetic. It ought to be obvious to
everyone that a prophetic passage about the temple does not require the
actual physical existence of a temple in Jerusalem. When Daniel (in
Babylon after 586 BC) wrote prophetically about a temple (e.g., Dan. 9:27
and 12:11), no temple was in existence. When Ezekiel was told to measure
the temple and write extensively about it (Ezek. 40–48), the temple had
been destroyed over a decade earlier and did not exist. In Revelation 11,
John is simply instructed to measure *the temple in his vision* and this does
not require the existence of the Jerusalem temple. Whether or not there
was a temple in existence when John received this vision is not relevant
and, therefore, Revelation 11 simply has nothing to do with the dating of
the book of Revelation.

The Internal Evidence: (2) The Number of the Beast/Nero

A second line of internal proof for preterism is the number of the beast as "666" in Revelation 13:18. This number (666) is said to be the numerical value of Nero's name. The idea is that if the "666" is referring to Nero, then the writing of Revelation must have been during his reign.

To arrive at this conclusion, one must use the mystical approach to interpretation, a hermeneutically unsound way of handling the Scriptures. Nowhere in Scripture is any number given specific theological meaning. After analyzing data from antiquity, John J. Davis concluded that the "exegetical method of ascribing theological values to numbers is of Greek origin and finds its development primarily among the Gnostics, Neo-Pythagoreans, and Jewish allegorists."[31] This approach found its way into Christianity by means of church fathers who were clearly influenced by Greek thinking.

It is true that in the Revelation passage that the reader is instructed to "calculate" the beast's number (13:18). Over the years, many attempts have been made unsuccessfully to identify the Antichrist by using number mysticism (called "gematria" by its proponents). But when the time comes, the 666 will no doubt be significant in identifying the Antichrist.

Modern preterism's use of number mysticism puts this view on shaky ground. In this case, preterists use a Hebrew spelling of Nero's name (Nero Caesar). In order for the numerical value of the name to add up to "666," the name must be transliterated into the Hebrew, which would be rather strange to John's Greek-speaking audience. One wonders why the preterists try to be so literal with this number when so many of the numbers in Revelation are dismissed as symbolic.

Aside from being another example of preterism's dual hermeneutics, there are numerous other problems with such an approach. Andy Woods observes that (1) preterists must resort to shifting to Hebrew letters from the original Greek; (2) Nero had numerous names, and there is no conclusive evidence that the title Nero Caesar would be the proper one; (3) the preterists's calculations are built upon a defective spelling of the word *Caesar*; and (4) there are actually three possible Hebrew equivalents to one of the Greek letters in question.[32] All of this calls into question the whole confusing approach.

It must also be noted that this use of number mysticism to arrive at Nero as the Antichrist was never seen in the history of the church until the middle of the nineteenth century. Over the years dozens of people have been identified as the Antichrist using the method of number mysticism. This alone demonstrates the highly subjective nature of the approach and why the Bible student must stay away from it.

In this case, in spite of great efforts by many within preterism, this internal proof for an early date is no proof at all. In passing it should be noted that Nero simply does not line up well with the description of the character and career of the Antichrist found in Revelation 13, and this obvious reality has forced preterism to allegorize much of that chapter.

The Internal Evidence: (3) The Seven Kings

The third preterist internal evidence for an early date of Revelation is found in 17:10 where the "seven kings" are spoken of and where the sixth king is referred to as "one is." Preterists begin their discussion with the assumption that the text is describing seven Roman kings from the first century. They then argue that the sixth king is Nero. They make this assumption even though their interpretation basically ignores Daniel's prophecies, which form the backdrop for Revelation 17. Complicating their proof are the many different ways used to count the Roman kings. In order for Nero to be the sixth king, certain kings are not counted (ones with short reigns) and the starting point must be adjusted to arrive at Nero. There are so many difficulties with this scheme of things that there is ample reason to just set aside the whole approach. Even R. C. Sproul seems less than enthusiastic about this internal proof for an early date for Revelation.[33]

Based on Daniel 7, it is better to understand this sixth king (kingdom) as referring to the sixth empire that was in existence at the time, namely Rome. And the seventh one that is yet to come is looking at the future empire of the Antichrist, which John indicates will be notable but very brief. This is consistent with the way that Daniel used kings and kingdoms interchangeably in his prophecies. To try and find Nero in the passage is futile and it is not exegetical.

The Internal Evidence: (4) The Late Date

The late date (AD 95) for the writing of Revelation also has a line of sup-portive internal evidence. One line of evidence has to do with the spiritual conditions of the seven churches that John wrote to in Revelation 2 and 3.

The question is, "Do the spiritual conditions of these churches best fit first- or second-generation churches?"

When several of the churches are analyzed, it seems far better to view these churches as second-generation churches, which are being written to long after AD 70. If that is so, then preterism is damaged beyond repair. In having John write the Revelation, the Lord apparently selected seven churches because they represented *settled* spiritual conditions that can be true of local churches any time and any place. They were not always in the spiritual situation that they were in when John wrote to them, but most likely had come to those conditions over a period of time.

The church at Ephesus (Rev. 2:1–7) got a mixed review from the Lord of the churches. Jesus commended them for their perseverance in the faith and for their successful resistance of false apostles and of the heresy of the Nicolaitans. These commendations all reflect a time element, since matters such as persevering require time. However, the Lord Jesus also condemned them for departing from their "first love," which also seems to require time in order for this to become their settled condition. If John wrote to them around AD 65 (as the preterists insist), then Paul was writing at the same time to Timothy (1 and 2 Timothy), who was leading the Ephesian church. In fact, one could argue that 2 Timothy was written after John wrote Revelation (according to preterism) and yet, there is no statement by Paul of the highly significant spiritual failure of the Ephesians leaving their "first love" nor any mention of the sect of the Nicolaitans, which was apparently bothering the churches of Asia Minor (cf. Rev. 2:6, 15). Also, it is interesting to note that John does not mention the apostle Paul, who played a crucial role in the establishing of the church at Ephesus as well as others in Asia Minor. Hitchcock explains the omission this way:

> On his third missionary journey Paul headquartered in Ephesus for three years and had a profound ministry there. If John wrote in AD 64–67, then the omission of any mention of Paul in the letters to the seven churches of Asia Minor is inexplicable. However, if John wrote 30 years later to second-generation Christians in the churches, then the omission is easily understood.[34]

Two other churches merit some mention as well, namely the churches of Smyrna and Laodicea. Evidence points to the fact that the Smyrna church did not exist during the days of Paul.[35] If this is so, then that church did not come into existence until after the death of Paul (died around AD 67) and the preterist date for the writing of Revelation.

Notice that in his writings, Paul did refer to other churches in Asia Minor, such as Laodicea, Colossae, and Hierapolis (cf. Col. 1:2; 4:13) but made no reference to Smyrna. The absence of any reference to Smyrna in Paul's writings and the statement of Bishop Polycarp point to a late date for the writing of Revelation, at least to some time well after 70.

Bible students are well aware that the church at Laodicea was in the worst spiritual condition among the churches, according to the Lord. Its condition at the writing of Revelation was that the believers there were very wealthy and saw themselves in need of nothing (Rev. 3:17), indicating a deep spiritual poverty. And yet, their condition of spiritual "lukewarmness" was not mentioned by the apostle Paul when he spoke of them in Colossians 4. But the main matter is a historical one. The Laodicean church would not have had time to become wealthy (resulting in them settling into their lukewarm spiritual state) by the mid-60s due to the circumstance brought about by a devastating earthquake that took place in 60. Laodicea was destroyed by the earthquake of 60 and was not seen as a city of great wealth just a few years later when John allegedly wrote Revelation. As Hitchcock notes:

> *Because the rebuilding of Laodicea after the earthquake occupied a complete generation, and because there is no numismatic [coin] evidence from the decade of the AD 60s, it is highly problematic for preterists to claim that Laodicea was rich, wealthy, and in need of nothing in AD 64–67. During those years the city was in the early stages of a rebuilding program that would last another 25 years. However, if Revelation was written in AD 95, the description of Laodicea in Revelation 3:14–22 would fit the situation exactly. By this time the city had been completely rebuilt and was basking in the pride of its great accomplishments.*[36]

The seven churches of Revelation and their spiritual conditions favor a late date. Preterists cannot allow for the writing of Revelation after 70 (or even 68/69) and thus are locked into their position on the date of the writing of Revelation. But the external evidence points to a late date and the internal evidence, though not as weighty, also points to a post-70 writing of the book.

THE BASIC POSITIONS AND PROBLEMS:
4. THE "TIMING TEXTS" IN REVELATION

Very important to the preterist position are the "timing texts." These are verses which allegedly lead the interpreter to the conclusion that prophecies would be fulfilled soon after they were given. For example, Revelation 1:1 speaks of events which *"must shortly take place"*; or where Jesus said, *"I am coming quickly"* (2:16; 3:11; 22:7, 12, 20, emphasis added). Preterists insist that these words require that the fulfillment take place in the first century, shortly after they were prophesied. They see this as a key interpretive clue; that is, that the fulfillment must take place within a short time frame of the writer's contemporaries.

However, these words are not to be understood as chronological indicators telling the reader *when* the Lord is returning. Rather, they are to be taken as qualitative indicators describing *how* the Lord Jesus will return. He will return "suddenly." The word is communicating the idea that when the events of the Lord's return take place, they will occur rapidly once they begin. The emphasis is on the manner in which He returns and not the time in which He will return.

Thomas Ice has done a fine job in pulling together some of the important lexical information pertaining to this matter.

A form of the Greek word for "quickly" (tachos) is used eight times in Revelation (1:1; 2:16; 3:11; 11:14; 22:6–7, 12, 20). Tachos and its family of related words can be used to mean "soon" or "shortly," as preterists believe (relating to time), or they can be used to mean "quickly" or "suddenly," as many futurists contend (the manner in which action occurs). In the Bible, the tachos *family is used both ways.*[37]

Dr. Ice observes that lexicographers generally do not support the preterist interpretation, noting that the lexicons give very strong support for the futurist understanding of this important word:

The leading Greek lexicon in our day is Bauer, Arndt, and Gingrich *(BAG), which lists the following definitions for* tachos: *"speed, quickness, swiftness, haste" (p. 814). The two times this noun appears in Revelation (1:1; 22:6), it is coupled with the preposition* en, *causing this phrase to func-*

tion grammatically as an adverb revealing to us the "sudden" manner in which these events will take place. They will occur "swiftly." The other word in the tachos family used in Revelation as an adverb is tachus, which all six times occurs with the verb erchomai, "to come".... BAG gives as its meaning "quick, swift, speedy" (p. 814) and specifically classifies all six uses in Revelation as meaning "without delay, quickly, at once."... BAG (and the other lexicons also agree) recommends a translation descriptive of the manner in which an event will happen (Revelation 2:16; 3:11; 11:14; 22:7, 12, 20).[38]

Not only is there this strong lexical support, but there is solid grammatical support for the futurist position as well, as is seen in Blass-Debrunner.

Blass-Debrunner, in the section on adverbs, divides them into four categories: 1) adverbs of manner, 2) adverbs of place, 3) adverbs of time, 4) correlative adverbs (pp. 55–57). The tachos family is used as the major example in the "adverbs of manner" category. Interestingly, no example from the tachos family is listed under "adverbs of time."... Greek scholar Nigel Turner also supports this adverbial sense as meaning "quickly." Not only is there a preponderance of lexical support for understanding the tachos family as including the notion of "quickly" or "suddenly," there is also the further support that all the occurrences in Revelation are adverbs of manner.... These adverbial phrases in Revelation can more accurately be translated "that when these events begin, they will take place with 'rapid fire' sequence or 'speedily.'"[39]

These so called "timing texts" found in various verses in Revelation do not, in fact, tell us *when* these things will happen but instead tell us *how* they will occur. They, therefore, do not support the preterist position.

THE BASIC POSITIONS AND PROBLEMS:
5. THE "TIMING TEXTS" IN MATTHEW

As noted earlier, the "this generation" of Matthew 24:34 is understood by preterists to "require" a first-century fulfillment and is a basic part of its foundation. Two other verses in Matthew are also used by preterists to prove that the Lord had to have come in the first century. These Scriptures are Matthew 16:28, where Jesus declares that some of His listeners would "not taste death until they see the Son of Man coming in His kingdom," and Matthew 10:23, where He says that "you shall not finish going through the cities of Israel, until the Son of Man comes."

Let's observe the context of these two verses in Matthew. The Lord's statement found in 16:28 is explained in the very next event, which is the transfiguration. Three of the apostles did indeed see the Lord in His splendor as He will appear in His glorious, kingly reign in the Messianic kingdom. The subject of Jesus' statement is that of the Messiah's coming in *His kingdom*. For preterists to see this as Christ's "coming" in judgment in AD 70 is simply leaving the normal meaning of words. It is His glorious coming kingdom being referred to and not a coming judgment. The Lord is not promising that the kingdom will be instituted in the lifetimes of the apostles, but that they will get a "preview" of what it would be like when the kingdom was established.

"Jesus was not saying," wrote John Walvoord, "that the second coming would occur before those of His generation tasted death. He was introducing, rather, the transfiguration of chapter 17, which anticipated, in vision, the glory of the Son of man coming in His kingdom."[40]

Apparently Peter, one of those eyewitnesses to the transfiguration, understood that this was a preview of Christ's glory which would be seen in His kingdom. Peter recalls the transfiguration in 2 Peter 1:16-18 right after he has discussed the need for believers to diligently add to their faith certain virtues so that they would have an abundant entrance (reward) when Christ set up that eternal kingdom. The establishing of the eternal kingdom did not happen in 70, nor did Christ come in His kingdom at that time. Contrary to preterism, Matthew 16:28 is not teaching a first-century coming of Jesus Christ in judgment.

The commissioning of the apostles and their persecution is the setting of Christ's statement in Matthew 10:23, which reads, "But whenever they persecute you in this city, flee to the next; for truly I say to you, you shall not finish going through the cities of Israel, until the Son of Man comes." Preterists insist that this verse is clear and requires the Lord's return in 70, even though there have been many interpretations of this controversial verse from all theological camps. The commissioning of the apostles in this section (Matt. 10:1-23) actually has two parts to it; the first having to do with their present situation (vv. 1-15) and the second looking at a future time of wider ministry (vv. 16-23). Jesus makes the statement in verse 23 as part of the section dealing with their wider ministry in the future. Looking toward the future, the Lord refers to the coming of the Son of Man, which He uses elsewhere in reference to His powerful and glorious second coming (cf. Matt. 24:27, 30 and especially Matt. 16:27 and 19:28: "The Son of Man is going to come in the glory of His Father"; "The Son of Man will sit on His glorious throne"). Since Matthew 10:23 uses the same terminology, many commentators believe that this verse is looking at the same period of time, namely, the end of the tribulation period when the Son comes to judge the world and to establish His kingdom.

The primary point being made by the Lord is that the evangelization of the rebellious nation of Israel will not be finished by them but will await His return, which is the point made by Paul (cf. Rom. 11:25-29) and the prophets (e.g., Zech. 12:10). F. F. Bruce summarizes the thought of the Lord's statement. "It means, simply, that the evangelization of Israel will not be completed before the end of the present age, which comes with the advent of the Son of man." He then notes that the apostles's "mission, in the form in which they pursued it, was brought to an end by the Judean rebellion against Rome in AD 66, but it would be unwise to say that *that,* with the fall of Jerusalem four years later, was the coming of the Son of man of which Jesus spoke."[41]

Israel rejected the message of the apostles, who then turned to the Gentiles with the gospel of Christ. But *the requirement* that must be fulfilled before the Son of Man could return was Israel's repentance (cf. Matt. 23:39). This will be accomplished in the tribulation period as well as by the Second Coming itself, and this is apparently what the Lord was stating in Matthew 10:23.

THE BASIC POSITIONS AND PROBLEMS:
6. THE OLIVET DISCOURSE

Central to the position of preterism is their interpretation of the Lord's Olivet Discourse (Matthew 24–25). They view most all of these prophecies of the Lord Jesus as being fulfilled in 70 with the Roman destruction of Jerusalem. Thus Gentry wrote:

A simple reading of Matthew 24:34 lucidly reveals that all *of the things Christ the Great Prophet mentions up to this point—that is, everything in verses 4*

through 34—will occur in the same generation as the original disciples.
. . . All of these signs do, in fact, come to pass in the era before AD 70. . . .
Thus the Great Tribulation and all of its attendant signs belong to the first
century.[42]

Three Basic Observations

The discussion surrounding this one passage of Scripture is extensive and
detailed, and these few pages can only briefly summarize some of the
issues; a greater discussion and refutation of the preterist position can be
found in other places.[43] Before looking at several specific matters, three
general observations can be made about the preterist position on the
Olivet Discourse.

First, the key matter of the unconditional, everlasting Abrahamic
covenant is not part of their discussion. As was observed earlier (see chapters 2 and 3), all of Bible prophecy is based on this covenant and its sub-
covenants, which were guaranteed by God on oath and must, therefore, be
fulfilled as given. Also, many of the prophecies given in the Old Testament
dealing with the reign of the Messiah, which fulfill God's covenant
promises, are basically ignored.

Second, the details of Matthew 24 simply do not support the position
of preterism. As noted earlier in this chapter, Sproul acknowledged that
the events surrounding the Lord's coming are taken figuratively. Many of
the details of Matthew 24 must be allegorized by preterism in order for it
to try and prove its points. And when passages such as 2 Thessalonians 2,
Revelation 13, and Zechariah 12–14 that parallel Matthew 24 provide
many more details about the events and persons of the tribulation time,
the preterist position becomes more untenable.

Third, when Matthew 24 is taken with such key passages as Zechariah
12–14, as it should be, it becomes apparent that the coming of Christ
being described is to deliver a repentant Israel and not to judge a faithless
Israel. The emphasis of preterism is on God's judgment, which does not go
well with the great prophecies of Israel's restoration and salvation. Also,
Luke 21:18, which is part of a parallel section to Matthew 24, explicitly
states that the terrible events of the tribulation are to bring about Israel's
salvation. In that verse, Jesus said when these various signs and events took
place that they were to "lift up your heads, because your redemption is
drawing near."

The Context of Matthew 24 (Matt. 23:35–39)

Important to the discussion of Matthew 24 is the preceding section of 23:35-39. This section comes after Christ's severe denunciation of the religious leaders of Israel who were largely responsible for the nation's rejection of Jesus as the Messiah. As a result, judgment would fall on them—and it did, in 70. But equally clear is that Christ foretells a time when Israel will repent (23:39). In fact, the repentance of Israel is the one key event that must be in place in order for Christ to return. This is a fact that is also given by Daniel (cf. Dan. 12:7). Stanley Toussaint's discussion of Matthew 24:39 is helpful.

> *The verse is introduced with* gar, *which helps to explain the desolation of Israel's house in verse 38. In some way the abandonment of Israel's house is related to the absence of the Lord Jesus. Preterists would agree with this assertion. The problem for the preterists is the last half of the verse, "You shall not see me until you say, 'Blessed is He who comes in the name of the Lord!' That the Lord is dogmatic about this is seen in the Greek construction of* ou me *with the aorist subjunctive. By no means would they see the Lord until Israel makes the grand pronouncement of Psalm 118:26. . . . The Greek term* ho erchomenos, *the Coming One, is also significant because it is messianic. . . . In other words, this coming is to be identified with the triumph of the Second Advent as portrayed in Psalm 118.*[44]

Dr. Toussaint then notes that in context, the "you" of verses 38 and 39 must be looking at the same people Israel. Verse 38 refers to the judgment of God on Israel for their rejection of Messiah, but verse 39 looks at their future repentance. Dr. Toussaint writes:

> *Jews would hardly call the horrible decimation of life at that cataclysmic event a* blessed *coming of the Messiah. Rather verse 39 describes Israel's future repentance when as Zechariah 12:10 says they shall mourn for their great sin. This becomes important because the clear deduction is Israel's repentance* precedes *His coming.*[45]

This future salvation of national Israel is an emphasis of many Scriptures, but one that is absent from the preterist discussion of Matthew

24. Jesus was clear that they would not "see" Him again until they had repented. This repentance would be evident by their changed attitude toward Him, which is reflected in Psalm 118. To propose, as preterists do, that there is a "coming" of Christ in 70 not only reinvents the idea of His "coming" but also ignores the mandatory prerequisite of His coming, namely the repentance of Israel.

Understanding the "Abomination of Desolation" (Matt. 24:15)

To try and illustrate the preterist approach to Matthew 24 and also to respond to some specific issues, three matters will be mentioned: first, the "abomination of desolation" (24:15); second, the "coming" of Christ (24:3, 27, 37, 39); and finally the "signs in heaven" (24:2–31).

The Lord Jesus said the "abomination of desolation" (24:15) was one of the clear indicators to alert Israel that the tribulation had come and that His return would be soon. Jesus specifically quoted from Daniel (cf. 9:27; 11:31; 12:11), which sets the boundaries for the meaning of this term. Since no such event, as described by Daniel, actually took place during the temple's destruction in 70, preterists are not in agreement among themselves on what is being referred to by this phrase. They do seek to find some historical support from Josephus but to no avail.[46]

Some preterists think the "abomination" refers to the unrighteous acts of wicked zealots who invaded the temple prior to the Roman taking the temple while others believe it refers to the destroying of the temple by the Romans because the "stone-by-stone dismantling" of the temple surely involves its "desolation."[47] Still others believe it is the corrupting of the temple by apostate Israel. But none of these ideas really fits the scriptural teaching, which is why preterists retreat to Josephus to find their evidence.

The Bible presents the "abomination" as a specific event centering on an individual in the holy place itself. This is what the Scriptures speak of and not a general defiling or the presence of unclean Gentiles in the temple. It must be remembered that in 70 no image was set up in the temple, no man sat in the holy of holies and proclaimed himself to be deity, no period of three-and-one-half years took place between the "abomination" and the coming of the Messiah, and no time existed for Israelites to flee the city after the temple's destruction by the Romans, something required by the Matthew 24 text. The differences between Matthew 24 and

Vespasian's destruction of the temple are great.

There must be specific correspondence between Daniel's statements and Jesus' statement. Daniel presents to his readers a clear picture of the "abomination of desolation" when he tells of such an act as it would be perpetrated by Antiochus Epiphanes. There would need to be the defilement of the temple proper by unclean sacrifices to *another god* in the middle of the seven year tribulation period. Jesus' words are expanded on by Paul (2 Thess. 2:4) and John (Rev. 13:3–17) who tell us that a person occupies the holy place and that there is worship of that person (the Antichrist) along with Satan. Could anything be more defiling than that? This enforced worship will center in the newly rebuilt temple in Jerusalem where Antichrist will present himself as deity (cf. 2 Thess. 2:3b, 4, 9). The "abomination of desolation" did not occur with the temple's destruction in 70 but awaits a future fulfillment in the newly built temple that Daniel speaks about (9:27).

Understanding the Coming of Christ (Matt. 24:27, 37, 39)

A second matter to consider is the "coming" of the Lord Jesus. Preterists claim that this took place in 70 with a "judgment coming" of the Lord Jesus who did not, however, visibly appear at that time.[48] This doctrine is both arbitrary and contrary to the use of *parousia* (coming) and to the context.

In context, the disciples specifically asked the Lord for signs related to "Your coming" (24:3), and so He speaks of His "coming" in His response. Most everyone agrees that the disciples' questions were based on Zechariah 12–14, where all the matters mentioned by the disciples (Jerusalem's destruction and the Messiah' coming) were found. In Zechariah, the Messiah would come and His presence would be clear and obvious to both believers and unbelievers. Concerning the Lord's "coming," preterists assign two very different meanings to the phrase "thus shall be the coming of the Son of Man" (24:3, 27, 37, and 39). They propose a "judgment coming" as well as the second coming. However, Christ is not actually seen at the "judgment coming" because He is not visibly present. Some preterists correctly see 24:37 and 39 speaking of the second coming of Christ.

Toussaint successfully argues that the meaning of *parousia* is clear and consistent.

If the coming of the Son of Man in Matthew 24:37, 39 is the Second Advent, one would expect the identical clause in 24:27 to refer to the same event. The word would also have the same meaning in 24:3. It must be the Second Advent in each case. Furthermore, the word parousia *as found in the New Testament is always used of an actual presence. It may be employed of the presence of persons as in 1 Corinthians 16:17; 2 Corinthians 7:6–7; 10:10; Philippians 1:26; 2:12; and 2 Thessalonians 2:9. In each of the above cases the person is* bodily *present. In all of the other cases* parousia *is used of the Lord's presence at His second coming. . . . The only occurrences in the Gospels of* parousia *are in Matthew 24. It would seem that they, too, refer to a yet future coming of Christ.*[49]

Significantly, the *Bauer-Arndt-Gingrich Greek Lexicon* defines *parousia* as "presence" and "coming, advent." The lexicon "cites all four uses of *parousia* in Matthew 24 as a reference to Christ's second coming," Ice reports. He adds: "Kittel's dictionary, in concert with *BAG*, tells us that the core idea of the word means 'to be present,' 'denotes esp. active presence. . . .' Kittel describes *parousia* as a technical term "for the 'coming' of Christ in Messianic glory."[50]

When the disciples asked the Lord about the His "coming" (presence), the usual meaning of the word along with Zechariah's prophecy of the actual coming/presence of the Messiah would certainly have affected both their understanding and their questions. It is very hard to believe that Jesus would not have corrected their thinking and would not have made the matter of His "coming" crystal clear. If He were to come in 70, in a non-literal return in judgment where He would not be visibly present, the Lord Jesus would have told His followers. And furthermore, Jesus underscores the unmistakable nature of His "coming" when He likens His coming to the spectacular lightning flashes going across the sky. His "coming" will be a powerful, glorious, and unique event, visible to all and which no one can mistake for something else (24:27). There will be no speculation or debate about His coming when He does return in this powerful and glorious act. The preterist position on a dual "coming" (where one is not an actual presence of Christ) is at best artificial.

Understanding the Signs in Heaven (Matt. 24:29–31)

The Lord Jesus declared that at His coming there would be amazing cosmic signs in the heavens (24:29-31). He stated that sun, moon, and stars would cease giving their light, plunging the earth into darkness and that the heavens would be shaken. And these phenomena would cause all the tribes of the earth to mourn. Then, in the midst of this darkness, the sign (the *shekinah* glory?) of the coming Son of Man would appear. R. C. Sproul admits the difficulty of this section for those holding to the preterist position:

> *This passage describes the* parousia *in vivid and graphic images of astronomical perturbations. It speaks of signs in the sky that will be visible and the sound of a trumpet that will be audible. Perhaps no portion of the Olivet Discourse provides more difficulties to the preterist view than this one.*[51]

And it is indeed a difficult portion for the preterists who admit that no such cosmic signs took place at the destruction of Jerusalem. They attempt to explain it by pointing out that "sky" can be translated "heaven" and that cosmic disturbances are sometimes "a dramatic way of expressing national calamity or victory in battle."[52] They contend that these cosmic disturbances actually picture an event in heaven when the Son of Man enters the heavenly throne room and executes judgment. The "sign" of the Son of Man is that this rejected One is now in heaven as is evidenced by the destruction of the temple on earth.[53] Preterists limit the "mourning" at this event to the tribes within Israel who grieve over being the brunt of God's wrath and mourn the loss of land, temple, government and friends.[54] Sproul argues, "The graphic language used by Jesus to describe the attending events is metaphorical and consistent with the poetry of fervor used by Old Testament prophets."[55]

This preterist explanation of Matthew 24:29–31 not only illustrates the danger of allegorizing, it fails to acknowledge the Old Testament texts that the Lord was using as a basis for His statements. Matthew 24:29 reflects the prophecy of Joel, who describes the day of the Lord, which will be characterized by cosmic events such as darkness brought about by the diminishing of sun, moon, and stars (Joel 2:1–10, 30–31; 3:12–17). In this context of the "day of the Lord," Joel says that at that time God will "restore the fortunes of Judah and Jerusalem" and that He is entering into judgment on "behalf of My people and My inheritance, Israel" (3:1–2).

In this passage, the Lord is delivering His people Israel. God is judging these enemies of Israel because of their mistreatment of His people and He will be "a refuge for His people and a stronghold for the sons of Israel" with the result that "Jerusalem will be holy" (3:16–17). The Lord uses nature, as He often has done, to terrify and crush His enemies. What is being described by Joel did not take place in AD 70. Why run to fanciful allegorizing when it is clear from the plagues on Egypt, darkness on the land at the time of the crucifixion, signs in the sky with the shaking of Mount Sinai at the giving of the law, and other events that God does indeed use His power in nature to impress mankind? Why allegorize and leave normal language when there is no compelling reason in the text to do so?

Another passage that forms the background to Jesus' statement is found in the prophet Zechariah. Most everyone would agree that the mourning that is mentioned in 24:30 reaches back to Zechariah 12:10. But the mourning found in Zechariah is not about losing the temple, land, and friends. Rather it is a mourning that comes about because of Israel's clear understanding of what they did to their own Messiah. Because of the working of the Spirit, the nation of Israel mourns over their treatment of Messiah. Toussaint calls the mourning, "a repentant lamentation by Israel because it results in the purification of the nation" (Zech. 13:1). He then notes,

> *The context of Zechariah 12:10 is most significant. Rather than prophesying the destruction of Jerusalem, it is predicting the opposite. . . . It looks ahead to God's future deliverance of Israel when Jerusalem will again be surrounded by enemies. "In that day" is prophetic of a time of deliverance of Israel, not judgment.*[56]

In the larger section of Zechariah 12–14, the term "in that day" or similar wording occurs nineteen times and is "that classical eschatological formula"[57] which speaks of Messiah's day. This section is focused on the repentance, cleansing, and deliverance of Israel by the Lord God. After noting that this section of Zechariah looks at the distant prophetic future, David Baron makes this significant statement:

> *Neither can we, without doing great violence to the prophecy, interpret it [to refer to] the taking of Jerusalem by Antiochus Epiphanes, as some do, nor to*

the destruction of the city and the temple by the Romans; for . . . in none of those calamitous events in the past history of Israel did God in the person of the Messiah visibly appear on the Mount of Olives with His angelic hosts as the Deliverer of His people and the destroyer of many nations which were gathered against them; nor was the spirit of grace and supplication ever yet poured out upon the Jewish nation, so that they might look upon and recognize "Him whom they have pierced"; nor has the Lord, from any of those past events onward become "King over the whole earth" (chap. 14:9); not to mention many other great and solemn events which are predicted in these chapters, which cannot be allegorized or explained away.[58]

In Zechariah 14, the Lord is seen fighting against those nations that come against Jerusalem (14:3), which did not occur in AD 70. Great signs will accompany this time including the splitting of the Mount of Olives (14:4–5) and unique cosmic signs (14:6–7), including darkness, which also did not occur in 70. The end result of all of these signs and the Lord's coming will be the security and safety of Jerusalem and the reigning of Messiah over all the earth (14:9), none of which occurred in 70.

SOME FINAL OBSERVATIONS

The discussion could go on and it does in a number of other books. Several observations can be made as a result of this brief study.

1. The hermeneutical approach of preterism is eclectic, giving it the flexibility to move in and out of allegorization or literal interpretation as it needs to. This kind of interpretive approach essentially makes the interpreter the final authority.
2. The view of preterism fails to adequately deal with the Abrahamic covenant which is the basis for prophecy. Without the boundaries set by the biblical covenants, preterists can wander wherever they choose.
3. Preterism diminishes the wonderful passages about the Lord's coming in glory and power to establish His kingdom and reduces the "blessed hope" of Christ's return to almost nothing. It diminishes those texts that tell of a gracious, covenant, keeping God who returns in awesome majesty to fulfill His oath and save His wayward

people Israel, as well as all believing people. It replaces this glorious coming with a naturalistic coming of the Roman armies.

Two final observations. First, the position of preterism that all (or almost all) was fulfilled in the past forces it to hold to ideas that are simply unrealistic; such as that the new heavens and new earth have already been established, the danger of apostasy is passed, the "last days" have come and gone, that Satan has been bound and judged, and a host of other views. Second, it forces all Scripture into its postmillennial mold where the world is to become Christianized and dominated by the law of God. This pre-understanding prohibits them from letting the Scriptures speak normally. Preterism deprives many portions of Scripture of any real meaning and impacts the way in which a believer today lives the Christian life and how that believer views the future workings of Christ.

CHAPTER TEN

THE KINGDOM

OF  God

The pastor looked at his congregation and declared enthusiastically, "We are kingdom people, and we must invest our lives right now in doing the work of the kingdom! It is to us that God has committed this work, and the expansion of His kingdom depends on our obedient and dedicated labor."

The congregation nodded in agreement, even though they were not exactly sure what this meant or what they should do. It certainly sounded right and biblical, and they knew that a positive response was appropriate. Most in the congregation had forgotten that two weeks earlier the pastor taught them that the kingdom would come only when Jesus returned to the earth, but this apparent contradiction between his two sermons did not register. No one asked, "Is the kingdom present, or is it something future? Is the kingdom on this earth, or is it in heaven?"

Like many others, this congregation had learned to live with certain unclear concepts. And the term *kingdom of God* is one such concept. The word *kingdom* is often employed by Christians, but many use the term without having a clear understanding of its meaning or usage in the Bible.

The kingdom of God is the great theme of the Scriptures. God is the eternal King who rules now and shall rule in the future. It is in the kingdom of God that the purposes of God are fulfilled. And since the term *kingdom of God* is an important concept in all the millennial views, as well as in the study of future things in general, it is important to define the term and note the distinct ways it is used in the Scriptures.

DEFINING THE TERM: *KINGDOM OF GOD*

Since the phrase "kingdom of God" is scriptural, any definition must be based on a careful investigation of the Bible. In arriving at an understanding of the kingdom of God, all of Scripture must be examined. Any view of the kingdom that rests in large measure on a single text should be viewed with suspicion. For example, using the statement "the kingdom of God is within you" (Luke 17:21 KJV) as the starting point for defining the kingdom will most likely lead to an incorrect and unbalanced view. Not only would the view be built on a single text, but it would rest on a text that is subject to several diverse interpretations.

To get a clear picture of the kingdom of God, a large number of Scripture portions need to be studied. Since a divine kingdom is mentioned in the Bible more than two hundred times, it is impossible in one chapter to include every reference. But it is possible to look at enough biblical material to understand the basic definition and distinctions of the kingdom of God.

When we speak of a "kingdom," certain elements are included in our understanding of that term. "The normal use of the term *kingdom* denotes a dominion or physical sphere of rule involving a ruler, a people who are ruled, and a physical territory where the rule takes place."[1] As it is used in the Scriptures, the term *kingdom of God* refers to the rule of the sovereign God over His creation. In both the general concept of a kingdom and in the biblical idea of the kingdom of God, three essential elements are found.

A Sovereign, Authoritative Ruler

There must be a ruler. This ruler must have the authority and power to rule. In the biblical concept of the kingdom of God, that ruler is our sovereign God. King Jehoshaphat expressed it well in 2 Chronicles 20:6: "O Lord, the God of our fathers, art Thou not God in the heavens? And art Thou not ruler over all the kingdoms of the nations? Power and might are in Thy hand so that no one can stand against Thee."

He recognized the sovereign authority of God to rule over the entire universe. The sovereign authority of God to rule is discussed throughout the Scriptures, all the way to the book of Revelation, where the question of rulership over the earth is settled once and for all. The apostle John refers to the "throne" of God some thirty times. The term *throne* speaks of the seat of authority. God is seen as the sovereign ruler, who has great power and authority in His rulership. A kingdom, then, must have a ruler who has the authority to rule.

A Realm to Rule

There must be a realm of rule. This element of a kingdom focuses on the subjects to be ruled and not on the authority possessed by the ruler. In the kingdom of God, God exercises His rule over those in the heavens and on the earth. Some have attempted to prove that the kingdom of God looks abstractly at the authority to rule and not at the domain or the subjects being ruled.[2] It is true that the idea of the kingdom can have an abstract shade of meaning. But when passages are studied in their contexts, inevitably an authority over someone or something is found. A kingdom cannot really exist without subjects.

> It is true that one may think of regal authority as something possessed but not actually exercised. The New Testament, however, has a word for this. Before His ascension our Lord said, "All power (exousia) is given unto me in heaven and in earth" (Matt. 28:18). . . . The "power" is essential to the "kingdom" but the kingdom is more than the power.[3]

If there is only authority but no subjects in a realm, then by definition no kingdom really exists.

The Exercising of Authority

In a kingdom there must be the actual exercising of authority. In theory, of course, one might propose that a ruler could temporarily leave his realm of authority and still be viewed as a ruler. But there can be no kingdom in a full and complete sense without the active exercising of that authority. God does actually exercise His power and authority over the realm of His creation.

In 1 Chronicles 29:11–12, King David includes all three of these essential elements when he speaks of the kingdom of God:

Thine, O Lord, is the greatness and the power and the glory and the victory and the majesty, indeed everything that is in the heavens and the earth; Thine is the dominion, O Lord, and Thou dost exalt Thyself as head over all. Both riches and honor come from Thee, and Thou dost rule over all, and in Thy hand is power and might; and it lies in Thy hand to make great, and to strengthen everyone.

The biblical concept of the kingdom of God, therefore, includes a ruler who has authority to rule, a realm of subjects that He rules, and the actual exercising of the rulership.

DISTINCTIONS IN THE CONCEPT OF THE KINGDOM OF GOD

In order to come to an understanding of the kingdom of God, certain distinctions need to be observed. When reading through the Bible, some notable differences regarding the kingdom of God initially may seem to be contradictory. But they are not; they are simply different aspects of a wonderfully diverse concept.

A distinction needs to be observed in relation to *the beginning of the kingdom* of God. In some passages the kingdom is said to be something that has always existed, whereas other portions indicate that it has a definite beginning in the future (Pss. 10:16; 145:13; Dan. 2:44; Matt. 6:10). The Psalms tell us that the Lord is the eternal ruler over an everlasting kingdom; on the other hand, Jesus encouraged His followers to pray for the kingdom to come. And Daniel foretold a day when the kingdom would begin, indicating that it was not presently in existence.

So one way to distinguish between these two kingdoms is to note whether or not the kingdom has a starting point. The Scriptures speak of the kingdom as being a present reality (no starting point) and yet something that will not begin until a future time. The psalmist speaks of the Lord as presently ruling as a king (Ps. 29:10), but Zechariah says that He "will be" the king (Zech. 14:9). Daniel is in agreement with Zechariah as he speaks of the day when the Son of Man will rule after all the kingdoms of man are destroyed (Dan. 7:13–14).

Another difference is the distinction in *the scope of the kingdom.*[4] Sometimes the Bible speaks of the kingdom as being universal in its scope, including all created things. David declared that "the Lord has established

His throne in the heavens, and His sovereignty rules over all" (Ps. 103:19). There is absolutely nothing outside that kingdom. Yet, on the other hand, the kingdom is also revealed as *earthly* in its scope. When God establishes such a kingdom, it will encompass the whole earth (Dan. 2:44–45), and Christ will rule from His throne in Jerusalem (cf. Isa. 24:23; Zech. 14:4–9).

Finally, there is the distinction in *the administration of the kingdom*.[5] The kingdom sometimes is presented as the rule of God directly, with no human mediator ruling on God's behalf. God administers His own rule over any or all parts of the creation (Ps. 59:13; Dan. 4:34–37). In contrast to this, God's rule is also administered indirectly through a human mediator. For example, in Psalm 2 the Messiah is that mediator who will rule over the nations of the earth. He stands in God's place, since He is identified by God as "My king" and any who oppose Him will be subject to the wrath of God. So God the king can rule directly or indirectly.

These notable differences in the concept of the kingdom of God are not contradictions at all. The supposed contradictions disappear and the fuller picture of the kingdom of God comes into focus when we understand that a number of aspects to the kingdom of God are revealed in the Scriptures. Before these various aspects of the kingdom of God are viewed, however, one other distinction is sometimes made concerning the kingdom of God; namely, there is a distinction between the "kingdom of heaven" and the "kingdom of God."

The phrase "kingdom of heaven" is found only in Matthew's gospel. In the parallel accounts in Mark and Luke, this phrase is rendered "kingdom of God" (e.g., compare Matthew 13 with Mark 4 and Luke 8). It is best, therefore, to understand these phrases as interchangeable and not as two different aspects of the kingdom. But why the difference in Matthew?

The reason Matthew used "Kingdom of Heaven" is because he was writing his gospel to the Jews. Jewish people were and are sensitive about using the name "God" in vain so they try to avoid using the term whenever they are writing or speaking; they tend to use the term only within the confines of the synagogue or in religious discussions. . . . Matthew, writing to Jews and aware of Jewish sensitivities, used the expression "Kingdom of Heaven" so that it would be more readily acceptable to his Jewish readers. However, Mark wrote to Romans and Luke wrote to Greeks who did not have these sensitivities so they used the expression "Kingdom of God." What Matthew meant by the "Kingdom of Heaven" is no different from what Mark and Luke meant by the "Kingdom of God."[6]

These terms, therefore, are not expressing differences in the concept of the kingdom of God but rather are synonymous ideas.

THE VARIOUS ASPECTS OF THE KINGDOM OF GOD

As Scripture discusses the rule of God over creation, various aspects of the kingdom become obvious. If we are going to understand God's kingdom rule, these must be distinguished. It also becomes clear that the context in which the kingdom is discussed will play a large part in determining which aspect is in view.

1. The Universal Kingdom of God

The universal kingdom of God is the rule of God over the entire universe. In this kingdom nothing happens outside of the will of God because He is sovereign and in control (1 Chron. 29:12; Ps. 145:13). This sovereign control is eternal, as the prophet Jeremiah declared: "He is the living God and the everlasting King" (Jer. 10:10). This rule is usually direct and is sometimes evidenced through supernatural manifestations (Ex. 11:9; 20:18-20; Deut. 4:32-40; Dan. 6:26-27). But He also rules indirectly through individuals (Prov. 21:1; Isa. 10:5-6; Jer. 25:8-12) or through the elements of nature (Ex. 14:21; Ps. 148:8).

This aspect of the kingdom of God would, therefore, be the broadest expression of the kingdom of God. His is an eternal, sovereign rule everywhere over the entire creation.

2. The Spiritual Kingdom of God

The spiritual kingdom of God is the rule of God over all those who are believers, that is, those who have experienced the regenerating work of the Holy Spirit. Anyone from Adam until now who has been born again is part of this phase of God's kingdom (Col. 1:13). When Jesus spoke to Nicodemus about entering into the kingdom by the new birth, this is the aspect of the kingdom He was referring to (John 3:1-10). The true church of Jesus Christ is this aspect of the kingdom of God.

Note, however, that the spiritual kingdom was in existence before the church began on the day of Pentecost. In addition, it will continue to exist after the church departs at the rapture.

3. The Theocratic Kingdom of God

The term *theocratic* simply means the "rule of God." This phrase, therefore, speaks of God's rule over a temporal, human kingdom. The title is rather general and may not be the best designation. However, it is used here to speak of God's rule over the earth (in contrast to His rule over the universe) and of His indirect administration (in contrast to direct ruling) through human mediators.

Even more specifically, it refers to God's rule over the nation of Israel. This aspect of the kingdom was established at Mount Sinai when Israel entered into a covenant relationship with God and agreed to keep God's law. This law code became the constitution of the nation of Israel. After the Israelites left Mount Sinai, they entered and possessed Canaan. God established no new human leader after the death of Joshua, since it was His intention to rule the nation through the Mosaic law, which was administered through the priests.

But disobedience and failure marked this period of time. It lasted for a little more than three hundred years, at which time Israel demanded a king. The human administrators of the kingdom then became the kings of Israel and Judah. But this aspect of the theocratic kingdom ended in failure also. It's depicted visually with the departure of the *Shekinah* Glory, a symbol of the presence of God.

> *With the departure of the Shekinah Glory from the temple (Ezek. 8:4; 9:3; 10:4; 10:18; 11:22, 23), God marks the close of the theocratic kingdom in Israel's past history. . . . The "times of the Gentiles" began, in which Israel is set aside until Messiah should come.*[7]

With the end of the theocratic kingdom, the focus of attention was on the future, when Messiah would come and bring in the kingdom promised to David.

4. The Mystery Form of the Kingdom of God

In Matthew 13 the Lord Jesus spoke to His followers about the mysteries of the kingdom. The word *mystery* in the Bible has to do with the revealing of divine truth that was previously unknown. Obviously the Old Testament spoke a great deal about the kingdom of God, but Jesus taught His disciples truth about the kingdom that was previously unrevealed in the Old Testament. The Old Testament anticipated the fulfillment of the great messianic kingdom, but what it did not anticipate was Israel's refusal to accept their King and His kingdom and what would take place after that rejection. As Dwight Pentecost wrote, "The mystery was the fact that when the One in whom this program was to be realized was publicly presented He would be rejected and an age would fall between His rejection and the fulfillment of God's purpose of sovereignty at His second advent."[8]

This aspect of the kingdom of God exists between the two advents of Christ, or more specifically between the time when Jesus was rejected by the nation of Israel until the time Israel accepts Jesus as the Messiah. In this mystery form of the kingdom the "Ruler is God. The ruled are people on the earth who have related themselves in a positive, neutral, or negative way to 'Christendom' (including true believers, professing people, rejecters, and even opponents). The time is the period between His comings."[9] Unlike the spiritual kingdom, unbelievers are a part of this aspect of God's kingdom.

5. The Millennial Kingdom of God

This aspect of the kingdom of God is yet future and, as the name implies, will last for a thousand years. This facet of God's kingdom will fulfill the great eternal, unconditional covenants of the Old Testament, particularly the Davidic covenant (2 Samuel 7). As was discussed in previous chapters, this kingdom will be on the earth, where Jesus Christ will physically, literally rule after His second coming. This aspect of the kingdom of God is sometimes called the messianic kingdom, since the ruler will be the Messiah.

This is the kingdom that John the Baptist declared was "at hand," and this is the kingdom that was offered to the nation of Israel by both John the Baptist and Jesus. It was this aspect of the kingdom that was rejected by the nation when they spurned the Lord Jesus. But in the future time of the tribulation, Israel will once again be offered this kingdom. At that time they will accept it, and Jesus will rule on the throne of David. The characteristics of this facet of the kingdom will be dealt with later.

6. The Eternal Kingdom of God

This aspect of the kingdom might well be included in the previous section, but because of certain factors it is kept distinct. Daniel 2:44 declares that the "God of heaven will set up a kingdom which will never be destroyed. . . . It will itself endure forever." This kingdom spoken of by Daniel comes into existence only *after all* the kingdoms of man are totally removed from the earth. This kingdom of God does not coexist with human kingdoms.

In Revelation 5, the apostle John had a vision of the Lord Jesus (the Lion-Lamb of Judah) receiving the right to judge and rule the world. This is prior to His second coming. After Christ returns and rules, the Lord Jesus (the King of Kings and Lord of Lords) will destroy all human kingdoms and establish His own. This, of course, is the millennial kingdom, which lasts for a thousand years. But how can it last for a thousand years and be said to "endure forever"? The answer is that there are two distinct phases to God's kingdom after the second coming.

The first phase is the millennium, in which the Messiah reigns on this present earth in order to fulfill completely the covenant promises given primarily to Israel. The second phase is the eternal state, in which God reigns over a new heaven and new earth that is free from all opposition to His rule, as it was at the very beginning when the universe was created. In one sense the eternal kingdom of God is a restoration of paradise lost. Referring to these as two phases of a future "forever" kingdom is an attempt to emphasize some differences that exist while making clear that once Jesus Christ returns at His second coming, no created being will ever again establish a kingdom and rule anywhere in the universe.

In 1 Corinthians 15:23-28, the apostle Paul looks at these two phases of the future, eternal kingdom. He teaches that, at the end of the millennial reign, Jesus "delivers up the kingdom to the God and Father" (v. 24). Jesus does this after He has rendered inoperative every enemy, including rebellious men, evil angels, and death (vv. 25-26). Paul says that all of Jesus' enemies will be put "under His feet" (v. 25), which is an ancient figure for the total defeat and subjection of one's foes. The dominion over the earth that Adam lost in the fall will be fully recovered by Christ. When this occurs, Christ will turn over the kingdom rule to the Father for the eternal reign over a new heaven and new earth. Paradise will be restored. What God originally intended when He created this universe will finally, completely, and eternally come to pass.

This is the great goal: God's ruling over a redeemed people in a perfect environment that is free from all enemies and opposition. Although interpreters differ on who will actually rule in the eternal kingdom of God, it is probably best to see the triune God as reigning. "Christ will continue to reign, because His reign is eternal (Rev. 11:15), but He will reign with the Father in trinitarian glory, subject to the Trinity in that way eternally designed for Him."[10] The eternal kingdom of God is the final phase of the kingdom of God and will fulfill Daniel's prophecy that "the God of heaven will set up a kingdom which will never be destroyed" (Dan. 2:44a).

THE CHURCH AND THE KINGDOM OF GOD

After viewing these various aspects of the kingdom of God, it should be apparent that the *church* and the *kingdom of God* are not equivalent terms. Although some use the terms as though they were interchangeable, they should not be so used. Certain, clear distinctions ought not to be blurred. But this does not deny any relationship between the church and the kingdom of God. The church does have a relationship with certain aspects of the kingdom.

The church is part of the *universal kingdom*, since the church is part of the creation over which God rules. The church is the *spiritual kingdom of God* in this present age, though the spiritual kingdom of God was in existence before the church began at Pentecost and will continue to exist after the church is removed from the earth at the rapture. But the church has no part in the *theocratic kingdom*, since that kingdom began at Mount Sinai and included the nation of Israel only. The church is part of the *mystery form of the kingdom* because this aspect of the kingdom exists between the two advents of Christ. But they are not equivalent ideas because the mystery form of the kingdom encompasses a slightly longer period of time and includes unbelievers. The church also has a part in the final future aspects of the kingdom of God. As the bride of Christ, the church will have a prominent place in the *millennial kingdom* as well as in the *eternal kingdom*.

Even this brief survey of the various aspects of the kingdom of God should make clear that phrases such as "we are kingdom people" need further definition. It is important to carefully study the context of a passage in which the word *kingdom* is found in order to determine precisely what truths about the kingdom of God the writer was talking about.

VARIOUS ASPECTS OF THE KINGDOM OF GOD

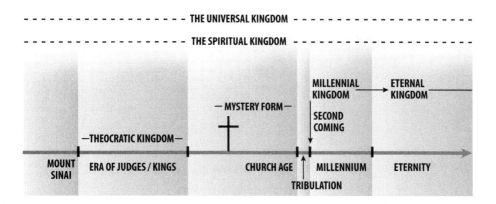

But when all is said and done, what a glorious future lies ahead for the children of God! What an honor to be redeemed by the King and to be a part of the present kingdom of God, as well as anticipating participation in the eternal kingdom of God! These realities should motivate us to represent our King in an excellent way right now while living daily in "enemy territory." And they should motivate us to be waiting expectantly for the return of King Jesus.

CHAPTER ELEVEN

AN OVERVIEW
OF
Future Events

A person's first flight in an airplane is always a memorable one. After getting past the fear, he or she is always impressed with the view. The world takes on a brand-new look from several thousand feet up, and the relationship between buildings, trees, roads, and rivers takes on new meaning. Likewise, in the military, reconnaissance missions are flown over enemy lines to obtain information on the strength, position, and movement of enemy forces. Those flights provide the "big picture," giving a perspective that would not be possible from the ground.

As we turn our attention to many of the details of future events, it is helpful to first get the big picture. Without an overview clearly in mind, it is possible to get lost in all the details. This quick "flyover," which is from the perspective of pretribulational premillennialism, will highlight the relationships between seven key prophetic events. These will be detailed in parts three and four.

1. THE RAPTURE OF THE CHURCH

The first event in the sequence of upcoming end-times events is the rapture of the church out of this world. The Lord Jesus will return from heaven and will suddenly and supernaturally remove the church (1 Thess. 4:13–18). Jesus will not return all the way to the earth as He will at the second coming but, rather, will meet believers in the air. Christians who are alive at this time will be caught up to meet the Lord Jesus and will at that moment receive their glorified bodies.

Those Christians who have died since the church began at Pentecost will also be involved in the rapture, having their physical bodies raised from the dead. These Christians have been with the Lord since their death, but only now do they receive their resurrected, glorified bodies (1 Cor. 15:51–53). This will be part of the "first resurrection" (Rev. 20:5–6).

All Christians who are part of the church, the bride of Christ, will be taken by the Lord to heaven and will be with Him there (John 14:1–3).

2. The Judgment Seat of Christ

Immediately following the rapture of the church, the judgment seat of Christ will take place in heaven. All those who are involved in the rapture (church saints) will also be involved in this event (Rom. 14:10; 1 Cor. 3:11–4:5; 2 Cor. 5:10). This will be a time when the Lord Jesus evaluates the works of those who are His people. The issue at the judgment seat is not the salvation of the individual, since that matter has already been settled. The issue at the judgment seat of Christ is the works of Christians. If the works done during their life are good and acceptable to Christ, they will receive reward. If their works are considered worthless, there will be a loss of reward, but not the loss of salvation. A variety of rewards will be given, and they apparently have some impact on life and responsibility during the final kingdom of God.

Following the judgment seat of Christ and before His second coming to the earth, the marriage of the Lamb (Christ) will take place (Rev. 19:9). This event eternally unites the newly rewarded church with the Lord Jesus.

3. The Seven-Year Tribulation (the Seventieth Week of Daniel)

After the church is removed from the earth at the rapture, the world will experience a period of time commonly called the tribulation. There could well be a short period of time between the rapture and the actual beginning of the tribulation during which some necessary alignments and developments take place. Based on Daniel 9:24–27, this period begins when the man known as the Antichrist signs a treaty with the nation of Israel. The Antichrist will seem at first to be the protector of Israel, but he will turn out to be the great persecutor of Israel. The seven-year Tribulation is divided into two distinct parts of three and a half years each. These two parts have significant events and judgments. There are two primary purposes for the tribulation.

The first and great purpose of God is to save the nation of Israel (and many Gentiles as well) and bring them under the new covenant, which is the covenant of salvation. To bring Israel to the point where they will respond in a positive way to God's gracious offer of salvation, God will employ many miracles. He will also allow intense persecution to come upon Israel, which will cause Israel and others to come to faith in Christ. It will be a time of unprecedented salvation, and it is likely that no other seven-year period in human history will rival the great numbers of people who are redeemed (Rev. 7:9–17).

The second purpose of the tribulation is to judge wicked people and nations. The unrighteous have willfully and arrogantly refused to live in obedience to the Creator. And while God is slow to anger and full of mercy and grace (Ex. 34:6–7), eventually unrepentant sinful people and wicked angels must be dealt with. As a result, the tribulation will be an unprecedented time of trouble and judgment on this earth (Revelation 6–18; Matt. 24:4–28). In three series of judgments, close to 80 percent of the world's population will perish, and life on this planet will be chaotic. The Lord Jesus noted that if God had not limited the length of the tribulation no human being would make it through that time alive (Matt. 24:22).

The tribulation will also be a time of unique activity for Satan as well. Using the Antichrist, Satan will attempt to destroy God's people, thwart God's purposes, and cause all on the earth to worship him. His hatred for God will be focused on the people of God and will be seen in his aggressive attempt to put all of God's people to death. Satan will successfully deceive many on the earth through his use of amazing and powerful signs and wonders. Multitudes will follow him (Matt. 24:21–24; 2 Thess. 2:1–12; Rev. 13:1–18). But all this will be to no avail. When the time is right, the Lord Jesus will return to the earth and seize control over this planet once and for all.

4. THE SECOND COMING OF CHRIST TO THE EARTH

The terrible time of tribulation will come to an end when the Lord Jesus comes in power and glory from heaven to the earth. This coming will be a universal revelation as both those saved (during the time of tribulation) and unsaved witness this event. Many will respond with sorrow as they realize that their judgment is at hand. Others will rejoice because they understand that His coming will bring to an end the kingdoms of mankind and will inaugurate the millennial kingdom of the Messiah. Five important events occur in connection with the second coming of the Lord Jesus. They are, in order:

1. *The judgment of the living Gentiles.* Although literally billions of people perish during the tribulation, millions are still alive at the end, and it is necessary for them to be judged to determine whether they can enter the millennial kingdom. The first group to be so evaluated is the Gentiles. In what is commonly called the "sheep and the goats judgment" (Matt. 25:31–46), saved Gentiles (the sheep) are allowed into Messiah's kingdom, whereas the unsaved (the goats) are not allowed entrance but, rather, are cast into hell.

2. *The judgment of Israel* (cf. the parable of the ten virgins in Matt. 25:1–11). This also is a judgment to determine which Israelites will enter into Messiah's kingdom. Saved Israelites (the wise) are allowed in, whereas unsaved Israelites (the foolish) are refused entrance into the kingdom of Messiah.

3. *The resurrection and rewarding of Old Testament saints and the saints who perished in the tribulation* (Rev. 20:4–6; Dan. 12:2, 13; Rev. 6:9). It is at the second coming that these people are given their resurrected bodies and are rewarded according to the works that they have done.

4. *The binding of Satan* (Rev. 20:1–3). When the Lord Jesus returns, He will have Satan cast into the Abyss, where he will be completely restricted. He will not be able to exercise any influence during the thousand-year reign of Jesus Christ on this earth. When the Scriptures speak of the binding of Satan, this includes the host of demons that do his bidding.

5. *The actual establishing of the messianic kingdom.* Daniel 12 suggests that there will be a seventy-five-day period between the second coming

and the beginning of the messianic kingdom. It may be that during these weeks the administration of the kingdom is established and the borders of the nations are defined.

AN OVERVIEW OF FUTURE EVENTS

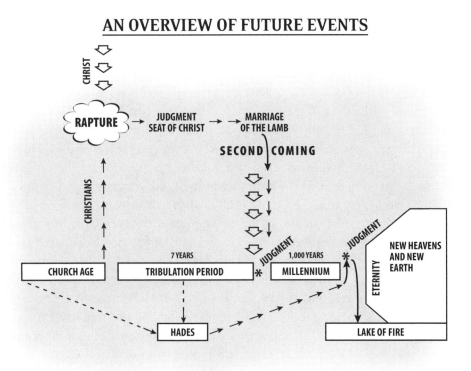

5. THE MILLENNIAL KINGDOM OF JESUS CHRIST

Once all the enemies of Christ are removed and all necessary resurrections and judgments take place, the wonderful period of the millennium will begin. The great unconditional covenants given centuries earlier will now be fulfilled. Every promise made by God will be accomplished, and Israel in particular and Gentiles in general will enjoy the blessings of Christ's rule.

The millennial kingdom will be characterized by righteousness, peace, and joy. All people everywhere will worship the Lord Jesus, who will be present in His glory. The curse that was placed on the creation at the fall of mankind will be removed, causing the desert and all of the earth to bloom and become fertile. Because of this, mankind will experience an unprecedented prosperity that will reach to every individual. Apparently very long life spans will characterize the kingdom. This, coupled with the absence of disease, will cause the population of the earth to increase rapidly. Also, the removal of the curse will immediately affect the animal kingdom. Animals will once again universally be vegetarians. No longer will lions eat lambs; rather, they will nap together in peace and harmony.

When the messianic kingdom begins, only believers will inhabit the kingdom, and they will gladly worship the King. But even though all are believers at the beginning, the kingdom will be made up of people with two different types of bodies: resurrected bodies and mortal bodies. Those with resurrected bodies received them either at the time of the rapture (church-age saints) or at the second coming (Old Testament and tribulation saints). The other group is made up of those who made it alive through the tribulation and as believers entered the messianic kingdom. However, their bodies were not changed, and thus they will marry and reproduce. As the kingdom period proceeds, the children born into the millennium, like children in every other age, must come to the place where they personally respond to the Lord. In this environment of truth and righteousness, most will probably become believers and follow Him, but others will not. Only a few will actually be outwardly rebellious and receive the Lord's rod of iron (Ps. 2:9; Isa. 11:4); most will worship the Lord Jesus Christ. But the millennial kingdom will have more and more unbelievers as time goes on. It is these unbelievers that Satan, when he is released from the Abyss for a short time at the end of the Millennium, will find willing to rebel against the rule of King Jesus (Rev. 20:7–10).

6. The Judgments of the End Times

After the messianic/millennial kingdom is over and before the final eternal kingdom of God begins, three judgments will take place (Rev. 20:7–15; 1 Cor. 6:3).

First is the final judgment of Satan and the fallen angels. They will be cast into the lake of fire, and there they will spend eternity.

Second, unbelievers will be judged at the great white throne judgment. All unbelievers from every age will be resurrected at this time and forced to face their Creator God. Because of their sinful actions, their unbelief, and their refusal to receive His gift of eternal life, they will be cast forever into the same lake of fire as Satan (Rev. 20:12–15).

The third judgment will be that of the heavens and the earth. The present heavens and earth have been contaminated by sin and by the presence of wicked beings, and this necessitates their cleansing. The judgment of fire will completely destroy the old heavens and earth and prepare the way for the creation of a new heaven and a new earth (2 Peter 3:7–10).

One other event might occur at this time as well. If some believers die during the millennium (the Scriptures do not specifically address this issue), it is logical that they be resurrected in preparation for the eternal state.

7. THE ETERNAL STATE (THE ETERNAL KINGDOM OF GOD)

It was God's purpose from the very beginning to rule over and fellowship with people and with angels. His rulership was challenged, and His fellowship was marred by the entrance of sin and rebellion. But with the death of Jesus Christ on the cross to pay for sin and satisfy the wrath of God, fellowship was once again a reality. And with the defeat of the usurper Satan and the collapse of all the kingdoms of mankind, the Lord Jesus is King of Kings and the kingdom is now delivered over to the Father. In the eternal kingdom of God, there will be a fullness of joy, full and unhindered fellowship, and meaningful living on a new earth (Rev. 21:1–22:5). This will forever be the experience of those who are the children of God.

PART THREE

Understanding
THE
COMING
Prophetic Events

CHAPTER TWELVE

THE *Pretribulational* RAPTURE VIEW

Those future events that are important to us are always eagerly anticipated. Watch children during those final two weeks before Christmas—they can hardly contain their excitement and enthusiasm as they look forward to the moment when they can unwrap those beautiful and mysterious presents. Then there is the young couple who faithfully marks each day off their calendar as they anticipate departing on a luxurious cruise ship for a week of fun in the sun. Although they may not exhibit the raw enthusiasm of children prior to Christmas, the anticipation is just as real. The student who has put in four long years of study shares this same sense of eager anticipation as graduation day approaches.

The same is true for believers in Jesus Christ as they anticipate an upcoming event far more significant than cruises, Christmas presents, or graduation. The apostle Paul encourages believers to look forward to "the blessed hope and the appearing of the glory of our great God and Savior, Christ Jesus" (Titus 2:13). We are to be eagerly anticipating the day when the Lord Jesus returns to take us home to be with Him. That event is commonly referred to as the rapture of the church.

THE RAPTURE, ACCORDING TO THE SCRIPTURES

The supernatural removal of the church of Jesus Christ out of this world is called the rapture. The term *rapture* comes from the Latin word *rapturo*. This is the Latin translation of the Greek verb "caught up," which is found in 1 Thessalonians 4:17. The word denotes a sudden, irresistible act of carrying off by force. In that passage the apostle Paul teaches that true believers in Christ will suddenly be caught up into the air by the power of Christ and will meet Him in the air. This idea of the sudden removal of God's people through powerful, divine activity has no parallel in Old Testament literature. In the New Testament, a number of passages speak of Christ's coming for His church.

1. *John 14:1–3.* The night before His crucifixion, Jesus told His disciples that He was going to leave them shortly, which would break their physical fellowship with Him. This revelation caused great distress in the hearts and minds of His followers, but Jesus went on to promise that He would come back again and bring them into a place of permanent fellowship, namely the "Father's house." Jesus said, "And if I go and prepare a place for you, I will come again, and receive you to Myself; that where I am, there you may be also" (v. 3).

Several important truths are found in these verses. First, Jesus went literally and bodily into heaven, and He will return in the same manner after the necessary preparations are made. He will not send an angel but will come Himself. Second, the promise is made to His followers, not to mankind in general. Jesus was speaking to His disciples, who also represent the church. Third, when He returns He will take His followers to the Father's house, which is in heaven. The promise is to take the church ("receive") to the place where He made the preparations for permanent fellowship. This promise was new revelation to the disciples, for they were anticipating the establishment of the kingdom on earth. The idea of first going to heaven as a group of the Lord's people was a truth that Jesus had not previously shared with them. The disciples learned that they (the church) would not remain on this earth, for the earth is not the hope of the church. John 14 is the first mention of the rapture event in the Scriptures.

2. *Titus 2:13.* According to this passage, the future hope of the believer is the return of the Lord Jesus in glory. The believer is to live in anticipation of that time when Christ will appear. He or she is to live anticipating the return of the Lord Jesus, not looking for the tribulation or some other event.

3. *Philippians 3:20.* Paul informs the believers at Philippi that they will be taken to the place of their citizenship (which is heaven) at the time of the rapture, when the Lord Jesus appears. Their physical bodies will experience change at that time by the power of the Lord and will be made like Christ's body.

4. *1 Corinthians 1:7.* In the opening of this letter, the apostle Paul exhorted the Corinthian believers to live dedicated lives in light of the coming of the Lord Jesus. The apostle John also uses the Lord's coming to motivate Christians to holy and dedicated service in 1 John 3:1–3.

5. *1 Corinthians 15:51–53.* In this important rapture passage, Paul says that the truth of the rapture is a mystery. "Behold, I tell you a mystery; we shall not all sleep, but we shall all be changed, in a moment, in the twinkling of an eye, at the last trumpet" (vv. 51–52). The word *mystery* appears in the New Testament several dozen times and refers to a newly revealed divine secret that was not revealed in the past and that would not be discovered without divine revelation. The church itself is said to be a mystery; therefore, truths and events related to the church are sometimes said to be mysteries.

We know that the resurrection of the body was not a mystery, since the Old Testament Scriptures speak of the bodily resurrection of believers. And it was not a mystery that there would be believers on the earth when the Lord comes back. The mystery found in this passage is the truth that some believers will not experience death but, rather, will be caught up to meet the Lord in transformed, immortal bodies. The idea of receiving a resurrection body without first dying was new truth never before given.

6. *1 Thessalonians 4:13–18.* Without a doubt this is the central passage on the rapture of the church. It contains many facts and details necessary to coming to an understanding of this important truth. The six verses read:

But we do not want you to be uninformed, brethren, about those who are asleep, that you may not grieve, as do the rest who have no hope. For if we believe that Jesus died and rose again, even so God will bring with Him those who have fallen asleep in Jesus. For this we say to you by the word of the Lord, that we who are alive, and remain until the coming of the Lord, shall not precede those who have fallen asleep. For the Lord Himself will descend from heaven with a shout, with the voice of the archangel, and with the trumpet of God; and the dead in Christ shall rise first. Then we who are alive and remain shall be caught up together with them in the clouds to meet the Lord in the air, and thus we shall always be with the Lord. Therefore comfort one another with these words.

THE RAPTURE EVENT

As far as end-time prophetic events are concerned, the rapture of the church is the first to take place. It is an event to which no signs or indicators are attached. We are not told to look for certain signs in order to correctly anticipate the time of the rapture. There are no signs; the rapture event itself is what is to be anticipated.

The rapture is a supernatural event. The sudden removal of the true church from the world can happen only as a result of the power of God. When the church is removed from this earth, believers will meet Christ in the air, which is one of the facts that distinguishes the rapture from the second coming of Christ to the earth.

The Three Inaugural Sounds

According to Paul's description, the rapture will be accompanied by several audible sounds: Christ's *shout*, the archangel's *voice*, and the *trumpet of God*. Some believe that these three sounds are to be understood as one great signal from heaven. Though it is true that the sounds will be heard for only a short moment in time, there do seem to be three distinct sounds. In light of this great signal from heaven, it hardly seems possible that the rapture will be an entirely silent event.

It may well be that unsaved people are aware that something unique, supernatural, and amazing is taking place, but they will not understand its meaning and significance. This was the case on the Damascus road when Saul of Tarsus fell before the risen Christ, seeing His glory for a brief moment and also hearing the words spoken to him by the Lord. Those traveling with Saul knew something had taken place, but did not understand the words spoken or comprehend the event (Acts 9:7; 22:9). Similarly when the voice of the Father was heard after Jesus' triumphal entry into Jerusalem (just one week before His crucifixion), many heard the voice but apparently did not understand the words, for they thought it was thundering or that perhaps an angel had spoken (John 12:28-30). Perhaps there will be a similar phenomenon on a worldwide scale at the rapture of the church. Unbelieving people will know something startling has taken place but will not understand it. And it may be that the magnitude of the event and people's awareness of it will open the door to renewed interest in spiritual matters—both good and bad.

The first sound at the rapture is the shout. The word means "a shout of command" and implies both authority and urgency.[1] The shout probably comes from the Lord Himself, even though the text is not specific on the matter. Neither does the text declare the content of the shout. However, it is certainly possible that the command shouted out will be like the one given to the apostle John when he was told, "Come up here" (Rev. 4:1). Or it may be the command found in John 5:28-29, ordering those who are dead to come forth from their graves.

The second sound mentioned is the voice of the archangel. The only other reference to the archangel occurs in Jude 9. There he is identified as Michael. Michael is either the leader of the holy angels or one of the primary leaders. Since he and other angels have been commissioned to protect the people of God (Dan. 12:1; Heb. 1:14), it may be that he is present to protect the saints of God from Satan and his forces as they pass through his domain. Satan is referred to as the "prince of the power of the air" (Eph. 2:2), and God's people will be passing through these dangerous regions. No indication is given as to what is said by Michael, but perhaps it is a word of victory.

The third sound is said to come from a trumpet belonging to God. Since the days when Israel was camped down at Mount Sinai, trumpets were used to call God's people together for assembly. Moses was instructed to make two silver trumpets to be used for notifying people of upcoming events and "for summoning the congregation" (Num. 10:2). This eschatological blast from God's trumpet summons the church of Jesus Christ to heaven and to fellowship in the Father's house. It parallels the "last trumpet" of 1 Corinthians 15:52. Not every mention of a trumpet of God, however, refers to this particular event of the rapture. Just as there were a number of reasons why trumpets were blown in Israel, a variety of trumpets are blown in the end times to signal the conclusion of certain events or the gathering of certain peoples.

With these three sounds from heaven being heard all over the earth, calling both living and dead saints to glory, we can assume that unbelievers will most likely be conscious of the fact that something dramatic and supernatural is taking place. How they may explain it is another matter.

The Clouds in the Air

As Paul describes the rapture event, he informs the Thessalonians that believers will be caught up in the *clouds* to meet the Lord. This parallels Jesus' ascension into heaven, when He was received up into the clouds (Acts 1:9). Clouds can, of course, refer to literal clouds that may carry rain. However, clouds are also used figuratively in the Bible to refer to the presence and glory of God (e.g., Ex. 14:19-24; 16:10; 19:9, 16; 20:21; 40:34-38). It is best in this rapture passage to understand the clouds as referring to the visible presence and glory of the Lord. At the rapture, it is the glorious Lord Jesus who appears and brings the saints into the presence of His glory.

Paul further describes the meeting with the Lord as being "in the air" (1 Thess. 4:17). This phrase tells us in general terms that the meeting takes place somewhere between the heavens and the earth. What is significant about this is that it distinguishes the rapture from the second coming, when the Lord Jesus actually comes down to the earth.

THE PARTICIPANTS IN THE RAPTURE

The most significant participant at the rapture is the Lord Jesus. We are told that the "Lord Himself" will come for the church (1 Thess. 4:16). He will not send angelic messengers to call the saints home, but He will personally come down from heaven where He has been at the Father's right hand to bring His church home to glory. The event is a very personal one for the Lord.

The people involved in the rapture are believers, but more specifically they are said to be those who are "in Christ" (1 Thess. 4:16). Those who are "in Christ" are the ones who have been placed into the body of Christ by the Holy Spirit (1 Cor. 12:13). This work of Spirit baptism did not begin until the day of Pentecost. It was on that day (Acts 2) that the church of Jesus Christ began. Therefore, only those who are part of the church, the body of Christ, will be part of the rapture event, for they are the only ones who are "in Christ."

The rapture will include all believers from the day of Pentecost to the rapture event itself. There is no indication in the rapture passages that some true believers in the church will not participate. In fact, Paul pointedly declares that "all will be changed" and given glorified bodies at the rapture (1 Cor. 15:51). True believers are those who have believed that Jesus died and rose again, and these without exception are seen as being involved in the rapture. Being "in Christ" means that no Old Testament saints will be participants, since they have not been placed into the church, the body of Christ, by Spirit baptism. And, of course, it also means that no unbeliever will be part of the rapture.

That the rapture will include living believers, as well as believers who have died, was not so obvious to the Christians at Thessalonica in the early days of the church. Paul had taught them about the rapture, and they were looking forward to its taking place at any moment. They were anticipating being caught up to meet the Lord. But they became deeply disturbed when some of their number died. Apparently they had concluded that the rapture was for living believers only and did not know what was to become of these departed loved ones. Paul wrote to assure them that they need not worry about these deceased fellow believers, for all those who "sleep in Jesus" (a euphemism for believers who have died) will be caught up to meet the Lord also. In fact, he pointed out the order of the rapture: deceased believers will go first, followed by living believers (1 Thess. 4:13–17). Later, in writing to the Corinthian church, Paul made clear that resurrection is very much a part of the rapture (1 Cor. 15:51–53). Believers who have previously died and who, therefore, are with the Lord in heaven return with Him to the meeting in the air (1 Thess. 4:17). At that moment ("in the twinkling of an eye") they receive their resurrection bodies, which are fit for eternal living. At the same time, living believers exit the earth in their mortal bodies. Those bodies are instantly made immortal without having to pass through death. This is the mystery that Paul spoke of in 1 Corinthians

15:51. The end result is that "all" believers experience a change at the rapture.

RESULTS OF THE RAPTURE

A number of important results are connected with this grand event. One result is that the promise of Christ to come back for His own is fulfilled. He guaranteed to His followers that the day would come when they would enjoy an unbroken fellowship with Him in the Father's house. He will be true to this commitment, as He always is.

A second result of the rapture will be the completion of our salvation. Although Christ fully paid the redemption price for our salvation, the reality is that we are not yet fully saved. Romans 8:23 reminds us that we are "waiting eagerly for our adoption as sons, the redemption of our body." Our physical bodies are the place where sin manifests itself and where the flesh resists the working of the Holy Spirit (Rom. 6:6; Gal. 5:16–17). These physical bodies are in the process of decaying and dying, which is simply a manifestation of the results of sin in the created world. Christ's death included the redemption of the body, but that aspect of our salvation has not yet taken place. It will take place at the rapture, when the body will be made like that of the Lord's and will live forever. The "flesh" will no longer be around to promote sin. This final phase of our salvation will complete our liberation from the power and effects of sin.

A third result of the rapture will be the uniting of all believers. The truth of the rapture was given to bring comfort to those believers who have experienced separation from loved ones (1 Thess. 4:18). Christians have legitimate hope and encouragement because the rapture will unite all believers someday at that meeting in the air.

THE TIME OF THE RAPTURE: PRETRIBULATIONISM

There is general agreement among premillennial scholars on what will take place at the rapture and who will participate in it. However, there is significant disagreement on one important question. The controversial question in relation to the rapture is, "When does the rapture event take place?" When, in relation to the tribulation period (the "Seventieth Week of Daniel"), does the Lord Jesus return to remove His church from the earth?

A number of solutions have been proposed. These solutions place the rapture in varying relationships to the tribulation period, so the various views are known by such titles as the "pretribulational rapture" view or the "posttribulational rapture" view. Our analysis of the time of the rapture will begin with pretribulationism, the view that the rapture takes place *before* the tribulation begins. Four other rapture views will be dealt with in the next two chapters.

No rapture view is without some difficulties, and that is why detailed arguments continue to be set forth by proponents of differing views.[2] However, the pretribulational rapture view seems to be the strongest and the one most consistent with a literal hermeneutic.

THE PRETRIBULATIONAL RAPTURE

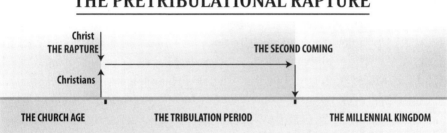

Seven major issues will be discussed in support of a pretribulational rapture of the church. Although a detailed analysis of all ideas cannot be given, certain issues are pivotal in deciding when the Lord Jesus will return in glory for His church, and these need to be mentioned.

1. The Scriptural Distinction Between the Church and the Nation of Israel

The position of pretribulationism depends to a large degree on maintaining a clear distinction between the church and Israel. Pretribulationism does not deny that some similarities exist among the saints of God of all ages, but it asserts that the church is not identical with Israel. The clearer the distinction made between Israel and the church, the clearer the necessity of a pretribulational rapture of the church. The truth is that God is dealing with two distinct programs for two distinct groups (Israel and the church). This makes it highly unlikely that they will be dealt with simultaneously.

The church began on the day of Pentecost (Acts 2) and is made up of believing Jews and Gentiles—to them God has given great and precious promises. On the other hand, the nation of Israel was given many promises by God in the eternal, unconditional covenants of the Old Testament. As we have seen in earlier chapters, these covenant promises were made and ratified with Israel and must be fulfilled to Israel. The church did not take over the covenant promises made to the nation of Israel. So, with the beginning of the tribulation period, God's focus returns to national Israel and the fulfilling of these covenant promises made so many centuries ago. The covenants find their ultimate and final fulfillment in the millennial kingdom, and the tribulation period is a necessary period of preparation to get Israel ready for Messiah's coming. It would seem most logical that God will first complete His program with the church, remove the church at the rapture, then resume His program with national Israel. Otherwise, during the tribulation period there would be two distinct groups of redeemed people—the church (the body of Christ) and national Israel in covenant relationship with God—witnessing for two distinct programs of God. Although such could be possible, it does not seem likely.

Furthermore, it does not seem scriptural. According to Romans 11:25–27, the spiritual blindness that presently characterizes national Israel will be removed, and salvation will come to the people sometime in the future. This spiritual blindness was a special judicial act of God because of the nation's rejection of Jesus as Messiah (called a "mystery" because it was a new dimension of Israel's blindness to the will and Word of God). Paul points out that the spiritual blindness is "partial," which means that it is not universal and that some Jewish people can be saved now. But it also indicates that most will not see the truth about Jesus the Messiah. He goes on to say that this spiritual blindness will not go on forever. It will last "until" the fullness of the Gentiles is completed (v. 25).

This "fullness of the Gentiles" refers to Gentile blessing and opportunity in this age, which came about as a result of the failure and unbelief of Israel. This unique opportunity given to the Gentiles began at Pentecost (Acts 2) and will continue until the rapture. At the rapture, the fullness of the Gentiles is completed and the spiritual blindness of Israel is removed. The removal of Israel's judicial blindness does not mean that Israel will immediately turn to the Lord Jesus as Savior and Messiah, but it does mean that they will be in a position to respond favorably to the truth and be restored by God to the place of blessing. This process will go on throughout the tribulation period and culminate at the second coming. Israel as a whole (not every single individual) will turn to the Lord and be redeemed under the new covenant.

Paul's instruction clearly points to a wonderful future for ethnic Israel. In his discussion he refers to the unconditional covenants of the Old Testament, which are part of God's program for Israel. The clear contrasts between Israel and the church make it most logical that during the tribulation period God will be dealing with just one of these two groups, namely Israel.

2. The Nation Israel and the Stated Purposes of the Tribulation

It is right and natural to assume that God has a purpose in whatever He does. Sometimes He may not choose to explain His purposes to His creation, but sometimes He does, as in the case of the tribulation period. *The first, and most likely the greatest, purpose for the tribulation is to prepare the nation of Israel for the Messiah* and the messianic (millennial) kingdom. The second major purpose is to execute judgment on the wicked and in the process to take back the earth from Satan and those who do his will. It should be noted that God does not need seven years or even seven seconds to execute judgment on the wicked, so judgment is probably not the primary reason for the period of tribulation. Time is required, however, to bring vast numbers of people to faith in Jesus, and that would suggest the primacy of the first purpose.

The primary purpose of preparing Israel for her Messiah and His kingdom is evidenced in a number of passages. For example, this period is viewed as the "time of Jacob's trouble" (Jer. 30:7 KJV). Whereas this does not mean that other nations will not be involved, it does suggest that Israel is the focus of this tribulation period. Other passages show that the tribulation has a definite Jewish character (e.g., Deut. 4:30; Dan. 12:1; Ezek. 20:37; Zech. 13:8–9; Matt. 24:15–20). The important focus of this period is the coming of salvation to Israel and, consequently, to the Gentiles as well (e.g., Dan. 9:24; Ezek. 36:25–36; 37:1–14; 39:21–29; Jer. 31:31–34; Mal. 4:4–6; Rom. 11:25–28; Rev. 7:4–14). As a nation, Israel has never come under the new covenant of salvation. It is absolutely essential for Israel to become partakers of the new covenant before there can be a final and complete fulfillment of the covenant promises of the Old Testament.

Perhaps no passage explains this primary purpose for the tribulation in such a detailed way as Daniel 9:24–27. This key passage clarifies our understanding of the purposes for the tribulation period. Daniel 9 records the concerned prayer of Daniel as he viewed his people Israel in their Babylonian captivity, which was brought about by their idolatry and disregard for the law of God. The nation had experienced defeat, the destruction of Jerusalem and the temple, and captivity in a foreign land. Daniel not only confessed the sins of his people Israel but interceded for them, calling upon God to fulfill His promise to restore Israel back to her land. Although Daniel and other godly people realized that Israel did not deserve blessing and restoration, they knew that God had made certain promises. The prophet Jeremiah had predicted seventy years of captivity, and though that captivity period was almost over, there did not seem to be any movement toward restoration.

Deeply concerned that God's promise might not be fulfilled, Daniel prayed. Daniel's lengthy prayer focused on the two subjects of the people of Israel and the city of Jerusalem. His prayer again and again shows concern for "Thy city Jerusalem, Thy holy mountain . . . Jerusalem and Thy people . . . Thy desolate sanctuary . . . Thy city and Thy people" (vv. 16–19). John C. Whitcomb emphasizes the nature of Daniel's requests:

> It is of great importance that we recognize what Daniel prayed for—and what he did not pray for. He did not pray for the spiritual well-being of the church, the Body of Christ. He did not pray for the spiritual prosperity of the saints of all ages. He did pray for "Thy city Jerusalem, Thy holy mountain." . . . This distinction is highly important because God's answer is just as specific as Daniel's prayer. The answer sent by God through Gabriel centers exclusively on Jerusalem and Israel, and thus bypasses the entire church age.[3]

In answer to his prayer on these two matters, the Lord sent the angel Gabriel with a message concerning Israel's future (vv. 24–27). Gabriel informed Daniel that God was going to have special dealings with Israel for "seventy units of seven" (which because of the context is commonly understood to mean 70 times 7, or 490 years).[4] Daniel was told that this 490-year period would be made up of three distinct divisions. The first unit of seven sevens (forty-nine years) is the period of time for the rebuilding of the city of Jerusalem (v. 25a); the second unit of sixty-two sevens (434 years) comprises the time from the rebuilding to the coming of the Messiah (v. 25b). This, of course, brings the total to sixty-nine sevens (483 years), leaving one unit of seven (seven years) yet to be discussed in the passage.

After the second division of time but before the final division (of seven years), two key events will transpire: the death of the Messiah, and the destruction of the city of Jerusalem (v. 26). Placing these two events after sixty-nine weeks but *before* the seventieth week seems to indicate a gap of time. This allows for, but does not require, the church age. But since the last week is disconnected from the first sixty-nine weeks, the question arises as to when this final week takes place. The answer given is that when "he" (probably the Antichrist) makes a covenant with Israel, the last week begins. This passage will be discussed further in relationship to the discussion on the tribulation period.

THE SEVENTY WEEKS OF DANIEL

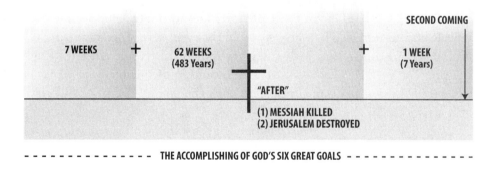

Most important in Daniel 9 is what God says He will accomplish by the time the 490 years have run their course. In verse 24 six goals are given: "(1) to finish the transgression; (2) to make an end of sin; (3) to make atonement for iniquity; (4) to bring in everlasting righteousness; (5) to seal up vision and prophecy; and (6) to anoint the most holy place." We need to remember that all six of these goals are earthly as they relate to Daniel's people (Israel) and Daniel's holy city (Jerusalem).

The first three goals were accomplished by Christ's work on the cross, which dealt with the sin issue fully and completely. However, these goals (which relate to the new covenant) have not been applied to Israel as a nation.

The fourth goal looks at a time when everlasting righteousness will be experienced by national Israel. Israel, as a nation, has not at any time embraced this righteousness that comes from the Lord God. When will such righteousness be experienced by Israel?

> If "everlasting righteousness" based on the atoning work of Christ is to be brought in for Israel as a nation, it must be brought in while Israel is still constituted as a nation. . . . The only possible point in time when this could occur and remain within the time parameters offered (i.e., with the 490 years) would be at the end of the Great tribulation and at the inception of an earthly kingdom.[5]

The fifth goal related to the sealing up of vision and prophecy most likely looks at that time when the glorified Christ is present with His people, fulfilling all prophecies and making visions and prophecies unnecessary.

The sixth goal is "to anoint the most holy." The term *most holy* is frequently used in the Bible of the Holy of Holies in the tabernacle and the temple and should also be understood in that way here. This anointing is most likely in connection with the great millennial temple spoken of by the prophet Ezekiel (Ezek. 40–48). The anointing of this most holy place will probably take place in connection with the second coming of Christ at the very end of the "seventy weeks."

This significant passage in Daniel clearly states God's intentions in relation to Israel. The fulfillment of these six goals, while made possible by the work of Christ on the cross, have not been fulfilled to national Israel. God plans on saving and restoring Israel in the future. There remains just the one week (seven years) for the fulfilling of these goals. It is clear then that the purposes of God for the last week (the tribulation) are established, and their focus is definitely on Israel and on bringing Israel back to the Lord her God. It is admitted by all that the church of Jesus Christ has been redeemed and, therefore, does not need to be regenerated and to enter into the new covenant.

The primary purpose of the tribulation simply does not involve the church, but it most certainly involves Israel. This also holds true for the *second purpose: bringing judgment on evil people and nations for their unbelief and sin.* The church is made up of believers, and the sins of the church have been cared for by the Lord Jesus. The church will not be brought into judgment, because the Lord took our judgment on Himself (John 5:24). The church does not need to be punished or purified, having already entered into that wonderful work of propitiation accomplished by the Lord Jesus at Calvary.

The focus of Daniel 9:24–27 is exclusively Jewish. The passage deals only with those matters concerning the Jewish people, not the church. The covenant is made with Israel; it is the Jewish temple that is rebuilt with its accompanying sacrifices. It is the desecration of that temple with the "abomination of desolation"; and it is the repentance and blessing of Israel in their land that is in view. Daniel 9:24–27 is the definitive revelation on the purposes of God for this final seven years.

The conclusion is that, since the church does not fit into the declared purposes of God for the tribulation, the church will not be a part of that period of time. There is simply no need for the church to be present during a time when God focuses so completely on the nation of Israel.

3. The Church: Excluded from the Wrath of God

There is general agreement among all rapture views that God has promised the church of Jesus Christ exemption from the future wrath of God. This wrath of God must not be understood in terms of uncontrolled, irrational human anger but, rather, as God's controlled, passionate feeling against the sin and rebellion of His creatures. It is the settled indignation of God that focuses on the sinner some time in the future.[6]

Concerning this future wrath, the promise of God is wonderfully clear. The apostle Paul writes that "God has not destined us for wrath" (1 Thess. 5:9). However, there is considerable debate on how God will keep the church from the coming wrath and also on how long the wrath of God actually lasts.

God's promise of exemption does not mean that the church will avoid all trials, troubles, and persecution. In fact, the Scriptures are quite clear that times of tribulation and difficulty await the church (e.g., John 15:18–20; 1 Thess. 3:3; 2 Tim. 3:12; 1 Peter 4:12–16). But this kind of tribulation and persecution is not the future wrath of God. The church is exempted from this terrible divine wrath.

A unique time. The Scriptures teach that the tribulation is a unique period of time in all of human history in that the world experiences the wrath of God as never before.

> *There are four classic scripture passages which speak of the time as being more severe in suffering than any other in history. Because there can be only one such time, all four must refer to the same period. . . . "Then shall be great tribulation, such as was not since the beginning of the world to this time, no, nor ever shall be" (Matt. 24:21). . . . Jer. 30:7 . . . "Alas! for that day is great, so that none is like it." Daniel 12:1: ". . . and there shall be a time of trouble, such as never was since there was a nation even to that same time.". . . Joel 2:2: "A day of darkness and gloominess. . . . there hath not been ever the like, neither shall be any more after it."*[7]

Only one time can be said to be "unique," otherwise "unique" has lost its meaning. The future time of wrath is unprecedented in its intensity. Not only do these verses emphasize the uniqueness of the coming day of the wrath of God, they also use some key eschatological terms interchangeably—which will be an important point later on.

But just why is this upcoming tribulation period different from all other periods of time in human history? First, it will be a worldwide reality and not simply localized death and destruction. There have always been terrible times of carnage and destruction in various places on this planet but not a time when it was literally a universal experience—except for the universal flood in Noah's day. With earth's population now in the billions, this tribulation period will be unrivaled in terms of the sheer number of people who perish during this relatively short period of time.

Second, the magnitude of supernaturalism will be unprecedented. Signs, wonders, and supernatural phenomenon from God and from Satan will awe those living during this time. Now and then God has intervened in human experience with the miraculous, but never to the degree that will be seen during these final seven years.

In light of this unique future time of wrath, God's promise of exemption for His children is highly significant and extremely comforting.

Seven years of wrath. When is the wrath of God poured out on the earth? It is displayed throughout the seven years of tribulation and not simply in the last part of Daniel's seventieth week. This is a crucial point in the debate concerning the timing of the rapture and will be addressed in the upcoming discussion of other rapture views (chapters 11 and 12). However, one important matter can be included here. During His ministry on earth, the Lord Jesus taught that all people will face Him sometime, either as the One who gives life or as the judge. Concerning the matter of judgment, He declared that the Father "has given all judgment to the Son" and that the Father "gave Him authority to execute judgment, because He is the Son of Man" (John 5:22, 27). This declaration establishes an important foundational point when interpreting the book of Revelation, namely that all divine judgments come from the Son of God.

In the heavenly scene of Revelation 4 and 5, the Father who sits on the throne has a scroll in His hand; it is sealed with seven seals. The significance of the seals is that they keep the scroll secure; that is, no one can change the scroll or tamper with it. In this heavenly scene it becomes clear that no one in all the universe has the authority to take the scroll and to break its seals except for the Lion-Lamb of Judah (the Lord Jesus Christ). When Christ takes the scroll and begins to break the seals (Revelation 6–8), the judgments begin to fall on the earth. This is the beginning of God's judgments—the wrath of God.

God's wrath is seen in all the judgments on the scroll, which includes the three series of judgments—the seals, the trumpets, and the bowls—in the book of Revelation. God's wrath includes those judgments that are direct supernatural acts (such as the great disturbances in the heavens and the one-hundred-pound hailstones devastating the earth), as well as those forces, elements, and individuals that God uses in an indirect way (such as war, famine, the Antichrist, and Satan).

> *The activity of the* whole *period proceeds from the activity of the worthy Lamb; it is He who breaks the seals (Rev. 5:11–14; cf. Rev. 6:1, 3, 5, 7, 9, 11). One cannot exegetically classify various kinds of wrath and distinguish their recipients, and thus avoid the conclusion that the whole seventieth week is a time of God's retributive wrath.*[8]

The protection and removal of the church. If it is true that the wrath of God encompasses the entire seven-year period, then the removal of the church of Jesus Christ would take place prior to this period of time.

Several passages point to the protection and removal of the church during these days of the wrath of God.

First, in 1 Thessalonians 1:9–10, after Paul praises the believers at Thessalonica for, among other things, their patient, confident looking for the coming of the Lord ("to wait"), he says that the Lord Jesus "delivers us from the wrath to come." The word *deliver (rhuomai)* carries with it the idea of rescuing from something by a forcible act.[9] The word puts an emphasis on "the greatness of the peril from which deliverance is given by a mighty act of power."[10] This powerful rescue by the Lord Jesus at His coming (the rapture) does not include everyone on this planet but only believers. We are rescued by a mighty act of God's power. Paul uses the present participle, which emphasizes Jesus' office and work as our deliverer. In one sense, our rescue began when His death and resurrection obtained our deliverance from God's wrath (Rom. 5:9–10). As Renald Showers writes,

God's resurrection of Jesus from the dead guaranteed that the already obtained deliverance of church saints from future wrath would never cease to be a present reality. It meant that Jesus would always be available to execute that deliverance through a mighty act of power-drawing or snatching them out to Himself before the future wrath comes.[11]

First Thessalonians 1:10 says that Christ will deliver believers "out from" *(ek)* the coming wrath of God. This word emphasizes the completeness of our rescue by Christ—we are rescued out of the time of distress itself.

Second, 1 Thessalonians 5:9–10 also points to the removal of the church by rapture prior to the time of God's future wrath. Here the apostle Paul comforts the believers with the truth that "God has not destined us for wrath, but for obtaining salvation through our Lord Jesus Christ, who died for us, that whether we are awake or asleep, we may live together with Him." In these verses Paul speaks of God's sovereign determination of the believer's future. Paul emphatically states that it is *not* God's intention for the believer to experience wrath. This clear guarantee that believers will not experience His wrath agrees with other portions of Scripture (e.g., John 5:24; Rom. 5:9–10; Col. 1:13).

This negative assertion seems clearly to assure that believers will not have part in the coming Great tribulation, when God's wrath falls upon a Christ-rejecting world (Rev. 6:15–17; 14:10; 19:15). They are looking forward not to the coming of that day when God will display His wrath in divine judgment but to the coming of the Lord Himself who will deliver them from the very presence of sin.[12]

In this passage, Paul makes a sharp distinction between the believer and the unsaved, speaking of the Christian ("you," "we") in contrast to the unbeliever ("they," "them"). These two groups have different destinies—one for salvation and the other for judgment. Quite clearly it is God's sovereign intention to keep His children safe. It is the Lord Jesus who brings us salvation and guarantees our safety. This is true not only of our eternal salvation, which keeps us safe from the terrible penalty of eternal damnation, but also of a temporal aspect to our salvation, keeping us safe from the wrath of God that will be revealed in the tribulation. The death of the Lord Jesus delivered believers from all forms of God's wrath. It is at the rapture event that the final phase of the believer's salvation will take place as resurrection bodies are received. It is God's sovereign will, according to the apostle Paul, that believers be removed from the time of God's wrath and be given their completed salvation.

A third significant passage is Revelation 3:10, where the apostle John records the words of Christ to the church at Philadelphia: "I also will keep you from the hour of testing, that hour which is about to come upon the whole world, to test those who dwell upon the earth." Protection is promised to believers, to keep them from (*ek*) the hour of testing. There is considerable debate on the meaning of the Greek word *ek*. Some feel that the use of the word indicates that the church will be protected from the time of testing by being removed from the earth. Others believe that the word suggests that the church will be protected *through* the time of tribulation. However, it should be observed that the promise is not that believers will be kept from testing but that they would be kept from the "hour of testing." This hour of testing refers to the tribulation period. The promise is to keep the church from the time period of testing, which necessitates actual removal from the time period itself and not preservation through it. The means of the removal from this universal time period of testing is the rapture prior to the beginning of the tribulation.

4. The Concept of the Imminent Coming of Jesus Christ

The word *imminent* is not found in the Bible but has become the word to express the theological idea of the "any-moment" coming of the Lord Jesus Christ. The word itself speaks of something that is about to happen. Showers explains:

> *An imminent event is one that is always hanging overhead, is constantly ready to befall or overtake a person, is always close at hand in the sense that it could happen at any moment. Other things* may *happen before the imminent event, but nothing else* must *take place before it happens. If something else must take place before an event can happen, that event is not imminent. The necessity of something else taking place first destroys the concept of immanency.*[13]

The imminent coming of Jesus Christ means that there are no signs or events that must take place prior to His return. He could return at any moment. The imminent coming of the Lord is not the same thing as the soon coming of the Lord. Though imminent, it may or may not be soon. In the first century, the apostles spoke of the Lord's coming as imminent, but as it has turned out Jesus did not come soon after their pronouncements. Today also the Lord's return can be at any moment, but it may not be soon.

As the New Testament writers addressed the matter of the return of the Lord Jesus at the rapture event, they used terms that anticipated this as an any-moment event—no intervening events had to take place. So they encouraged their readers to be watching and waiting for the Lord's return and to be comforted and challenged by this prospect. The second coming of Christ, however, has the distinction of *not* being seen as an imminent event; a number of signs and events must take place prior to it—signs such as the appearance of the Antichrist and the setting up of the Abomination of Desolation (cf. 2 Thess. 2:3-4; Matt. 24:15). But the rapture *is* an imminent event, and the church is exhorted to look for the Lord's appearance, not for certain events or signs. Keeping this distinction in mind is vital to a consistent interpretation.

> *Passages demanding imminency would refer to the rapture, whereas passages demanding signs would refer to Christ's second coming. Failure to recognize*

this distinction and trying to see the rapture and the second coming as a single event has forced certain writers into the dilemma of having a second coming that is imminent in some passages and not imminent in other passages. Surely the Spirit of God cannot be accused of contradicting Himself.[14]

As the New Testament passages on the rapture were written, no signs were given that must be fulfilled. Rather, there seems to be a consistent belief and anticipation that the Lord Jesus might well return within the lifetime of the writers and recipients. A normal reading of a number of Scripture passages leads to the conclusion that the writers of the New Testament believed in imminency. Here are seven key passages.

James 5:7–9. In these verses James exhorts his Jewish Christian readers to live righteously in light of the Lord's return, setting aside certain sinful practices. He gives his exhortation based on the nearness of the Lord and the possibility that He could return at any moment: "The coming of the Lord is at hand. . . . Behold, the Judge is standing right at the door."

Two key phrases in these verses are "at hand" or "drawing near" (v. 8) and "standing" (v. 9). Both verbs are in the perfect tense, which emphasizes action that is completed. Therefore, in verse 8 James is declaring that the Lord Jesus "has drawn near," indicating that He may well appear at any moment. The verb "standing" in verse 9 is better translated "has taken a stand." The picture James paints is that of the Lord Jesus standing right at the door with His hand on the knob, ready to fling the door open at any moment and appear to us. The opening of this door may not be soon, but it is certainly seen as an imminent event. And because the Judge could appear at any moment, these believers are to live correctly.

1 Thessalonians 1:10. This verse was observed earlier in the discussion of the church's exemption from the wrath of God. But it also supports the idea of the any-moment return of Christ in Paul's use of the present infinitive "to wait." The apostle commends the Thessalonian Christians for continually, expectantly looking for the Lord's return. *Wait* is a word that "carries with it the suggestion of waiting with patience and confident expectancy."[15] It was the Lord they were waiting for, not certain signs and events. Paul commends them for their anticipation of the coming of the Lord and does not correct them, telling them that certain events must first transpire.

1 Corinthians 1:7. Here again Paul praises believers for "awaiting eagerly the revelation of our Lord Jesus Christ." They were anticipating the coming of the Savior, not signs, such as the terrible days of wrath or the appearing of the Antichrist. Their eager anticipation of the Lord's return points to their belief in imminency.

Philippians 3:20–21. Once again the apostle Paul speaks of the Lord's return in the context of proper Christian living. He encourages the Philippian Christians to live in a manner that pleases the Lord and accurately reflects their heavenly citizenship: "We eagerly wait for a Savior, the Lord Jesus Christ; who will transform the body of our humble state into conformity with the body of His glory."

Wait is a compound word that speaks not only of anticipating the Lord's arrival but of an intense focus on that event. In the context of Philippians 3 the apostle has encouraged believers not to look back but to focus intently on the finish line of the future. It is noteworthy that Paul includes himself in the eager anticipation of the Lord's return. Even though Paul was getting older and was facing possible death when he wrote Philippians, he still believed that he might see the Lord without dying first.

1 Thessalonians 4:15. In this key rapture passage Paul states, "For this we say to you by the word of the Lord, that we who are alive, and remain until the coming of the Lord, shall not precede those who have fallen asleep." In using the personal pronoun "we," Paul includes himself in the group of living believers who will be caught up first to meet the Lord in the air. "The Greek construction makes very clear and emphatic here that Paul is not talking simply about those who are alive at the *parousia* but about those who survive until the *parousia.* He thus betrays the expectation that he and his contemporary Christians will remain alive until Christ comes."[16]

In a number of passages Paul's wording strongly suggests his belief that he might see the Lord's return and not die, but, since he did not know the exact time of the Lord's coming, he could not be sure.

Consequently, in speaking of the return of the Lord Jesus, the Apostle sometimes associates himself with the one class, looking forward to resurrection, as in 2 Cor. 4:14, sometimes with the other, looking forward to change, as in 1 Cor. 15:51, 52 and 1 Thess. 4:15. . . . He shared in what should be the attitude of each generation of Christians, the desire for, and the expectation of, the Parousia of the Lord Jesus. . . . His example and his words alike teach us to be prepared to meet death with unflinching courage, but, above all things, to look for the Parousia of the Lord.[17]

Paul clearly expected the Lord to return at any time, and throughout his ministry he instructs believers in this truth.

Titus 2:13. Again in the context of righteous living, Paul says that we should be "looking for the blessed hope and the appearing of the glory of our great God and Savior, Christ Jesus." Christians are reminded to have a glad expectancy as they anticipate "the blessed hope," the glorious appearing of the Lord Himself. This is the proper anticipation, not the terrible days of the tribulation, which certainly would not be viewed by anyone as a blessed hope. Paul's accompanying exhortation to godly living makes sense only if the Lord's return is imminent.

1 Corinthians 16:22. Paul concludes his first letter to the Corinthian Christians with this statement: "If anyone does not love the Lord, let him be accursed. Maranatha." It is the word *maranatha* that is of interest and importance here. The term is made up of three Aramaic words that, when put together, mean "Our Lord, come."[18] Many scholars have concluded that this Aramaic term, especially since it is used in a letter written to a Greek-speaking church, was probably a well-known term in the early Christian community, with a fixed meaning. It apparently conveyed the theology and hope of the early Christians that the Lord Jesus could return at any time.

It would appear, then, that the fixed usage of the term "Maranatha" by the early Christians was a witness to their strong belief in the imminent return of Christ. If they knew that Christ could not return at any moment because of other events or a time period that had to transpire first, why did they petition Him in a way that implied that He could come at any moment?[19]

Even more Scriptures suggest that the writers and recipients did anticipate an imminent return of the Lord (e.g., Rom. 13:11-14; 1 Cor. 15:51-53; Phil. 4:5; 1 John 2:28-3:3). It is difficult to get around the conclusion that the early church really did anticipate the Lord's return at any moment. They were eagerly looking for the Savior, but clearly they were not looking for signs. They were motivated to godliness because they believed that Jesus could return at any moment. If they thought that the

Lord's return was far off, their tendency would be toward sinful, careless living—just as Jesus Himself taught (Matt. 24:48-49). The concept of imminency is a strong argument for the pretribulational rapture of the church.

5. The Distinction Between the Events of the Rapture and the Second Coming

Some similarities between rapture passages and second coming passages are apparent. This, of course, would be expected because in both groups of passages the same Lord Jesus is coming from heaven to deal with human beings. But similarities between the two events does not mean that they are the same or that they take place at the same time. There are enough differences between the rapture passages and the second coming passages that a claim can legitimately be made that they are two different events. Although this would not prove a pretribulational rapture of the church, it would certainly allow for it, and it would also cast significant doubt on a posttribulational rapture. When comparing the main passages dealing with the rapture (1 Thess. 4:13-17; 1 Cor. 15:51-53; John 14:1-3) with those on the second coming (Joel 3:12-16; Rev. 19:11-21; Zech. 14:1-5; Matt. 24:29-31) certain differences can be observed.

1. At the rapture the saints meet Christ in the air, whereas at the second coming the Lord descends to the Mount of Olives. In none of the second coming passages is there a reference to the meeting in the air.
2. At the rapture the Lord comes to bless His people with the final aspect of their salvation. No judgment is found in any of the rapture passages. In clear contrast, the emphasis of the second coming passages is on the judgment that will fall on the unbelievers of this world. Judgment is not associated with the rapture, but it is very much a part of the second coming.
3. In connection with the rapture, there is no mention of the millennial kingdom being established after this return of Christ. But the second coming passages emphasize the establishing of Christ's kingdom. The reason for the second coming is the setting up of the long awaited messianic kingdom.
4. At the rapture both living saints and those who have died previously receive glorified bodies. Both groups are involved and both receive

bodies that will live forever. In the second coming passages no one is said to receive a glorified body. In fact, there is no reference to the translation of living saints at the second coming.

5. The rapture occurs before the wrath of God is poured out on the world, whereas the second coming follows this time of wrath in the Day of the Lord.

6. The coming of the Lord in connection with the rapture is seen as imminent, whereas numerous signs and events must take place prior to the second coming.

7. At the rapture the Lord returns to heaven with His saints (to the "Father's house"), but at the second coming the Lord Jesus descends and remains on the earth.

8. At the rapture all believers will be removed from the earth, leaving for a moment in time unbelievers only on the earth. However, at the second coming, with its accompanying judgments, all unbelievers will be removed from the earth. Only believers will remain to enter into the messianic kingdom.

These eight contrasts point to the strong possibility that two different events are in view. They open the door to a pretribulational rapture of the church and also raise some serious questions about a posttribulational rapture of the church.

An additional note should be added at this point. Three primary words are used in the New Testament for the Lord's return: *parousia* ("coming"), *apokalypsis* ("revelation," or "unveiling"), and *epiphania* ("appearing"). Some have tried to use these words to establish the timing of the rapture. But they are not technical words and do not help in settling the issue of when the rapture will take place. But the differences just observed between the two events of the rapture and the second coming do suggest that we are looking at two separate events that could be separated by the seven-year period of tribulation.

6. An Interval Needed Between the Rapture and the Second Coming

Several events found in the Scriptures seem to take place after the rapture but before the second coming: (1) the judgment seat of Christ; (2) the marriage of the Lamb; and (3) the salvation of people after the rapture who will then populate the earth during the millennial kingdom. The pretribulational rapture of the church provides the necessary time for these events to take place (as does the midtribulational rapture view), but they pose serious difficulties for the posttribulational position.

When the Lord Jesus returns at the rapture, He promised that He would take His followers to the "Father's house" in heaven (John 14:1-3). Jesus promised that He would receive believers to Himself, which means that they will be taken *from* their abode on the earth *to* the place where He dwells, namely, heaven. He does not take them to the earth because He promised to take them to heaven and also because there are several important events for the church saints to participate in prior to the second coming. Those events include (1) the rewarding of believers, (2) the marriage of the Lamb, and (3) the salvation of those who will enter the millennial kingdom in nonglorified bodies.

First, they are to be rewarded. The rewarding of believers is connected closely to the Lord's return in a number of Scripture passages (e.g., 1 Peter 5:4 and Rev. 22:12). This rewarding of believers in the church is commonly called the "judgment seat of Christ" (or the "bema"). Its purpose is not to determine the eternal destiny of believers, because that has been determined already. The reason for this time is to reward believers for their faithful service to the Lord during their days on earth (1 Cor. 3:11-4:5; 2 Cor. 5:10).

This event apparently takes place in connection with the rapture but prior to the second coming because, at the second coming, these believers have already been rewarded. The church has been rewarded in Revelation 19:8, where John states that "it was given to her [the church] to clothe herself in fine linen, bright and clean; for the fine linen is the righteous acts of the saints." The garments represent the rewards. The fact that the bride is wearing her beautiful garments indicates that she has already received her rewards for her deeds of righteousness. The time of this event is clearly right before the Lord Jesus descends from heaven to conquer the world as King of Kings and Lord of Lords. The judgment seat of Christ, therefore, must take place prior to the second coming but after the church is taken to heaven by the Lord Jesus. This rewarding of believers assumes that some length of time must be involved. And a rapture that occurs before the final seven years allows for that needed time.

Second, the marriage of the Lamb must take place; this event seems to require some time between the rapture and the second coming. According to Revelation 19:7–9, there will be great joy in heaven when this event takes place. The text of Revelation 19 places the marriage in heaven, not on the earth or in the clouds.

The marriage of the Lamb is a very important event to the Lord Jesus, since He has given His life for her "that He might present to Himself the church in all her glory, having no spot or wrinkle or any such thing; but that she should be holy and blameless" (Eph. 5:27). At the marriage, believers (the church) are united forever with Him, "that where I am there you may be also" (John 14:3) and "thus we shall always be with the Lord" (1 Thess. 4:17).

> *The implication is evident that those in heaven who compose the "bride" are already translated or resurrected and their righteous acts determined and rewarded. . . . If the church is to be judged, rewarded, and joined to Christ in the symbol of marriage before the Second Advent, an interval of time is required.*[20]

The third event that requires some time between the rapture and the second coming is *the salvation of those who will enter the millennial kingdom in non-glorified bodies.* At the rapture event all believers on the earth are removed, leaving no believers at all. Yet, when Jesus Christ comes back at His second coming, large numbers of believers populate the earth. It is clear that they come to faith in Christ after the rapture but before the second coming. At the second coming these living believers are not said to be changed—they will not receive glorified bodies. This will make it possible for them to repopulate the earth in the millennial kingdom.

> *The Scripture declares emphatically that life on earth in the Millennium relates to a people not translated and not resurrected, a people still in their mortal bodies. Isaiah 65:20–25 declares of the inhabitants (of Jerusalem): "they will build houses and dwell in them; they will plant vineyards and eat their fruit. . . . They will not toil in vain or bear children doomed to misfortune; for they will be a people blessed by the Lord, they and their descendants with them." The passage closes with a description of millennial conditions. . . . Obviously, only a people in mortal flesh build houses, plant, work and have offspring.*[21]

The pretribulational position has no problem with this reality. At the rapture all believers are removed from the earth, and the tribulation begins. The gospel is preached during the seven years of the tribulation, and many come to faith in the Lord Jesus Christ. Although many will be martyred for their faith in Christ, many others will make it to the end of the tribulation alive. Since there is no evidence that these living ones receive glorified bodies, they will enter the millennial age in their natural bodies. These people will fulfill the statements of Isaiah and other prophets concerning the millennial age.

Those holding to the midtribulational rapture position have no real problem with this issue, because people have three and a half years to be saved before the second coming of Christ. Those who believe in the posttribulational position, however, do have a major problem with this issue. If all believers are raptured and glorified at the time of the second coming, then there are no believers with nonglorified bodies to enter the millennial kingdom. Because they put the rapture and second coming at the same moment, no time is available between these events for people to be saved. Because this is a significant problem for the posttribulational view, it will be discussed in more detail in the next chapter.

EVENTS BETWEEN THE
RAPTURE AND THE SECOND COMING

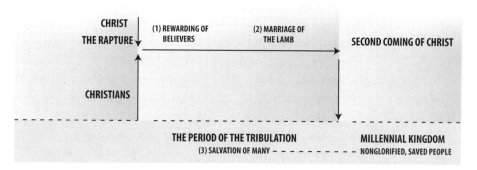

The evidence of Scripture is that these events take place between the rapture and the second coming and that some reasonable amount of time is needed for there to be a fulfillment of them. These events, therefore, support a pretribulational rapture of the church.

7. The Lack of Evidence for the Church's Presence in the Tribulation

The Scripture passages that deal with the tribulation period contain no specific reference to the church of Jesus Christ. The tribulation passages in both the Old and New Testaments refer to Israel and to Gentiles and to people who are saved, but they do not refer to the church. The word for "church" (*ekklesia*) is not used, and specific terms used of the church, such as "the body of Christ" are not found in these passages.

Some would argue that this is just an argument from silence, which is no real argument at all, and, to some degree, they have a point. Nevertheless, it is possible that the reason for no mention of the church is that it is not there! It is not only possible, but it is likely that this is the case, since many passages speak about the coming period of the tribulation and all of them fail to mention the church specifically.

There are, of course, saved people in the tribulation. But all saved (or elect) people are not in the church, and to be elect does not automatically make one a part of the church. "The question is not whether there are any elect in the tribulation but whether that portion of the elect that is called the church, the body of Christ, is ever mentioned."[22] If no evidence exists that the church is in the time of tribulation, there is a strong probability that it is not there. And if the church is not there, it has been removed suddenly and supernaturally by the Lord Jesus at the rapture. Several portions of Scripture illustrate what has already been said.

Daniel 9:24–27 (which explains the Seventieth Week of Daniel) is one of the most important passages on the tribulation. It explicitly says that these years involve Daniel's people and Daniel's city—Israel and Jerusalem. That was true of the first sixty-nine weeks (483 years), and consistency would require that it will also be true of the seventieth week (last seven years) as well. Nowhere in that key passage is the church seen or hinted at.

Revelation 6–19 gives an amazing amount of detail regarding the tribulation period. In that section Israel is spoken of many times, as are the nations of the earth. And although there are references to the elect and to the saints, the church is not mentioned—either by its usual word, *ekklesia*, or by phrases such as "the body of Christ" or "the bride of Christ."

Yet in Revelation the apostle John does speak of the church more than twenty times in chapters 1–3 and once in the benediction in 22:16. But none of these uses and others (such as "the bride") place the church on the earth during the tribulation. Matthew 24:31 speaks of "the elect" being gathered from all over the world at the end of the tribulation period. But this verse fails to identify those elect as a part of the church, and this would be necessary to prove that the church is on the earth during the tribulation. The elect of Matthew 24:31 is a reference to living saints on the earth at the time of the second coming, probably both Jews and Gentiles.

The Seven Strong Arguments for A Pretribulational Rapture

The seven lines of argument given in this chapter emerge out of a study of a number of key Scripture passages. The distinction between the church and the nation of Israel, the stated purposes for the tribulation found in the Scriptures, the church's exemption from the future wrath of God, and the concept of imminency are strong arguments for the rapture taking place before the final seven years of tribulation. An analysis of the rapture and second coming passages reveals some striking differences between the two events—differences that make the pretribulational position a viable one.

These arguments, combined with (1) the need for some amount of time between the rapture and second coming because of three important events and (2) the lack of specific evidence for the church being in the time of tribulation, present a good case for the pretribulational rapture of the church.

Some Implications of a Rapture Before the Tribulation

In conclusion, three points of a practical nature ought to be highlighted.

First, the writers of the New Testament always discussed the rapture in the context of godly living. The truth of the rapture was to bring about changes in the way believers thought and lived. The truth of the Lord's return was to help Christians become more loving, diligent, generous, and righteous and less impacted by sin and by Satan's world system. In all of our theological discussion and analysis of the rapture (as important as these things are), the end result ought to be a movement toward greater godliness in our personal lives.

The second point is a reminder to pretribulationists that the rapture is a signless event; therefore, we are not to be looking for signs. The unwise practice of setting dates and the habit of finding fulfillment of prophecy in current events must cease. This has caused harm to many of God's people, cast suspicion on God's Word, and brought considerable embarrassment to the cause of Christ. To see certain events or situations as possibly setting the stage for the fulfillment of prophecies is legitimate, but to declare a particular event as a fulfillment of prophecy (without direct validation by Gabriel or some other heavenly messenger) is not legitimate. We must be careful and wise in how we view the events in our world and how we relate them to the inspired Word of God.

A third point relates to the charge by some opponents of the pretribulational rapture view that it breeds an escapist mentality as well as social irresponsibility. It is difficult to answer such a charge because it contains a mixture of truth and error. It is perhaps true that some have developed a "bunker mentality," withdrawing from life around them, hoping desperately for the rapture to come to remove them from all their troubles and pain. But that attitude certainly has not generally characterized pretribulational believers over the years who have served Christ and their fellow man effectively and faithfully. Nor was it the attitude of the writers of the New Testament, who saw the any-moment coming of the Lord as a strong incentive for action. This dynamic truth motivated them to reach out to others in a variety of ways. It enabled them to live vibrant and useful lives in spite of sufferings and pain. For example, the apostle Paul was possessed with a desire to see Christ and be part of the living at the rapture event, and yet his life was spent in "toil and labor" as he served Christ energetically.

The rapture ought to shape the attitude of believers today in similar ways. The any-moment return of our Lord should energize us to serve faithfully and enthusiastically because the Judge is right now standing at the door with His hand on the knob. Maranatha!

CHAPTER THIRTEEN

THE
Posttribulational
RAPTURE VIEW

W e all tend to admire those people who agree with us. Such people are obviously unbiased individuals who possess great knowledge and insight. Their agreement with us is a testimonial to their clear thinking and powers of evaluation. We do not, however, usually hold those who disagree with us in such high regard. This chapter and the next evaluate views that differ from a pretribulational rapture position. The doctrinal positions will be questioned but not the sincerity, intelligence, or spirituality of those who hold to them. We need to appreciate fellow believers who differ on some of the details of the rapture.

This chapter will feature posttribulationism, one of the most widely held rapture views. In chapter 14, three views concerning the rapture of the church will be discussed: (1) the partial rapture view; (2) the midtribulational rapture view; and (3) the pre-wrath rapture view. Some lengthy books have been written promoting these various positions, so two chapters cannot handle all the many points and details. But the major points of each view will be stated and evaluated.

THE DISTINCTIVE BELIEFS OF POSTTRIBULATIONISM

As the name *posttribulation* indicates, the rapture is believed to occur after the great tribulation comes upon the world. "Posttribulationism teaches that the rapture and the second coming are facets of a single event which will occur at the end of the tribulation when Christ returns. The church will be on earth during the tribulation to experience the events of that period."[1] Posttribulationism differs from pretribulationism on a number of basic issues: the nature of the tribulation, the distinction between the church and Israel, the doctrine of imminency, a time element between the rapture and the second coming, and the meaning of certain eschatological terms.

In any major position on the rapture, differing ideas and thoughts will exist among those holding to that particular position. This is true of pretribulationism and midtribulationism, and it is also true of posttribulationism. In fact, within posttribulationism four distinct viewpoints need to be mentioned before one analyzes the posttribulational view. These are discussed in some detail by John Walvoord and will be summarized here.[2]

Classic Posttribulation

First, "classic posttribulationism" holds that the church has always been in the tribulation because, during its entire existence, it has suffered persecution and trouble. The tribulation is not a future event but an ongoing present reality. In this view, therefore, the events of the tribulation are not understood in a literal or futuristic way. The tribulation prophecies have already been fulfilled in the life of the church over the centuries. Interestingly, because there are no future prophetic events that must be fulfilled, this form of posttribulationism believes in the imminent return of the Lord even though they see the rapture and second coming as a single event.

This view has some major interpretive problems in key passages such as Daniel 9:24–27 and Revelation 19. It does not have many adherents today because of its inconsistent approach to the interpretation of Scripture. Both the literal and allegorical approaches are employed, making the interpreter the final authority. "The classic view is rejected because of its inconsistent application of interpretive principles of the Bible, its inability to explain problems, and its subjective character that permits the interpreter to explain away any problem that exists."[3]

Semiclassic Posttribulationism

The second viewpoint, "semiclassic posttribulationism" agrees with classic posttribulationism that the tribulation is a contemporary event. However, it posits that some events are future and await fulfillment. Because there are still some unfulfilled prophecies, the second coming (and the rapture) cannot be an imminent event.

Some adherents of this view hold to a future seven-year period of time prior to the second coming, but others do not. There is considerable disagreement among those who hold this view on how literally to take the prophecies related to the tribulation. There is also a lack of clarity on the sequence of events leading up to the second coming and on the purpose of a rapture at all. In addition, this view has the major problem of mixing the literal approach to interpretation with the allegorical, which is the reason significant disagreement exists among adherents.

Futuristic Posttribulationism

A third view is that of the "futurist posttribulational" position. In the twentieth century the futurist approach became a major view within posttribulationism. In the past those who held to a posttribulational position were not futurists—futurism within posttribulationism is relatively new. George Ladd, in his book *The Blessed Hope*, promoted the idea that there was a future period of seven years that immediately preceded the second coming. These seven years of tribulation would be experienced by the church before it was removed from the world at the rapture, which would occur at the time of the second coming.

This approach takes a far more literal approach to key passages in Daniel and Revelation, though it does not make a clear distinction between the church and the nation of Israel.

Dispensational Posttribulationism

The fourth viewpoint within the posttribulational position is "dispensational posttribulationism"—a futurist approach with a different twist. Usually those who are posttribulationists do not hold to a clear distinction between the church and national Israel in God's program. But Robert Gundry, in his book *The Church and the Tribulation*, attempts to combine a dispensational interpretation with posttribulationism.

This attempt has forced Gundry to come up with some unusual exegetical and logical arguments and to redefine some eschatological terms and ideas. Although he sees a distinction between the church and Israel, he says that the church lives through the tribulation period. The church is exempt from the wrath of God because most of the terrible events in the tribulation are a result of Satan's wrath, not God's. Understanding that the idea of an any-moment coming of Christ would neutralize the posttribulational position, he aggressively denies the doctrine of imminency.

These four posttribulation positions emerge out of differing arguments and approaches. In fact, there is such diversity among them that they actually contradict one another. To hold to one view makes it impossible to hold to another. If an individual held to the dispensational posttribulation position, he would actually be rejecting the classic posttribulation position. Even though they are both labeled as posttribulational views, both cannot be correct. With such diversity within these particular viewpoints, it is impossible to say that one particular position is the view of posttribulationism, and this makes it somewhat difficult to present or refute posttribulationism. However, certain major features, or lines of evidence, are fundamentally true of the position, and these will be discussed.

SUPPORT FOR THE POSTRIBULATIONAL POSITION

The Historical Argument

The first line of evidence is the historical argument. Many writers who support the posttribulation position have spent a considerable amount of effort trying to show that the pretribulation position is recent and is to be rejected because it is not the historic teaching of the church. About one-third of Ladd's *The Blessed Hope* deals with the historical argument for posttribulationism. The feeling is that demonstrating the recency of pretribulationism would help establish the validity of the posttribulation view. One posttribulation author notes,

> *About 1830 . . . a new school arose within the fold of Premillennialism that sought to overthrow what, since the Apostolic Age, have been considered by all pre-millennialists as established results, and to institute in their place a series of doctrines that had never been heard of before. The school I refer to is that of "The Brethren" or "Plymouth Brethren," founded by J. N. Darby.*[4]

The point is that if it is new, then it is most likely not valid.

Generally it is believed that Darby was the one who formulated the pre-tribulational view in the early 1830s. Others have attempted to show that Darby did not really originate the view but that pretribulation rapture theory was first created by Emmanuel Lacunza (1812) or Edward Irving (1816) or Margaret MacDonald (1830).

Irving and MacDonald are not the kind of persons most would want as the founders of their viewpoint. Edward Irving was a man whose orthodoxy was doubtful, and Margaret MacDonald had her vision (which allegedly was the source of pretribulationism) under demonic influence. A number of anti-pretribulation writers want to tie these individuals to the pretribulation position since such an association would tend to discredit pretribulationism. In his book *The Great Rapture Hoax,* MacPherson wrote, "It may be a bit unsettling to realize that the Pre-tribulation rapture's birthplace is Port Glasgow, Scotland, that the date on its 'birth certificate' is 1830, and that a young Scottish lassie originated it."[5] The same author emphasizes that Margaret MacDonald's "revelation" of the rapture as being a separate event from the second coming was absolutely unique and unheard of prior to the spring of 1830. Her visions and views are seen as highly significant.

> *Margaret's two-stage revelation has influenced evangelicals and fundamentalists as much as anything else has influenced them during the last 150 years. Just think: the popular Pre-Trib rapture view—reflected in countless books, pamphlets, magazines, sermons, songs, poems, paintings, slogans, bumper stickers, movies, crusades, TV and radio ministries, Christian schools, etc.— was actually set in motion in 1830 by a young, publicity-shunning girl in Scotland!*[6]

Tracing the origin of the pretribulation view back to Darby or possibly to some others of questionable theology has been an important emphasis in the arguments of the posttribulation position. If such an argument can somehow set aside the pretribulation position, it becomes somewhat easier to establish the posttribulation point of view.

The Nature of the Tribulation Period

A second line of argument for posttribulationism has to do with the nature of the tribulation period. Some posttribulationists see the entire present age as the tribulation, whereas others view it as a time in the future. Though there is a significant difference between these two viewpoints, posttribulationists agree that the church was promised persecution and tribulation. The idea is that, since the church is clearly promised tribulation, it is impossible to say that the church must be raptured prior to the tribulation period.

Some posttribulationists do believe that there is an unprecedented time of trouble ahead known as the "wrath of God," but they also believe that the church will be preserved through this time while remaining on the earth.[7] The church, then, will be protected in tribulation (particularly the "wrath of God") but not removed from such times. Sometimes posttribulationists will make a distinction between God's wrath and the wrath of Satan.

The Nature of the Church

A third line of argument used by posttribulationists concerns the nature of the church. Generally, posttribulationists have not held to a clear distinction between the church and the nation of Israel in God's program. Rather, they tend to include believers of all ages in the church. Since believers are certainly seen in the tribulation period, they conclude that the church is clearly there also.

This has been an important point in the reasoning of posttribulationists, except for the more recent view of Robert Gundry. If the church is defined as "the elect of all ages," there is no good reason to believe that it will be absent from the tribulation. However, if a clear distinction is made between the church and Israel, then a pretribulational view becomes far more likely. This is a major issue in determining the time of the rapture.

Terminology Regarding the Return of the Lord

A fourth argument comes from the terminology used in relation to the return of the Lord. The three key words *apokalypsis* ("revelation"), *epiphania* ("manifestation"), and *parousia* ("presence") are seen as strong indicators of a posttribulational position.

> *What is important to note about these terms is, first, that each is clearly used to describe the posttribulational return of Christ and, second, that all three also designate an object of the believer's hope and expectation. . . . If, then,*

believers are exhorted to look forward to this coming of Christ, and this coming is presented as posttribulational, it is natural to conclude that believers will be present through the tribulation.[8]

This is a critical issue for posttribulationists. They must prove that the rapture and second coming passages are so similar that one must conclude that these passages are speaking of the same time and the same event. The use of these three words is, therefore, significant to the position. Connected with this is the need to show similarities between the events, such as references to clouds and trumpets in each.

Denial of the Doctrine of Imminency

A fifth argument used by many posttribulationists is the denial of the doctrine of imminency. If the Lord's return can occur at any moment as defined by pretribulationism, then a posttribulation rapture is not possible. Therefore, emphasis is placed on the signs that precede the Lord's return and on understanding "imminence" as describing an event that is near but not necessarily without known intervening events.[9]

The Interpretation of Matthew 24–25

A sixth argument is based on the Olivet Discourse in Matthew 24–25. Proponents argue that Matthew 24:31 is a conclusive statement that the rapture takes place at the end of the tribulation, in connection with the second coming of Christ. In this verse the "elect" gather with the blowing of a trumpet. Since 1 Corinthians 15 and 1 Thessalonians 4 also record a gathering of the elect and a trumpet blowing, they conclude that the rapture is in view in this verse as well.

These are not the only lines of argument presented by those holding to a posttribulational rapture position, but they are the main ones. It is now our task to analyze these six areas of discussion.

AN ANALYSIS OF THE POSITION

The Historical Argument

Several points can be made in answering the historical argument made by posttribulationism that pretribulationism is a new doctrine.

THE POSTTRIBULATIONAL RAPTURE THEORY

RAPTURE

SECOND
COMING

THE TRIBULATION PERIOD

It must be acknowledged that J. N. Darby was instrumental in formulating pretribulationism in its modern form. But in spite of great effort by several writers, no clear evidence exists that Darby got his views from Margaret MacDonald or Edward Irving.[10] In fact, it is highly unlikely that either one of these was actually pretribulational in his or her viewpoint. Irving in 1831 declared that the rapture would take place at the time of the seventh bowl—which most agree is at the end of the tribulation—if anything, making him a posttribulationist. MacDonald's ideas about the rapture are very unclear. It is true that she may not have been a traditional posttribulationist, but there are no clear statements proving that she held to a pretribulational rapture.[11] Darby undoubtedly arrived at his position primarily from the study of Scripture and perhaps from ideas presented by writers much earlier than him.

The charge that pretribulationism is new and therefore invalid is not true on two counts. First, as we will see, the concept of the rapture as a distinct event from the second coming did not begin with Darby or with those who lived at that time. Second, simply because something is new does not make it invalid. If that were true, futuristic posttribulationism might be considered invalid because the positions expounded by Ladd and Gundry are quite recent.

We must keep in mind that there has been a history in the development of systems of theology. Certain areas of theology have been discussed and developed at different times, and the area of eschatology has only recently been carefully addressed and formulated.

Each era of church history has been occupied with a particular doctrinal controversy, which has become the object of discussion, revision, and formulation, until there was general acceptance of what Scripture taught. The entire field of theology was thus formulated through the ages. It was not until the last century that the field of Eschatology became a matter to which the mind of the church was turned.[12]

This is not to say, of course, that up until the last century no one in the church had ideas about eschatology. But a precise formulation of eschatology has been a recent development, and this would include views within all the rapture positions. It is, therefore, less than fair or accurate to say that pretribulationism ought to be set aside because it is a recent doctrinal formulation.

Having said this, however, it must be observed that J. N. Darby did not originate the idea that the rapture and the second coming were two distinct events and that the rapture removed the church from the tribulation period. But that is not the opinion of a number of posttribulationists, as the following quote demonstrates:

Before 1830 Christians had always believed in a single future coming, that the catching up of 1 Thess 4 will take place after the Great tribulation of Matthew 24 at the glorious coming of the Son of Man when he shall send His angels to gather together all of His elect.[13]

That 1830 was the starting date for the pretribulation rapture view is simply not accurate. Other writers prior to Darby taught that the Lord will come and deliver His people prior to the tribulation. Although an extensive study is not possible here, several citations demonstrate that an imminent return of Christ prior to the second coming was believed in by others long before Darby.[14]

As early as 1687, Peter Jurieu, in his book *Approaching Deliverance of the Church* (1687), taught that Christ would come in the air to rapture the saints and return to heaven before the battle of Armageddon. He spoke of a secret rapture prior to His coming in glory and judgment at Armageddon.[15] About fifty years later, Philip Doddridge's commentary on the New Testament (1738) and John Gill's commentary on the New Testament (1748) both used the term *rapture* and speak of it as imminent. It is clear that these men believed that this coming will precede Christ's descent to the earth and the time of judgment. The purpose was to preserve believers from the time of judgment.

James Macknight (1763) and Thomas Scott (1792) taught that the righteous will be carried into heaven, where they will be secure until the time of judgment is over.[16] Although a detailed chronology is not given by these writers, it is evident that they did see a distinction between the rapture and the second coming and saw the rapture as preceding the time of judgment. Why did these and other writers begin to speak of a rapture that was distinct from the second coming and see believers removed from the earth prior to the judgments? The answer is that once a literal approach to interpreting the Scriptures began to be rediscovered, these truths started to emerge.

Quite significant is the fact that more than a thousand years before Darby the writings of one known as "Pseudo-Ephraem" (4th–7th century AD) spoke of the saints being removed from the earth and taken to be with the Lord prior to the judgments of the tribulation. He taught that there were two distinct comings and that the church was removed before the tribulation.[17] Such witnesses who lived long before Darby blunt the charges that are often leveled against pretribulationism.

THE ARGUMENT FROM THE NATURE OF THE TRIBULATION PERIOD

It should always be remembered, however, that the main issue is not historic quotations but, rather, the teaching of the Word of God. What the church fathers and other ancient writers did or did not teach does not settle the matter. What the writers of the Bible taught is of supreme importance. Exegesis of the relevant biblical texts and a theology that is consistent with known biblical truth must be the bases for conclusions on this matter.

All the rapture views agree that *the church has not been exempted* from persecution and tribulation. The Lord Jesus Himself declared, "In the world you have tribulation" (John 16:33). The word *tribulation* is used here by the Lord Jesus in a nontechnical, noneschatological way. Other writers of Scripture also use the word in such a way (e.g., Mark 4:17; Rom. 5:3; 2 Cor. 1:4). But there is a great difference between persecution and the great tribulation. It is one thing to say that the church will experience persecution and tribulation yet quite another to say that it will go through the time of God's wrath.

The Scriptures declare that there is coming an unprecedented time of trouble, when the wrath of God is poured out on the world. The wrath of God is the controlled, but passionate, judgments of God against evil that will result in His reclaiming for Himself the creation and bringing it under His dominion. This is not the same as general persecution, which can occur throughout this age. The problems faced in the rapture question are (1) when does the wrath of God begin, and (2) how is the church protected from God's wrath?

Rapture Question 1: When Does God's Wrath Begin?

In answering the first question, futuristic posttributionists seem to confine the outpouring of the wrath of God to the very end of the Seventieth Week, when it is poured out on unbelievers only. The other terrible judgments in the tribulation, according to some, are demonstrations of the wrath of Satan and the wrath of man. But as we saw in our study of supports for the pretribulational rapture, the evidence is strong that divine wrath is poured out throughout the entire period. The judgments recorded by the apostle John in Revelation 6–19 do not come from Satan or man but from the scroll in the hand of the Lord Jesus (Rev. 5). It is the Lord Jesus who breaks the seals, as the One to whom all judgment has been given (John 5:22). As He breaks each seal, judgment comes, showing that each is divine in character. It is abundantly clear that the One in charge of all the judgments is the Lord Jesus Christ. He may choose to use Satan and mankind as His agents, but there can be no doubt as to the source of these judgments.

It is also instructive to observe that God's wrath is seen very early in the tribulation period in the breaking of the first seal judgments, which are said by Christ to be the "beginning of birth pangs" or sorrows (Matt. 24:8). In Revelation 6, a large number of people on the earth die in the first four seal judgments. These seal judgments include famine, disease, wild beasts, and the sword (war). Many scholars are convinced that when John wrote these words, he had Ezekiel 14:21 in mind: "For thus says the Lord God, 'How much more when I send My four severe judgments against Jerusalem: sword, famine, wild beasts and plague to cut off man and beast from it!'" The context of Ezekiel 14:21 (vv. 12–21) indicates that these four things are expressions of God's wrath. This verse is but one of many that identify these four as the wrath of God (cf. Lev. 26:21–28; Deut. 11:17;

28:20-26; 32:22-25; Jer. 15:1-9; 16:4-11; 19:7-9; Ezek. 5:11-17; 6:11-12; 7:3-15; Num. 11:33; 16:46; 25:8-11).

In passage after passage they are identified as God's wrath against sin. They are never identified as Satan's wrath or man's wrath. So the rich Old Testament background to the book of Revelation points to the seals as being evidence of God's wrath. These apparently come early in the Seventieth Week, giving proof of the presence of His wrath during the entire tribulation period. It is best to conclude that the wrath of God is not isolated to a short moment at the end of the tribulation but that it covers the entire seven years.

Rapture Question 2: How Is the Church Protected from God's Wrath?

The second question concerns how believers are protected from the wrath of God. Posttribulationists believe that the church is protected in the midst of divine judgment, whereas pretribulationists believe that the church is removed out of the time of wrath. In deciding which position is correct, several matters should be discussed.

Why would God want His people to experience His wrath? The church's sins have been taken care of by the work of Christ on the cross, and judgment for sin is no longer a future expectation of believers (e.g., John 5:24). In the Scriptures mentioned above, the wrath of God is clearly focused on sin and sinful creatures. What, then, would be the purpose of preserving the church through God's wrath and then removing the church at the end as Christ descends to earth?

> The tendency of posttribulationism to blur the scriptural description of the tribulation arises from the necessity to defend posttribulationism from certain contradictions. One of these is the question as to why saints of the present age who are perfectly justified by faith, given a perfect position of sanctification, and declared to be in Christ, should have to suffer the "great day of his wrath" in the tribulation. While Christians can be disciplined and chastened, they cannot justly be exposed to the wrath of God.[18]

Since the wrath of God focuses on sin and since there is no purpose for keeping the church in the midst of it (either for salvation or sanctification), it seems better to understand that the church is removed from the time of the tribulation.

How will God protect His people from His wrath when some of the judgments are universal in their scope and there is no indication that anyone on the earth is exempt from them? Revelation 3:10 reminds us that the hour of testing is coming upon "the whole world, to test those who dwell upon the earth." It would seem that the universal nature of at least some of the tribulation judgments points to the need to remove the church from the world if judgment is to be avoided. It is hard to imagine how God's people will not be deeply affected by worldwide famines, wars, earthquakes, and other judgments. If posttribulationism is correct, then no believer will lose his life during these judgments. But it is clear that incredible numbers of people lose their lives during this time of judgment, and there is simply no evidence that God will protect believers in the midst of them.

Furthermore, in Matthew 24:22, Jesus said that "for the sake of the elect those days shall be cut short." If God is shielding His people from death during this time, why is it necessary to cut the days of tribulation short? If God were preserving His people in the midst of wrath, it would make no difference if the tribulation were seven hours, seven years, or seven decades in length. The Lord's statement would suggest that believers, along with the world, are being impacted by these judgments.

Robert Gundry, a posttribulationist, responds by saying that "the tribulation of the seventieth week has to do, then, not with God's wrath against the sinners, but with the wrath of Satan, the Antichrist and the wicked against the saints."[19] But as we have seen, such an idea does not align itself with the fact that all the judgments of the seals (and thus the trumpets and bowls) are divine judgments (Revelation 5). They all come from the worthy Lamb, who alone has the authority to break the seals. Furthermore, we know from Scripture that large numbers of believers do die during the seven years of tribulation.

It would not seem likely that any believer would be comforted with the idea that he will not die in God's wrath but instead will perish in the wrath of Satan or the Antichrist. A condemned murderer would not be greatly encouraged with the news that he would not die in the electric chair but would instead die by lethal injection. He would rejoice, however, if he were transferred out of his death-row cell. Deliverance of the church out of the time of trouble seems to align better with the Scriptures than preservation within the tribulation.

The teaching of Paul in the Thessalonian letters points to removal from the time of wrath, rather than preservation in this time of tribulation. As we observed, Paul praised these believers for their expectant waiting for the Lord's return and then encouraged them in 1 Thessalonians 1:10 by telling them that the Lord Jesus delivers His church saints from the coming eschatological wrath. The word *deliver* (*rhuomai*) has the thought of being rescued from danger by a powerful act. The verb is used with "from" (the Greek preposition *ek*), which is used "to denote separation" and also "to introduce the place from which the separation takes place."[20] "It is used especially with 'verbs of motion,' such as *rhuomai*, the verb Paul used in participial form for Christ's ministry of delivering church saints from future wrath by separating them from it, not by sheltering or protecting them from the wrath while they are in its midst."[21] Paul's words of encouragement to the Thessalonian believers seem best understood as deliverance out of the coming time of wrath and not preservation within it.

The central passage of 1 Thessalonians 4:13–18 also has a contribution to make on the matter of deliverance out of the time of wrath. Because loved ones had died, the believers at Thessalonica were sorrowful. Paul wrote to comfort and encourage them by reminding them of the truth of the rapture, letting them know that these who had died would participate in the rapture by being resurrected at that time. If Paul had previously taught them a posttribulation rapture, we can reasonably assume that they would have been told to rejoice that these deceased loved ones would now escape the tribulation. Missing the wrath of God would be something to rejoice about! But if he taught them a pretribulation rapture, they could well have been distressed when loved ones died, thinking that they would miss the rapture event. This is especially true if they believed that the resurrection of these dead would not take place until after the tribulation period, based on Daniel 12:1–2—the only resurrection Scripture available to them. Perhaps that is why Paul explicitly told them that living believers "shall not precede" those who have died.[22] Paul's words of encouragement fit well with the idea that he had previously taught a pretribulation rapture.

The passage in 1 Thessalonians 5:9–10 also points to the removal of believers out of the time of tribulation. In 5:2–8, Paul contrasts the destinies of the saved and the unsaved, and their futures are markedly different. The unsaved face the judgments of the Day of the Lord, but believers will not be overtaken by that day. Then, as we noted in our discussion of pretribulationism, Paul states emphatically that it is not the will of God for the believer to experience wrath. We have the clear guarantee that believers will not experience His wrath. Instead, it is God's sovereign intention to complete the salvation of believers:

> *Because Christ's death for church saints caused their salvation from the future wrath of God, and because Christ's death has already been accomplished once for all (Rom. 6:9–10), the salvation of church saints from the future wrath of God has already been obtained. Their future experience of this already obtained deliverance is certain.*[23]

The salvation spoken of in this context is the deliverance from the wrath of God that is poured out in the day of the Lord. Paul's words best fit with the idea of being delivered out of the time of tribulation.

The tribulation is best understood as a full seven years of divine wrath. And in light of the kind of salvation that Jesus has purchased for us, it is best to see that the believer is delivered out of that time of wrath and not simply preserved through it.

The Argument Based on the Nature of the Church

There has been general agreement among all involved in the rapture discussion that the clearer the distinction made between the church and the nation of Israel, the more likely one will hold to a pretribulational position. The following two quotes from a pretribulationist and a posttribulationist (Walvoord and Moo, respectively) affirm this:

> *If the term church includes saints of all ages, then it is self-evident that the church will go through the tribulation, as all agree that there will be saints in this time of trouble. If, however, the term church applies only to a certain body of saints, namely, the saints of this present dispensation, then the possibility of the translation of the church before the tribulation is possible and even probable.*[24]

> *If a radical disjunction between Israel and the church is assumed, a certain presumption against the posttribulational position exists, since it would be*

inconsistent for the church to be involved in a period of time that, according to the Old Testament, has to do with Israel.[25]

It is clear, then, that a person's view of the nature of the church and Israel plays an important role in the position taken on the rapture and the tribulation. Having two distinct groups of God's people speaks to the idea of two distinct programs. That which applies to one group may not (and probably would not) apply to the other. If the church is distinct from Israel, it is likely that God's program for Israel will not involve the church. That is not to say that similarities do not exist or that there is not commonality in some places, but it is saying that they are not the same. Similarity and sameness are not equivalent ideas. This issue of the church and Israel has been discussed in the first four chapters and cannot be repeated here. However, several matters can be briefly mentioned.

Pentecost: The Church's Birthday

The church began on the day of Pentecost (Acts 2), not with Abraham or Adam. The church is not found in the Old Testament and, therefore, cannot be defined as "the elect of all ages." During His ministry, Jesus declared, "I will build My church" (Matt. 16:18). He did not say, "I have been building My church." The building of the church was something that would take place in the future. In Acts 1:5, after His resurrection, the Lord predicted that the Holy Spirit would come and baptize His followers. The apostle Peter said that this prediction was fulfilled on the day of Pentecost (Acts 11:15ff.). Spirit baptism, according to 1 Corinthians 12:13, places a believer into the body of Christ (the church). Since this ministry of the Holy Spirit did not exist prior to the day of Pentecost, it was not possible until then for anyone to enter the church.

Thus the church of Jesus Christ did not exist until Pentecost (Acts 2), and Jesus did not assume His position as head of the body until after His resurrection and ascension (cf. Eph. 1:22; 5:23; Col. 1:18). The body could only exist when there was a functioning Head.

That the church is a "mystery" also points to its distinction from Israel. The New Testament uses "mystery" to refer to divine knowledge that was not revealed by God in the past, and that people could never have discovered on their own, but that God has now revealed (e.g., Rom. 16:25–26; 1 Cor. 2:7–8; Eph. 3:4–9; Col. 1:26). The idea of regenerated Jews and

Gentiles being united and equal in one body was not known in the Old Testament. The Old Testament did reveal that Gentiles would be saved, and it clearly revealed the priority place occupied by Israel. But the unity and equality of the body was new and unrevealed until God gave this truth to the apostles. The revealing of this mystery, which took place shortly after the actual beginning of the church, points to a distinction between the church and the nation of Israel.

The Abrahamic Covenant and the Nation of Israel

The Abrahamic covenant and the other biblical covenants also strongly suggest a distinction between Israel and the church. As was discussed in chapters 2 and 3, these unconditional, eternal covenants were made and ratified with the nation of Israel and not with the church. The fact that significant portions of them remained unfulfilled necessitates a future fulfillment that will definitely involve Israel but not the church.

It is not surprising to a pretribulationist that the church is not mentioned in key tribulation passages, since the stated purposes of the tribulation period have to do with God's distinct people Israel. If the focus of the Seventieth Week of Daniel is on Israel and if the church is distinct from Israel, then it is very likely that the events of the tribulation do not include the church. Daniel 9:24–27 specifies that the seventy weeks (490 years) have to do with the land and people of Israel, not the church. The church did not exist during the first sixty-nine weeks, and it would be consistent for God to deal only with the land and people of Israel in the seventieth week also.

In Revelation 6–19 and Matthew 24–25 the church (*ekklesia*), the body of Christ, is never mentioned. These two key tribulation sections not only do not use the word for church (*ekklesia*) but do not use "the body of Christ" or similar terms. Although some would simply dismiss this as an argument from silence, remember that the writers certainly had the vocabulary to include these "church words." And it must be acknowledged that perhaps the reason these passages do not mention the church is because the church is not there.

These passages, of course, do use "saints" and the "elect," but those terms simply refer to saved people without necessarily including them as a part of the church. There were saved people prior to the beginning of the church on the day of Pentecost, and it is not surprising to find saved people after the church departs this world at the rapture, especially when we keep in mind that the great purpose of the tribulation period is to bring Israel and many Gentiles into a saving relationship with the Lord.

THE ARGUMENT CONCERNING THE TERMINOLOGY

The key argument for the posttribulationist has to do with the terms and events found in the rapture and second coming passages. To establish his position, the posttribulationist must demonstrate that these passages refer to the same event and the same time. As we noted, the three words used in connection with the Lord's return are not technical terms and do not, in and of themselves, prove the timing of the rapture. The only thing that can be established is that these words are used of both events. Now if the posttribulationist cannot demonstrate that rapture and second coming passages are so similar that they must be seen as identical, then other rapture positions become possible. Two lines of argument against the posttribulational idea (that the rapture and second coming passages refer to the same event, occurring at the same time) point to some important differences in both the time of these two events and the events themselves.

Dissimilarities Among the Rapture Passages

The first line of argument has to do with some significant dissimilarities among the rapture passages (John 14:1–3; 1 Cor. 15:51–55; 1 Thess. 4:13–18) and the second coming passages (Joel 3:12–16; Zech. 12–14; Matt. 24:29–31; Rev. 19:11–21).

1. In the rapture passages the Lord Jesus returns in the air and translates all believers, whereas in the second coming passages He returns to the earth, and there is no translation at all.
2. In the rapture passages Jesus returns to heaven (the "Father's house") with the translated saints, whereas at the second coming Jesus returns with the saints to the earth.
3. The rapture passages present the Lord's coming as a time of blessing and salvation for the saints with no mention of judgment at all, but the second coming passages focus on the Lord's coming in judgment on His enemies.
4. The rapture passages do not make any reference to the establishing of the messianic kingdom, whereas the second coming passages are

immediately followed by a discussion of the establishing of that kingdom.

5. In the rapture passages only believers are involved, and they are glorified, but in second coming passages all people are involved, and no one is glorified.

6. In the rapture passages the Lord comes before the time of wrath, whereas in the second coming passages He comes at the conclusion of the time of wrath.

7. In the rapture passages no signs are given before this event can take place, although many signs are given as preceding the second coming.

These dissimilarities speak against the rapture and the second coming as being the same event, occurring at the same time.

The Need for a Time Interval Between the Events

The second line of argument has to do with events that occur between the rapture and second coming that necessitate an interval of time between the two. This was discussed in the previous chapter on the pretribulational rapture. To summarize, the rewarding of believers (the judgment seat of Christ), the marriage of the Lamb, and the salvation of people after the rapture are the three intervening events between the rapture and the second coming.

Revelation 19 places the marriage of the Lamb in heaven immediately before the second coming. The bride (which represents the church) is wearing white linen, said to be the righteous deeds of the saints. She has, therefore, been rewarded, which means that the judgment seat of Christ (where believers are rewarded) has already occurred. It is highly unlikely that these events will take place in connection with a posttribulational rapture. If so, the church would be raptured out of the world at the end of the tribulation and immediately return to the earth with Christ and yet be involved in the judgment seat and the marriage in a moment of time. It is true that God can do anything He wants, but it is also true that He would make these events meaningful to His people, which would seem to require that some amount of time would elapse.

The third event that must take place after the rapture is the salvation of people who will enter the messianic kingdom in nonglorified bodies.

The Old Testament prophets are clear that there is a need for people in their mortal bodies to enter the millennial kingdom. This reality poses a major problem for those who are premillennial and posttribulational. When the rapture takes place, every believer is removed from the earth and glorified. If the rapture were to take place at the end of the tribulation, there would be no one left to enter the kingdom in nonglorified bodies and repopulate the earth. Who will stand before the Lord Jesus at His second coming at the "sheep and goat judgment" when there are no "sheep" left on the earth?

This presents posttribulationists with a huge problem, and they have not as yet come up with any solid scriptural solution. Some have suggested that unsaved people will enter the millennial kingdom, whereas others speculate that the celibate 144,000 will be the nonglorified who enter the kingdom. These seem out of keeping with the teachings of a number of Scriptures on this issue.

THE ARGUMENT CONCERNING IMMINENCY

If the church must go through the tribulation period, then Christ cannot come at any moment. Posttribulationists have argued that imminency could not have been true in the early church because necessary events first had to occur, such as the spread of the gospel, suffering because of persecution, the performing of great works, and Christ's promise that Peter would grow old and die (John 21:18–19). It is true that certain events had to transpire at the very beginning if the church was to be formed and the gospel was to be proclaimed. But none of the things presented by posttribulationism mandates a great length of time ,nor does it prohibit the maturing church to anticipate an any-moment return of Christ. Leon Wood concludes:

> By the time the "watching" and "hoping" passages were written, . . . the church was well under way, persecution had been suffered, marvelous works had been performed, and the gospel message had been spread far and wide. As for Peter, by the time he penned the words, "But the end of all things is at hand" (1 Pet. 4:7), sufficient years had passed to satisfy Jesus' words about Peter growing old.[26]

These events, therefore, do not prohibit the writers from speaking of the Lord's coming as imminent, since nothing had to be fulfilled by the time they wrote.

In chapter 10 (under "4. The Concept of the Imminent Coming of Jesus Christ") we looked at several passages that spoke of the coming of the Lord as imminent. The exhortations to wait, watch, and hope take on real meaning only if the Lord's coming could be at any time. It must be remembered that "imminent" does not mean "soon." Events *may* happen before the Lord returns, but no events *must* take place. All nonpretribulation views have numerous signs or events that of necessity must take place prior to the Lord's return, but this does great damage to the concept of imminency. The idea of some posttribulationists that *imminency* means that "the glorious return of Christ *could* take place within any limited time period"[27] does not do justice to the doctrine. It can be concluded that it is the pretribulational position that most comfortably fits this New Testament teaching.

THE ARGUMENT BASED ON THE OLIVET DISCOURSE

The Olivet Discourse (Matthew 24–25) has a number of important contributions to make to our understanding of future things. However, let's focus on the presence or absence of the rapture in Christ's words in Matthew 24:31. Here the Lord says, "And He will send forth His angels with a great trumpet and they will gather together His elect from the four winds, from one end of the sky to the other."

Many posttribulationists say that the gathering of the elect, along with the mentioning of clouds and a trumpet, equates this event (the second coming) with the gathering of saints at the rapture. To many it is a clear reference to the rapture. If it is, then Christ has associated it with His second coming. But several observations argue against this.

1. Matthew 24:30–31 contains no reference to the resurrection or glorifying of any saints, which is a critical part of the rapture.
2. The discourse is in answer to questions about the future of Israel and the millennial kingdom, not the church. It would be quite surprising for the Lord to speak about the rapture because it was a subject that

He had never talked about. The first mention of the rapture (John 14) would be given two days later.

3. The attempt to relate the second coming in the Olivet Discourse with the rapture in 1 Thessalonians 4 is not convincing. Simply because trumpets and clouds are found in both does not equate them.

Concerning this third point, Bible scholar Paul Feinberg has correctly stated:

> *That there should be similarities between passages dealing with a posttribulation return of Christ and a pretribulation rapture of the church should not surprise us. While the two events are different, they are not entirely dissimilar. The two events may be similar, but they are not the same. . . . The fact that there are differences . . . is more significant than the similarities.*[28]

Feinberg then goes on to point out some of the differences: (1) the angels gather the elect together in Matthew whereas it is the Lord Himself who catches the believers up, (2) the believers ascend in Thessalonians but not in Matthew, and (3) absent from Matthew is any word of the resurrection and glorification of believers. Enough dissimilarity exists to mute the claim that the rapture is present in Matthew 24.

POSTTRIBULATIONISM DIFFICULTIES

The clear rapture and second coming passages have enough differences to make any of the rapture positions a possibility. But posttribulationism finds itself faced with several difficult theological problems that make it less attractive:

- the need for nonglorified bodies to enter the millennium and the presence of "sheep" at the "sheep and goat" judgment;
- the problem of exemption from the wrath of God;
- the need for adequate time to include the three events that occur after the rapture but before the second coming;
- the distinction between the church and Israel with its unfulfilled covenant promises;

- the combining by some of a literal hermeneutic with the allegorical approach; and
- the doctrine of imminency.

Though not problem free, the pretribulational view handles all these issues with a greater ease and consistency.

CHAPTER FOURTEEN

OTHER RAPTURE
Views

THE PARTIAL RAPTURE VIEW
THE MIDTRIBULATIONAL RAPTURE VIEW
THE PREWRATH RAPTURE VIEW

Within the church, the great majority hold to either the pretribulation or posttribulation view of the rapture. It is often said that the "majority rules," but, although that may be true in politics, it is not necessarily true in theology. Having more people on your side does not validate a theological position. A widely held teaching must be evaluated on its biblical and theological merits.

This chapter will present the three rapture theories that would be considered minority views. Sincere people, who are committed to the Word and who love Christ's appearing, hold these positions; thus, we will discuss and evaluate the arguments for (1) the partial rapture view, (2) the midtribulational rapture view, and (3) the pre-wrath rapture view.

THE PARTIAL RAPTURE VIEW

Distinctive Beliefs

Within the ranks of pretribulationism is the view that only some of the believers in the church will be taken in the rapture, which will be prior to the tribulation. This view, which was first articulated in the midnineteenth century, teaches that only faithful, spiritual Christians will be taken by Christ at the rapture: "Partial rapture teaches that only those believers who are 'watching' and 'waiting' for the Lord's return will be found worthy to escape the terrors of the tribulation by being taken in the rapture."[1] Those Christians who enter the tribulation period because they were unprepared (because of their worldliness and carnality) will either be raptured sometime during the tribulation or at its end or will entirely miss being raptured.

Partial rapture advocates believe that several groups of believers will be raptured during the tribulation. These are the ones who, after entering the tribulation, turn their lives around spiritually. The tribulation will be a time of purging these believers from their sin and carnality. After this they can be raptured. Being raptured, therefore, is seen as a reward for being faithful to Christ. These times of rapture are seen in Revelation 7:9–14; 11:2; 12:5; and 16:15. If a believer is not an "overcomer," that believer will not be raised until after the millennial kingdom, thus missing out on great blessing.

THE PARTIAL RAPTURE THEORY

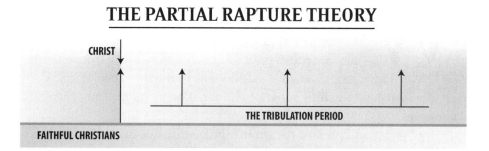

One example from Matthew illustrates the approach. In 24:40–51, God's people are exhorted to "be on the alert, for you do not know which day your Lord is coming. . . . You be ready too; for the Son of Man is coming at an hour when you do not think He will" (24:42, 44). Those who choose not to be alert and watching will be dealt with severely (24:51). Partial rapturists have pointed out that the text speaks of two women who are at the mill; one will be taken and the other left (24:41). They argue that the word for "take" (*paralambano*) is also used in John 14:3 for the rapture and that Matthew 24 is teaching that one woman is taken up in the rapture and the other woman is left to go into the tribulation. On the surface they seem to have a point, but upon further analysis the text itself does not bear out this position.

First, the focus of Matthew 24 is on the period of tribulation itself and not on the time prior to the tribulation. The two women in the text are already living in the tribulation period, not in the church age looking ahead to the tribulation. Second, the context has to do with the nation of Israel in the end times, not the church. Third, the Greek word *paralambano* is not a technical term for the rapture. It is used in a variety of ways in the New Testament and cannot be made to stand for the rapture event. Fourth, the powerful removal of believers at the rapture is simply not found in this passage. The kind of event described by Paul in 1 Thessalonians 4 is not seen in this passage.

This text in Matthew 24 is dealing with those days immediately before Christ's second coming to the earth. Therefore, it is better to understand the text as teaching that the woman at the mill who was taken away was taken away in judgment, whereas the woman who remained was left to enter into the millennial kingdom.

An Analysis of the Position

The partial rapture view is based largely on Scripture portions that emphasize the need to be waiting and watching for the Lord's return. There is blessing and reward for those who are faithful. The primary passages used to present this position are Matthew 24:40–51; 25:1–13; Luke 20:34–36; 21:36; 1 Corinthians 9:27; Philippians 3:10–12; 1 Thessalonians 5:6–10; 2 Timothy 4:8; Titus 2:13; Hebrews 9:24–28; and Revelation 3:3–11. Although this view might initially seem to have significant support, a careful analysis of these Scriptures shows that such is not really the case. In referring to many of these passages, Walvoord comments,

> *In citing these passages, little distinction is observed between references to Israel and references to the church, and passages referring to the second coming of Christ to establish the millennial kingdom are freely applied to the rapture, or translation. . . . A study of these passages as interpreted by the partial rapturists will show the confusion of interpretation.*[2]

Aside from this general observation about the manner in which Scripture texts are approached, there are some specific reasons for rejecting the partial rapture theory.

First, this view has problems in relation to the doctrine of salvation. The believer in Jesus Christ is justified by faith, not by works. All aspects of our salvation are because of the grace of God. The translation and resurrection of believers is the future part of our salvation, and we receive that aspect of our salvation by God's grace and power and not by our good works. Yet, in the partial rapture theory, this aspect of our salvation is based on merit, at least to the extent that the future aspect of our salvation is postponed.

The translation and resurrection of the church is a part of its salvation provided by grace and is a reward only in the sense that it is a fruit of faith in Christ. To accept a works principle for this important aspect of salvation is to undermine the whole concept of justification by faith through grace, the presence of the Holy Spirit as the seal of God "for the day of redemption" (Eph. 4:30), and the entire tremendous undertaking of God on behalf of those who trust Him.[3]

Second, this viewpoint contradicts the plain teaching of Scriptures that all believers are included in the rapture. In 1 Corinthians 15:51, Paul declares that "we shall all be changed." This rapture passage speaks of two categories of believers (the living and the dead) and states that all will be involved. There is no indication of exclusion. In 1 Thessalonians 4:13–17, the apostle says that those involved in the rapture are the ones who are "in Christ," whether living or dead. Those who are raptured are those who "believe that Jesus died and rose again." He does not divide believers into the watching and not watching categories of the partial rapture position.

Third, this view of the rapture contradicts a correct understanding of a key rapture passage, 1 Thessalonians 5:9–10. As we saw in an earlier study of these verses, Paul teaches that the sovereign will of God is that His children not experience His wrath but, rather, that they obtain deliverance. Paul then gives them additional encouragement concerning their removal from the earth before the time of wrath when he says, "that whether we are awake or asleep, we may live together with Him." Those who are awake and those who are asleep have often been interpreted as living and dead believers. Paul, of course, does speak of these two categories of believers in relationship to the rapture event. In 1 Thessalonians 4, Paul contrasts living and dead believers and uses the Greek word *koimao* when speaking of the dead believers ("those who are asleep"). But in 1 Thessalonians 5:10, Paul has chosen to use the Greek word *katheudo* to speak about those who are "asleep." This word is rarely, if ever, used in the New Testament for death. And in this context it refers to one who is not being watchful and alert.

The context defines its meaning since it has been used in verses 5 and 6 to describe the state of unwatchfulness against which Paul is warning. In the same way, the verb in verse 10 for "awake" . . . has been used in verse 6 to describe the state of alertness that Paul enjoins. Unless sound exegetical procedure is to be thrown to the winds, verse 10 cannot be seen as a description of living and dead Christians. Rather it refers to watchful and unwatchful believers. Hence Paul asserts that the Thessalonians have an inalienable hope that is theirs whether they watch for it or not. The believer's destiny, he insists, is not the wrath of the Day of the Lord but rather deliverance from it to live "together with" Christ. This is true "whether we are awake or asleep."[4]

Paul, of course, is very concerned that believers live godly lives, waiting eagerly for the Lord to return. But in these verses he makes the point that all believers will be taken by the Lord in spite of how watchful and alert they may be. "He has urged the Thessalonians to watch, but he also gives them assurance that the rapture is certain and does not depend on their watchfulness. All of the church will be raptured; there is no partial rapture."[5] These verses alone are a powerful argument against the partial rapture position.

Fourth, this theory divides the body of Christ, separating believers. The unity of the church has been created by God, and this vital, organic union between Christ and believers cannot be broken.[6] The New Testament doctrine of the oneness of the body of Christ stands against the partial rapture idea.

In conclusion, the theological and exegetical problems connected with this view have caused very few to embrace it. To its credit, the view certainly encourages Christians to live holy lives. But the view itself does not align well with the truths of Scripture related to salvation, the church, resurrection, and the rewarding of believers. In much of its interpretation of specific Scripture passages, it fails to make basic and necessary distinctions, such as those between Israel and the church, and the rapture and the second coming.

THE MIDTRIBULATIONAL RAPTURE VIEW

The two primary positions on the timing of the rapture continue to be the pretribulational view and the posttribulational view. A less popular, but mediating, view is that of midtribulationism.

Distinctive Beliefs

This view places the rapture at the middle of the seven-year tribulation period, or after three and one-half years have elapsed. As Ryrie explains, "In this view, only the last half of Daniel's Seventieth Week is tribulation. That is why midtribulationalism is sometimes described as a form of pretribulationalism, since it teaches that the rapture occurs before the tribulations of the last half of the seven years."[7]

One supporter of this view prefers that it be called the "midSeventieth Week theory of the rapture," noting that his view "is popularly known as the midtribulational theory, but such a term gives rise to a possible misunderstanding"—that Seventieth Week proponents are really advocating a pretribulational rapture of the church.[8]

The midtribulational rapture theory agrees with the pretribulational view in that the rapture and the second coming are viewed as two distinct events separated by a period of time. There is also agreement on the fact that the church is removed out of the world and taken to heaven prior to the time of the wrath of God. Those holding to the midtribulational viewpoint offer several lines of evidence.

1. The church has been promised persecution and tribulation, since all who live godly will experience such things. This leads to the conclusion that tribulation is in harmony with the calling of the church. Therefore, the church can expect to experience the troubles of the first half of the Seventieth Week.
2. In both Daniel and Revelation the focus is on the last half of the Seventieth Week.[9] It is during these last three and a half years that the Antichrist becomes world dictator, the Abomination of Desolation is set up in the Jerusalem temple, and the greatest judgments are poured out on the earth (cf. Dan. 7:25; 9:27; 12:7, 11; Rev. 11:2; 12:6, 14; 13:5).

3. Some great event occurs at the midpoint of the Seventieth Week that dramatically affects life on this planet. It is concluded that this event must be the rapture of the church. Most midtribulationists have connected the rapture with the sounding of the seventh trumpet in Revelation 10:7 and 11:15. It is argued that the seventh trumpet (which is the last one in the series of seven) is the same "last" trumpet mentioned in 1 Corinthians 15:52, where the rapture of the church is being discussed. The church is thus seen as being removed at that point in time.

Connected with the sounding of the seventh trumpet is the account in Revelation 11 of the two witnesses who are taken to heaven and who are said to symbolically represent the church. Concerning this third point, the seventh trumpet is believed to begins the great tribulation, because Revelation 11:18 also declares that God's wrath has now come. "'Wrath' is a word reserved for the Great tribulation. . . . The Day of Wrath has *only now come* (11:18). This means that nothing that precedes in the Seals and Trumpets can rightfully be regarded as wrath."[10]

In this view, therefore, God's wrath is poured out only in the second half of the Seventieth Week, known as the great tribulation. The seal judgments that come earlier in the book of Revelation as well as the first six trumpet judgments are not seen as a part of God's wrath but instead are declared to be the wrath of man or the wrath of Satan. The church will experience the wrath of man and Satan in the first half of the tribulation, but not the wrath of God in the second half. It is the seventh trumpet that initiates the great tribulation and signals the removal of the church from the earth at the rapture.

Those holding to a midtribulational view find it necessary to disprove the idea of imminency.[11] Obviously one cannot hold to a midtribulational rapture and believe in the imminent return of the Lord, since the first half of the Seventieth Week has notable and still-to-be-fulfilled events that serve as clear signs pointing to the soon coming of Christ. The Seventieth Week begins with the signing of a treaty between the Antichrist and the nation of Israel. And, according to the midtribulational view, the terrible judgments of the seals and six of the trumpet judgments take place before the midpoint of the tribulation. None of these is secret and unobserved by the world; therefore, it is necessary for midtribulationism to deny the imminent return of the Lord. In this they resemble posttribulationism.

THE MIDTRIBULATIONAL RAPTURE THEORY

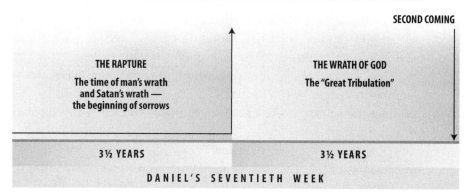

Midtribulationism differs from pretribulationism in a number of other ways, including seeing an overlap in God's dealings with Israel and the church and finding the rapture in Christ's Olivet Discourse (Matthew 24 and 25). But the heart of the view is the teaching concerning the seventh trumpet of Revelation.

An Analysis of the Position

Midtribulationists who say that the midpoint of the tribulation is extremely important are correct. When we look at this in our upcoming discussion of the tribulation period (chapter 15), we shall see that at the midpoint the Antichrist breaks his treaty with Israel, sets up the Abomination of Desolation in the Jerusalem temple, and becomes the dictator of the world who is worshiped by all people. Furthermore, at the midpoint Satan is cast out of heaven, and the great persecution of Israel begins.

But although the midpoint is an extremely important time, there is no convincing text that places the rapture at that point. The texts that speak about these midpoint events do not address a taking away of saints at that time.

The claim by midtribulationists that the seventh trumpet of Revelation 11 is the same as the last trumpet of 1 Corinthians 15:52 is tenuous at best. In *The Rapture Question*, Walvoord reminds us, "The Scriptures are full of references to trumpets," adding, "to pick out of all these references two unrelated trumpets and demand their identification because of the word

last is certainly arbitrary. Others, with no conviction relative to pre-tribu-
lationalism versus midtribulationalism, reject the identification.[12] Noting
that "in Jewish apocalyptic literature, trumpets signaled a variety of great
eschatological events," Charles Ryrie concludes, "the seventh trumpet is a
trumpet of judgment, while the trumpet in 1 Corinthians is one of resurrection and deliverance. That they indicate the same event is a gratuitous
assumption."[13]

This point is important and comes from the texts of Scripture involved.
The seventh trumpet is the last one in a series announcing judgments on
the earth, whereas the trumpet of 1 Corinthians 15 (and 1 Thessalonians
4) is a call to believers in Christ to meet the Lord and experience the completeness of their salvation. One announces judgment and the other
announces salvation, and they are not the same. The trumpet of 1 Corinthians 15 is probably called "the last" because it is signifying the completion of a program, namely, God's dealings with the church on earth.

Those of us in school settings know that a number of "last" bells ring
throughout the school day. The last bell for the eight o'clock class rings,
but that is not the last bell of the day. "Last" must be understood in relationship to the context in which it is found. Furthermore, it must be noted
that the seventh trumpet of Revelation 11 is not the last trumpet sounded
in the tribulation. In Matthew 24:31 a great trumpet is blown in connection with the gathering of the elect at the second coming. In the midtribulational scheme of things, this is three and a half years after the seventh
trumpet. This trumpet sounding in Matthew 24 is damaging to the position of midtribulationism.

Another point of dispute is whether the seventh trumpet begins the
wrath of God. The midtribulational position holds that the wrath of God
begins to be poured out on the earth with the sounding of the seventh
trumpet, said to occur at the midpoint of the tribulation. Several important points need to be made in answering this claim.

First, Revelation 6:16–17 records the response of people on the earth
who are experiencing the judgments of the seals: "They said to the mountains and to the rocks, 'Fall on us and hide us from the presence of Him
who sits on the throne, and from the wrath of the Lamb; for the great day
of their wrath has come.'" The seal judgments precede the trumpet judgments, and the Scriptures tell us that the wrath of God is present in the
seal judgments. God's wrath has already come—long before the seventh

trumpet. God's wrath, therefore, has been poured out well before the middle of the tribulation and the midtribulational rapture. In fact, a study of the seal judgments and the first six trumpet judgments shows that the world is so devastated by wars, famines, earthquakes, and many other terrible judgments that a minimum of one half the world's population perishes. Wrath is certainly present.

A second point in answering the midtribulational position is that the wrath of God encompasses the entire period of Daniel's Seventieth Week and not just the last half. It has already been seen in our study that all judgment has been given to the Lord Jesus (John 5:22). And in the heavenly scene of Revelation 5, the Lord Jesus is given the sealed scroll, which contains all the judgments of the tribulation. It is the Lord Jesus who breaks the seals and releases judgment on the earth. All the judgments (seals, trumpets, and bowls) come from the scroll and the One who breaks all the seals. All are demonstrations of divine wrath.

The midtribulationists (and others) try to say that what we are observing in the first part of the tribulation is human wrath and Satan's wrath but not God's wrath. They seem to be assuming that in order for judgment to be God's judgment it must be a direct supernatural act, such as hailstones from heaven. But that is not true.

God has often used indirect means in His judgments. For example, the prophets tell us that God used nations such as the Assyrians and the Babylonians to execute His judgments (e.g., Isa. 7:17ff.; Jer. 25:8ff.; Dan. 9:7). God's wrath is evidenced in such things as famines, plagues, and wars (cf. Ezek. 14:21). All agree that Armageddon is a demonstration of the wrath of God, and yet God uses the nations of the world, Israel, and Satan to accomplish His purposes. It is incorrect to say that a judgment is a divine judgment only if it comes directly from God. All the judgments of the seals, trumpets, and bowls are judgments from God, and they encompass the entire Seventieth Week. If that is so, then the church will be raptured out of this world before the Seventieth Week in order to escape seven years of the wrath of God.

A number of other issues cast doubt on the validity of the midtribulation position. These matters have been dealt with elsewhere and cannot be discussed at this time. They include the confusing of God's programs with the church and Israel,[14] the denial of imminency,[15] and the spiritualization of some prophecies.[16] The case for a midtribulational rapture is not strong, but the evidence against it seems substantial. Some of the same issues will be discussed in connection with the next rapture view.

THE PRE-WRATH RAPTURE VIEW

A more recent position concerning the time of the rapture is a view known as the pre-wrath rapture. This position is fundamentally a variation of the midtribulation view with a number of similarities to posttribulationism. However, it does contain a number of unusual features that set it apart from either of those two positions. A number of issues have already been dealt with in connection with those two viewpoints but will be mentioned again here as the pre-wrath view is discussed.

Distinctive Beliefs

Pre-wrath proponents believe that the church will be raptured out of the world about three-fourths of the way through the Seventieth Week of Daniel. "According to this position, the church will go through the first half and a significant part of the second half of the 70th week before being removed from the earth."[17]

Essential to this view is the division of the Seventieth Week into "three major, distinct, and identifiable periods of time: the 'beginning of sorrows,' the Great tribulation, and the Day of the Lord."[18] These three sections are not to be confused with each other, nor do they overlap. The third period within the Seventieth Week—the Day of the Lord— is the only time that experiences the wrath of God. Therefore, it is from this period only that the church is promised exemption and deliverance by rapture.

Based on 1 Thessalonians 1:10 and 5:9, the pre-wrath rapture proponents are convinced that "the Scriptures unquestionably teach" that God has not destined believers for His wrath.[19] This means that God will supernaturally remove His people out of this world prior to the time of wrath and not simply protect them in the midst of His wrath. The question is, of course, when does the wrath of God begin?

The pre-wrath view teaches that Daniel's Seventieth Week begins with the signing of the "covenant of death" between the Antichrist and the nation of Israel. The first half of this final "week," which covers three and a half years, is the "beginning of birth pangs" (Matt. 24:8). During this period the first four seal judgments are poured out on the earth.

According to the pre-wrath view, this period is not to be called the time of tribulation: "A clear fact emerges from an examination of the word *tribulation* as used in the Bible. In a prophetic context, it is used to describe only the period of time that begins in the middle of Daniel's Seventieth Week—never of the first half of it."[20] Instead, the four seal judgments are the wrath of man.[21]

After the first four seal judgments come upon the world, the midpoint of the Seventieth Week is reached. The Antichrist, who has been the protector of Israel, now breaks his covenant with Israel and begins to persecute her. He sets up the abomination of desolation in the Jerusalem temple, and "the great tribulation" begins.[22] The pre-wrath rapture view stresses two things at this point that are critical to its position:

1. The great tribulation is completely separate from the eschatological "Day of the Lord." This is important to the theory because the wrath of God is certainly part of the Day of the Lord. So to keep wrath out of the great tribulation, these two terms must be kept completely separate. The wrath of the great tribulation is the wrath of Satan.
2. The great tribulation will be cut short by the Lord. The great tribulation is so terrible that God will intervene and reduce its length from three and a half years to a period of perhaps a year and a half or two years. Marvin Rossenthal writes,

The Lord Himself teaches [that] the Great Tribulation is shortened. It is less than three and one-half years in duration. It begins in the middle of the Seventieth Week, but it does not run until the end of the Seventieth Week.... It is cut short.[23]

At the end of the shortened great tribulation, Christ will come and rapture His people out of the world. It is then that the wrath of God will break forth as the Day of the Lord comes upon the world.

The pre-wrath view sees the second coming and the rapture as one event, lasting about a year and a half, with four comings of Christ within the confines of that one second coming. At the first of these four comings Christ returns to take His people to heaven. At the second, which ends the Seventieth Week, He will descend to earth, bringing salvation to Israel, and will remain on earth for six days before returning to heaven. In the pre-wrath scheme of things, a thirty-day period of reclamation of the earth by the Lord will occur when the bowl judgments are poured out following the end of the Seventieth Week. The third of the four comings takes place after the thirty-day period, when Christ returns with His angels to defeat the Antichrist at Armageddon. This victory will be followed by a forty-five-day period, after which Christ will return to heaven. At the fourth coming Christ will return to the earth with His bride to rule the world during the millennial kingdom.[24]

THE PRE-WRATH RAPTURE THEORY

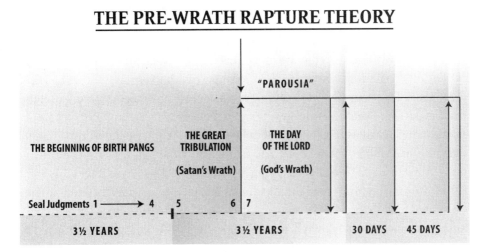

The pre-wrath rapture position has a number of unique ideas, as well as some viewpoints found in other rapture theories. All of these matters cannot be dealt with, but the most important in evaluating the validity of the position will be discussed.

An Analysis of the Position

In responding to the pre-wrath rapture position, numerous issues need to be addressed. Some matters are not significant to the pre-wrath view, such as the identification of Adolf Hitler as the Antichrist.[25] However, some matters are essential to the claims of adherents and must be discussed. To do this in a reasonably clear and concise manner, two general areas will be addressed: (1) the three divisions of the Seventieth Week proposed by the pre-wrath view, and (2) the matter of the wrath of God and the Seventieth

Week. A number of other interpretive and exegetical issues are important and could easily be included in this analysis, but if the pre-wrath rapture view fails on these two foundational matters, it has lost its case.

Analyzing the Three Divisions of the Seventieth Week

According to the pre-wrath position, there are "three major, distinct, and identifiable periods of time: the 'beginning of sorrows,' the Great Tribulation, and the Day of the Lord."[26] It is essential to the pre-wrath position that this three-part division of the Seventieth Week remain intact and without any overlap. If this three-part division is shown to be incorrect, then the pre-wrath view is significantly and perhaps fatally hurt.

Some serious doubts are immediately raised about this three-part division when we observe that both Daniel and Revelation reveal that the Seventieth Week has two parts to it; namely, two halves of three and a half years each. For example, in speaking of the coming persecution of Israel in the Seventieth Week, Daniel reveals that it will last for "time, times, and half a time" (Dan. 7:25). The book of Revelation also speaks of this persecution and says that it will last for "time and times and half a time" but then goes on to define that as being a period of 1,260 days (Rev. 12:6, 14). When we understand that the nation of Israel, along with the rest of the ancient world, followed a lunar calendar system (a month is thirty days, and a year is 360 days), then we see that the 1,260 days of Revelation 12 translates into three and a half years, or exactly half of the Seventieth Week.

Another example of the twofold division of the Seventieth Week is seen in the key matter of the covenant that is made between Israel and the leader known as the Antichrist. The signing of this covenant begins the Seventieth Week, but it is broken at the midpoint, thus dividing the week into two equal parts. As a result of this and other events, the Antichrist will rule the world for a period of forty-two months (three and a half years), demanding worship from all people (Rev. 13:5).

Although these examples do not conclusively prove that there could not be three parts to the Seventieth Week, suspicions are justifiably raised concerning the existence of three highly significant but diverse periods. The texts of Daniel and Revelation, which give important chronological indicators, never speak of the three divisions as found in the pre-wrath rapture view.

Several crucial issues impact this claim of three divisions.

First, the use of the word tribulation. The word *tribulation* is used popularly to refer to the entire seven years of Daniel's Seventieth Week. The pre-wrath view rejects this usage of the word and states that the word "should properly be omitted from an honest consideration of the time of the rapture of the Church."[27] Isolating the term *tribulation* to several years in the second half of the Seventieth Week is important to this view. However, honest and sincere scholars do legitimately use the term in reference to the entire seven-year period. The issue is not honesty but exegesis and interpretation. For example, some believe that Matthew 24:9, where the Lord says that "they will deliver you to tribulation," chronologically fits into the first three years because, in Christ's discourse, it precedes the setting up of the abomination of desolation (24:15), which occurs at the midpoint. Though this is a much discussed point, some do believe that the "tribulation" of 24:9 fits into the first half.

Furthermore, it would seem to be legitimate to use the term because certain events that take place during both halves of the Seventieth Week are associated scripturally with tribulation.

The Hebrew words for "tribulation" in the Hebrew Old Testament and the Greek word for "tribulation" in the Septuagint and Greek New Testament associate the concept of tribulation with the following things: (1) birth pangs (2 Ki. 19:3; Jer. 6:24; Jn. 16:21). (2) Sword, famine, and pestilence (2 Chr. 20:9; Job 15:20–23; Acts 7:11). (3) Removal of peace and nations warring against nations (2 Chr. 15:5–6). (4) Persecution of saints during that part of the 70th week that will precede the Abomination of Desolation of the middle of that week (Mt. 24:9, cf. Dan. 9:27). The Bible thereby associates the concept of tribulation with the same kinds of things included in the "beginning of birth pangs" . . . of Matthew 24:4–9 and the first four seals of Revelation 6:1–8.[28]

A large number of terms are used for judgment in the Old Testament, and many of these are used in passages that speak of God's future judgment. These terms are often used interchangeably and cover the entire seven-year period. In doing a study of these Old Testament terms for trouble and tribulation, Randall Price says,

While the Seventieth Week of Daniel is clearly divided into two equal periods of three-and-one-half years, and escalation or intensification is evident (as the

Olivet Discourse details), the Old Testament does not distinguish the time of tribulation into periods of "lesser" and "greater" (i.e., "Great") tribulation. Rather, it considers this experience of tribulation in its entirety as unparalleled in Israel's history.[29]

It is interesting to observe that even the term "great tribulation" used by Christ (Matt. 24:21) suggests that there must be a lesser time of tribulation, which would be associated with the beginning of birth pangs, that takes place in the first half of the Seventieth Week. The same author concludes that Daniel's use of these terms points to the entire seven-year period as tribulation.

Daniel's use of tribulation terms sees the entire Seventieth Week as a period of wrath. . . . Daniel understood that the Desolation which will occur from the middle of the Seventieth Week is connected with the covenant that also commenced this period. Therefore, the entire Seventieth Week must be of a desolating character.[30]

It is true that the focus of the Scriptures is on the second half of the Seventieth Week, and the term "great tribulation" certainly applies to that terrible time. This is reasonable and to be expected, since the focus of the Seventieth Week discussion is on Israel, and Israel lives in reasonable peace and safety during the first half while under the protection of the Antichrist. It is only at the midpoint that Israel faces intense persecution and the judgments of God increase greatly as the world rushes toward the second coming. But, contrary to the pre-wrath statement, it is not wrong to use the term *tribulation* in reference to the entire period of seven years.

Second, the Day of the Lord as distinct and separate from the great tribulation. The view of the pre-wrath rapture is that these are two distinct and completely separate periods of time within the last half of the Seventieth Week. But that is probably not the case, since they are really two designations that, in part, share the same events during the same time.

Notice that both of these times are said to be unprecedented times of trouble. As Leon Wood aptly observes, it is only possible to have one time that is "unprecedented." "There are four classic Scripture passages which speak of the time as being more severe in suffering than any other in history. Because there can be only one such time, all four must refer to the same period."[31] The four passages that speak of this unique degree of trouble are Matthew 24:21, Daniel 12:1, Joel 2:1–2, and Jeremiah 30:7. In Matthew 24:21 the Lord Jesus, apparently quoting Daniel 12:1, says that it is in the great tribulation (the second half of the Seventieth Week) that this unparalleled time of trouble takes place. Joel 2:1–2, however, says that this unparalleled time of trouble takes place in the Day of the Lord. There can be only one unparalleled time of trouble, which suggests that we are looking at the same time frame. As the Day of the Lord and the great tribulation are viewed in Scripture, we see that great trouble is true of both of them. The Day of the Lord is a time of trouble (Zeph. 1:14–15), as is the great tribulation (Matt. 24:21; Dan. 12:1).

> *Isaiah 2, 13 and Zechariah 14 are three important chapters that suggest the Day of the Lord also covers the same period as the Great Tribulation. An example is seen in Isaiah 2 where the language of Isaiah echoes the events of the sixth seal of Revelation 6:12–17. . . . A further example is seen in a comparison of catastrophic cosmic phenomenon in Isaiah 13:6–13 and the sixth seal of Revelation. . . . The events of these chapters clearly parallel each other. In addition, Zechariah 14 parallels events from the persecution of the Jews, which arises out of the Abomination of Desolation at the midpoint, to the second coming of Christ at the end of the tribulation. Therefore, the parallel language and content of these passages renders the conclusion that the Day of the Lord is not separate from the Great tribulation.*[32]

This is an important point because the concepts found in the eschatological passages of the New Testament did not materialize out of nothing; rather, they are rooted securely in the writings of the Old Testament. Parallel language is highly significant.

The two terms also have the concept of "birth pangs" associated with them (cf. Isa. 13:6–9; Jer. 30:6–7; 1 Thess. 5:2–3). The expression "that day" is used for both (Isa. 2:12–21; Zeph. 1:7–10, 14–15; Jer. 30:7; and Dan. 12:1 in the Septuagint). And both are associated with the future spiritual restoration of Israel (Deut. 4:27–30; 30:1–3; Jer. 30:7–9, 22; Zech. 12:2–3, 9–14; 13:1–2; 14:1–3).

> *These comparisons demonstrate that several of the same concepts and terms are associated with the Day of the Lord, the Time of Jacob's Trouble, and the*

Great Tribulation in the Scriptures. These consistent associations . . . indicate that the Day of the Lord will cover or at least include the same period as the Time of Jacob's trouble and the Great Tribulation.[35]

The claim of absolute distinction between these terms, which is foundational to the pre-wrath scheme of things, is simply not supportable. These two terms (along with "the time of Jacob's trouble" found in Jeremiah) are actually used of the same time frame, referring at least to the final three and a half years of the Seventieth Week.

A word now needs to be said about the way phrases and words are used. It is, of course, important to accurately define words and phrases in order to come to an understanding of the text of the Bible. However, wrong conclusions can be reached if a narrow definition is assigned to a word that is actually quite broad in its meaning.

For example, take our English word *club*. A "club" is defined as a "stout stick or staff." But a "club" is a little more than a stout stick to a golfer, who just spent a great deal of money on his new set of golf clubs. A "club" is also an organization that exists for some specific purpose; joining the Lions Club has nothing to do with a stout stick. To a gambler, a "club" is a playing card with black markings shaped like a three-leaf clover, and he would much prefer having an "ace of clubs" than a stout stick. If I were to say, "Here is the club," I could mean any of the above, and the context of the situation would have to determine what "club" means. Obviously, it would be unwise to arbitrarily assign a meaning to the word and declare that, since it quite legitimately means "a stout stick," it must mean that wherever it is found. We immediately see that we would reach some wrong conclusions.

This is a constant temptation faced by those who interpret the Scriptures. And it seems apparent that defining a word narrowly and applying it broadly has been done in a number of places by proponents of the pre-wrath rapture view.

Third, the shortening of the great tribulation. Another essential element for the pre-wrath position is to shorten the great tribulation from three and a half years to a shorter period of time. This must be done to have a year or so available for the appearance of the Day of the Lord during the second half of the Seventieth Week, which the pre-wrath view sees as the only time when God's wrath is poured out on the earth. Because the pre-wrath view allows no overlap between the great tribulation and the Day of the Lord and because there is no wrath of God in the great tribulation, it is essential to shrink the great tribulation so that God's wrath may then appear in the next segment of time identified as the Day of the Lord. When speaking about the great tribulation, what did Jesus mean when He said, "And unless those days had been cut short, no life would have been saved" (Matt. 24:22)? As we have seen, the pre-wrath view says that the original period of time of three and a half years for the great tribulation was shortened.[34] But this is probably not what the verse is saying.

The approach of the pre-wrath proponents on this important issue reveals a logical fallacy, Karleen notes:

> *We have no indication what the time period is shortened from and what it is shortened to. It is perfectly reasonable to assume that it might be shortened from ten years to seven, or from seven to three and one-half. In this the author has demonstrated the fallacy of the false dilemma again. The author has allowed only one choice—that the period is shortened from three and one-half years to a smaller duration. The Bible does not limit the reader to that one choice.*[35]

In addition, the verb "shortened" ("cut off") is used by Jesus to teach that God had already decreed in the past that the great tribulation would last three and a half years. Jesus' point is that, if God had chosen to let this terrible time of intense judgment last any longer than the three and a half years, no human being would survive. In Matthew 24:22 and the parallel passage in Mark 13:20, the verbs are aorist tense, which normally has no time significance. This is true except when in the indicative mood with the augment; then they express past time.[36] That is the case here. So Jesus is teaching that the decree of God, made in eternity past, had already determined that the great tribulation would be just three and a half years and not some longer period of time. This interpretation is verified by noting what the Scriptures say about the length of the great tribulation.

Finally, Jesus was not teaching the shrinking of the great tribulation from three and a half years to about two years, because the great tribulation covers the entire three-and-a-half year period. The great tribulation begins at the midpoint of the Seventieth Week, because Jesus connects its beginning with the setting up of "the Abomination of Desolation" in the Jerusalem temple (Matt. 24:15–21; cf. Dan. 9:27).

As observed earlier, the statement of the Lord in Matthew 24:21 echoes the words of Daniel 12:1—both passages speak of the unique time of trouble for Israel and the world. Daniel 12:6–7 reveals the length of time involved. In those verses an angel asks how long the events of Daniel 12:1 would last. His question is answered by another being who said it would be for "a time, times, and half a time." As we saw earlier, this phrase designates three and a half years. So the angel is told that the great tribulation will last for three and a half years. When this time period is over, God will have accomplished His purpose of breaking the rebellious, apostate spirit of Israel and bringing the nation back to Himself (cp. Dan. 12:7 with 9:24).

It is interesting that Daniel 12 not only teaches that the great tribulation will last for three and a half years but reinforces the idea that the purpose of this period is to bring Israel back to the Lord, something that does not involve the church. It is worth noting that in Daniel 12:7 the one giving the answer to the angel's question confirmed the validity of his answer on oath, raising his hands toward heaven. As John Whitcomb points out, "The two hands raised to heaven emphasizes the tremendous solemnity of the oath being uttered."[37] Renald Showers adds an insightful observation:

> *Since he put his answer in the form of an oath, and since he based that oath on the eternal God who is sovereign and truthful, he asserted the truthfulness and reliability of his answer in the strongest way possible. He affirmed the absolute certainty of the Great tribulation's lasting for three and one-half years, until Israel's rebellion against God ends at the end of the 70th week.*[38]

Revelation 12 corroborates the idea that the great tribulation will last throughout the last three and a half years of the Seventieth Week. In that chapter the apostle John tells of the persecution of Israel (the woman) by Satan (the dragon). He reveals that this terrible persecution of Israel will last for 1,260 days and "time and times and half a time" (12:6, 14), which is the entire second half of the Seventieth Week. Israel will receive protection by fleeing into the wilderness (12:14). This is the same point that Jesus made in Matthew 24. He declared that at the midpoint of the Seventieth Week, when the abomination is set up in the temple, that great persecution would break out on Israel. He warned Israel to flee to the wilderness areas when they saw that event take place because terrible persecution would erupt.

This persecution of Israel will last throughout the great tribulation (for 1,260 days, or three and a half years) and not for a shorter length of time. This is further verified by Daniel 7:21-25 and Revelation 13:5-7, which teach that the persecution of Israel led by the Antichrist will last for forty-two months (three and a half years), continuing until the Lord returns and delivers His people at the second coming.

Several things can be concluded:

- The "shortening" does not refer to the shrinking of the three and a half years of the great tribulation but refers to God's decision in the past not to allow this terrible time of persecution to be any longer than three and a half years.
- The key chronological passages of Daniel 7, 9, 12, and Revelation 12 and 13 all speak of this time as three and a half years.
- The pre-wrath claims on this point are unfounded, leading to the conclusion that the pre-wrath view is in serious trouble because the system depends on a three-part division of the Seventieth Week.

Fourth, the beginning and the length of the Day of the Lord. The pre-wrath rapture view teaches that the Day of the Lord begins about three-fourths of the way through the Seventieth Week and continues until the second coming, or a little beyond. This Day of the Lord is seen lasting about a year, or perhaps two. Again this view has established a position that does not fit all the facts of Scripture. Although a detailed analysis of the Day of the Lord is not within the scope of this study, certain truths need to be clarified:

1. The future Day of the Lord is greater in length than one or two years.
2. The Day of the Lord has two aspects.
3. The starting point for the Day of the Lord will come unexpectedly.

First, the Scriptures indicate that the future Day of the Lord is greater in length than a year or two. The Day of the Lord includes the elements of judgment on the nation of Israel, judgment of Gentile nations, and the coming of Messiah to deliver and restore Israel (e.g., Isa. 30:23-25; 34:1-8; 35:1-10; Joel 2:28-32; 3:1-21; Zech. 14:1-21; Zeph. 3:8, 16-20). Though judgment is a major emphasis, the goal of the Day of the Lord is not judgment but the bringing in of the messianic kingdom.

Dozens of times, the Day of the Lord itself is said to include the time of blessing and salvation in connection with the coming and rule of Messiah.[39] So the full and complete Day of the Lord has elements of darkness (judgment) and light (blessing). This would mean that the Day of the Lord would include the time of judgment (the Seventieth Week) and time of Messiah's kingdom rule (the millennium). To be the Day of the *Lord*, it must "involve His rule of the world system during the Millennium," argues Showers. "How could the Day of the Lord fully demonstrate who He is— the sovereign God of the universe—without the sovereign exercise of His rule in visible form over the entire world?"[40] If this is correct, the length of the Day of the Lord is not simply a year or two, as proposed by the pre-wrath rapture view.

Second, the Day of the Lord has two aspects—a broad sense and a narrow sense. The broad, or extended, sense is the one just discussed, that is, the Seventieth Week followed by the millennial reign of Messiah. The narrow sense of the Day of the Lord looks at the very specific time when Christ will return to earth with the great judgments that accompany that moment in time. For example, Zechariah 14 and Joel 3 speak of the Day of the Lord as being that day when the Lord returns to fight against the armies that have gathered to fight against Israel. We understand that He will do this at the second coming (Rev. 19:11–21). This is the time that is referred to as the great and terrible Day of the Lord.

> *We should note that Joel 3:14–15 indicates that the sun, moon, and stars will be darkened when the narrow Day of the Lord is near. Those heavenly bodies will be darkened before "the great and terrible Day of the Lord to come." It is obvious from this that Joel 3 and 2 are referring to the same Day of the Lord. We can conclude, then, that the narrow day of Joel 3 and Zechariah 14 is to be identified with the great and terrible Day of the Lord—the day on which Christ will come to the earth.*[41]

The pre-wrath rapture view has followed the lead of posttribulationism and focused exclusively on the narrow aspect of the Day of the Lord. Here is one illustration of the point made earlier, that of taking a legitimate (but narrow) definition of a term and applying it everywhere the term is found. This has led to the erroneous conclusion that the Day of the Lord is a very short period of judgment at the end of the Seventieth Week. What is true is that the narrow aspect of the Day of the Lord is simply the climax of the judgment aspect of the broad Day of the Lord.

Third, the starting point of the Day of the Lord is unexpected and has distinct elements. The pre-wrath view has it beginning with the breaking of the seventh seal (Rev. 8:1), which is seen about three-fourths of the way through the Seventieth Week. But based on 1 Thessalonians 5, several distinct elements of that day argue against that idea. Of that day the apostle Paul wrote: "The day of the Lord will come just like a thief in the night. While the unbelievers are saying, 'Peace and safety!' then destruction will come upon them suddenly like birth pangs upon a woman with child" (vv. 2–3).

> *The comparison lies in the suddenness and unexpectedness of both events. The thief comes suddenly and at a time that cannot be predetermined; so the Day of the Lord will come suddenly when people are not expecting it.* . . . *The coming of the thief at* night *simply serves to emphasize his secretive and unannounced coming.*[42]

Paul is making the point that no forewarning is given to the world for the beginning of the Day of the Lord. This makes good sense if the Day of the Lord starts when the Seventieth Week begins, since there will be no previous warnings given. The element of surprise, which is emphasized by the comparison, is clearly there. Such would not be the case if the Day of the Lord did not begin until approximately three-fourths of the way through the Seventieth Week, since Christ's great sign of the "Abomination of Desolation" (at the midpoint), several years of great tribulation, and numerous other signs and events would have just transpired. It would not seem that the coming of the day would be sudden or unexpected as Paul taught.

Paul also teaches that the unbelieving people on whom the day suddenly breaks forth will be saying "Peace and safety" when it happens. "'Peace' here points to circumstances that do not evoke a feeling of alarm; 'safety' has the thought of being unshaken, secure from enemies and danger. . . . They feel that everything is safe and secure and see no outward evidence to dispute the feeling."[43] Immediately before the Day of the Lord overtakes them there is a worldwide feeling of security. This fatal delusion will be shattered by the sudden, unexpected coming of the Day of the Lord.

When will mankind possibly be saying "Peace and safety" and really believing that such exists? Before the Seventieth Week is certainly a possibility. Perhaps man's efforts at attaining world peace will achieve a certain amount of success and people will feel secure from destructive wars. We, of course, cannot be sure what will cause this worldwide feeling of security. But it seems highly unlikely that three-fourths of the way through the Seventieth Week that people will be saying such things. According to the pre-wrath view, the sixth seal will have just been broken, which will result in earthquakes and great cosmic disturbances that will cause incredible terror to the inhabitants of the earth (Rev. 6:12–17). In fact, more than one-fourth of the world's population will have recently been destroyed by famines, disease, and widespread warfare on the earth. It does not seem likely that the people of the world would be saying "Peace and safety" when more than a billion people have recently perished and incredible cosmic disturbances are taking place. But it would make sense for them to be saying "Peace and safety" if the Day of the Lord begins at the start of the Seventieth Week, well before the terrible events that take place throughout the Seventieth Week.

The pre-wrath rapture view does not align itself well with the beginning and length of the Day of the Lord as portrayed in the Scriptures. This is a critical matter to this viewpoint, since it rests squarely on the theory that the Seventieth Week has three distinct parts to it.

Analyzing the Wrath of God and the Seventieth Week

As we have seen already, the pre-wrath rapture view holds that the wrath of God is confined to approximately a year or two at the end of the Seventieth Week. In this view the wrath of God begins with the seventh seal judgment. But the evidence is that the wrath of God actually encompasses the entire Seventieth Week period and not just a short period of time at the end of the Seventieth Week. The duration of the wrath of God has been dealt with in our previous discussions of the pretribulational view and the posttribulational view. In those discussions, several key points were made that apply to the pre-wrath position. Those points and several others will be considered.

First, the judgments recorded by the apostle John in Revelation 6–19 come from Christ, not from Satan, the Antichrist, or mankind. It is the Lord Jesus, as the One to whom all judgment has been given, who breaks the seals (John 5:22; Rev. 5:1–14). As Jesus breaks each seal, judgment takes place, showing the divine character of each judgment. He is clearly in charge of all the judgments. The pre-wrath view counters this by saying that if the seals are God's wrath then God must be held responsible for the activities of the Antichrist (the first seal) as well as other evil matters.[44] But this does not ring true with the sovereignty of God.

> *This view of the seals demonstrates a faulty understanding of God's sovereignty. God is active in all the affairs of the universe. . . . Weren't Satan's activities toward Job under God's control? Wasn't Babylon, as a persecutor of Israel under God's control? The Old Testament actually describes God as raising up Babylon to discipline His people. Orthodox theologians have regularly stated that God controls human and angelic affairs but still cannot be charged with sin. It is theologically consistent for God to control the events of the first five seals and still not be chargeable with sin. Here, as elsewhere, God uses human beings and angels to bring about His purposes.[45]*

God may choose to use Satan and evil men as His agents, but there is no doubt as to the source of these seal judgments during the early days of the Seventieth Week. The Scriptures reveal how God time and again used evil men to accomplish His purposes, so it should not be surprising that such is the case during the Seventieth Week. Take, for example, the pharaoh of Egypt who did so much harm to Israel. God clearly takes credit for raising him up. The Lord states that He knew and created the personality of Pharaoh to accomplish His purposes (cf. Ex. 9:13–16 and Rom. 9:17–22). God does use Satan and the Antichrist to accomplish His great purposes during the Seventieth Week, and this is consistent with what He has done in the past. An interesting illustration of this is found in Revelation 17:17, where the forces of the Antichrist destroy the apostate religious system. The text says that "God has put it in their hearts to execute His purpose by having a common purpose." We can conclude that all the seal, trumpet, and bowl judgments (Revelation 6–16) are divine judgments even though God may use Satan and people as His agents.

Second, the wrath of God is seen throughout the Seventieth Week as we understand the nature of the first four seal judgments, which bring about the death of one-fourth of the world's population. These seal judgments include famine, disease, the sword (war), and wild beasts.

Ezekiel 14:12–21 says that these four things are expressions of God's wrath. And as noted in chapter 13 (see the discussion under "The Argument from the Nature of the Tribulation Period"), Ezekiel 14 is but one of many passages in the Old Testament that identify those four things as evidences of the wrath of God. The Old Testament background to the book of Revelation points to the seals as being evidences of God's wrath. The Old Testament does not identify these as the wrath of Satan or mankind, which is what the pre-wrath rapture view holds. The seal judgments occur prior to the midpoint of the Seventieth Week, making a strong statement for the wrath of God being in the first half of the Seventieth Week.

Third, the wrath of God is seen in the seal judgments because of the statement made in connection with the sixth seal in Revelation 6:16–17. At the breaking of the sixth seal, the terrified people of the earth will cry out for the mountains and rocks to fall on them, declaring that the great day of God's wrath "has come" (Gk: *elthen*). It is the position of the pre-wrath rapture that this is the people's pronouncement that the wrath of God is about to begin and that this sixth seal is a forewarning of the soon arrival of the Day of the Lord, which will bring the wrath of God.[46] The pre-wrath view cannot allow the verb "has come" to refer to a present (or past) situation since God's wrath is still something future. It is taught that the breaking of the seventh seal begins the Day of the Lord and the outpouring of the wrath of God.

However, does the word *elthen*, which is in the aorist tense, refer to something in the future? The other five times it is used by John in Revelation, none are futuristic. In examining the occurrences of *elthen* in Revelation that involve the action of people (5:7; 7:13; 8:3; 17:1, 10; 21:9), we find that every one of them describes an event that occurs prior to the time of speaking. None is futuristic.[47]

> *While* elthen *may be an ingressive or a dramatic aorist, it could just as well be constantive or complexive. This would mean that the wrath of God has come, not just in the sixth seal, but in the six seals viewed as a whole. . . . It may be that with the increased severity of the judgments, people are just beginning to recognize that this is not simply a stroke of bad luck, but the outpouring of God's wrath.*[48]

The context is important in determining the meaning of the statement that the wrath of God "has come." The statement of these terrified people on the earth at the breaking of the sixth seal is on the basis of events that they have experienced, not on the basis of events that will take place. The great earthquake and cosmic disturbances are not seen as the wrath of Satan or man but, rather, the wrath of God.

> *The verb* elthen *("has come") is aorist indicative, referring to a previous arrival of the wrath, not something that is about to take place. Men see the arrival of this day at least as early as the cosmic upheaval that characterize the sixth seal (6:12–14), but upon reflection they probably recognize it was already in effect with the death of one-fourth of the population (6:7–8), the worldwide famine (6:5–6), and the global warfare (6:3–4).*[49]

The wrath of God is evidenced in all of the seal judgments, not simply the seventh one. The cry of those experiencing the sixth seal indicates that the wrath of God was being experienced and had been experienced in the past.

There are a number of lines of argument showing that God's wrath is to be found throughout the Seventieth Week. However, just *one more argument will be included at this time: the concept of "birth pangs."* The judgments of the end time Seventieth Week is often expressed by the figurative language of the travail connected with childbirth (e.g., Isa. 13:8–9; 66:7–8; Jer. 22:23; 48:41; Hos. 13:13; Mic. 4:9–10).

> *On the one hand, the figure is applied to the experience of tribulation because its application to males or to the nation of Israel, is tantamount to reducing them to the helpless state of women at the time of birth. On the other hand, the involuntary and uncontrollable nature of birth-pangs, as well as their intensification leading ultimately to a time of deliverance, well pictured the concept of a time of divine judgment that must run its course until the promise of new life could be experienced.*[50]

So the term *birth pangs* (*odin*), which is used by the Lord Jesus (Matt. 24:8) and the apostle Paul (1 Thess. 5:3), has a rich Old Testament heritage. The Lord Jesus placed the beginning of the birth pangs in the first half of the Seventieth Week. He said that they would begin prior to the midpoint when the "Abomination of Desolation" is set up in the Jerusalem temple. The apostle Paul (using the same word) states that these birth pangs begin when the Day of the Lord begins. This would fit exactly with the Lord's teaching and place the beginning stages of the birth pangs in the first half of the Seventieth Week. In fact, Paul's statement would place their inception at the start of the Seventieth Week.

But according to the pre-wrath position, the Day of the Lord (with the wrath of God) starts three-fourths of the way through the Seventieth Week. So an attempt is made to distinguish between Paul's use of the term and the Lord's use of it. "What becomes abundantly clear is this: The time immediately prior to the Day of the Lord is likened to a woman in travail (hard labor), but the first part of the Seventieth Week is likened to a woman with beginning birth pangs," writes pre-wrath proponent Marvin Rosenthal.[51]

But there is no linguistic basis for making such a significant distinction. The use of the same term rather points to the same event and the same time. The birth pangs that represent the judgments of God are seen in both halves of the Seventieth Week. In fact, J. Randall Price says Jesus' statement in the Olivet Discourse about the birth pangs (Matt. 24:8) indicates "specifically that the events of the first half of the tribulation (vss. 4–7) are merely the 'beginning,' with the expectation of greater birth-pangs in the second half (the 'great tribulation'). Based on this analogy, the entire period of the Seventieth Week is the experience of birth pangs."[52]

Jesus, in general terms, described the birth pangs as famines, wars, earthquakes, and false religions. These line up with the first seal judgments in Revelation 6, leading us to conclude that they are the same. The apostle Paul said that the Day of the Lord will come suddenly on this world like birth pangs comes upon a pregnant woman. The pregnant woman, of course, realizes that she is going to experience labor but does not know the exact moment.

Paul used the singular form of "birth pang" with a definite article—"the birth pang." "It is a woman's very first birth pang, not the later hard labor pangs, that comes suddenly at the start of the painful process of giving birth. Thus . . . Paul was teaching that the beginning of the broad Day of the Lord will be characterized by the very first birth pang."[53]

The fact that the birth pangs are at the beginning (or at least in the first half) of the Seventieth Week and that they are often associated with the wrath of God in the Day of the Lord (e.g., Isa. 13:8–9) leads us to conclude that God's wrath is found in the first half and, therefore, throughout the

Seventieth Week. If the latter stages of the birth pangs in the second half of the Seventieth Week are seen as God's wrath, the wrath of God is also in the first half, since it is the same "birth" that is in view. The birth pangs go all the way through the Seventieth Week and culminate in the salvation and rule of the Messiah.

REVISITING THE RAPTURE QUESTION

In concluding this brief analysis, it has been seen that the pre-wrath rapture view rests on its threefold division of the Seventieth Week and on its theory that the wrath of God is found only in the Day of the Lord, which is a period of a year or two in the second half of the Seventieth Week. In light of a number of linguistic, exegetical, and theological considerations, we conclude that the base on which this view rests has significant problems. The problems are so significant that the view is untenable.

Although chapters 12-14 have devoted much space to the various views concerning when the rapture will take place, the discussion has been necessary, as every believer will be personally involved at this grand event. Each answer to the rapture question contains some positive ideas that should cause study and meditation on the Word of God. No view is problem free. But some views seem to have problems that are so pervasive that real doubt is cast on their validity. Of all the views, it is our conclusion that pretribulationism best handles the combined theological, exegetical, and hermeneutical considerations.

Again, in all of this discussion we must not forget that the doctrine of the rapture was not given to stimulate a combative spirit among the saints but, rather, a worshipful spirit toward the Lord Jesus. This doctrine is to bring comfort and encouragement, not animosity. It remains the blessed hope to all those who love His appearing. "Amen. Come Lord Jesus" (Rev. 22:20).

CHAPTER FIFTEEN

Daniel's

SEVENTIETH WEEK

(THE TRIBULATION PERIOD)

I f you are a sports fan, you know that the final few minutes—or even seconds—of the game can be the most dramatic. These moments are often filled with daring or desperate strategies by coaches and players. Every football team has its "two-minute offense," when normal plays and procedures are set aside and risks are taken in order to score quickly. Likewise in basketball, even the players are amazed at how much can happen in the final sixty seconds. Most fans can remember games when last-second heroics or errors have brought the "thrill of victory" or the "agony of defeat."

In sports, the final moments can be crucial and often are unique. So it is with those final moments of man's rule and existence on this earth. After thousands of years of human history, it is the final seven that are so crucial and so unique. Daniel's "Seventieth Week" (the tribulation) is, of course, no game. It is a deadly serious spiritual battle between the Lord and Satan. It decides who will be worshiped as ruler of the world and determines the eternal destiny of billions of human beings. In one sense this contest is simply a continuation of what has been going on since the fall of Satan and man. But it is carried on with much greater intensity because it is clear to all that time is running out.

Unlike many sporting events, however, there is no question about the outcome of this spiritual contest between the Lord and Satan. The Lord Jesus wins. He returns to this planet as the conquering King of Kings and

Lord of Lords, the righteous and powerful ruler of the universe. But it is the events of those seven years leading up to His triumphal return that we now want to investigate.

Throughout the Scriptures a great deal of information can be found about this period of time and the time that follows it. The sheer amount of information and the varying opinions about a number of the details make an exhaustive study of Daniel's "Seventieth Week" (the tribulation) an impossibility in this chapter. Of course, some issues related to this period of time have already been discussed in the chapters on the various rapture views and do not need to be repeated at this point. Not every Scripture portion can be dealt with here, and concerning those that are discussed there may be valid differing opinions on a number of details.

THE TERMINOLOGY OF THE TRIBULATION

The Scriptures employ several terms when referring to the seven years prior to the second coming of Christ. These terms reveal something of the nature of this period of time.

1. *The Day of the Lord.* The phrase "Day of the Lord" is used in the Bible to emphasize special interventions of God in human history. His victory over His enemies and His sovereignty over the universe are emphasized. The phrase is used in a noneschatological sense when in past times the Lord's authority over the world was demonstrated by His executing of judgment on Gentile nations and on Israel. The phrase is used of the future as well—the Lord will intervene in human history to judge the nations, discipline Israel, and establish His rule in the messianic kingdom (e.g., Isa. 30:23-25; 34:1-8; 35:1-10; Joel 2:28-32; 3:1-21; Zeph. 3:8, 16-20; Zech. 14:1-21).

As we observed in the previous chapter (related to the pre-wrath rapture view), the future Day of the Lord includes darkness (judgment in the Seventieth Week) and light (blessing in the messianic kingdom). We also observed that the judgmental aspect of the Day of the Lord includes a broad aspect (the entire seven-year period of Daniel's Seventieth Week and a narrow aspect (the actual event of the second coming and the judgments that are part of the coming).

2. *The tribulation and the great tribulation.* These terms refer to that future time of unique suffering and trouble that will be experienced by Israel and the Gentile world (e.g., Deut. 4:30; Matt. 24:9, 21, 29; Rev. 7:14). From an earlier discussion, it was concluded that the word *tribulation* can legitimately be used for the entire seven-year period of Daniel's Seventieth Week and that the term *great tribulation* should apply to the second half of the week. The terms will be used this way in our discussion.

3. *The time of Jacob's trouble.* This phrase is used by the prophet Jeremiah (30:7) and focuses on the unparalleled time of trouble and suffering that will be experienced by the nation of Israel. The "time of Jacob's trouble" (KJV) and the Day of the Lord are both declared to be the time of unparalleled trouble for Israel. Since there can be only one such time, it is concluded that these two refer to the same period. The "time of Jacob's trouble" has the same characteristics as the Day of the Lord, and this reinforces the conclusion that they refer to the same period of time, namely, the seven-year tribulation period.

4. *The wrath of God.* This phrase is used to refer to the entire tribulation period, since only the wrath of God could qualify as "the unparalleled time of trouble" (e.g., Zeph. 1:15; 1 Thess. 1:10; 5:9; Rev. 11:18; 15:1; 16:1). Satan's wrath and man's wrath may be terrible indeed, but they cannot compare to the wrath of God. Since unparalleled trouble is going to be experienced and since it covers the entire period of tribulation, then we conclude that the wrath of God speaks of the entire tribulation.

5. *The Seventieth Week of Daniel.* This term is based on Daniel 9:24–27, where Daniel was informed that God was going to have seventy weeks (490 years) of special dealings with Israel in order to accomplish six great purposes. The final week of seven years (the Seventieth Week) is yet future and is commonly called the tribulation.

There are perhaps several dozen other designations for this final seven years, all of which emphasize it as a time of great trouble and distress, particularly for the nation of Israel.[1]

THE BEGINNING AND THE LENGTH OF THE TRIBULATION

The removal of the church at the rapture precedes the tribulation, but there is no direct connection between the two events. There could well be a short period of time (perhaps weeks or months) between the rapture and the beginning of the tribulation. The tribulation period itself begins when the Antichrist signs a seven-year covenant with the nation of Israel (Dan. 9:27 and Isa. 28:14–22). This covenant is made to guarantee the security of Israel and is *the* event that marks the beginning of the last seven years prior to Christ's return.

The length of the tribulation (seven years) is based on Daniel 9:24–27. As we have observed in previous discussions, this is a vitally important portion of Scripture. Daniel 9 records the prayer of Daniel, who was greatly concerned about the future of the people of Israel and the city of Jerusalem. At the time of this prayer, the nation had been in Babylonian captivity for almost seventy years, and Daniel knew from Jeremiah's prophecies that the captivity was supposed to last only seventy years. He acknowledged that God was right and just in disciplining Israel but also pointed out that God's credibility was at stake (if God did not take the people back to the land). Daniel pleaded with God to fulfill His commitment to restore Israel.

As Daniel prayed for his people and his city, the angel Gabriel was sent to inform him that God was going to have 490 years (seventy "weeks") of special dealings with Israel. When the 490 years had run their course, God would have accomplished six great goals related to Israel. Daniel was told that *after* the sixty-ninth week was over and *before* the seventieth would begin, two significant events would take place: (1) the Messiah would be cut off, and (2) the Jerusalem temple would be destroyed. As history bears out, the sixty-nine weeks have run their course, the Messiah was killed, and Jerusalem was destroyed. But what has not taken place is the final seven years (one "week") of God's special dealings with Israel. These final seven years are yet future but will not begin until the covenant between Israel and the Antichrist is signed.

THE PRIMARY PURPOSES OF THE TRIBULATION

God always has excellent reasons for doing what He does. He, of course, does not always share His purposes with His creatures, but often He does. And while He certainly has not revealed all of His purposes for this seven-year period, He has given two major reasons for the existence of this period of time.

First, it is the purpose of God to judge wicked, unbelieving men and nations for their sinfulness. The creature will be held responsible to the Creator for violating His laws and standards. During the days of the tribulation, God will deal with all the nations of the world (e.g., Ps. 2:5; Jer. 25:30–32; Zech. 12:3; 2 Thess. 2:12; Rev. 3:10; 6:15). In the three series of judgments in the tribulation (the seals, trumpets, and bowls), the nations of the earth will receive deserved retribution for their wickedness. These judgments are another step in dealing with sin in preparation for the Messiah's reign of righteousness on earth. But it is clear that God could judge sinners completely in a matter of moments and does not need seven years. This suggests that judgment, though important in the plan of God, is not the main reason for the seven-year period of tribulation.

The second, and probably the greatest, purpose of God in the tribulation is to bring salvation to the nation of Israel, preparing them for the messianic kingdom. The Scriptures indicate that the tribulation has a definite Jewish character (e.g., Jer. 30:7; Dan. 9:24; 12:1; Matt. 24:15–20).

Daniel 9:24–27 is a central passage on the matter of God's purposes related to Israel and the period of tribulation. The six great goals of God revolve around "Daniel's people" and "Daniel's holy city." Daniel had prayed passionately about his people and his holy city, and God answered his prayer concerning these two matters. The Lord said that He was committed to accomplishing these six specific purposes during a 490-years period which will be finalized in the last seven years. These verses clearly place Israel at the center of God's purposes for the tribulation. The six goals (mentioned in 9:25) are as follows.

1. "To finish the transgression." The word "transgression" focuses on the deliberate rebellion and apostasy of Israel. This willful rebellion will be brought to an end by the great events of the tribulation, and Israel will turn to the Lord in faith.

2. "To make an end of sin." The vain, sinful national existence of Israel will come to an end when they repent and mourn for their sin in the tribulation and turn to their Messiah.

3. "To make atonement for iniquity." This purpose is undoubtedly looking at the cross of Jesus Christ, since it is the only thing that takes care of sin. This is, of course, the basis for Israel's cleansing and being brought into the new covenant. The total and complete payment for sin was in the past at the cross, but it will be in the future that the provision of the cross will be applied to the nation of Israel (cf. Zech. 12:10; 13:1; Isa. 59:20–21; Ezek. 36:25–27; Jer. 31:31–34).

4. "To bring in everlasting righteousness." The nation of Israel and the city of Jerusalem are in view in Daniel 9, and neither one becomes righteous (holy) until their repentance. Messiah's righteous kingdom is not established until His people turn to Him during the tribulation. Then Messiah's righteous kingdom can come.

5. "To seal up vision and prophecy." This goal indicates a complete fulfillment of prophecy coupled with the idea that there will be no additional prophetic information given. With the repentance of Israel in the tribulation, the Lord Jesus can return in His glory and establish the forever kingdom of God, reclaiming the earth from the usurper, Satan, and bringing about the complete restoration of man as prophesied.

6. "To anoint the most holy." This has to do with the anointing of the most holy place (i.e., the temple) at the return of the Messiah. The final fulfillment of God's six goals for the seventy weeks is based on the work of the Lord Jesus on the cross. Once the full and complete redemptive price for sin was paid, it then became possible for God to act and restore Israel and to fulfill His covenant promises to them. The restoring of Israel will be the focus of the tribulation period.

As the terrible events of the tribulation unfold, and especially as the Jewish people enter into the great tribulation, they will suffer terrible persecution at the hands of the Antichrist, and they will begin turning to their Messiah, who centuries before died for them. God will use those terrible times and wicked individuals to pull the spiritual blinders off the nation.

As Fruchtenbaum says of Daniel 12:7, one goal of the tribulation is "to break the power or the will of the Jewish nation." The tribulation will continue and will not end until this happens. "God intends to break the will of the holy people in order to bring about a national regeneration."[2] Israel will become a believing nation and God will have fulfilled His great purpose (cf. Ezek. 39:22; Jer. 31:31–34; Mal. 4:5–6; Rom. 11:25–27).

We should not forget that all this is linked with the covenant promises made by God to Israel in the Old Testament. Many of those unconditional, eternal promises have not yet been fulfilled and await Israel's national regeneration. It is only as a saved nation that Israel can enter into the Messiah's kingdom and experience the blessings of the Abrahamic covenant.

SOME KEY PERSONALITIES IN THE TRIBULATION

Probably all would agree that God and Satan are the key persons involved in the great conflict of the tribulation. But the Scriptures speak of a number of human personalities who play significant roles in that unfolding drama known as the Day of the Lord.

The Man Called "Antichrist"

The most significant (though evil) individual who appears in the tribulation is the man commonly called the Antichrist. The Scriptures refer to him using a number of different titles that reveal something of his character. It is interesting that the title people use most often of him (the Antichrist) is really used only once in the Bible (1 John 2:18). The title itself, however, is a good one because it says something significant about his character and intentions.

The Greek preposition *anti* can carry with it the idea of opposition. For example, if someone is against a labor union forming at their company, he might be called antiunion. The Antichrist is very much against the Lord Jesus Christ and His purposes. The same preposition can convey the idea of "in place of" or being a substitute. That would also hold true of the Antichrist, since it seems that he will be Satan's substitute messiah.

He is known by other names as well. In 2 Thessalonians 2:3 he is referred to as the "man of lawlessness." This title emphasizes his personal wickedness as he lives outside of the laws established by God. In Revelation 13 and 17, he is frequently called "the beast," which sees him as wildly hostile to God and might also suggest his deep depravity. In Daniel 7:8 he is called the "little horn." Quite often the Old Testament used this term to describe power, such as a king's. Although the term itself does not tell us much about him, Daniel 7 does speak clearly of his pride, aggressiveness, and hostility to the true God.

He will be a man of great ability who is empowered uniquely by Satan (cf. Dan. 7:8-26; 9:26-27; 11:36-45; 2 Thess. 2:3-10; Rev. 13:1-9; 17:8-14). The Scriptures suggest that he will be blessed with great leadership ability, being one who can solve complex problems facing the world and being able to control situations. He will be intelligent, possessing an understanding of economics and political matters. He will be a man who is militarily powerful and brilliant. He has great oratorical ability, and this, coupled with his craftiness, will enable him to persuade multitudes to follow him. But behind him stands Satan, who gives him supernatural abilities and the authority to rule nations. The Scriptures suggest four phases to his career in the tribulation.

The *first phase* will actually be prior to the start of the tribulation, when he is the leader of some powerful western nation. In Daniel 7, the "little horn" (the Antichrist) is seen coming out of a restored Roman Empire, which means that the Antichrist comes from the West and not from Russia, Israel, or some other part of the world. The coming together of this western federation of nations (a restored Roman Empire) seems to take place after the tribulation begins. According to Revelation 6:2, early in the tribulation the Antichrist goes out to conquer. In Daniel 7:8 and 20 the Antichrist conquers three nations and possibly subdues seven others. It is likely that these are the same event. If so, the Antichrist enters into his covenant with Israel before he is the ruler of the restored Roman Empire. This would suggest that when he signs the covenant with Israel (which starts the tribulation) he is the ruler of one nation—one that is powerful enough to guarantee the safety of Israel.

The *second phase* of his career will take place during the first half of the tribulation, when he is the ruler of the restored Roman Empire. During his rise to power he will make enemies who will assassinate him near the midpoint of the tribulation (cf. Rev. 13:3, 12, 14). But, much to the astonishment of the world, he is restored to life and becomes the object of worship (along with Satan).

This worldwide adulation launches the *third phase* of his career, as he (for forty-two months) rules as dictator of the world (Rev. 13:5-7). He will achieve what hundreds of despots have only dreamed of—total domination of the world. It does not appear that this phase will be without trouble, but he will clearly have trouble on his hands at the end of the tribulation when the Lord Jesus returns.

THE CAREER OF THE ANTICHRIST

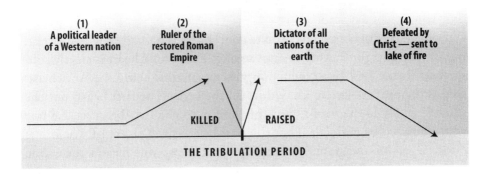

(1)	(2)	(3)	(4)
A political leader of a Western nation	Ruler of the restored Roman Empire	Dictator of all nations of the earth	Defeated by Christ — sent to lake of fire

KILLED   RAISED

THE TRIBULATION PERIOD

The *fourth phase* of his career is his defeat by Christ. He will then become the first occupant of the lake of fire (Rev. 19:20).

The Man Called the "False Prophet"

Revelation 13:11–18 reveals another person who is prominent in the tribulation, called a "beast." This second beast elsewhere is called the "false prophet" (Rev. 16:13; 19:20; 20:10), and he is apparently subservient to the first beast (the Antichrist). The evidence is that he is a religious leader—he is called a false *prophet*, and his activities are clearly religious in nature. He will have the ability to work miracles, which will be important in deceiving the unbelieving world into worshiping the Antichrist.

The miracles and signs that he will perform, such as calling fire down from heaven, will probably be used as evidence to validate his claim to be the Elijah who would come before "the great and terrible day of the Lord" (Mal. 4:5–6). If so, the claim will be made and promoted that the Antichrist is the true Messiah. This is confirmed when we remember that a primary focus of attention during the last half of the tribulation is on the temple in Jerusalem, where the image of the Antichrist (the "abomination of desolation") is set up and worshiped. The False Prophet, with his use of miracles and wonders, leads the world in worshiping the image of the Antichrist and kills those people who will not do so (Rev. 13:13–15).

His power will come from Satan, and his authority will be delegated to him from the Antichrist. The evidence from Revelation 13 is that economics and religion will be inseparably linked together during this time. Those who refuse to worship the Antichrist not only face death but will not receive the "mark of the beast" (666), which is essential for any buying or selling.

Some have suggested that this second beast is actually the Antichrist, but the support for that view is not strong. The second beast is clearly subservient to the first beast, which argues against his being the Antichrist, who is the most powerful individual on the earth. The first beast, not the second, will rule the world, and this points to the first beast as the one who claims to be Messiah. That the first beast is the object of worship is evidence of his messianic claims. The first beast will have a messianic appeal to the unbelieving Jewish nation and fit the role of Satan's false messiah. Therefore, it is best to see the second beast functioning in an Elijah-like role with delegated authority from the Antichrist ("exercises all the authority of the first beast in his presence," Rev. 13:12), leading the world in the worship of the Antichrist.

The 144,000

God is not going to abandon the planet to Satan, the Antichrist, and the False Prophet but will raise up those who bear witness to His power and greatness. The most prominent such group is the 144,000 (Rev. 7:1–8; 14:1–5). Several important statements are made about this group.

First, they are Jewish people. The text states that this group comes "from every tribe of the sons of Israel" (7:4) and then goes on to detail that 12,000 come from each of Israel's twelve tribes. Covenant theologians, who insist on the church being "spiritual Israel," believe that the 144,000 represent the church in the tribulation. But this view is foreign to Revelation 7 and to the use of the word *Israel* in the New Testament. One commentator on Revelation points out:

> No clear-cut example of the church being called "Israel" exists in the NT or in ancient church writings until AD 160. Galatians 6:16, in which "the Israel of God" can and probably does refer to some group other than the church as

a whole, is no exception. This fact is crippling to any attempt to identify Israel as the church in Rev. 7:4. . . . The approach is so misconceived that it does serious violence to the context. . . . It cannot be exegetically sustained. The 144,000 are declared to be from Israel, not from any other group.[3]

Second, they are "bond-servants of our God" (Rev. 7:3). This statement specifically declares that the 144,000, along with the angels who are speaking, are servants of God. They are not servants of Satan or the Antichrist. This tells us that they are saved individuals. We are not told when they are saved, but most likely it will be in the early days of the tribulation because the event being described in Revelation 7 is probably in the first half of the tribulation. The fact that they are called servants of God also reveals that they will minister for the Lord in some way. Most likely they will be the primary evangelists for God during the greater part of the tribulation. When teaching about the days of the tribulation, Jesus said that the "gospel of the kingdom shall be preached in the whole world for a witness to all the nations, and then the end shall come" (Matt. 24:14).

Immediately after the vision of the setting apart of the 144,000 in Revelation 7:1–8, John sees (vv. 9–17) the results of the ministry of the 144,000—a great multitude of saved people will come from every nation on the earth, which would seem to line up well with the statement of Jesus in Matthew 24. These 144,000, then, will be important instruments in the hand of God as He fulfills His purpose of bringing salvation to mankind during the terrible days of the tribulation.

Third, they are sealed. The concept of "sealing" has several meanings in the Bible, but the primary one is that of security. Sealing made something secure (e.g., the tomb of Jesus was sealed for the purpose of keeping it safe from tampering). The 144,000 are kept secure and protected from the judgments of God that will fall on the world and from the wrath of Satan. In light of their ministry of propagating the gospel and the successful persecution of believers by the forces of Satan in the tribulation (cf. Dan. 7:25; Rev. 13:7), such protection would be absolutely essential.

We can conclude, then, that the 144,000 are Jewish evangelists who will be kept secure by God as they proclaim the gospel during the days of the tribulation. But the 144,000 are not the only ones God will use to represent Him in those days.

The Two Witnesses

According to Revelation 11, God will raise up two special individuals in the tribulation, who will bear testimony for Him. They will be given the ability to work powerful miracles (vv. 5–6), which will validate their ministry to the people of Israel as being from God. Their ministry is centered in the city of Jerusalem, which is identified in the text by the phrase "where also their Lord was crucified" (v. 8). Though the content of their message is not given, the fact that they are clothed in sackcloth (v. 3) suggests that their emphasis will be similar to that of John the Baptist, who also wore sackcloth (Matt. 3:4). Sackcloth is a sign of mourning and repentance. "It may be concluded, from their distinctive dress, that the two witnesses are announcing the same message as John did, that of repentance, because the King is coming."[4]

The two witnesses are often identified by commentators as Elijah and Moses or Enoch. But support for these ideas is not particularly strong. Since they are not identified in the text, we should refrain from trying to identify them with any particular historical person. They are simply two Jewish prophets who will be used uniquely by God in the terrible days of the tribulation. Their ministry is said to last for a period of 1,260 days (one-half of the tribulation period, Rev. 11:3). But in which half of the tribulation period will they minister?

As one might suspect, there is a division of opinion on this matter. It is not a crucial issue, but their ministry seems to fit best into the second half of the tribulation, when the temple of Jerusalem is dominated by the worship of the Antichrist, as led by the False Prophet (Rev. 11:2).

Because this duration [1,260 days] corresponds exactly to one-half of the tribulation, and because the last half of the tribulation is specifically in the immediate context (11:2), it is logical to conclude that this witnessing activity takes place during that period. These two people, whatever their identity, will begin their work at the time when the Antichrist breaks his treaty with Israel and will continue throughout the difficult months of his oppression and persecution. The unusual power with which they are endowed by God will be necessary so that they will be able to continue, since the Antichrist surely will oppose them with the greatest severity.[5]

These two witnesses are said to fulfill Zechariah 4:11–14. In that vision, the prophet Zechariah saw two lampstands that were supplied continuously with oil from two olive trees. It communicates the truth that the empowerment of the Holy Spirit of God (the olive oil) is needed in order to minister as lights (the lampstands) for the Lord. The two witnesses of Revelation 11 will clearly operate in the power of God—a ministry that will be accompanied by the working of powerful miracles.

Revelation 11:7 states that when they have completed their ministry the two will be put to death by the Antichrist. This terrible act will cause the unbelieving world to rejoice and celebrate. But, much to their amazement, the two witnesses will be raised from the dead and taken to heaven. Their resurrection, like that of the Lord Jesus, will give clear testimony to the fact that the Father approved their ministry.

These two miracle-working servants of God are lights for the Lord in the morally and spiritually dark city of Jerusalem. The two witnesses are a reminder that even in the worst of times God does not leave Himself without witnesses.

EVENTS OF THE TRIBULATION

Understanding the individual events of the tribulation and how they relate to the whole is not easy. It is not always clear how the various personalities, judgments, events, and battles fit together. Our task in fitting all these things together would have been made easier if the apostle John had concluded the Revelation with some sort of chart. (Imagine the difference if he had left us just one PowerPoint slide!) But, since such is not available, we must attempt to plot the events of the tribulation in a manner that seems to fit with what has been revealed through the apostles and prophets. For the sake of analysis, the tribulation will be divided into three parts: (1) events of the first half; (2) events at the midpoint; and (3) events of the second half.

Events of the Tribulation: The First Half

The events occurring during the first half of the tribulation will involve the nation of Israel, the Antichrist, and Satan.

1. *The nation of Israel.* When the tribulation begins, Israel is back in their ancient land. Ezekiel, along with other prophets, saw that in the end times the nation would be restored to their land by the Lord Himself (e.g., Deut. 30:4–5; Ezek. 20:40–44; 34:11–13; 36:22–36; 37:1–14). When the nation returns, however, it will not be as a nation of believers. Ezekiel indicates that Israel will first come back to their land, then they will come back to the Lord:

> *"For I will take you from the nations, gather you from all the lands, and bring you into your own land. Then I will sprinkle clean water on you, and you will be clean; I will cleanse you from all your filthiness and from all your idols. Moreover I will give you a new heart and put a new spirit within you."* *(Ezek. 36:24–26)*

Apparently many in the nation will return to their ancient worship system, which was centered in the Jerusalem temple and which involved animal sacrifices. The temple must, therefore, be rebuilt, though not necessarily before the start of the tribulation. How the Jewish people will be able to do this (in light of the Islamic holy places that are located on the temple mount) and when they will rebuild the temple are not revealed. The Scriptures simply inform us that at the midpoint of the tribulation the temple will exist and the Levitical sacrificial system will be in place (cf. Dan. 9:27; Matt. 24:15), but it does not tell us how long it has been going on.

During the first half of the tribulation, Israel will be living in peace and safety because of the covenant they have made with the powerful Western leader, who is the Antichrist. He is able to guarantee their security, and they will live in relative peace in spite of many terrible things happening elsewhere in the world.

2. *The judgments of God.* God's judgments begin when Christ breaks the seals on the scroll (Rev. 5:1–6:1). The first six seal judgments will take place probably during the first half of the tribulation. They are described by Christ as the "beginning of birth pangs" (Matt. 24:8). When the Lord Jesus answered His disciples' questions about the signs of the second coming, He spoke in general terms about judgments and other matters that would precede His second coming. In Matthew 24:4–8, He spoke of judgments that will be found in the first half of the tribu-

lation—famines, earthquakes, false messiahs, wars, and persecutions. This general description of judgment is detailed by John as he describes the seal judgments (Rev. 6:2–17).

The world will experience the following judgments in the first half of the tribulation:

SEAL 1: The Antichrist, the false messiah, appears and goes forth to conquer. Although no open warfare is mentioned, he does wear a crown, which is the sign of a victor. It may be that this refers to his conquering of the three kings and his subduing of seven others in the forming of the Western federation of nations (the restored Roman Empire) revealed in Daniel 7:8, 20–24.

SEAL 2: With the opening of this seal, total, open warfare breaks out on the earth (cf. Matt. 24:6–7). The "great sword" given to the rider on the horse speaks of an unprecedented kind of conflict all over the world.

SEAL 3: The rider on a black horse represents worldwide famine (cf. Matt. 24:7). He holds a pair of scales in his hand, which was used for weighing food. The scarcity of food is evidenced in very high prices for grain. Famine is often the direct result of war. And since the wars are great, the famine will be great also—perhaps found in places where famine is not usually experienced.

SEAL 4: The breaking of this seal brings incredible destruction to the world's population, as one-fourth will perish in this judgment. Men will be killed "with sword and with famine and with pestilence and by the wild beasts of the earth" (Rev. 6:8). These four agents of death are specifically said to be God's "four severe judgments" (Ezek. 14:21). The number of deaths will be staggering if the tribulation begins with five or six billion people on the planet.

SEAL 5: This seal is different from the others because it focuses on the death of believers during these days. These believers have been martyred because of their loyalty to the Lord and His Word. Many,

many people will come to faith in Christ during those first years of the tribulation, but probably few will make it through alive.

SEAL 6: This seal is probably broken near the middle of the tribulation (and may introduce the final three and a half years—the great tribulation). It brings amazing and powerful upheavals on the earth and in the heavens. A great earthquake convulses the crust of the earth, and "every mountain and island were moved out of their places" (Rev. 6:14). This will be accompanied by great cosmic disturbances affecting the sun, moon, and stars (vv. 12–13). So great are these events that a terrified humanity cries out to the rocks and mountains to hide them from the wrath of God.

These seal judgments are said to be the "beginning of birth pangs" (Matt. 24:8). The term *birth pangs* is used to describe the judgments of God throughout the entire tribulation. It is used many times in the Scriptures (e.g., Isa. 13:8–9; 26:17–18; Jer. 22:23; Hos. 13:13; Mic. 4:9–10) and suggests a number of things about God's judgments in the tribulation.

First, birth pangs are unique pains. Although a woman will experience pain in many ways in her life, the pains of delivery are unique..Similarly, earth has often endured the pains of war, famine, and disease, but these pains in the tribulation will be unique—perhaps because of their intensity and location. Second, once birth pangs begin, they do not end until the baby is born. So also, once the tribulation judgments begin, they will not stop until the kingdom of the Messiah is born into the world. Third, birth pains become more intense as the time for birth draws near. The judgments of the tribulation become more severe as the period proceeds. Fourth, birth pangs come closer and closer together as time goes on. The judgments of the tribulation appear to have greater amounts of time between them toward the beginning, but they come closer together as the second coming of Christ approaches. This may be one reason that mankind does not immediately identify the first seal judgments as coming from God. With months and months between each seal, people may see them as natural, though terrible, events. Fifth, in both cases, when the birth pains have run their course, new life is experienced.

3. *The activities of the Antichrist.* As we have already observed, the tribulation begins when the Antichrist signs a covenant with the nation of Israel guaranteeing the people's safety. After that the Antichrist consolidates his power over the ten other Western nations (the restored Roman Empire) and rules for most of the first three and a half years of the tribulation. With this power, he is able to function well as Israel's protector.

4. *Religions in the World.* First, the nation of Israel will return to its ancient levitical worship system, and the Jerusalem temple will once again become the center of Jewish religious life. Second, in the absence of any indication to the contrary, it seems safe to assume that all the other major religions and cults of the world will continue to exist during the first half of the tribulation. Third, an apostate church (in the absence of the true church of Jesus Christ) grows in power and influence. Revelation 17 reveals information about an unfaithful woman (a harlot). This designation is in contrast to a faithful bride (19:7–8) and suggests one who claims loyalty to Christ but is unfaithful to Him. This religious system (the harlot) is a politically powerful, wealthy, and aggressive persecutor of true believers. During the first half of the tribulation, there is a close connection between this apostate church and the Antichrist, since she is seen riding on the beast (17:3). This may even indicate that the woman (the apostate church) actually has control of the Antichrist for a period of time. But, in any case, a close connection exists between religion and politics (which has usually been the case, unlike the American way of thinking).

The apostate church is not only politically influential but very wealthy (Rev. 17:4). She is described as the "mother of harlots," (v. 5) and the use of the plural would suggest that this religious system is ecumenical, made up of numerous groups. It is quite clear that this religious system is responsible for the death of many true believers in Christ during those days (v. 6). The apostate church will itself come to a violent end at the hand of the Antichrist and his followers (vv. 16–17). This ecumenical religious system apparently is centered in Rome, since it is identified with the city that was ruling the world in the apostle John's day (v. 9). This system cannot exist past the middle of the tribulation, since at the midpoint the Antichrist will require worship from all people. It seems probable that its destruction will come at about that time.

5. *True believers in Jesus Christ.* One of the major purposes of the tribulation is to save people. Mankind's apathy and unconcern about spiritual matters will be swept away during the tribulation when the world is startled by supernatural signs and shaken by cataclysmic events. In that setting many will turn to Jesus Christ for salvation. The 144,000 will probably come to faith during this time, along with multitudes of others, as evidenced by the large numbers who will be martyred for their faith (cf. Rev. 6:9–11; 17:6).

At the Holy Spirit will be very active during the days of the tribulation, since it is He who regenerates people, giving them eternal life (cf. John 3:5–8; Titus 3:5). The Holy Spirit is not removed from the world at the rapture event, as some have taught. It is His ministry of restraining sin that is removed. But the omnipresent Spirit is present on the earth saving millions of people.

Events of the Tribulation: The Midpoint

Some notable differences exist between the first and second halves of the tribulation because of the important events that transpire at the midpoint. These all take place about the same time, but no clear order of events can be established.

1. *The nation of Israel.* For three and a half years the nation will have experienced a notable degree of peace. But that will change when the treaty with the Antichrist, who has secured this peace, will be broken. At the middle of the tribulation the Antichrist will end true worship in the temple and substitute an idol of himself in the temple (cf. Dan. 9:27; Matt. 24:15; Rev. 13:14–15). This "abomination of desolation" will begin the intense persecution of the nation of Israel by the Antichrist.

At this time there may be a great invasion of Israel by hostile forces (Ezekiel 38–39). Some equate this battle with Armageddon at the end of the tribulation, whereas others place it at the beginning of the tribulation. In this battle, Israel is faced with overwhelming odds. But God will intervene for Israel and destroy this invading force, much like He destroyed the armies of Pharaoh so many centuries ago. The result of this battle is that Israel will begin to know the Lord as never before (39:21). It may be a key event in the spiritual restoration of the nation of Israel.

2. *The activities of the Antichrist.* For the first half of the tribulation, the Antichrist has been ruling over the Western nations, but something happens now that launches him into his role as world ruler and causes the people of the world to worship him. Apparently the Antichrist dies violently and suddenly, since it is said that he has a "fatal wound" and that this fatal wound came from "the sword" (Rev. 13:3, 14). But he will come back to life (vv. 3, 12, 14) and be worshiped worldwide. It is probably then that his idol is erected in the temple. Of this action, Cohen writes:

> *A man proclaims himself to be this world's deity and is accepted as such by the unregenerate population of the globe (Rev. 13:8. . . . What is the explanation for this immense effect? It can only lie in an equally immense cause— the resuscitation of the Beast. With this in mind it cannot be far amiss to place the resurrection of the Beast shortly before his entering into the temple to proclaim himself "God" which occurs at the midpoint of the week.*[6]

3. *The activity of Satan.* Satan has always had access to heaven even though he rebelled against God. However, at the midpoint of the tribulation, he is forcibly removed from heaven by Michael and the holy angels. Revelation 12:7–12 records that this causes great joy in heaven, as the "accuser of the brethren" is defeated in battle and banished from heaven forever. But while heaven no longer has to endure Satan's presence, the earth is not so fortunate. At this time a solemn warning is given to the people of the earth because Satan's removal from heaven causes him to realize that his time is short (v. 12). As a consequence, Satan goes forth with "great wrath"—wrath that targets the nation of Israel. His renewed and intense persecution of Israel (primarily through the Antichrist) will last for 1,260 days.

4. *Religions in the world.* At the midpoint of the tribulation the world will be worshiping Satan and the Antichrist (Rev. 13:4–5). Recall that at the midpoint of the tribulation the Jewish worship in the temple is brought

to an end and also that the apostate church (the harlot) is destroyed. This would cause us to conclude that from the midpoint on there is only one approved religion in the world and that all others religions are forbidden. Only the worship of the Antichrist (and Satan) will be permitted.

Events of the Tribulation: The Second Half

This one-world religion impacts everyone, from the nation of Israel and true believers in Christ to the Antichrist himself, and leads to God's judgments, including the final battle on earth prior to Jesus' return.

1. *The nation of Israel.* The Scriptures leave no doubt that the second half of the tribulation will be a terrible time of persecution for the nation of Israel (cf. Matt. 24:9–24; Rev. 12:6, 13–17). The Lord will instruct the people of Israel to flee into the wilderness, where they will receive help. Satan and the Antichrist will make war against those who are Jewish believers for 1,260 days, until the Lord Jesus returns and rescues them. It is during this half of the tribulation that God's great purpose of redeeming the nation of Israel takes place.

2. *The activities of the Antichrist.* According to Revelation 13:5–7, the Antichrist will rule the world for a forty-two-month period. His world dictatorship will be during this second half of the tribulation. It seems that for most of this time the world follows after him, but it may be that toward the end significant rebellion against his rulership takes place. This will lead to Armageddon.

3. *True believers in Jesus Christ.* Revelation 7 reveals that vast numbers are saved during this time, with most of them being martyred for their faith (vv. 9–14). The 144,000 will be spreading the gospel throughout the world and most likely are God's instruments for the salvation of many (Matt. 24:14). Much to the distress of the followers of the Antichrist, the "two witnesses" will be bearing witness for the true God in the unholy city of Jerusalem. Much of the world will lie in the power of the Evil One, yet God will have His witnesses, and many will turn to Him.

4. *The judgments of God.* The three series of judgments (seals, trumpets, and bowls) succeed one another; that is, the seals are followed by the trumpets, and the trumpets are followed by the bowls (Rev. 6:1–17; 8:1–9:21; 16:1–21).

The trumpet and bowl judgments take place in the second half of the tribulation. When the Lord Jesus breaks the seventh seal (8:1), the trumpet judgments begin (v. 6). These judgments are more severe than the first six seal judgments and come in answer to the prayers of the saints of God (vv. 2–5).

TRUMPET 1: When this trumpet sounds, one-third of the vegetation of the earth will burn up. The effect on the food supply and the resources of the earth will be staggering. There must also be a considerable loss of human life as a result of this judgment.

TRUMPET 2: The sounding of this trumpet causes one-third of the sea to be turned into blood. Consequently, one-third of the sea creatures die, and one-third of the ships on the sea are destroyed.

TRUMPET 3: The third trumpet brings great destruction to the fresh waters of the earth. One-third of these waters are contaminated in some way, which will be disastrous to life on this planet.

TRUMPET 4: The fourth trumpet brings judgment on the sun, moon, and stars. One-third of each is darkened, which will cause unbelievable disaster to the world. How this darkening will take place is not clear, but there is no doubt about the end result.

TRUMPET 5: This trumpet is also called the "first woe" (9:12) because it causes even greater suffering than the previous judgments. With the blowing of this trumpet, locustlike creatures emerge out of the Abyss and torment people as they roam the earth. Most likely they are particularly evil demonic beings who have been kept in confinement until this moment. For five months they torment people but are not allowed to kill anyone (v. 5).

TRUMPET 6: Things get worse with the blowing of this trumpet, said to be the "second woe." An army of 200,000,000 men from the east will destroy one-third of mankind (9:13–21). Demonic involvement is apparent in this judgment also. This army from the east may well be a prelude to the great battle of Armageddon.

TRUMPET 7: The seventh trumpet is known as the "third woe" (11:14–15). With the sounding of the seventh trumpet, words from heaven indicate that the world is only a short time away from the second coming: "The kingdom of the world has become the kingdom of our Lord, and of His Christ; and He will reign forever and ever" (v. 15). The seventh trumpet, the third woe, and the seven bowl judgments are all the same thing.

The sounding of the seventh trumpet, which will bring to an end the wrath of God (cf. Rev. 10:7; 15:1, 8; 16:17), brings forth the seven bowl judgments, which target the Antichrist and his followers. These are the most intense judgments of them all.

BOWL 1: The pouring out of this bowl brings terrible sores on all those who follow the Antichrist (Rev. 16:2).

BOWL 2: This bowl turns all the seas into blood, causing the death of all creatures in the seas.

BOWL 3: When this bowl is poured out, all the fresh waters of the earth are turned to blood.

BOWL 4: The content of the fourth bowl gives power to the sun to bring terrible heat on the earth, causing intense suffering. The text makes clear that people know that these judgments come from God, but they blaspheme Him anyway and refuse to repent of their evil (16:9, 11, 21).

BOWL 5: The pouring out of this bowl brings a supernatural darkness over the kingdom of the Antichrist.

BOWL 6: With the emptying of this bowl, the river Euphrates is dried up, and demonically inspired men head for their own destruction to a place called Armageddon (16:16).

BOWL 7: This final judgment brings about the greatest convulsions in nature yet. A massive moving of the earth's crust will be accompanied by huge one-hundred-pound hailstones falling from heaven.

5. *The battle of Armageddon.* Although the phrase "battle of Armageddon" is a familiar one, it is also somewhat misleading for two reasons. First, it is not a single battle but, rather, a whole series of conflicts that culminate with the second coming of Christ. "The Greek word *polemos,* translated 'battle' in Revelation 16:14, signifies a war or campaign, while *mache* signifies a battle, and sometimes even single combat."[7] The word selected by John, *polemos,* in Revelation 16 indicates that Armageddon is really a campaign made up of numerous conflicts among a number of nations over a period of time at the end of the tribulation.

A second reason the phrase "battle of Armageddon" is somewhat misleading is that this final end-time conflict is not geographically isolated to the region around the plain of Megiddo. Revelation 14 teaches that the land area involved in this end-time campaign is actually about 180 miles in length (v. 20). Several other locations are mentioned in the Scriptures other than Megiddo; namely Jerusalem, the valley of Jehoshaphat (an area east of Jerusalem), and Edom (Isa. 34, 63; Jer. 49; Joel 3; Zech. 12; 14). So the many armies that gather are apparently spread out over a much larger area than the plain of Megiddo. John calls this area of land the "winepress" of God's wrath.

No one Scripture outlines the order of events at the very end, and this makes the construction of an exact chronology difficult. A number of Scripture writers contribute pieces of information about the movement of nations from all four points of the compass, but no one writer has put all of it together. Thus, a number of theories have been developed. In fact, some six or seven basic theories try to explain the movement of armies and the sequence of battles in the very last days of the tribulation.[8]

We do not know for sure, but it may be during the forty-two months when the Antichrist is ruler of the world that he establishes his headquarters in the

EVENTS OF THE TRIBULATION PERIOD

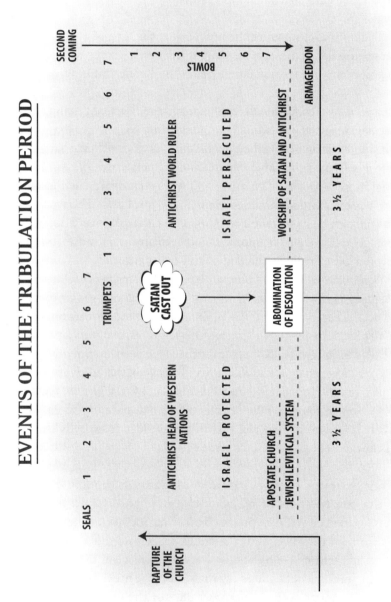

Jerusalem area. And although he technically rules the world, considerable unrest seems to develop against his rule. This unrest, combined with existing nationalism, brings a challenge to the rulership of the Antichrist. Apparently, the sixth bowl judgment, by some supernatural means, opens the way for armies from the east to challenge his authority. Other nations also head for Palestine with the intention of overthrowing the Antichrist.

As these armies gather and carry on warfare with one another, the "sign of the Son of Man" appears in the heavens (Matt. 24:30). With the realization that Jesus Christ is about to return, hostilities toward one another cease, and these armies unite against the Lord. But they, of course, are unable to resist His coming and are utterly destroyed by the King of Kings (Rev. 19:11–21).

The Lord Jesus treads "the great wine press of the wrath of God"—which is the huge land area where these final events take place (14:19–20). The nations are slaughtered in the "wine press," and the blood is said to be as high as the horses' bridles (v. 20). The victorious Lord Jesus will seize the Antichrist and the False Prophet and will throw them alive into the lake of fire (19:20).

End of the Tribulation: The Second Coming of Christ

With the return of the Lord Jesus Christ to the earth, the six great goals found in Daniel 9:24 will find their fulfillment. As we have seen already, the tribulation was primarily designed by God to bring His covenant people Israel back to Himself. The outpouring of the supernatural, combined with the witness of the 144,000, as well as the witness of many other believers, will be used to bring many Jewish people (as well as Gentiles) to the Messiah. But the spiritual eyes of many others in Israel will not be opened until the second coming itself. Along with this spiritual awakening of many in Israel, a number of significant happenings occur when the Lord Jesus returns in power and great glory.

1. *Jesus Christ brings salvation to many in Israel.* The terrible oppression and persecution of Israel during the second half of the tribulation period will have God's desired effect on the nation. The stubborn, rebellious will of the Jewish people will be broken, and they will seek the Lord their God and come to saving faith in the Lord Jesus.

In His scathing denunciation of the religious leaders of Israel at the end of His ministry (Matt. 23:1–39), Jesus pronounced judgment on that generation and declared that Israel would not see Him again *until* they declared, "Blessed is He who comes in the name of the Lord" (v. 39).

Jesus will not come back to the earth until the Jews and the Jewish leaders ask Him to come back. Just as the Jewish leaders led the nation to the rejection of the Messiahship of Jesus, they must some day lead the nation to the acceptance of the Messiahship of Jesus. This, then, is the twofold basis of the second coming: Israel must confess her national sin and then plead for Messiah to return, to mourn for Him as one mourns for an only son. Until these two things happen, there will be no second coming.[9]

This acceptance of the Messiahship of Jesus when He returns in power and glory is seen in Zechariah 12:10 and 13:9, where that prophet says,

"And I will pour out on the house of David and on the inhabitants of Jerusalem, the Spirit of grace and of supplication, so that they will look on Me whom they have pierced; and they will mourn for Him, as one mourns for an only son, and they will weep bitterly over Him, like the bitter weeping over a first-born. . . . They will call on My name, and I will answer them; I will say, 'They are My people,' and they will say, 'The Lord is my God.' "

These passages reveal that God is going to accomplish His purpose of saving the nation of Israel. Many Jewish people will believe and be saved during the tribulation (as a result of the ministry of the 144,000), but many more in Israel will respond to Him at the second coming. As the apostle Paul declared, "and thus all Israel will be saved," and he observed that the time of this national regeneration would be when "the Deliverer will come from Zion, [when] He will remove ungodliness from Jacob" (Rom. 11:26).

It is important to remember that God is saving Israel because of the covenant commitments He made to Abraham and Abraham's descendants. Paul said that this salvation is based on God's covenant with Israel: "And this is My covenant with them, when I take away their sins" (v. 27). Paul is referring to the *new covenant*, a subcovenant of the Abrahamic covenant (see chapter 2).

In Jeremiah 31:31–34, God promised that He would make a "new covenant" with the houses of Israel and Judah. This was the salvation aspect of the Abrahamic covenant that would be based on Christ's death on the cross. But national Israel never has entered into the new covenant. The terrible events of the tribulation will break their stubborn will and open their spiritual eyes, causing them to accept gladly the Lord Jesus as their Savior and Messiah, and bring them into the new covenant.

2. *Jesus Christ reclaims the world for God by defeating the enemies of God.* The tribulation period ends with the return of Christ in power and glory (Rev. 19:11–21). All the enemies of God who have defied His authority and tormented His people will face destruction.

Apparently, as the nations gather in Palestine, they will be alerted to the second coming of Christ by the "sign of the Son of Man," which will visibly appear in the heavens (Matt. 24:30). Jesus said that His coming would be observed by all on the earth (unlike the rapture) and likened it to lightning flashing across the sky (Matt. 24:27). All people will realize that something of monumental importance is about to happen, and their response will be that of "mourning."

At that moment the Jewish people face terrible destruction, and only the powerful coming of the Lord will save them. The Lord Jesus returns and fights against the nations gathered in the "winepress of the wrath of God" (Zech 14:3–4; Rev. 14:17–20) and totally destroys them (Rev. 19:19–21). He then captures the Antichrist and the False Prophet and immediately dispatches them to the lake of fire (Rev. 19:20). Satan, the evil mind and power behind these wicked men, is captured, bound, and placed in the Abyss, the place for the confinement of demons (Luke 8:30–31; Rev. 20:1–3).

With the defeat of God's enemies, believing Israel is regathered to the land in preparation for Messiah's kingdom. This regathering is necessary in order to fulfill the *Palestinian (land) covenant,* another subcovenant of the Abrahamic covenant. With the removal of God's enemies from the land, believing Israel will now experience the fulfillment of God's land promise (cf. Deut. 29:1–30:20; Isa. 11:11–12:6; Jer. 16:14–15; 23:3–8; Ezek. 11:14–18; 37:1–28).

3. *Jesus Christ establishes Himself as king.* When Jesus comes again, He returns as King of Kings (Rev. 19:16) with the purpose of reestablishing the throne of David and fulfilling the *Davidic covenant* (see chapter 3). It is God's declared purpose to establish a kingdom that will last forever (cf. Dan. 2:44; 2 Sam. 7:16; 1 Chron. 17:14). Jesus has never sat on the throne of David to fulfill this covenant, but that will change when He returns.

Seventy-five days will pass from return until the actual beginning of the millennial (messianic) kingdom (cf. Dan. 12:11–12). Apparently these seventy-five days are preparatory to the millennial kingdom and will involve such things as the removal of the abomination of desolation from the temple, the judgments of those who made it through the tribulation alive (see the next chapter), and the resurrection and rewarding of tribulation and Old Testament saints. Once these and other matters are settled, the messianic age can begin.

CHAPTER SIXTEEN

THE COMING JUDGMENTS
AND
Resurrections

A farmer, who was an unbeliever with a particular dislike for Christians, would purposely work on Sundays in his field across from the little country church. Those who attended the church were somewhat upset by the plowing, cultivating, and fertilizing that went on each Sunday. In the early fall he chose to harvest his crop only on Sundays. The farmer wrote a letter to the editor of the local paper pointing out that he had worked that field only on Sundays and yet had one of the highest yields in the whole county. He challenged the editor to have Christians explain this.

The editor's reply was simple and succinct: "God does not settle all of His accounts in the month of October."

We applaud that editor's response because we intuitively believe that bad behavior of any kind should be judged—that unbelieving farmers ought to reap what they sow. Although we may not always like the idea of being judged ourselves, we generally feel that there ought to be justice in this universe of ours.

The Scriptures do reveal that all people, whether believers or unbelievers, are accountable to God. And although the prospect of evaluation and judgment may be an uncomfortable thought to many, the reality is that the creature is accountable to the Creator. Some resist the idea of God's role as judge, contending that God is a God of love. He is that, of course, but He is also holy. And if God is holy, then there are moral absolutes. And if there are moral absolutes, then God will justly judge His creatures for violating those moral absolutes. There is a time of judgment for every person.

> *When we regard God as the author of our moral nature, we conceive of Him as holy; when we regard Him in his dealings with his rational creatures, we conceive of him as righteous. He is a righteous ruler; all his laws are holy, just, and good. In his moral government He faithfully adheres to those laws. He is impartial and uniform in their execution. As a judge he renders unto every man according to his works. He neither condemns the innocent, nor clears the guilty; neither does He ever punish with undue severity. Hence the justice of God is distinguished as* rectoral, *or that which is concerned in the imposition of righteous laws and in their impartial execution; and* distributive, *or that which is manifested in the righteous distribution of rewards and punishments.*[1]

This judgment of God, however, will not occur as one general judgment in which all people stand before Him. There is no one "Great Judgment Day." Actually, a number of different judgments will take place at different times in the future.

THE ONE WHO JUDGES

The Judge in the end times is the Lord Jesus Christ. All judgment has been given to the Son of God, and all those who do not come to Him as the giver of life will have to face Him as their Judge (cf. John 5:21–23, 27). Jesus declared that His judgments will be just and fair, and He will act in harmony with the will of the Father (v. 30). During His earthly ministry He was not a respecter of persons—He was not impressed by wealth, status, or power. And that will hold true in the future as well (Isa. 11:4–5).

It is said of Jesus that His eyes are like a flame of fire, which emphasizes that He sees all and knows all (Rev. 1:14; 2:18). It is essential that the judge knows everything and that He cannot be fooled. This also means that He will not inadvertently overlook facts or issues.

He is holy (Rev. 3:7). There is nothing sinful or shady in His judgments because He will judge according to the moral absolutes of God. When people stand before Him, they will not be able to manipulate, deceive, or bribe this judge. These realities, of course, do not mean that Judge Jesus is cold, austere, or uncaring. It is also true that He is full of love, grace, and mercy and that He does not delight in the death of the wicked (Ezek. 33:11; Eph. 2:4–5). But all people, at one time or another, will stand before the Lord Jesus.

THE COMING JUDGMENTS

When a person stands before the Lord, he or she comes not to learn of his eternal destiny, for one's presence in or absence from the future kingdom of God has been settled during that person's earthly life. What, then, is the purpose of the future judgments?

In answering this question, we will look at the approaching future judgments in three groups: (1) the judgment at the rapture; (2) judgments at the second coming; and (3) judgments after the millennial kingdom.

The Judgment at the Rapture

Immediately after the church is removed from the world at the rapture, the "judgment seat of Christ" will take place (2 Cor. 5:10). What is this "judgment seat"? The Greek word *bema* is used by the apostle Paul to describe this judgment. A *bema* was a seat or raised platform where a judge sat as he made his decision regarding a case (e.g., Matt. 27:19; John 19:13; Acts 18:12). This word was also used in connection with the platform on which the umpire or referee sat during the Olympic games or the Isthmian games at Corinth. This was the place where the winners of the various events received their rewards. The apostle Paul seems to have this idea of reward in mind as he speaks of the "judgment seat of Christ." This, then, is actually a place of rewarding, not punishing.

When will this judgment take place? The fact that the Lord Jesus rewards His servants in connection with His coming indicates that the judgment seat of Christ will take place shortly after the rapture (1 Cor. 4:5; Rev. 22:12). Furthermore, the Lord taught that rewarding takes place at the time of resurrection, which is an important part of the rapture (Luke 14:14). Also, when the Lord Jesus returns to the earth at His second coming with His bride, the church, the bride is already rewarded (Rev. 19:8). This places the rewarding of the church sometime after the rapture but before the second coming. It will take place in the sphere of the heavenlies.

Who will be present at the judgment seat of Christ? This judgment involves the same people who were involved in the rapture, namely, believers from the church age. In the contexts where the judgment seat of Christ is discussed (Rom. 14:10-12; 1 Cor. 3:10-4:5; 2 Cor. 5:1-10), it is believers who are being encouraged and exhorted. For example, in the 1 Corinthians passage, it is clear those who have built on the foundation of Jesus Christ will be at the "judgment seat." This clearly is a reference to church age believers. In fact, the only ones who are said to be at the judgment seat of Christ are church age believers. This would mean that unsaved people are not a part of this judgment, and it also means that saints from the Old Testament will not participate.

What are the bases for the evaluation and rewarding? The believer's works will be examined by the Lord Jesus to determine if rewards will be given. The apostle Paul (in 1 Cor. 3:10-15) uses the illustration of constructing a building. He informs believers that all have received a foundation on which to build. That foundation, which is given to the believer, is none other than the Lord Jesus. The believer builds daily on that foundation and has a choice of building materials. The issue is not if believers will build but with what they will build. At the judgment seat their works will be tested by fire. Some of the building materials are perishable (wood, hay, and straw), whereas others are not (gold, silver, and costly stones). The works that please and honor God will not be burned up but will bring a reward. When the Lord Jesus evaluates the lives of believers at the judgment seat, His evaluation will be based on several factors.

First, the extent our lives and ministry follow the Word of God. The Scriptures, with their commands and principles, will form the objective standard used by the Lord. He will not evaluate us on the basis of our experiences or traditions but on His revealed truth. The study and application of God's Word is a key to our rewarding. How seriously we have taken the Master's instructions will be an important factor in our rewarding.

Second, the extent we have been faithful stewards of all that He has entrusted to us. We have been given spiritual gifts, natural abilities, material resources, training, and opportunities for service. The Bible reminds us that "it is required of stewards that one be found trustworthy" (1 Cor. 4:2). This concept of faithful stewardship and rewarding is developed by Christ in several of His parables (e.g., Matt. 25:14-30; Luke 19:11-27). Believers must always remember that they are held accountable for what has been given to them, not what has been given to another.

Third, our motives (cf. 1 Cor. 4:5). The Lord is not interested only in what we do but also why we do it (or do not do it). Those who live and serve with a desire to please and honor Christ will receive great reward. Those who live and serve motivated by self-promotion, financial gain, or some other improper goal will not receive rewards.

What is the result of the rewarding at the judgment seat of Christ? Negatively, there will be a loss of reward and a sense of shame (cf. 1 Cor. 3:15; 1 John 2:28). It is God's desire to reward His children, but He will withhold reward from those who have lived sinful, self-centered lives. "We will not only be rewarded for the good in our lives at the bema but will have to face Jesus' response to the useless and sinful realities as well. . . . There are passages that point to the presence of a negative aspect in the believer's judgment."[2] Again and again the Lord Jesus and the apostles challenged believers to avoid the loss of reward, inheritance, and rest and to gain a full reward. This is one of the motivations consistently given to believers so that they might daily live their lives to honor Jesus Christ.[3] Although there may be the loss of reward, the apostle Paul is clear that this will not involve the loss of salvation: "If any man's work is burned up, he shall suffer loss; but he himself shall be saved, yet so as through fire" (1 Cor. 3:15).

There are many positive results of the judgment seat of Christ. Those who are rewarded have opportunity to serve Christ in greater ways in His future kingdom (e.g., Matt. 25:19–23; Luke 19:16–19), experience a special joy and fellowship (Matt. 25:21, 23; 1 Peter 4:12–13), receive divine commendation (Matt. 25:21), and obtain a variety of "crowns" (e.g., 1 Cor. 9:25; 1 Thess. 2:19; 2 Tim. 4:8; James 1:12; 1 Peter 5:4). These rewards will carry with them positive consequences in Christ's millennial kingdom and possibly His eternal kingdom.

What place does the believer's sin have at the judgment seat of Christ? One of the marvelous truths of the New Testament is that the believer in Jesus Christ has been justified by faith. Jesus' death on the cross fully paid the penalty of sin so that the one who receives God's gift of salvation will never face the judgment of God that results in banishment forever from His presence (cf. John 5:24; Rom. 3:21–25). However, sinful living on the part of a believer will have an effect on what transpires at the judgment seat of Christ.

THE COMING JUDGMENTS AND RESURRECTIONS

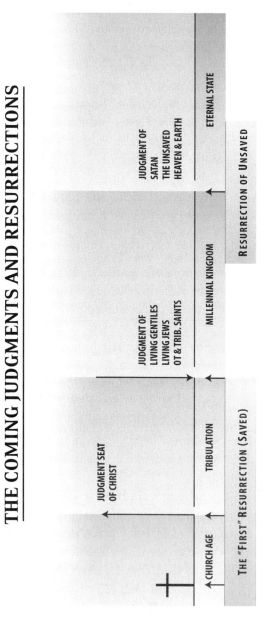

CHURCH AGE | TRIBULATION | MILLENNIAL KINGDOM | ETERNAL STATE

JUDGMENT SEAT OF CHRIST

JUDGMENT OF
LIVING GENTILES
LIVING JEWS
OT & TRIB. SAINTS

JUDGMENT OF
SATAN
THE UNSAVED
HEAVEN & EARTH

THE "FIRST" RESURRECTION (SAVED)

RESURRECTION OF UNSAVED

The Judgments at the Second Coming

When the Lord Jesus returns at His second coming to establish the millennial kingdom, three judgments will take place.

First, the judgment of Gentiles at the end of the tribulation (Joel 3:1–2; Matt. 25:31–46). Upon His return to the earth, Jesus will judge those Gentiles who have made it through the tribulation alive. These living Gentiles will be gathered to a place near Jerusalem (the valley of Jehoshaphat) to determine their spiritual condition. Those who are the righteous among the Gentiles (the "sheep" in Matthew 25) will be welcomed into Messiah's kingdom, but those who are unsaved (the "goats" in Matthew 25) will be sent away into everlasting punishment.

The internal, spiritual condition of the Gentiles is revealed externally by the way in which they treated Israel during the great tribulation (cf. Rev. 12:13–16). This is a valid proof of true righteousness because of the terrible persecution that Israel will endure during the second half of the tribulation. As Ryrie explains:

> *For a Gentile to treat any Jewish person with kindness during the tribulation will place his life in jeopardy. No one will do this merely out of a beneficent attitude, but only out of a redeemed heart. . . . Those whose good deeds prove the presence of saving faith will enter the kingdom.*[4]

These saved Gentiles will enter the kingdom in their earthly bodies and will be a part of repopulating the earth during the millennial kingdom.

Second, the judgment of the Jewish people who are living at the end of the tribulation period. When the Lord Jesus returns, He will defeat His enemies at Armageddon. At that time the people of Israel will be regathered from all over the world to the land of Israel (Matt. 24:31). The Lord will then determine which are saved and which are unsaved. The righteous of Israel will be allowed to enter into the messianic kingdom and to experience the fulfillment of God's covenant commitments to the nation. But the "rebels" in Israel (the unsaved) will be cut off and will not be allowed into the kingdom (cf. Ezek. 20:34–38; Matt. 25:1–30). As with the Gentiles who enter the kingdom, these Jewish believers will not receive immortal bodies. Rather, they will remain in their earthly bodies and will be part of the repopulation of the earth.

Third, the judgment of the Old Testament and tribulation saints (Daniel 12:2–

3; Matt. 16:27; Rev. 20:4–6). These believers who died either in the tribulation or millenniums earlier in Old Testament times will be rewarded when raised from the dead. Daniel 12:2–3 is set in the context of the tribulation and speaks of the resurrection and rewarding of the saints of God. This takes place immediately after the tribulation. Daniel 12:2–3 speaks of the resurrection of both the righteous and the unrighteous without indicating that any time exists between the two. Daniel 12:13 shows that Daniel (an Old Testament saint) will be raised and rewarded at the time under discussion; namely, the time immediately after the tribulation. When Daniel 12 is combined with Revelation 20:4–6, we are able to see that the righteous are raised and rewarded before the millennial kingdom, whereas the unrighteous are raised after the thousand-year reign of Christ.

It would appear that the ones raised from the dead and rewarded at the second coming include both Old Testament saints and tribulation saints. According to Revelation 20:4–6 those resurrected (and rewarded) at this time are part of the "first resurrection." This has caused some confusion since many believers had already been resurrected when the church was raptured some seven years earlier. However, the words *first resurrection* refer to a category of resurrected people rather than a chronological order. Those involved in the "first resurrection" are believers.

> *The term "first" is used more to characterize the occasion as to kind, namely a resurrection of the righteous, than as to number in sequence. This idea makes the resurrection of the wicked, which does not occur until after the millennium, the second resurrection, corresponding in name to the "second death," as noted in Revelation 20:6, 14. The term "second" here again carries a connotation basically in respect to kind, rather than sequence.*[5]

Thus, the "first resurrection" has to do with those who are resurrected to life eternal (cf. John 5:29). There are several points in time when believers are raised to eternal life, but all would be considered the "first resurrection."

Judgments After the Millennial Kingdom

When the thousand-year messianic kingdom is over, three more final judgments will take place. They are necessary in order to prepare for the eternal kingdom of God, which will follow the millennial kingdom of Christ. With these, God's judgments are completed.

The first judgment is that of Satan and the fallen angels (Rev. 20:10). The Scriptures reveal that Satan and his angelic followers will be judged for their sin and rebellion (2 Peter 2:4; Jude 1:6–7) and that believers will be involved in their judgment (1 Cor. 6:3). Satan's fate was sealed for all time at the cross, but it is not until after the millennium that he is cast forever into the lake of fire. Satan's judgment has several stages. Halfway through the tribulation he will be cast out of heaven and confined to the earth. At the beginning of the millennial kingdom, Satan will be bound and thrown into the Abyss. He will be released at the end of the Millennium for a short period of time. The rebellion that he brings about will be brief, and he will then be cast into the lake of fire, which will be his final, eternal judgment.

The second judgment will be the destruction by fire of the present heavens and earth (2 Peter 3:10). This passing away of the present universe is anticipated in several passages of Scripture (e.g., Matt. 24:35; Rev. 20:11). Because of the remaining elements of the curse placed on creation and because of the presence of sin in the universe, this destruction is necessary. Once the present heavens and earth are destroyed, God will create a new heaven and earth (21:1).

The third judgment to take place after the millennial kingdom but before the eternal state begins is the judgment of the unsaved. This judgment is commonly referred to as "the Great White Throne" judgment because of its description in Revelation 20:11–15. All unsaved people from every age will be resurrected at this time and will stand before the Lord Jesus to be judged (cf. John 5:22, 26–29). These individuals are referred to as "the dead," in contrast to believers, who are called "the dead in Christ." When these unsaved people appear before the Lord, two books will be opened:

> *The Book of Life which will be opened at the Great White Throne judgment will not contain the name of anyone who will be in that judgment. The books of works which will also be opened will prove that all who are being judged deserve eternal condemnation (and may be used to determine degrees of punishment).*[6]

These books are not, of course, needed to jog the Lord's memory but are there as positive evidence to all concerned that the judgment being executed is fair and right. These unsaved are thrown into the lake of fire, which is said to be the second death.

CHAPTER SEVENTEEN

THE FUTURE Kingdom OF God

While hiking deep in a wilderness area, a city dweller came across a magnificent waterfall. He stood admiring this genuinely beautiful sight, greatly impressed not only with what was there but with what was not there. The roar of the cascading waters, the awesome beauty and color of the lush green trees, the brilliant hues of the many wildflowers—together they nearly overwhelmed his senses. He was almost equally impressed, however, with the absence of litter, traffic jams, and the incessant noise of his high-tech society. What was there and what was not there made this a powerful and memorable moment.

The wilderness experience of the city dweller will be the experience of all those who enter the marvelous future kingdom of God. We will be awed by what is there and happily impressed by what is not there. Once Jesus Christ destroys the kings and kingdoms of this world, He will establish the most magnificent kingdom ever seen on this earth.

THE DURATION OF THE FUTURE KINGDOM OF GOD

Daniel revealed that when the Lord establishes His future kingdom, it will not only bring to a final end all human kingdoms but it will be a kingdom that will endure forever—"the God of heaven will set up a kingdom which will never be destroyed, and that kingdom will not be left for another people; . . . it will itself endure forever" (Dan. 2:44).

This future kingdom of God will have two distinct phases. The first phase is the millennial kingdom of Christ, and the second phase is the eternal state. The millennial (messianic) kingdom is declared to be one thousand years in Revelation 20:4–6. The fact that this number is repeated six times in this passage indicates that this figure is to be understood literally. The second phase of the future kingdom of God is eternal (22:5).

THE PURPOSE OF THE FUTURE KINGDOM OF GOD

When God created Adam and Eve, He gave them "dominion" over the earth, establishing the theocratic kingdom in Eden (Gen. 1:26). However, when Adam and Eve sinned, they not only defected from God but handed the ruling authority over to Satan (cf. Luke 4:6). Ever since then Satan has operated as the ruler of this world (cf. John 12:31; 14:30; 16:11; 2 Cor. 4:4; 1 John 5:19). The Scriptures again and again reveal God's determination to reestablish His rulership over the earth through the Messiah, the Son of God (e.g., Ps. 2:7–9; Isa. 2:2–4; 9:6–7; 11:1–5).

God's great purpose in establishing His future kingdom on *this present earth* is to fulfill His many promises given in the Scriptures and to clearly demonstrate to all of creation that He alone is the sovereign God. It was on this earth that God was apparently defeated (in Eden and at the Cross), and it is on this earth where He must be clearly victorious, defeating all usurpers and establishing His rule. Closely connected with this is the need to fulfill His specific covenant promises to Israel. The promises given in the Abrahamic, Palestinian, Davidic, and new covenants are fulfilled in the millennial kingdom. The purpose of the millennial (messianic) kingdom especially relates to fulfilling these covenants made with Israel. The second (eternal) phase of the future kingdom of God will maintain God's sovereign ruling authority over a new heaven and a new earth.

CHARACTERISTICS OF THE MILLENNIAL KINGDOM

In the book of Revelation, John reveals that the length of the messianic kingdom will be a thousand years, but through the numerous prophecies found in the Old Testament we learn about the characteristics of the millennial (messianic) kingdom.

The Government of the Millennial Kingdom

Jesus the Messiah will reign as the King, fulfilling the Davidic covenant (cf. Ps. 2:1–9; Isa. 9:6–7; 11:1–2; 55:3, 11; Jer. 23:5–8; 33:20–26; Ezek. 34:23–25; 37:23–24; Luke 1:32–33). The Lord Jesus will rule over a united Israel, with Jerusalem as the center of His kingdom.

Israel will enjoy a special relationship with the King, since they are in a covenant relationship with Him. However, the Lord Jesus will also rule over the Gentile nations as their sovereign Lord (Ps. 2:8; Isa. 2:4; 42:1; Dan. 2:35; 7:14, 27). He will be the benevolent dictator of the entire earth.

Some Scriptures suggest the mechanics of Christ's rule during the millennium. For example, Jesus once promised to reward the Twelve by granting them the right to sit on twelve thrones ruling over the twelve tribes of Israel in His kingdom (Matt. 19:28). It would seem that each apostle will have a kind of jurisdiction (under Christ) over one tribal area in Israel. Also, some offer evidence (based on Ezekiel 34 and 37) for the idea that King David will have a special place of rulership under the Lord Jesus in the millennial age.[1] If this is accurate, David would be a prince who, under Christ, shares some of the duties in the millennial kingdom.

The Scriptures do teach that others will rule under Christ's authority in the messianic kingdom. For example, one of the rewards offered by the Lord Jesus to His faithful servants is the privilege of rulership when He returns (e.g., Luke 19:12–27; Rev. 5:10; 20:4). Faithful Christians may have the privilege of serving Christ in places of rulership over the Gentile nations scattered all over the earth (cf. 1 Cor. 6:2; 2 Tim. 2:12).

It would seem that part of the purpose of the seventy-five days between the second coming and the actual beginning of the millennial kingdom will be to establish governing authority over the nations of the earth. However, whatever the setup may be, Jesus is unquestionably the King of all kings and the Lord of all ruling authorities.

The Spiritual Characteristics of the Millennial Kingdom

The millennial kingdom will be a wonderfully spiritual time. *First and foremost, the risen, glorified Lord Jesus Himself will be present.* This fact alone sets this period of time apart from all others. When the apostle John saw this glorious Lord, he could do nothing but prostrate himself before Him. Certainly this will be the response of all the subjects of His kingdom.

Second, this is a uniquely spiritual time because Satan is bound (Rev. 20:1–3). With the removal of Satan comes the removal of his demonic forces and his world system. Even today the spiritual temperature would rise significantly if Satan and his world system were not around.

Third, the reign of Christ is characterized by righteousness (e.g., Isa. 11:4–5; 32:1; 33:5). His reign is not only declared to be one of righteousness but is also seen in the emphasis that He will rule with "a rod of iron," which means that sin will be restrained and dealt with severely (e.g., Ps. 2:9; Isa. 11:1–5; Rev. 12:5; 19:5). When the millennial kingdom begins, only righteous Jews and righteous Gentiles will be allowed to enter. They will retain their earthly bodies and their sin natures, as will the children born to them. But, in spite of the presence of the sin nature in these people, righteousness, not sinfulness, will be the prevailing atmosphere in Messiah's kingdom.

Fourth, because of the domination of righteousness on the earth, several wonderful consequences will appear. The world will be characterized by peace (cf. Isa. 2:4; 11:6–9; 32:18), joy (cf. Isa. 9:3–4), a full knowledge of the Lord (cf. Jer. 31:34), and a fullness of the Holy Spirit (cf. Joel 2:28–32).

Fifth, there will be a universal worship of the Lord Jesus, centered in the magnificent new temple in Jerusalem. This worship will no doubt be of a quality and depth never before seen on earth, as righteous Jews and Gentiles gladly come to Jerusalem to praise the great Savior King (e.g., Isa. 2:2–4; 11:9–10; Ezek. 20:40–41; 40:1–46:24; Zech. 14:16). And with the glory of the Lord once again present in the temple, the scene of worship will be best described by the word *awesome.* Jerusalem will be like a spiritual magnet drawing people to worship and praise the Lord.

Connected with the worship of Jesus Christ in the millennial kingdom will be animal sacrifices (cf. Ezek. 43:13, 27; 45:15, 17, 20; Zech. 14:16–21; Isa. 66:20–23; Jer. 33:18). That animal sacrifices are mentioned in connection with millennial worship has troubled some because they appear to be a throwback to the outdated Levitical worship and to diminish the work of Christ on the cross. But these sacrifices do not mean that there is a return to the Levitical worship system, and they do not detract from the cross.

Like the Old Testament temple that revealed the character of God through its rituals and provided a place for sinful men to approach God, the millennial temple will perform the same basic function for those under the new covenant. We who are in our resurrected bodies will apparently not need these sacrifices, but there will be sinful men in non-glorified bodies who will. These people (even if they are believers) can and do sin because of the presence of the old sinful flesh. Thus the need for cleansing and purification exists. Afterward, in the eternal kingdom on the new earth, there will be no sacrifices because there are no non-glorified people anymore, only resurrected people living in a new and glorious environment.

Animal sacrifices were never a means of removing sin in the Old Testament and they will not have and cannot have that function in the millennium. They may partially function as a memorial of Christ's death since God as the Great Educator regularly gives His people ways to remember His great deeds and provisions (1 Cor. 11:24; Lev. 2:2, 9; 5:12; Josh. 4:4–7). It would certainly be in keeping with the way God has worked in the past to give mankind a way of remembering that greatest of provisions, the cross. It may be that the sacrifices will be a visible way of maintaining fellowship with God much like we today need to be cleansed from sin. But it is most likely that the animal sacrifices are the means of providing ceremonial purification as sinful men approach the glorified Messiah in worship.

> *While the Old Testament sacrificial system was* effective, *it was not* expiatory. *In the words of Hebrews, it was effective for temporary ritual restoration, the "cleansing of the flesh" (Heb. 9:10,13), but it could not permanently expiate guilt by "taking away sins" (Heb. 10:4) or "cleansing the conscience" (Heb. 9:14). . . . The Savior offered Himself in place of guilty sinners to both* expiate *(remove guilt of sin) and* propitiate *(appease the righteous wrath of God against sin). . . . Under the present administration of grace—in which Christ is absent from the earth and our approach is in the heavenly realm—sanctification is possible under the spiritual provisions of the New Covenant (the Holy Spirit, the new heart). However, under the coming administration of the kingdom in which Christ will be present on the earth and approach will be at the Temple in Jerusalem, outward corporate "sanctification" (or ceremonial purification) will be necessary, as well as inward personal sanctification, under the full terms (spiritual and physical) of the New Covenant.*

> *Therefore, the literal interpretation of the sacrifices of the Temple of Ezekiel and their resumption during the Millennium have not been found to be blasphemous, but rather, to the God-ordained means to blessing in the theocratic kingdom. And though this Final Temple and its priestly service will be at the center of the blessings of this Messianic age its course will conclude when the 1,000 year reign of Christ over a restored Israel is complete (Rev. 20:7) and the eternal kingdom has begun with the creation of a new heavens and earth (Isa. 66:22; Rev. 21:1).*[2]

It will be a different system on earth during the millennial kingdom, and these sacrifices apparently have an important role to play. This age of the church and that age of the millennium will have many differences just as there are differences between this age and the Mosaic law period. But when the many statements of the prophets are put together, we must conclude that the millennial kingdom will be the most spiritual time ever witnessed on this earth.

The Physical Characteristics of the Millennial Kingdom

Although the millennial kingdom will be established on this present earth, the earth will be significantly changed.

First, the curse that was placed on the creation at the time of the fall of man (Gen. 3:17–19) will be lifted. The apostle Paul testifies that creation experiences futility and corruption because of the curse; that negative situation will continue until God finishes saving mankind (Rom. 8:19–23). One result of the curse being removed is that peace will come to the animal kingdom, which has been characterized by violence and death since the days of Eden (Isa. 11:6–9; 35:9; 65:25). All animals will once again be plant eaters, as they were in the original creation (Gen. 1:30). That carnivorous animals will no longer exist is seen in the fact that wolves and lambs live together and lions and oxen graze together.

The reversal of the curse will also enable the earth to once again be amazingly productive, being freed from thorns and thistles (e.g., Isa. 32:13–15). Much of the present earth is unproductive because it is desert, but the millennial kingdom will be characterized by an abundance of water, and the desolate, dry areas of the earth will blossom as the rose (Isa. 35:1–7).

Second, sickness and deformity will end (Isa. 33:24; 35:5–6; 61:1–2; Ezek. 34:16). It seems that the King will be a great healer and will remove disease and physical deformity from the earth. This will result in long life spans such that if someone dies at the age of one hundred they will be thought of as being cut off prematurely. The life span of those in their earthly bodies will rival those who lived in the days of Noah.

Of course, not all participants in the millennial kingdom will have earthly, mortal bodies. Millions of believers from the Old Testament era, the church age, and the tribulation will have resurrected, immortal bodies. But there is no reason to think that these two groups will not be relating to one another and interacting with each other during the millennium. The resurrected Lord Jesus had no problems teaching and fellowshipping with His disciples during the forty days after His resurrection.

With the earth being freed from the curse and becoming universally fertile, and with disease and death being almost nonexistent, we can understand why peace, prosperity, and a sense of well-being will characterize Messiah's kingdom (e.g., Isa. 25:8–9; 35:1–2; 30:23–25; 60:15; 61:7; Amos 9:13–15; Ezek. 36:29–30; Zech. 8:11–12; 9:16–17). This great millennial kingdom will last a thousand years, yet it is merely the first phase of the eternal, future kingdom of God.

THE ETERNAL PHASE OF THE FUTURE KINGDOM OF GOD

At the very end of the millennial kingdom and before the start of the final, eternal kingdom of God, a brief rebellion will be led by Satan (Rev. 20:7–9). Having been released from the Abyss, Satan is able to gather a large number of people against the Lord Jesus. These rebels are undoubtedly unsaved people. They were born in the millennial period and outwardly adhered to the principles of the Messiah's kingdom (no doubt fearing the "rod of iron"), but never came to personal, saving faith. We are not told why God allows Satan to be released, but it is perhaps to give a final, grand object lesson concerning the depravity of man. If nothing else, this rebellion at the end of the millennium demonstrates that man's real problem is his sinful, unregenerate heart, not his environment or his circumstances. These rebels have lived in Messiah's kingdom, a near-perfect environment. They cannot claim poverty, a lack of knowledge, bad circumstances, or an unfair judicial system as reasons for their rebellious behavior. Their problem is their sinful heart. This event underscores the truth that, when given the opportunity to rebel against the Lord God, sinful man will do it every time.

The rebellion is short-lived and completely unsuccessful. And those who participate in it are put to death, while their leader Satan receives his final judgment in the lake of fire (Rev. 20:9–10). After this the judging of all unsaved people at the great white throne judgment takes place, as well as the judging of the old heavens and earth. These events must take place before the final, eternal phase of the kingdom of God begins.

The end of the millennial phase signals the beginning of the eternal phase. The apostle Paul provides some important information about this transition in 1 Corinthians 15:24–28:

> *Then comes the end, when He hands over the kingdom to the God and Father, when He has abolished all rule and all authority and power. For He must reign until He has put all His enemies under His feet. The last enemy that will be abolished is death. For He has put all things in subjection under His feet. But when He says, "All things are put in subjection," it is evident that He is excepted who put all things in subjection to Him. And when all things are subjected to Him, then the Son Himself also will be subjected to the One who subjected all things to Him, that God may be all in all.*

Paul is speaking of the transition from the millennial phase of the future kingdom of God into the eternal phase of that kingdom. He points out that the Father put all things under Christ's authority, with the exception, of course, of the Father Himself. Now after all things, including death, come under Christ's authority, then Christ will transfer the kingdom to the Father, and God (including Christ) shall reign. Once the millennial kingdom is over, all things have come under Christ's authority, and the eternal phase of the final kingdom of God will begin.

> *The means by which all things are brought under subjection to God, so that He becomes all in all, is that Christ unites the authority that is His as King with the Father's after He has "put down all rule and all authority and power" (1 Cor. 15:24). God's original purpose was to manifest His absolute authority and this purpose is realized when Christ unites the earthly theocracy with the eternal kingdom of God. Thus, while Christ's earthly theocratic rule is limited to one thousand years, which is sufficient time to manifest God's perfect theocracy on the earth, His reign is eternal.[3]*

After Satan's power is finally broken and all people are finally resurrected, all the subjugation necessary has been realized. It is then possible to move into the eternal state, into a new world.

> *As we pass from chapter 20 into chapter 21 of the Apocalypse, therefore, we stand at the junction point between two worlds and between two kingdoms. It is the end of the "first" or "natural" order of things, and the beginning of the final order of things. . . . What will happen is succinctly described in St. Paul's classic passage on the subject . . . (1 Cor. 15:24, 28). This does not mean the end of our Lord's regal activity, but rather that from here onward in the unity of the Godhead He reigns with the Father as the eternal Son. There are no longer two thrones: one His Messianic throne and the other the Father's throne, as our Lord indicated in Revelation 3:21. In the final Kingdom there is but one throne, and it is "the throne of God and of the Lamb." (22:3)*[4]

When the earthly millennial kingdom is merged with the eternal kingdom, the eternal sovereignty of God is established. Satan's challenge and disruption of God's purposes so many millenniums ago will be answered finally and forever.

LIFE IN THE ETERNAL KINGDOM OF GOD

The Scriptures do not give us a great deal of information about this future aspect of the kingdom. Perhaps that is because we would not be able to really comprehend what it will be like, since it will be so far beyond our present experiences. However, the book of Revelation does give us some information about this eternal kingdom of God (21:1–22:5). Some interpreters see this section in Revelation as viewing the millennial period and not the eternal state. However, such an idea violates the literary order and chronological order of Revelation.

Revelation 20 has already spoken of the millennial period and discussed the final judgments. After discussing the final judgments it is highly unlikely that John would then revert back to a discussion of the millennial. Also, in Revelation 21, such things as sin and death are said to be excluded, which would not be true of the millennial period where both are present to some degree. Furthermore, the language in Revelation 21:1–22:5 is characterized by an eternal finality that would not be appropriate for the thousand-year millennial kingdom (e.g., 22:5—"they shall reign for ever and ever").

It seems best, therefore, to view Revelation 21:1–22:5 as giving information about the eternal kingdom of God, which follows the millennial kingdom. This section discloses several things about the eternal kingdom.

New Heavens and a New Earth

One of the final judgments following the millennial kingdom will be the destruction of the heavens and earth (2 Peter 3:7, 10; Rev. 20:11). When these have been destroyed, God will call into existence new heavens and a new earth. In the eternal kingdom, therefore, these new heavens and earth are not simply a renovation of the old heavens and earth but are, rather, the result of a definite act of creation. The word *new* (*kainos*) denotes something that is fresh or new in quality but not something that is strange or uniquely different.[5] This would suggest that the newly created heavens and earth will strongly resemble the previous ones that were destroyed by fire. Apparently the new earth will resemble the old with the main exception that there are no oceans on the new earth (21:1). Our present oceans are a result of God's judgment (Genesis 6–8), and there will be no evidence of judgment in the eternal kingdom.

The new earth will be the dwelling place of God's people. It would seem that the account of the original creation (Genesis 1–2) is a key in understanding the account of the re-creation (Revelation 21–22). God is going to do in the eternal state what He originally intended to do in the first creation. Mankind was created then to dwell on this earth, and that is where he will dwell in the eternal kingdom of God. This would suggest that in eternity, as in the original creation, man will be involved in various kinds of meaningful activity, learning and serving the Lord. The church will dwell on this new earth because the Scriptures teach that the church will be wherever Christ is, and He will be ruling in this eternal kingdom (cf. John 14:3; 17:24; Rev. 21:3). Israel will dwell on this new earth since the promises in the covenants guarantee an eternal dynasty, kingdom, throne, and blessing, and it would seem that an eternal earth is needed to fulfill these promises.

But why does God create new heavens? The answer may be found in Genesis 1, where we discover why He created the old heavens. Those were created to provide light for the earth and to mark time on the earth—days, months, and years. This would suggest that time will exist in the eternal state, which is seen by the fact that the tree of life bears fruit each month (Rev. 22:2).

Full, Unhindered Fellowship with God

We were created for fellowship with God. But even in our most worshipful moments, we sense the barriers and hindrances that exist because of sin. In the eternal kingdom no such hindrances will be experienced. It is said that we shall "see His face" and God Himself will "dwell among them" (Rev. 21:3; 22:4).

What Adam and Eve began to experience in the garden of Eden, the redeemed people of God will fully experience in the eternal kingdom. We will see His glory and begin to know the Lord as never before. This will cause a never-before-equaled quality of worship in our lives. Apparently, there is no temple in the New Jerusalem or on the new earth. None is really needed since the Lord Himself will dwell among His people (21:22). It is clear that we will then enjoy a quality of fellowship with the Lord that we cannot presently imagine.

Elements Missing from Our Present Experience

Sin has brought terrible and far-reaching results into human experience. Not only has sin brought separation from God, but it has affected mankind's mind, emotions, and physical body. Sickness, death, pain, and sorrow of all kinds have been the constant companions of mankind. But we are so used to sin and its effects that we find it hard to even imagine what life would be like without these things.

The wonderful truth is that in the eternal kingdom of God all aspects of sin and all consequences of sin are gone, including sorrow, death, and pain (Rev. 21:4). How liberating it will be not to face or experience death. How pleasant not to have the tears of sorrow, frustration, regret, anger, or disappointment run down our cheeks. The eternal kingdom will be wonderful because of what is not there.

A Beautiful City Called the New Jerusalem

After the creation of the new heavens and earth, the apostle John says that the beautiful holy city, the New Jerusalem, will descend from heaven to the earth. The city is of incredible size and beauty. It measures 1,500 miles long, 1,500 miles wide, and 1,500 miles high (Rev. 21:16). It is not only declared to be beautiful, like a bride adorned for her husband (v. 2), but it is said to have gates of pearl, buildings of pure gold, and foundation stones of precious gems (vv. 17–21). In it will dwell the Lord and His people. "This city will serve as the eternal abode of several groups. It will be inhabited by the entire Triune God, the entire angelic host, the church saints and the spirits of just men made perfect who are the Old Testament saints."[6]

It is felt by some that this glorious city came into existence prior to the millennial kingdom and became the dwelling place of the church saints after the rapture and judgment seat of Christ. It is believed that the church age saints (the bride of Christ) are joined by the Old Testament saints who are resurrected at the second coming. The city itself will not actually come down upon the earth during the millennial kingdom but will remain suspended over the earth.

> *This dwelling place prepared for the bride, in which the Old Testament saints find their place as servants (Rev. 22:3), is moved down into the air to remain over the land of Palestine during the millennium, during which time the saints exercise their right to reign. These saints are in their eternal state and the city enjoys its eternal glory. At the expiration of the millennial age, during the renovation of the earth, the dwelling place is removed during the conflagration, to find its place after the recreation as the connecting link between the new heavens and the new earth.[7]*

Whether or not this is the sequence of events is impossible to say, and there is a variety of strong opinions on the subject. What is clear, however, is that this awesomely beautiful city will be the significant place for life and worship during the eternal kingdom of God. And although there is much that we do not know about life in the eternal kingdom, we do know that our God's past creative acts are wondrous, and this leads us to conclude that His future creative work will be at least as beautiful and magnificent. It will definitely be worth waiting for.

PART FOUR

Understanding
THE
FUTURE OF THE
Individual

CHAPTER EIGHTEEN

DEATH AND
THE
Intermediate State

I

f invited to attend a party or asked to go to a funeral, most would quickly choose the party. After all, there is at least some hope for fun and laughter at the party, but the funeral only offers such things as tears, burdens, and some real uneasiness of mind and heart. Yet the counsel of wise King Solomon was that it is better to go to the funeral home ("a house of mourning") than to attend a party ("a house of feasting"). This is so, he explains, because parties tend to promote an empty, useless perspective on life, whereas it is at the funeral home that we face reality (Eccl. 7:2–6).

It is, of course, at this very point (of facing reality) that many wish to depart from Solomon's wisdom. Certainly death is not the most pleasant of subjects, and people prefer not to meditate on it because deep inside it brings fear and uneasiness. The biblical truth that "it is appointed for men to die once and after this comes judgment" (Heb. 9:27) pointedly reinforces what man intuitively seems to sense—that there is life after death, and it may not be pleasant. Since none of us has walked through the valley of death, there is a certain foreboding about it all. People generally prefer to suppress thinking about the inevitability and nearness of death.

It is not at all surprising, therefore, that there is a readiness to listen to ideas and philosophies that teach tranquility and peace after death. Many would try to calm people's fears and anxieties by assuring them that no eternal punishment awaits them. This may take the form of a television special that gives the testimonials of those who claim to have had wonderful and warm near-death experiences or that promotes such teachings as reincarnation. Even some within the church attempt to persuade others not to be unduly concerned about death, since God is a God of love; because of that, everyone will eventually be saved, and no one will really suffer forever in a place of torment.

It is certainly an understatement to say that death, the intermediate state, and eternity are not minor matters. In fact, of all the areas within eschatology, none matters more than this one. So, as we have done with all the other areas of eschatology, we must turn to the Word of God for final and definitive answers.

THE BIBLICAL VIEW OF DEATH

Though death is both real and inevitable, it is unnatural. When God created the heavens and the earth, death was not part of it. And that is why, eventually, death will be finally conquered (1 Cor. 15:26) and banished from the new creation—"And death and hades were thrown into the lake of fire" (Rev. 20:14). The Scriptures speak of three kinds of death: spiritual death, which is the separation of a created being from the Creator (e.g., Eph. 2:1); eternal death, which is the final, permanent separation of an unsaved person from God (e.g., Rev. 20:14); and physical death, which is the separation of the immaterial part of man from the material body (e.g., Gen. 35:18–19).

When a person dies physically they do not cease to exist; rather, their body and soul experience separation.

> *Physical death is a termination of physical life by the separation of body and soul. It is never an annihilation. . . . Death is not a cessation of existence, but a severance of the natural relations of life. Life and death are not opposed to each other as existence and non-existence, but are opposites only as different modes of existence.*[1]

As Stephen was being stoned to death, he looked into heaven and prayed for the Lord to receive his spirit (Acts 7:59). As Rachel died during childbirth, it is said that her soul was in the act of departing (Gen. 35:18). James teaches that at physical death there is a separation of the body from the spirit (James 2:26). In the Scriptures, life is not viewed merely as existence but as well-being. Death, therefore, is the loss of well-being, not the cessation of being.

THE INTERMEDIATE STATE

Death and the Believer

After the death of a believer and before his resurrection, he or she exists in the intermediate state. The Scriptures do not give a great deal of information about this condition. That is because the hope of the believer is the resurrection, when all will be complete, and not the intermediate state (between death and resurrection). However, some important certainties are given by the writers of Scripture about what happens to the believer at death.

First, believers are given the guarantee that nothing, including death, will ever separate them from their Lord Jesus Christ (Rom. 8:38–39). This assures them that they are not abandoned even for a moment at the time of physical death. Jesus, who said that He would never leave His people, will not do so.

Second, believers need not fear going through death because the Lord Jesus, who has already gone through death, is with us (Ps. 23:4). It is true that death is viewed as an enemy that still administers a painful sting, because loss of various kinds is experienced (1 Cor. 15:54–57). But Jesus has been victorious over death, and in the future He will destroy death. It is interesting to observe that the New Testament refers to the death of Christians in terms that are not frightening (e.g., "sleep," 1 Thess. 4:13–15).

Third, believers are assured that death brings them immediately into the presence of Christ. The believer is either in his physical body living on the earth or has left his material body and has gone into Christ's presence. There is no third option, such as purgatory or "soul sleep." The apostle Paul declared in the plainest of terms in 2 Corinthians 5:6–8 that at the moment a Christian dies and leaves this sphere of existence, he enters at once into the presence of the Lord Jesus. This passage nowhere suggests an intermediate state of unconsciousness or some sort of purgatory. Paul said that, while he continues at home in the body, he also continues away from home as regards the Lord Jesus (present tense); because of this, his fellowship was incomplete (v. 7). He added that a moment of time is coming (*aorist*) when this situation will be changed and he will be present with the

Lord and absent from the body, which is a rather clear reference to death (v. 8). This passage clearly teaches that at the moment of death the believer enters into a state of close fellowship with the Lord. "Both the tenses of the infinitives in verse 8 and the parallelism between verse 8 and verse 6 indicate that being present with the Lord does occur the moment one dies."[2]

Charles Hodge supports this interpretation and also shows that Paul's presence with the Lord is not a reference to the resurrection:

> *The apostle is speaking of the grounds of consolation in the immediate prospect of death. He says in effect that the dissolution of the body does not destroy the soul or deprive it of a home. His consolation was that if unclothed he would not be found naked. While at home in the body he was absent from the Lord, but as soon as he was absent from the body he would be present with the Lord. It is so obvious that the apostle is here speaking of what takes place at death.*[3]

Another passage that forcefully teaches that at death the believer goes immediately into the presence of Christ is Philippians 1:21–23. In this portion, Paul reveals the longing of his heart to be with the Lord Jesus Christ. He is well aware that the believers would greatly benefit from his ministry in their lives, and this gave him a desire to stay on earth. But in spite of his zeal for the salvation of people and his great desire to see Christians built up in their faith, he longed to depart and be with Christ. Paul would not have this longing if at death he entered purgatory or lapsed into a condition of nonexistence ("soul sleep").

The grammar of this passage emphatically teaches that at death a believer goes immediately to be with Christ.

> *The preposition* eis to *plus the infinitive shows "true purpose or end in view"—the strong desire which causes Paul's dilemma. Both infinitives* (analusai *and* einai) *have one construction, so are one thought, one grammatical expression. . . . In simple English, Paul's one desire has a twofold object: departure and being with Christ! If departure did not mean his immediate being with Christ, another construction would have been employed. It therefore seems impossible that soul sleep was in the mind of the Apostle, since he desired to depart from his body and to spiritually enjoy the presence of the Lord.*[4]

The apostle Paul's use of the two infinitives connected by the copulative "and" united by one definite article makes clear that he is putting these two ideas together. In the apostle's thinking, departure (death) meant that he was to be in Christ's presence. He sees that there are two possibilities for him, and he leaves no room for a third option.

At death the believer goes into the presence of Christ in heaven. Since at His ascension the Lord Jesus returned to the Father's house, it is there that the believer goes also. We should remember that when Jesus returns at the rapture to gather His church, those who have died previously will be coming with Him (1 Thess. 4:14). From this we can see that believers who died prior to the rapture (and thus prior to the resurrection) are with the Lord Jesus in heaven and will return with Him. Some theologians have suggested that, in this intermediate state, believers will possess some sort of temporary body. This idea is based in part on the fact that at the transfiguration of Christ, Moses appeared in bodily form even though the resurrection has yet to take place. But although the idea of a temporary body is not clear, it is clear that believers are with the Lord.

While on the cross Jesus promised the dying thief that he would be with Him in paradise that very day (Luke 23:43). The word *paradise* (a term that means "parks" or "gardens") is used three times in the New Testament for heaven, where Christ presently is manifesting His presence and glory. Some of the wonders of paradise, which were truly magnificent, were seen by Paul when he was caught up there (2 Cor. 12:2–4). Though there is undoubtedly so very much that we do not and cannot know about life immediately after death, it clearly is to be greatly preferred to this present existence. And yet the intermediate state for the believer will not be as wondrous as the time when the resurrection body is received and salvation is completed.

Death and the Unbeliever

The unbeliever also continues in conscious existence at the time of physical death. But his fate is not a pleasant one, as he experiences punishment in hell (hades). Some religious systems object to the idea of a conscious place of punishment called hell (sheol and hades). They point out that these words refer to the grave or a hole in the ground but never are equated with eternal punishment. Whereas it is true that these words can refer to the grave and generally to the place of the departed, it is also true that they are used as places of punishment. "Briefly, we may say that in the Old Testament Sheol usually means the grave, but sometimes the place of punishment, while in the New Testament Hades and Hell usually mean the place of punishment but sometimes the grave."[5]

Several Scripture passages reveal that these words are used as places of judgment and punishment for the wicked. Psalm 9:17 states that "the wicked will return to Sheol." Here "Sheol" is a place prepared for the wicked and is not simply the grave, since both righteous and wicked go to the grave. Proverbs 23:14 declares that "you shall beat him [the child] with the rod, and deliver his soul from Sheol." It is obvious that no amount of parental discipline can keep a child from the grave. Luke 16:23 tells of the rich man who died and "in Hades he lifted up his eyes, being in torment." His punishment, which follows his death, is clearly in view here. A number of other passages refer to a place where the wicked are conscious and punished in the intermediate state (e.g., Matt. 5:22; 11:23; 23:33).

Technically it is true that in the Scriptures hell is not seen as a place of eternal punishment. Hell will definitely come to an end when it is thrown into the lake of fire, but the lake of fire is clearly viewed as the place of eternal punishment (cf. Rev. 20:10, 14–15). Whether it is hell or the lake of fire, Scriptures give ample warning of the terrors that are ahead for those who will not repent and turn to the Lord Jesus for salvation and deliverance from judgment.

The Theory of "Soul Sleep"

It is the theological position of some groups (such as Seventh-Day Adventism) that there is no conscious existence between death and the resurrection. This concept of nonbeing during the intermediate state is partly based on verses that speak of death as "sleep." The view of "soul sleep" (or more accurately "soul extinction") rests squarely on a view of man's nature that denies a separate existence at death for the immaterial part of man (soul or spirit). It is not within the scope of this chapter to deal with the nature of man, demonstrating that soul and spirit can exist apart from the body. But when a person is correctly viewed as having both a material and immaterial part, it becomes clear that "sleep" is being used in a figurative way:

Everyone acknowledges, of course, that the body *does sleep until the resurrection, that is, it becomes unconscious, insensible. The sleep spoken of is that of the body, not of the soul. Those who teach soul sleep have simply confused the sleep of the body with that of the soul. Soul sleep is not taught anywhere in the Bible. In every instance in which the word sleep is used in connection with the dead the context makes it clear that it applies only to the body.*[6]

The nature of the body's "sleep" is that it will one day "wake up" in the resurrection. Thus, this figure of speech is not just euphemistic but illustrates a profound truth.

The doctrine of soul sleep is built on a metaphor, which is hermeneutically unsound. Death is certainly pictured as sleep in the New Testament, but one does not develop a doctrine from a figure of speech. It is evident that we are dealing with a word that speaks of appearance, not fact. The dead person appears to be asleep as the body lies there.

Some powerful Scripture portions destroy the concept of soul sleep if taken at face value. Two of these—2 Corinthians 5:6–8 and Philippians 1:21–23—have already been discussed. A number of other Scriptures can be added to these two. For example, Luke 16:19–31 relates the story of the rich man and Lazarus. In this passage Jesus pointedly teaches that at death these two men were not reduced to the common level of nonbeing. The story would not only lose its point, but it would be very misleading. Whether this is a parable or an actual event, it still teaches that there is life immediately after death, that life is lived in a conscious condition after death, that in the life after death the lost and saved are eternally separated, and that the lost have some memories of their earthly life.

The diversified conscious existence of the rich man and Lazarus pictured symbolically in this parable, therefore, must be a reflection of conditions during the intermediate state. As such, the parable confirms what we have learned from other New Testament passages, namely, that believers immediately after death go to be with Christ in order to enjoy a provisional happiness in His presence (provisional because their bodies have not yet been raised), whereas unbelievers at death go at once to a place of provisional punishment.[7]

Another significant passage is Luke 20:38, where the Lord Jesus answered the Sadducees' question about life after death. The Sadducees not only denied the idea of bodily resurrection but, according to Acts 23:8, denied that the soul existed after death. Jesus corrected both errors when He pointed out that Abraham, Isaac, and Jacob could not have been in the condition of nonbeing; they existed when God appeared to Moses at the burning bush (centuries after their physical deaths) because He identified Himself as their God. The three patriarchs were very much alive, though not living on the earth. Jesus then concluded that God is the God of the living.

Other passages that point to existence after death include Christ's declaration to the thief on the cross that he would be with Jesus that day in paradise (Luke 23:43) and Jesus' commitment (Luke 23:46) on the cross of His spirit into the Father's hand (which becomes quite meaningless if Jesus ceased to exist at His death).

In light of substantial evidence, the theory of soul sleep must be rejected as exegetically and theologically unsound. We conclude, then, that at death both the saved and unsaved experience continuing existence. Death is not the cessation of being; rather, it is the separation of body and soul. At death the believer, who is "in Christ" and can never be separated from Him, immediately goes into His presence. Although lacking the resurrection body, the believer consciously enjoys the glorious presence of Christ in paradise. On the other hand, the unbeliever consciously exists in a place of punishment. He will continue in this place of judgment until he is resurrected at the resurrection of the unsaved.

CHAPTER NINETEEN

THE FINAL

Eternal State

There are some things that the human mind finds difficult, if not impossible, to fully comprehend. We are, for example, given numbers and figures on a variety of subjects but often find it hard to really grasp what is being communicated to us. For example, someone tells you that the nearest star is 4.3 light years away (a light year being about 5,880,000,000,000 miles); you read that a computer chip the size of a thumbnail can contain three to four million words; and that the human eye has 130 million light-sensitive rods and cones that transmit one billion electrical impulses to the brain every second.

Understanding such facts is difficult for most of us because of the shear magnitude of the numbers involved. Eternity is something like this. We can speak of timelessness but find it hard to identify with the idea because that has not been our experience. We can discuss never-ending existence, but all we really know are beginnings and endings. The idea of eternity is simply beyond our full comprehension. So it is with a certain sense of inadequacy that we discuss the forever fate of mankind.

THE FINAL FUTURE OF THE BELIEVER

It was the prayer of the Lord Jesus that those who believed in Him would be with Him and see His glory (John 17). This prayer will be answered. The righteous will be with the Lord and experience eternal life, which is not simply endless existence but the life of God in its fullness (Matt. 25:46; John 17:3). The quality of life we will have then is something that we cannot fully appreciate now (e.g., Rom. 8:18; 1 Cor. 2:7–9). Following all the judgments and resurrections, God will create new heavens and a new earth. From what we can discern in Revelation 21 and 22, the focus of the eternal state will apparently be the new earth, as the Lord seems to be returning to the original plan of establishing something similar to the garden of Eden.

In our discussion "Life in the Eternal Kingdom of God" (see the final pages of chapter 17), we dealt with the final future of the believer. Although some differences will apparently exist between believers, all will experience fullness of joy and fellowship with the Lord and with others. There can be no doubt that the eternal experience prepared for believers by our powerful, loving, creative Lord is beyond our thinking—and beyond any computer-generated model!

THE FINAL FUTURE OF THE UNBELIEVER

The fate of the unbeliever is terribly different from that of the believer. Instead of being in a place of joy and fellowship, they will be in a place where they will experience suffering and loss. In His ministry, the Lord Jesus spoke a great deal about hell and warned people to avoid this place of judgment (e.g., Matt. 10:28; 11:21–24; 18:9; 25:41; Luke 16:19–31; John 3:36; 5:29). His use of the imagery of fire in reference to the fate of the wicked points to the conscious pain and misery of the unbeliever. Even though there was sorrow in His heart, Jesus spoke plainly and forcibly about the final future of the wicked.

> *Jesus taught that hell is a place (Matt. 24:51; Luke 16:28; cf. Rev. 21:8; Acts 1:25b) to be avoided at all costs (Matt. 5:22, 29, 30). He taught that it will be a place of enforced separation from His presence (Matt. 7:23; cf. 2 Thess. 1:8–9). As a place of darkness, its only sounds will be weeping and the gnashing of teeth (Matt. 8:12). Hell is a fate far worse than one's physical death (Matt. 10:28) and will contain punishments varying in severity (Matt. 11:22–24).[1]*

Concerning the final future of the unbeliever, the Scriptures teach that a number of realities will exist.

It may be said to consist in (a) a total absence of the favor of God; (b) an endless disturbance of life as a result of the complete domination of sin; (c) positive pains and sufferings in body and soul; and (d) such subjective punishments as pangs of conscience, anguish, despair, weeping, and gnashing of teeth, Matt. 8:12; 13:50; Mark 9:43, 44, 47, 48; Luke 16:23, 28; Rev. 14:10; 21:8. Evidently, there will be degrees in the punishment of the wicked. This follows from such passages as Matt. 11:22, 24; Luke 12:47, 48; 20:17.[2]

Apparently the purpose of the great white throne judgment (Rev. 20:11–15), with the presence of "the books," is to determine the degree of punishment to be suffered by those who did not respond to the revelatory light they had received. All who appear at that judgment will be eternally separated from the Lord, but there will be some differences between them.

When the realities of heaven are contrasted with those of hell, we become all the more sensitive to the terrible fate of the unbeliever.

If it is true that "at (God's) right hand are pleasures forevermore" (Ps. 16:11, NKJV), then what must be the condition of those who are separated from Him forever (Luke 13:27)? Would it not be miseries forevermore? For those who are faithful servants, there will be the master's happiness to share (Matt. 25:21, 23); for those who are unfaithful servants, there will be the "weeping and gnashing of teeth" (Matt. 25:30). Heaven will be a place of no tears, no death, no pain (Rev. 21:4); hell will be a place of only weeping, death and torment (Matt. 8:12; Luke 16:28). Heaven will be a place of light (Rev. 22:5), hell a place of darkness (Matt. 22:13). Heaven will be a place of companionship (1 Cor. 13:12; John 14:3), hell a place of loneliness (Luke 16:26). Heaven will be a place of varying rewards (Eph. 6:8; 1 Cor. 3:14; Rev. 14:13), hell a place of differing punishments (Rev. 2:23; Rom. 2:5–9; 6:23). Finally, heaven will be where Christ is (John 14:3); hell will be where He is not (Matt. 25:41; Rev. 22:14–15).[3]

The duration of the punishment of the wicked is eternal (cf. Matt. 18:8; 25:41, 46; 2 Thess. 1:9; Rev. 14:11; 20:10). In Matthew 25:46 Jesus declared that the wicked "will go away into eternal punishment, but the righteous into eternal life." He used the same word (Gk: *aionios*) when speaking of the eternal destiny of both the righteous and the wicked. Since one cannot legitimately have the same word mean two entirely different things in the one context, it must be concluded that Jesus was teaching that the duration of the righteous and the wicked are the same. If the righteous live forever in heaven, then the wicked live forever in hell. At this point we should note that hell is not actually the place of everlasting punishment. It is the lake of fire that is said to be the place of everlasting punishment, and it is into the lake of fire that hell will someday be cast (Rev. 20:14). Whatever the terminology used, the Scriptures teach that the punishment of the wicked is everlasting.

It is impossible for a sober-minded person to be casual about hell, and it certainly should not be the subject of jokes. It is a terrible place of punishment originally created for the Devil and the fallen angels. There is no way to exit hell once there. The only way to avoid the horrors of eternal separation from the Lord is to receive God's gracious gift of salvation in Christ. Those who embrace the Savior and receive eternal life are exempted from eternal damnation. How important it is for believers to carry the good news of Christ to unbelievers! How important it is for unbelievers to respond in a positive way to this powerful gospel that changes the final future of the individual.

THE CONCEPT OF ANNIHILATIONISM

In the past a number of nonevangelical groups (such as the Jehovah's Witnesses and the Seventh-Day Adventists) have taught that the wicked will be annihilated. These have been joined in recent days by several theologians within the evangelical church who proclaim that God will annihilate the wicked since He is too loving and kind to inflict everlasting misery on His creatures. It is the teaching of annihilationism that the unsaved will not exist forever—their judgment will bring about the cessation of their existence. This punishment is to be eternal in that the results of the judgment are eternal, but there is a clear denial that the punishment itself goes on forever.

The position of annihilationism probably comes primarily from a desire to defend the character and actions of a God who is loving and gracious. It is felt by annihilationists that God would have to be viewed as cruel and vindictive if He allowed people to suffer in torment forever and ever. In the opinion of some, God would be some sort of monster akin to Satan. With this as a basis, they attempt to modify the traditional interpretation of Scripture texts and to tie in the traditional view of eternal punishment with Greek philosophy.

Four Basic Issues

Although a great deal of space could be given over to a discussion of annihilationism, only a few basic responses can be given:

1. Logically, annihilation is not a punishment at all but something that could be quite desirable to the wicked. Nonexistence is certainly not an adequate punishment for sin, and the wicked would not feel constrained to cease sinning if that is all they faced. Boettner writes, "It implies a termination of consciousness and therefore of all pain and all sense of guilt or ill-desert. . . . For those who have an accusing conscience . . . it would in reality be a blessing."[4]

2. Annihilationists rely heavily on the position of *conditional* immortality—that people receive immortality from God only at salvation. Thus, the unbeliever who has not responded to God's offer of salvation does not possess immortality and is eventually annihilated. Annihilationists often point out that people do not automatically possess immortality, for it is said that only God possesses immortality (1 Tim. 6:16).

It is true, of course, that man cannot have immortality as God does, since man has a beginning, whereas God is eternal. But this hardly means that man was not created by God to live forever. As Louis Berkhof has argued, "Man's immortality is derived, but this is not equivalent to saying that he does not possess it in virtue of his creation."[5] We should also observe that to be immortal means "never to die." Thus, it becomes clear why Scripture teaches that immortality is not presently possessed by people but is seen as something future (1 Cor. 15:53). The term *immortality* actually applies to the material body. A believer does not receive immortality at the moment of conversion but awaits the resurrection, when "this mortal will have put on immortality." What the believer receives at the moment of conversion is eternal life, which is the life of God Himself (cf. John 17:3).

Although eternal life is conditioned on belief, that has nothing to do with the unbeliever existing forever. The unbeliever is in the condition of death, which is not cessation of being but separation from God.

3. The teachings of Scripture point to an eternal punishment. As we have already observed in Matthew 25:46, the Lord Jesus used the same word (*aionios*) to describe the eternal blessings of the righteous and the eternal punishment of the wicked. If the penalty of the wicked is not everlasting, then there is no reason to believe that the blessings of the righteous are everlasting either. The word *aionion* is used more than seventy times in the New Testament and always denotes indefinite, unbounded, eternal duration. In Matthew 25:46 there is no reason to see anything but the continued existence of both the righteous and the wicked.

The Lord Jesus also spoke of "everlasting fire" and "everlasting punishment" as He warned people of coming punishment, using the term *gehenna* (e.g., Matt. 18:8; 25:41; Mark 9:43). Gehenna was the name given to the valley south of Jerusalem, commonly called the Valley of Hinnom. It came to be equated with the fiery judgment of apocalyptic literature. Because human sacrifices were made there in the days of Ahaz and Manasseh (2 Kings 16:3; 21:6; 2 Chron. 28:3; 33:6) and because coming judgments would take place there (Jer. 7:32; 19:6), this valley came to symbolize the place of eternal torment and was so used by Jesus.

The Theological Dictionary of the New Testament rightly distinguishes between "gehenna" and "hades," or hell: "Hades receives the ungodly for the intervening period between death and resurrection, whereas Gehenna is their place of punishment in the last judgment; the judgment of the former is thus provisional but the torment of the latter eternal (Mark 9:43 and 9:48).[6]

Though this valley is used figuratively and symbolically, it is nevertheless figurative of fact and is a vehicle for conveying the meaning that the wicked will be punished in a place of torment forever. If the fire of *gehenna* is eternal and if this symbolizes punishment, then the punishment is eternal as well. If these teachings of the Lord Jesus do not teach that the punishment of the wicked continues eternally, it is difficult to see how He could have communicated that idea in a way that was any clearer. Other Scriptures combine with those of the Lord Jesus in teaching the everlasting nature of the punishment of the wicked (cf. Dan. 12:2; 2 Thess. 1:9; Jude 1:6–7, 13; Rev. 14:11; 19:3; 20:10).

4. Annihilationists commonly interpret words that speak of the destruction and punishment of the wicked as meaning the cessation of their being. For example, one key word for "destroy" used by annihilationists in that way is *apollymi*. However, *apollymi* does not mean annihilation but rather, "loss" or "ruin." For example, it means "lost" in the parables of Luke 15. It can be applied to that which has become "useless," as in the case of the wineskins in Jesus' parable (Matt. 9:17) or the idea of Judas Iscariot having already "perished" in John 17:12. In none of these passages would the idea of annihilation be appropriate, and it is questionable that it is ever used that way.

> *To destroy is to ruin. The nature of the ruin depends on the nature of the subject of which it is predicated. A thing is ruined when it is rendered unfit for use; and when it is in such a state that it can no longer answer the end for which it was designed. A ship at sea, dismantled, rudderless, with its sides battered in, is ruined, but not annihilated. It is a ship still. . . . A soul is utterly and forever destroyed when it is reprobated, alienated from God, rendered a fit companion only for the Devil and his angels.*[7]

Another word for "destroy" (*olethros*) is found in 2 Thessalonians 1:9. It becomes evident that this word also carries the idea of ruin or destruction but not that of total extinction.

> *The noun rendered "destruction" . . . does not imply annihilation but "carries with it the thought of utter and hopeless ruin, the loss of all that gives worth to existence." It does not denote loss of being but rather the loss of well-being, the ruination of the very purpose of their being. From 2 Thessalonians 1:9 it is clear that by destruction Paul does not mean physical annihilation but rather eternal separation from Christ of the lost. Destruction is the opposite of the salvation awaiting believers.*[8]

Other theological and exegetical points could be discussed, but they have been dealt with by other writers.[9]

Returning to the Biblical Issue

Although annihilation might appeal to human sentiment and human wisdom, it is not a doctrine that emerges from the teachings of Scripture. We must never forget that the Judge of the earth will always do what is right and will maintain the perfect and proper balance between love, justice, patience, and holiness. In the Gospels it seems that the Lord Jesus taught and warned people to escape from hell as much as—or more than—He encouraged them to enter the joy and blessings of heaven. Perhaps we should note His emphasis and make sure that people understand that there is not only a heaven to gain but a hell to avoid. If it is indeed true that people die and then face judgment (Heb. 9:27), it is important that we intercept them with the gospel before they experience death.

To hope that people may get another chance after death to receive Christ as Savior or that, if they fail to respond to the gospel now, they will be forever put out of existence is dangerous and unbiblical thinking. A final future, determined in the present, exists for all people. To those who do not receive Jesus Christ as their Savior, their final future is terrible indeed. But those who receive God's gracious gift of salvation based on the cross of Christ will experience a final future that is glorious beyond description.

AS WE AWAIT CHRIST'S APPEARING

At the beginning of this book we emphasized that Bible prophecy was given by God to have a positive effect on us as we live each day. Knowledge of the future was designed to greatly influence the present. That is so, we noted, for several reasons: (1) prophecy reminds us that our God is sovereign over people, nations, and angelic beings; (2) prophecy reinforces the truth that our God is good, having a glorious future in store for His children, because it gives us hope in a world characterized by hopelessness; (3) prophecy motivates us to holy living; and (4) prophecy encourages us to establish goals and priorities that are in line with future realities. It is God's desire to change the way we see life by allowing us some glimpses of what lies ahead.

It is possible, even with the opening emphasis of this book, to get lost in details, theories, and argumentations. All these things definitely have a place in our thinking, but they must not be allowed to negate God's intended purposes of Bible prophecy. In the final analysis our hearts, as well as our minds, should be one with the greatest theologian of the church who loved Christ's appearing and lived his life eagerly awaiting the Savior who will come from heaven (Phil. 3:20; 2 Tim. 4:8). Something is not quite right if we can evaluate all theories of the rapture but do not particularly care to see the One who is coming for us at that great event.

When we contemplate the future through the lens of God's Word, we cannot help but be awed by His wisdom, power, and love. He will reign in majesty and glory, and His children will experience fullness of joy. Bible prophecy is no child's fairy tale, and yet the endings are the same—"and they lived happily ever after."

PART FIVE

Appendices

AN OVERVIEW OF THE BOOK OF *Revelation*

"Write therefore the things which you have seen, and the things which are, and the things which shall take place after these things" (Rev. 1:19). Jesus' statement to John indicates the threefold division to the book of Revelation. The first division is "the things which you have seen" and has to do with John's initial vision of Christ (1:10-20), which follows the book's prologue. The second division, "the things which are," encompasses the letters to the seven churches found in chapters 2 and 3. The third division, which comprises most of the book (4:1-22:21), details "the things which shall take place after these things." This threefold division gives a basic chronological framework for the book of Revelation.

The first two divisions of Revelation cover the past and the present. In chapter 1, John records his vision of the living, glorified Christ and is reminded that the Lord Jesus is the sovereign Lord. Chapters 2 and 3 record letters written by the Lord of the church to the seven churches in Asia Minor. Clearly there were more than seven churches in Asia Minor when Revelation was written, so the question is why they are called the seven churches. The answer is that these seven historical churches were selected because they represent seven basic spiritual conditions that local churches in any age may be in. They accurately represent churches throughout the church age, from John's day until the rapture.

Not only are they representative of the congregations of John's day, but it can safely be concluded that, since the same spiritual circumstances surround believers throughout this present age, the seven churches are also representative of all congregations which shall exist during the entire church age. . . . Every segment within Christendom can see itself in these letters if it will but look. So the Scripture repeats seven times the admonition, "He that hath an ear, let him hear what the Spirit saith to the churches."[1]

There has been some discussion as to whether these churches are prophetical; that is, do they represent seven consecutive periods in the history of the church? Although there has been some support for this position from good and able expositors,[2] this view seems to lack the hermeneutical and exegetical clarity needed to make it strong. It is best to understand the seven churches as representative of the entire church age.

The third division (4:1–22:21) is the focus of Revelation and chronologically follows the age of the church (2:1–3:22) as is evidenced by the opening statement: "after these things" (4:1). This division begins with the marvelous, heavenly scene of the throne of God, where all authority for ruling and judging resides. The throne (which is symbolic of authority) is mentioned seventeen times in these two chapters because the great issue at this point is "Who has the authority to judge and rule the world and the universe." The Lord Jesus (the Lion-Lamb of Judah) is declared to be the only one worthy to judge and rule, and, therefore, to Him was given a scroll from the hand of the One on the throne. The scroll is the title deed of the universe (purchased by the blood of "the Lamb that was slain") and gives Him the authority to repossess the world and evict the squatter known as Satan.

Most of the chapters that follow (6:1–19:21) deal with the saving and judging work of Jesus, which will precede His return to the earth as King of Kings. These events around the throne occur after the Cross (the Lamb has been slain) but before the tribulation (the breaking of the first seal on the scroll, which begins the tribulation, has not been broken yet). Also, because of the presence of the twenty-four robed and crowned (rewarded) elders (4:4), it is likely that the church has already been raptured; therefore, this event in heaven follows the rapture of the church.

One's understanding of the tribulation period (discussed in 6:1–19:21) is largely determined by whether the three series of judgments (the seals, the trumpets, and the bowls) are sequential or simultaneous.[3] The evidence within Revelation strongly favors the sequential view; that is, the seven seal judgments are followed by the seven trumpet judgments, which are then followed by the seven bowl judgments. The idea of birth pangs discussed earlier would support the sequential view because each set of judgments is more severe and destructive than the one that preceded it.[4] When the seventh seal is broken, the trumpet judgments begin (8:1–2). The seventh trumpet is then connected to the bowl judgments, because with its sounding the bowl judgments, which are the end of God's wrath, come forth (10:7; 11:15; 15:1, 8; 16:17). This final set of judgments (the bowls of God's wrath) are said to be "the last" because with these judgments God's wrath is finished (15:1). So the text of Revelation does closely connect the three series of judgments from God.

AN OVERVIEW OF THE BOOK OF REVELATION

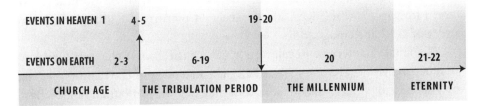

The tribulation period progresses as these three series of judgments unfold one after the other. Every now and then, the apostle John will pause to include new and important information. In chapter 7 he assures us that the tribulation is not simply a time of judgment but also of great salvation. In chapter 10, John is told by an angel that he must prophesy again (10:11). This is an interpretive key because it lets us know that, even though we have made our way through the entire tribulation period (having only the seventh and final trumpet judgment to come), some important truth needs to be given.

The information found in Revelation 11–14 seems to fit best into the second half of the tribulation. Chapter 11 reveals that God will raise up two witnesses who will testify for Him in Jerusalem for 1,260 days. Chapter 12 speaks of the removal of Satan from heaven and the 1,260 days of per-

THE CHAPTERS IN THE THIRD
DIVISION OF REVELATION (6–22)

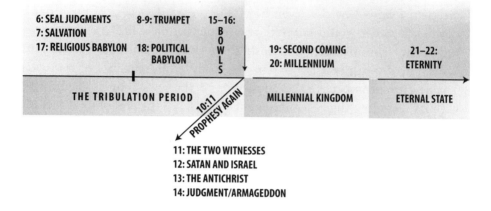

secution of Israel that will follow that removal. Chapter 13 focuses on the two beasts (the Antichrist and the False Prophet) who will dominate the world for forty-two months. And chapter 14 pictures the great final judgment of God at Armageddon.

The final chapters of Revelation speak of the end of the anti-God system of "Babylon" (chapters 17 and 18), the marriage of the Lamb, followed by His second coming to the earth (chapter 19), the millennial reign (chapter 20), and finally the eternal state (chapters 21 and 22).

APPENDIX TWO

CHRIST'S

Olivet Discourse

(MATTHEW 24-25)

A few days before His crucifixion, the Lord Jesus outlined the course of future events in the Olivet Discourse (so named because it was given on the Mount of Olives). Jesus had just denounced the religious leaders, pronounced judgment on that generation of Israel, and made clear that He would not return until Israel turned to Him (Matt. 23:1–39). Then, as His disciples showed some new work that had been done on the temple, Jesus declared that the temple itself was going to be destroyed.

After the Lord and His disciples left the temple area and crossed over to the Mount of Olives, the disciples were intrigued with the Lord's pronouncements and asked Him several questions. Their questions were most likely based on Zechariah 12–14. Their questions had to do with the destruction of Jerusalem and the temple, as well as His coming. There are differences of opinion among scholars as to the number of questions asked (two or three). But however many one chooses, the disciples probably believed that the destruction of Jerusalem and the coming of Messiah took place at the same time.

As the discourse is interpreted, these questions of the disciples must be kept in mind. The Lord is answering these questions of the disciples which focus on Israel. He is not speaking about the Church. Jesus speaks of "you" and "your" some twenty times in 23:34–24:15. In context, these words refer to Israel, which is sometimes represented by certain groups, such as the

369

apostles or the religious leaders. Aside from one brief statement (Matt. 16:18), the disciples had not been exposed to truth about the Church. And it is highly unlikely that they had even marginal understanding about "Messiah's *ekklesia*." In His answer, Jesus spoke of things that involved the Jewish people, such as the Sabbath (24:20), those living in Judea (24:16), the abomination of desolation (24:15), the gospel of the kingdom (24:14), and the presence of false prophets (24:11), which would be a problem for Israel (false teachers would be a problem for the church). In light of this, we should not see the church age in the Olivet Discourse, even as some have in 24:4–8.

Pretribulational writers agree in general that the Olivet Discourse is indeed future—that 24:15–28 refers to the second half of the tribulation and that 24:29–31 looks at the second coming. There is some disagreement on where 24:4–14 fits into the tribulation. Some view it as an overview of the entire period, with 24:4–8 looking at the first half and 24:9–14 viewing the second half of the tribulation.[5] Others view 24:4–14 as a reference only to the first half.[6]

Following the latter view, the discourse would be outlined as follows:

24:4–14; A Summary of the Entire Tribulation Period

The tribulation (Daniel's Seventieth Week) begins with God's judgments on the earth. The "birth pangs" begin at the start of the tribulation and grow in intensity until the Second Coming. The judgments mentioned in 24:4–8 parallel the "seal" judgments and do not refer to the events of this present age (unless Jesus is answering something not asked by the disciples). At 24:9, Jesus tells them that Israel will experience great persecution, which we know from Daniel 9:27 and Revelation 12:6–17 begins at the midpoint of the tribulation. Jesus then gives some general characteristics of the second half. But since the second half is the time of the greatest tribulation for Israel, Jesus then focuses on the second half of the Tribulation.

24:15–28: The Second Half of the Tribulation Period

This period begins with the great sign of the "abomination of desolation." This terrible desecration of the Jerusalem temple by the Antichrist and the False Prophet will be the unmistakable sign for the Jewish people to flee the land of Israel. At that time terrible persecution will break forth on

Israel. Also, the great outpouring of powerful and deceptive miracles will take place during this time. The Lord warned that there would be an unbelievable and massive destruction of mankind. In fact, He declared that if this period of time had not been cut short and limited to three and a half years, no flesh would survive.

24:29–31: The Second Coming of Christ

This will be an event witnessed by all mankind—believers and unbelievers alike. Prior to the return of Christ a sign will appear in the heavens indicating that Jesus Christ is now about to return. This warning will cause the unbelievers of the earth to mourn because they realize that they face immediate judgment. At this time the nation of Israel will be regathered from all over the world. The judgment that determines entrance into the kingdom will occur at this time.

24:32–25:46: Parables About Being Prepared

After answering the disciples' questions, Jesus gave six parables that were designed to warn and encourage. In fact, the greatest proportion of the Olivet Discourse is on the response to the truth He just gave. The Lord wanted His hearers to understand prophetic truth so that it might cause them to be prepared for what is to come. He emphasizes three matters: (1) to be watchful for His coming, being alert for end-time events; (2) to be prepared spiritually, making sure that He is indeed one's personal Savior; and (3) to be serving Him, making sure that He is the focus of life in all of our responsibilities and relationships. (Note that a more detailed discussion of some key points in the Olivet Discourse is given on pages 175–183).

Matthew is not the only source of information about the Olivet Discourse. This discourse is also recorded in Luke 21, but with a different emphasis. Luke records the Lord Jesus' answer to the disciples' question concerning the destruction of the Jerusalem temple and devotes less time to the questions dealing with the future events. The city of Jerusalem and the temple were destroyed by the Roman armies in AD 70, and the Lord does speak of that time. The following is a brief outline of Luke's record of the Olivet Discourse.

Luke 21:8–11. Luke parallels Matthew 24:4–8 and speaks of wars, famines, and earthquakes.

21:12–24. This section does not parallel Matthew's account but is unique to Luke. In 21:12 the Lord says that "before all these things" (a reference to the first days of the tribulation given in 21:8–11) certain other things will take place. These events would be fulfilled in the apostolic age. The language in this section is very similar to the language found in Matthew's account. However, similarity of language does not necessarily mean that the identical subject matter is being discussed. In their questions the disciples had lumped the destruction of the temple and the Lord's return together, assuming that they took place at the same time. But they did not/would not occur at the same time. What will occur in the future will resemble what took place in AD 70. It is not surprising that the language for both is similar. Furthermore, it seems that Luke's account is looking at AD 70 because it clearly leaves out any reference to the great tribulation or to the key sign event of the abomination of desolation. Jesus gives similarly sound advice to those living in Jerusalem in AD 70 when He warns those in Judea to flee to the mountains.

21:25–33. At this point, Luke returns in his recording of Christ's words to the events surrounding the second coming, including the Lord's promise that those who see the beginning of the signs will also see His return.

21:34–36. This is a brief statement on preparedness in light of the Lord's coming and parallels the extended section found in Matthew 24:42–25:30.

SOME
Definitions

Abrahamic covenant
An eternal, unconditional covenant made between God and Abraham in which God committed Himself to bless Abraham and to give his descendants a land, a posterity, and spiritual blessings.

Allegorical interpretation
A method of interpretation that disregards the historical context of a passage and treats the literal sense of a Scripture text as secondary to a deeper, more spiritual meaning.

Amillennialism
The view that there will be no earthly, literal millennium following the second coming of Christ.

Annihilationism
The teaching that the unsaved will not exist forever but will instead be judged by God, thus bringing about the cessation of their being. Their punishment is said to be eternal but their punishing is not.

Covenant
An agreement between two parties that bound them together with common interests and responsibilities.

Covenant theology
A theological system that interprets all of Scripture on the basis of two (or three) theological covenants: the covenant of works and the covenant of grace (and/or the covenant of redemption).

Davidic covenant
An unconditional covenant made with King David that is an expansion of the "seed promises" given in the Abrahamic covenant in which God promised David a dynasty, throne, kingdom, and rule that will last forever.

Day of the Lord
A phrase used in the Bible to emphasize special interventions of God in human history, including the future time when He will intervene to judge the nations, discipline Israel, and establish His rule in the messianic kingdom.

Dispensationalism
A theological system that approaches the Scriptures by seeing distinguishable stewardships of man under the authority of God. It is God who reveals His purposes to man and delegates responsibilities to him.

Eschatology
The doctrine or study of last things.

Great white throne judgment
The judgment of all the unsaved, which will take place after the millennial kingdom is over and which will consign them to everlasting punishment in the lake of fire.

Hermeneutics
The science of biblical interpretation, which sets forth the laws and principles that lead to the meaning of a Scripture text.

Intermediate state
The conscious experience of a person after physical death but before the resurrection. For the believer this will be in heaven, and for the unbeliever it will be in hell.

Judgment seat of Christ
An event that will take place in the heavenlies immediately after the rapture of the church, where church-age believers are evaluated and rewarded by Jesus Christ.

Kingdom of God
The rule of the sovereign God over His creation, a rule that has various aspects.

Literal interpretation
The grammatical-historical approach to the text of Scripture where the words of the passage are interpreted according to the accepted laws of language.

Messiah
A word coming from the Hebrew and meaning the "anointed one." In the Greek, the equivalent word is "Christ."

Millennium
A word that refers to the thousand-year reign of Christ. It comes from the Latin words *mille* (a thousand) and *annus* (year).

New covenant
An unconditional covenant, which is based on the death of Christ, in which God promises to bring salvation and the forgiveness of sins. This covenant will ultimately be fulfilled with Israel in the millennial kingdom.

Palestinian covenant
This unconditional covenant is an enlargement of the land aspect of the Abrahamic covenant, detailing the boundaries and other aspects pertaining to the land that Israel will eventually receive.

Postmillennialism
The belief that a golden spiritual age will come upon this earth (the millennium) because the world will progressively get better and better through the preaching of the gospel. It is at this time that Christ will return to the earth. This return is after the millennium is over.

Premillennialism

The view that Jesus Christ will return to the earth before the millennial kingdom is established. This kingdom will be on the earth and will fulfill God's covenant promises to national Israel.

Rapture

The sudden, supernatural catching away of the church to meet Christ in the air. Several theories are connected with the rapture event. The *partial rapture* view teaches that only spiritual Christians will participate in this event. The *pretribulational rapture* sees this event taking place prior to the tribulation, whereas the *midtribulational rapture* places it at the middle of the tribulation. The *pre-wrath* view places the rapture about three quarters of the way through the tribulation, and the *posttribulation rapture* sees the church removed at the end of the tribulation.

Theocratic kingdom

The rule of God over the earth indirectly through human mediators such as Moses, the judges, and the kings.

Tribulation

The final seven-year period of time (described in Scriptures such as Revelation 6–19) when God will pour out judgment on unbelieving Gentiles and disobedient Israel.

Wrath of God

God's passionate feeling against sin, which will lead to its inevitable punishment in a future day of judgment.

THE PROPHECIES

OF

A CHART OF THE PROPHECIES OF DANIEL

VISION	STATUE	FOUR BEASTS	RAM/GOAT	SEVENTY WEEKS	FINAL VISION
CHAPTER	2	7	8	9	11–12
BABYLON	Seen as the head of gold	Seen as the winged lion	———	———	———
MEDO-PERSIA	Seen as the chest & arms of silver	Seen as a bear raised up on one side	Two-horned ram that conquers many nations	70th week begins	4 kings of Persia
GREECE	Seen as the belly & thighs of bronze	Seen as a four-headed, four-winged leopard	Goat with a great horn ——— Four-horns grow ——— Small horn Antiochus IV		Rise & fall of the mighty king ——— Kingdom broken into four parts ——— Antiochus IV reigns
ROME I	Seen as the legs of iron	The terrible beast	———	Messiah killed and Jerusalem destroyed	———
ROME II	Seen as the feet of iron and clay – 10 toes	Ten horns on the terrible beast	———	Covenant made for one week (7 years)	Terrible time of trouble for Israel & world
THE ANTICHRIST	———	The little horn who conquers and dominates	———	The prince makes and breaks a covenant with Israel	The willful king powerful and blasphemous
GOD'S KINGDOM	The stone cut out without human hands	The Son of Man given the kingdom	———	The six great goals of God now accomplished	Blessed ones attain to the 1,335 days (the beginning of the millennial kingdom)

Notes

Introduction: The Critical Importance of Bible Prophecy

1. Larry Crabb, *Finding God* (Grand Rapids: Zondervan, 1993), 172.

Chapter 1: Interpreting Bible Prophecy

1. J. Dwight Pentecost, *Things to Come* (Grand Rapids: Dunham, 1964), 9.

2. Paul Tan, *The Interpretation of Prophecy* (Winona Lake, Ind.: BMH, 1974), 29.

3. Bernard Ramm, *Protestant Biblical Interpretation,* 3d rev. ed. (Grand Rapids: Baker, 1973), 121.

4. Elliott E. Johnson, "Premillennialism Introduced: Hermeneutics," in *A Case for Premillennialism,* ed. Donald K. Campbell and Jeffrey L. Townsend (Chicago: Moody, 1992), 17.

5. Pentecost, *Things to Come,* 13.

6. Thomas D. Ice, "Dispensational Hermeneutics," in *Issues in Dispensationalism,* ed. Wesley R. Willis and John R. Master (Chicago: Moody, 1994), 33.

7. Gary Cohen, *Understanding Revelation* (Chicago: Moody, 1978), 23–37.

8. Ramm, *Protestant Biblical Interpretation,* 30.

9. Johnson, "Premillennialism Introduced: Hermeneutics," 21.

10. Loraine Boettner, *The Millennium* (Philadelphia: Presbyterian and Reformed., 1958), 119.

11. Leon Wood, *The Bible and Future Events* (Grand Rapids: Zondervan, 1973), 24.

12. Merrill C. Tenney, *Interpreting Revelation* (Grand Rapids: Eerdmans, 1973), 101.

Chapter 2: The Abrahamic Covenant

1. Renald E. Showers, *There Really Is a Difference!* (Bellmawr, N.J.: Friends of Israel, 1990), 59.

2. Loraine Boettner, *The Millennium* (Philadelphia: Presbyterian and Reformed, 1958), 318–19.

3. Joel Green, *How to Read Prophecy* (Downers Grove, Ill: InterVarsity, 1984), 101.

4. Oswald T. Allis, *Prophecy and the Church* (Phillipsburg, N.J.: Presbyterian and Reformed, 1978), 33.

5. J. Dwight Pentecost, *Things to Come* (Grand Rapids: Dunham, 1964), 74.

6. John F. Walvoord, *The Millennial Kingdom* (Findlay, Ohio: Dunham, 1963), 150.

7. Walter C. Kaiser, *Toward an Old Testament Theology* (Grand Rapids: Zondervan, 1981), 93.

8. Robert B. Chisholm Jr., "Evidence from Genesis," in *A Case for Premillennialism,* ed. Donald K. Campbell and Jeffrey L.Townsend (Chicago: Moody, 1992), 54.

9. Showers, *There Really Is a Difference!* 62.

10. Kaiser, *Toward an Old Testament Theology,* 93.

11. Ibid., 94.

12. John F. Walvoord, *Israel in Prophecy* (Grand Rapids: Zondervan, 1988), 42.

13. Charles C. Ryrie, *Basic Theology* (Wheaton, Ill.: Victor, 1988), 454–55.

14. S. Lewis Johnson, "Evidences from Romans 9–11," in *A Case for Premillennialism,* ed. Campbell and Townsend, 220.

15. Showers, *There Really Is a Difference!* 66.

16. Ibid., 76.

17. Walvoord, *Israel in Prophecy,* 48.

18. Charles C. Ryrie, *The Basis of the Premillennial Faith* (New York: Loizeaux Bros., 1958), 53.

19. Johnson, "Evidences from Romans 9–11," 200–201.

20. Walvoord, *Israel in Prophecy,* 37.

Chapter 3: The Palestinian, Davidic, and New Covenants

1. J. Dwight Pentecost, *Things to Come* (Grand Rapids: Dunham,1964), 98.

2. Oswald T. Allis, *Prophecy and the Church* (Phillipsburg, N.J.: Presbyterian and Reformed, 1978), 58.

3. William E. Cox, *Biblical Studies in Final Things* (Philadelphia: Presbyterian and Reformed, 1967), 57–58.

4. Walter C. Kaiser, *Toward an Old Testament Theology* (Grand Rapids: Zondervan, 1978), 129.

5. Joel B. Green, *How to Read Prophecy* (Downers Grove, Ill.: InterVarsity, 1984), 104–5.

6. Loraine Boettner, *The Millennium* (Philadelphia: Presbyterian and Reformed, 1958), 119.

7. John F. Walvoord, *The Millennial Kingdom* (Findlay, Ohio: Dunham, 1963), 183.

8. Arnold Fruchtenbaum, *Israelology: The Missing Link in Systematic Theology* (Tustin, Calif.: Ariel Ministries, 1993), 585.

9. Alva McClain, *The Greatness of the Kingdom* (Chicago: Moody, 1968), 156.

10. Renald E. Showers, *There Really Is a Difference!* (Bellmawr, N.J.: Friends of Israel, 1990), 89.

11. Zane Hodges, "A Dispensational Understanding of Acts 2," in *Issues in Dispensationalism,* ed. Wesley R. Willis, John R. Master, and Charles C. Ryrie (Chicago: Moody, 1994), 174.

12. Showers, *There Really Is a Difference!* 90.

13. Craig Blaising and Darrell Bock, *Progressive Dispensationalism* (Wheaton, Ill.: Victor, 1993), 177–78.

14. For a more complete discussion, see Charles C. Ryrie, *Dispensationalism* (Chicago: Moody, 1995), chapter 9; and Willis, Master, and Ryrie eds., *Issues in Dispensationalism.*

15. Elliott Johnson, "Prophetic Fulfillment: The Already and Not Yet," in *Issues in Dispensationalism,* ed. Willis, Masters, and Ryrie, 191.

16. Hodges, "A Dispensational Understanding of Acts 2," 176–77, 178.

17. Johnson, "Prophetic Fulfillment," 189.

18. Charles C. Ryrie, "Update on Dispensationalism," in *Issues in Dispensationalism,* 23.

19. John F. Walvoord, *Israel in Prophecy* (Grand Rapids: Zondervan, 1988), 96.

20. S. Lewis Johnson, "Evidences from Romans 9–11," in *A Case for Premillennialism,* ed. Donald K. Campbell and Jeffrey L. Townsend (Chicago: Moody, 1992), 215.

Chapter 4: Dispensational Theology and Covenant Theology

1. Paul Enns, *Moody Handbook of Theology* (Chicago: Moody, 1989), 503.

2. Louis Berkhof, *Systematic Theology* (London: Banner of Truth Trust, 1941), 211–18.

3. Ibid., 277.

4. Renald Showers, *There Really Is a Difference!* (Bellmawr, N.J.: Friends of Israel, 1993), 16.

5. Berkhof, *Systematic Theology,* 265–71.

6. John F. Walvoord, *The Millennial Kingdom* (Findlay, Ohio: Dunham, 1963), 90–91.

7. Enns, *Moody Handbook of Theology,* 510.

8. Showers, *There Really Is a Difference!* 22–23.

9. Lewis Sperry Chafer, *Systematic Theology* (Dallas: Dallas Seminary Press, 1947), 4:156.

10. Showers, *There Really Is a Difference!* 20.

11. Charles C. Ryrie, *Dispensationalism* (Chicago: Moody, 1995), 28.

12. Ibid., 29.

13. Ibid., 41.

14. William E. Cox, *Amillennialism Today* (Phillipsburg, N.J.: Presbyterian and Reformed, 1980), 37.

Chapter 5: The View of Premillennialism

1. George E. Ladd, "Historical Premillennialism," in *The Meaning of the Millennium: Four Views,* ed. R. Clouse (Downers Grove, Ill.: InterVarsity, 1977), 27.

2. Harold Hoehner, "Evidence from Revelation 20," in *The Case for Premillennialism,* ed. Donald K. Campbell and Jeffrey L. Townsend (Chicago: Moody, 1992), 253.

3. Oswald Allis, *Prophecy and the Church* (Phillipsburg, N.J.: Presbyterian and Reformed, 1978), 238.

4. Floyd Hamilton, *The Basis of the Millennial Faith* (Grand Rapids: Eerdmans, 1942), 38.

5. Millard J. Erickson, *Millennial Views* (Grand Rapids: Baker, 1977), 104–6.

6. William Cox, *Amillennialism Today* (Phillipsburg, N.J.: Presbyterian and Reformed, 1980), 64–68.

Chapter 6: The Church and the Nation of Israel

1. Arnold G. Fruchtenbaum, "Israel and the Church", in *Issues in Dispensationalism* (Chicago: Moody, 1994), ed. Wesley R. Willis, John R. Master, and Charles C. Ryrie, 114.

2. Ronald E. Diprose, *Israel in the Development of Christian Thought* (Rome: Istituto Biblico Evangelico Italiano, 2000), 3.

3. Wayne Grudem, *Systematic Theology* (Grand Rapids: InterVarsity, 1994), 863.

4. Louis Berkhof, *Systematic Theology* (London: Banner of Truth Trust, 1941), 570–71.

5. William Cox, *Amillennialism Today* (Phillipsburg, N.J.: Presbyterian and Reformed, 1980), 37.

6. Diprose, *Israel in the Development of Christian Thought,* 102.

7. Ibid., 70.

8. Grudem, *Systematic Theology,* 859–63; Berkhof, *Systematic Theology,* 571–72.

9. Charles C. Ryrie, *The Basis of the Premillennial Faith* (New York: Loizeaux Bros., 1958), 53.

10. Diprose, *Israel in the Development of Christian Thought,* 71.

11. If there was an *implied* condition that Abraham had to leave his land and go to Canaan, then that was clearly fulfilled. We can only speculate what God would have done if Abraham had chosen to stay in Haran or in Ur. We suggest that God still would have fulfilled His covenant, though Abraham would have lost out on personal blessing that always comes with obedience.

12. For a fuller discussion of the biblical covenants, both their provisions and fulfillment, see chapters 2–3, as well as Arnold Fruchtenbaum, *Israelology: The Missing Link in Systematic Theology* (Tustin, Calif.: Ariel Ministries, 1992).

13. Berkhof, *Systematic Theology,* 571.

14. Cox, *Amillennialism Today,* 46.

15. Fruchtenbaum, *Israelology,* 118–20.

16. S. Lewis Johnson, "Paul and the 'Israel of God': An Exegetical and Eschatological Case Study," in *Essays in Honor of J. Dwight Pentecost* (Chicago: Moody, 1986), 183.

17. J. Dwight Pentecost, *Things to Come* (Grand Rapids: Dunham, 1964), 88.

18. Fruchtenbaum, *Israelology,* 126–27.

19. Gerhard Delling, "arche," *Theological Dictionary of the New Testament,* eds. Bromiley and Friedrich (Grand Rapids: Eerdmans, 1992), 81.

20. W. E. Vine, *Expository Dictionary of New Testament Words,* vol. 3 (London: Oliphants, 1963), 97.

21. Several helpful discussions can be found in S. Lewis Johnson's study of Romans 9–11 in *A Case for Premillennialism* (Chicago: Moody, 1992), and several sections in Arnold Fruchtenbaum's work *Israelology: The Missing Link in Systematic Theology* (Tustin: Ariel Ministries, 1993).

22. Johnson, "Paul and the 'Israel of God,'" 215.

23. Berkhof, *Systematic Theology,* 572.

24. Ibid., 571.

Chapter 7: The View of Amillennialism

1. David Reagan, *The Master Plan* (Eugene, Ore.: Harvest House,1993), 155.

2. Renald Showers, *There Really Is a Difference!* (Bellmawr, N.J.: Friends of Israel, 1993), 133.

3. John F. Walvoord, *The Millennial Kingdom* (Findlay, Ohio: Dunham, 1963), 6.

4. William Cox, *Amillennialism Today* (Phillipsburg, N.J.: Presbyterian and Reformed 1980), 1.

5. Ibid., 4.

6. Anthony Hoekema, "Amillennialism," in *The Meaning of the Millennium: Four Views,* ed. R. Clouse (Downers Grove, Ill.: InterVarsity, 1977), 178.

7. Millard J. Erickson, *Contemporary Options in Eschatology* (Grand Rapids: Baker, 1977), 83.

8. Cox, *Amillennialism Today,* 59.

9. Ibid., 62.

10. Anthony Hoekema, *The Bible and the Future* (Grand Rapids: Eerdmans, 1982), 228.

11. Hoekema, "Amillennialism," 161.

12. Hoekema, *The Bible and the Future,* 174.

13. Cox, *Amillennialism Today,* 5.

14. Hoekema, "Amillennialism," 172.

15. Walvoord, *The Millennial Kingdom,* 62.

16. Harold Hoehner, "Evidence from Revelation 20," in *A Case for Premillennialism,* ed. Donald K. Campbell and Jeffrey L. Townsend (Chicago: Moody, 1992), 247.

17. Hoekema, *The Bible and the Future,* 227–28.

18. Hoekema, "Amillennialism," 161.

19. John J. Davis, *Biblical Numerology* (Winona Lake, Ind.: BMH Books, 1971).

20. Stephen Carlson, "The Relevance of Apocalyptic Numerology for the Meaning of [*ciliath*] in Revelation 20" (PhD diss., Mid-America Baptist Theological Seminary, 1990).

21. Specifically, numbers are found in these verses in Revelation: 1:4, 11, 12, 16, 20; 2:1, 10, 12; 3:1; 4:4, 5, 6, 7, 8, 10; 5:1, 5, 6, 8, 14; 6:1, 3, 5, 6, 7, 8, 9, 12; 7:1, 2, 4, 5, 6, 7, 8, 11, 13; 8:1, 2, 6, 7, 8, 9, 10, 11, 12, 13; 9:1, 5, 10, 12, 13, 14, 15, 16, 18; 10:3, 4, 7; 11:2, 3, 4, 9, 10,

11, 13, 14, 15, 16; 12:1, 3, 4, 6, 14; 13:1, 3, 5, 11, 12, 18; 14:1, 3, 4, 8, 9, 20; 15:1, 6, 7, 8; 16:1, 2, 3, 4, 8, 10, 12, 13, 17, 19, 21; 17:1, 3, 7, 9, 10, 11, 12, 13, 16; 18:8, 10, 17, 19; 19:3, 4, 20; 20:2, 3, 4, 5, 6, 7, 8, 14; 21:1, 4, 8, 9, 12, 13, 14, 16, 17, 19, 20; 21:21; 22:2, 13.

22. Concerning these numbers, we note the following images and meanings:

   1. The seven *spirits* (Rev. 1:4; 3:1; 4:5; 5:6) and the seven *lamps* (4:5) apparently refer to the prominence/fullness of the Holy Spirit's activity in the world. This imagery is clearly based on Zechariah 3:9; 4:1–10; and Exodus 25:37.
   2. The seven *horns* and the seven *eyes* (5:6). This pictures Christ as the all-powerful sovereign as well as being omniscient. This imagery is also based on Zechariah 3 and 4 along with Daniel 7:20 and 8:5.
   3. The four *corners of the earth* and the four *winds of heaven* (7:1; 20:8). The four corners of the earth is a term to designate the four directions of the compass, thus the "whole earth," and the four winds represent God's destructive judgments that are being temporarily held back by the angels. This imagery is based on Jeremiah 49:36–38; Isaiah 11:12; Daniel 7:2.

23. Here are six reasons numbers should be interpreted literally in Scripture, and particularly in Revelation 20: First, the normal and universal use of numbers is not symbolic but is to indicate the quantity of something. To attach meanings to numbers (usually quite arbitrarily) is to engage in a highly speculative and subjective practice. On what basis can it be said that the number 10 "signifies completeness." Second, the vast majority of times (over 90 percent), apocalyptic literature uses numbers in the normal quantitative way. This calls into question the oft-repeated statement of amillennialism and postmillennialism that Revelation is filled with symbolic numbers. Third, only the number 7, on occasion, appears to have symbolic significance and even then it usually retains its quantitative meaning. Fourth, the phrase "thousand years" does not appear anywhere else in Revelation or in any other apocalyptic literature, and thus there is no possible symbolic meaning that can be brought in from some other source. Peter's use of the phrase, in 2 Peter 3:8, is not at all symbolic. He is not saying that a day equals a thousand years but simply reveals how much God can do in a single day. Peter's point only makes sense if he is using "day" and "years" in the usual sense of specific time markers. One must, therefore, look to the context of Revelation 19–22 and the larger context of the entire book of Revelation. Fifth, there is nothing within the final vision of John in Revelation 19–22 that compels one to abandon the normal use of numbers. In fact, other expressions in that context would argue for taking the one thousand years literally. (The point here is that John uses indefinite terms in Revelation 19–22, such as "a short time" and "forever and ever." And so, when he uses the specific phrase "1000 years" instead of some indefinite term, we would think that it should be understood specifically as numbers usually are.) Sixth, indefinite expressions are used in Revelation, where we are told that there are "thousands and thousands" around the throne (5:11) and a "great multitude" (7:9). John is obviously capable of expressing numbers in general, nonspecific ways. This he did not do when discussing the length of Messiah's kingdom. Seventh (in order to have a "complete" conclusion), the use of "thousand" does occur in Revelation in several places where multiples of "thousand" are given; such as 12,000 from each Israelite tribe. These uses seem to make a normal rendering of such statements as far more reasonable than a symbolic one.

24. Hoekema, *The Bible and the Future*, 228–29.

25. Cox, *Amillennialism Today*, 75–76.

26. Hoehner, "Evidence from Revelation 20," 257.

27. George Ladd, "Historical Premillennialism," in T*he Meaning of the Millennium*, 191.

Chapter 8: The View of Postmillennialism

1. John F. Walvoord, *The Millennial Kingdom* (Findlay, Ohio: Dunham, 1963), 22–23.

2. Loraine Boettner, "Postmillennialism," in *The Meaning of the Millennium: Four Views*, ed. R. Clouse (Downers Grove, Ill.: InterVarsity, 1977), 117.

3. Stanley J. Grenz, *The Millennial Maze* (Downers Grove, Ill.: InterVarsity, 1992), 66.

4. Loraine Boettner, *The Millennium* (Philadelphia: Presbyterian and Reformed, 1958), 64.

5. Ibid., 14.

6. Boettner, "Postmillennialism," 117–18.

7. Boettner, *The Millennium*, 68.

8. Grenze, *The Millennial Maze*, 74.

9. Boettner, *The Millennium*, 69.

10. Ibid., 82.

11. Ibid., 119.

12. David Chilton, *Paradise Restored: An Eschatology of Dominion* (Tyler, Tex.: Reconstruction, 1985), 226.

13. Gary North, *Unconditional Surrender* (Tyler, Tex.: Geneva Divinity School Press, 1983), 73.

14. Tremper Longman III, *Theonomy: A Reformed Critique* (Grand Rapids: Zondervan, 1990), 44.

15. Chilton, *Paradise Restored*, 214.

16. Greg Bahnsen, *No Other Standard* (Tyler, Tex.: Institute for Christian Economics, 1991), 11.

17. Greg Bahnsen, *Theonomy in Christian Ethics* (Phillisburg, N.J.: Presbyterian and Reformed, 1984), 84.

18. Gary North, *Millennialism and Social Theory* (Tyler, Tex.: Institute for Christian Economics, 1990), 23.

19. Millard Erickson, *Contemporary Options in Eschatology* (Grand Rapids: Baker, 1977), 72.

20. Renald Showers, *There Really Is a Difference!* (Belmawr, N.J.: Friends of Israel, 1993), 188.

Chapter 9: The View of Preterism

1. Kenneth L. Gentry Jr. and Thomas Ice, *The Great Tribulation: Past or Future?* (Grand Rapids: Kregel, 1999), 13.

2. R. C. Sproul, *The Last Days According to Jesus* (Grand Rapids: Baker, 2004), 25.

3. Ibid., 24.

4. Edward E. Stevens, *Steven's Response to Gentry: A Detailed Response to Dr. Kenneth L. Gentry* (Bradford, Penna.: Kingdom, 1997); as quoted by Sproul, *Last Days,* 155.

5. Thomas Ice, "The History of Preterism," in *The End Times Controversy,* ed. Tim LaHaye and Thomas Ice (Eugene, Ore.: Harvest House, 2003), 63.

6. Sproul, *Last Days,* 66.

7. Gary DeMar, "The Passing Away of Heaven and Earth"; http://www.preteristarchive.com/PartialPreterism

8. Robert Thomas, "The New Interpretation of Bible Prophecy," *The Gathering Storm,* ed. Mal Couch (Springfield, Mo. 2005), 45.

9. Norman L. Geisler, "Examining the Theology of Hank Hanegraff's book *The Last Disciple," National Liberty Journal,* May 2005, 4.

10. Walter Kaiser, "An Evangelical Response," in *Dispensationalism, Israel and the Church: The Search for Definition,* ed. Darrel L. Bock and Craig A. Blaising (Grand Rapids: Zondervan, 1992), 376; quoted by Thomas Ice, "The History of Preterism" in *The End Times Controversy,* ed. LaHaye and Ice, 65.

11. Thomas, "The New Interpretation of Bible Prophecy," 43.

12. Ibid., 35. See also Robert L. Thomas, *Revelation 1–7, Wycliffe Exegetical Commentary,* vol. 1 (Chicago: Moody, 1992), 29–40.

13. Ibid., 32–35.

14. Sproul, *Last Days,* 65.

15. Thomas Ice, "Hermeneutics and Bible Prophecy," in *The End Times Controversy,* ed. LaHaye and Ice, 67–81; Robert Thomas, "The New Interpretation of Bible Prophecy," 27–53.

16. Gentry and Ice, *The Great Tribulation,* 27.

17. Gary DeMar, *End Times Fiction: A Biblical Consideration of the Left Behind Theology* (Nashville: Nelson, 2001), 68; quoted in Thomas Ice, "Preterist 'Time Texts,'" in *The End Times Controversy,* ed. LaHaye and Ice, 92.

18. Thomas Ice, "Preterist 'Time Texts,'" in *The End Times Controversy,* ed. LaHaye and Ice, 92.

19. Randall Price, "Historical Problems with a First Century Fulfillment," in *The End Times Controversy,* ed. LaHaye and Ice, 380.

20. Sproul, *Last Days,* 132, 140.

21. Irenaeus, *Against Heresies,* 5.30.3. See also, Eusebius, *The History of the Church,* trans. by G. A. Williamson (New York: Penguin Books, 1989), 81.

22. Robert Thomas, *Revelation 1–7, Wycliffe Exegetical Commentary,* vol. 1 (Chicago: Moody, 1992), 21.

23. Mark Hitchcock, "The Stake in the Heart—The AD 95 Date of Revelation," in *The End Times Controversy,* ed. LaHaye and Ice, 128.

24. Ibid., 129.

25. Eusebius, *The History of the Church,* trans. by G. A. Williamson (New York: Penguin, 1989), 80–81.

26. Hitchcock, "The Stake in the Heart," 128–138.

27. Sproul, *Last Days,* 144.

28. Thomas, *Revelation 1–7,* 22.

29. Hitchcock, "The Stake in the Heart," 139.

30. Sproul, *Last Days,* 146.

31. John J. Davis, *Biblical Numerology* (Winona Lake, Ind.: BMH, 1968), 124.

32. Andy Woods, "Revelation 13 and the First Beast," in *The End Times Controversy,* ed. LaHaye and Ice, 246–47.

33. Sproul, *Last Days,* 189.

34. Hitchcock, "The Stake in the Heart," 147.

35. Ibid., 147–48. Hitchcock notes that Polycarp was the bishop at Smyrna. Yet in a letter Polycarp wrote to the Philippian believers in about AD 110, "Polycarp says that the Smyrnaeans did not know the Lord during the time Paul was ministering."

36. Ibid., 149.

37. Thomas Ice, "Preterist 'Time Texts,'" in *The End Times Controversy,* 103.

38. Ibid., 103–104.

39. Ibid., 104.

40. John F. Walvoord, *Matthew* (Chicago: Moody, 1974), 127.

41. F. F. Bruce, *The Hard Sayings of Jesus* (Downer's Grove, Ill.: InterVarsity, 1983), 109.

42. Gentry and Ice, *The Great Tribulation,* 65–66.

43. The most comprehensive source from the futurist position to date is *The End Times Controversy: The Second Coming Under Attack,* ed. Tim LaHaye and Thomas Ice (Eugene, Ore.: Harvest House, 2003).

44. Stanley Toussaint, "A Critique of the Preterist View of the Olivet Discourse," unpublished paper given at the PreTrib Study Group, 12 December 1996, Dallas, 3–4.

45. Ibid.

46. Larry Spargimino, "How Preterists Misuse History to Advance Their View of Prophecy," in *The End Times Controversy,* ed. LaHaye and Ice, 201–20.

47. Gentry and Ice, *The Great Tribulation,* 46.

48. Sproul, *Last Days,* 158.

49. Toussaint, "A Critique of the Preterist View," 7.

50. Thomas Ice, "The Olivet Discourse," in *"The End Times Controversy"* ed. LaHaye and Ice (Eugene, Ore.: Harvest House, 2003), 187.

51. Sproul, *Last Days,* 42.

52. Gentry and Ice, *The Great Tribulation,* 55.

53. Ibid., 58.

54. Ibid., 60.

55. Sproul, *Last Days,* 48.

56. Toussaint, "A Critique of the Preterist View," 9.

57. Eugene Merrill, *An Exegetical Commentary: Haggai, Zechariah, Malachi* (Chicago: Moody, 1994), 312.

58. David Baron, *Zechariah: A Commentary on His Visions and Prophecies* (Grand Rapids: Kregel, 2003), 422.

Chapter 10: The Kingdom of God

1. Paul Enns, *Moody Handbook of Theology* (Chicago: Moody, 1989), 639.

2. George E. Ladd, *Crucial Questions About the Kingdom of God* (Grand Rapids: Eerdmans, 1952), 79-83.

3. Alva McClain, *The Greatness of the Kingdom* (Chicago: Moody, 1968), 19.

4. Ibid.

5. Renald Showers, *There Really Is a Difference!* (Bellmawr, N.J.: Friends of Israel, 1990), 158-60.

6. Arnold Fruchtenbaum, *Israelology: The Missing Link in Systematic Theology* (Tustin, Calif.: Ariel Ministries, 1993), 605.

7. J. Dwight Pentecost, *Things to Come* (Grand Rapids: Dunham, 1964), 441-42.

8. Ibid., 143.

9. Charles C. Ryrie, *Basic Theology* (Wheaton, Ill.: Victor, 1988), 398.

10. John MacArthur, *1 Corinthians,* Macarthur New Testament Commentary (Chicago: Moody, 1984), 421.

Chapter 12: The Pretribulational Rapture View

1. D. Edmond Hiebert, *1 & 2 Thessalonians,* rev. ed. (Chicago: Moody, 1992), 211.

2. See, e.g., Gleason Archer, Paul Feinberg, and Douglas Moo, eds., *The Rapture: Pre-, Mid-, or Post-Tribulational?* (Grand Rapids: Zondervan, 1984).

3. John C. Whitcomb, *Daniel* (Chicago: Moody, 1985), 126.

4. Alva J. McClain, *Daniel's Prophecy of the Seventy Weeks* (Grand Rapids: Zondervan, 1969), 28-35.

5. Kenneth Barker, "Evidence from Daniel," in *A Case for Premillennialism,* ed. Donald K. Campbell and Jeffrey L.Townsend (Chicago: Moody, 1992), 145.

6. Hiebert, *1 & 2 Thessalonians,* 76.

7. Leon Wood, *The Bible and Future Events* (Grand Rapids: Zondervan, 1973), 54.

8. Paul Feinberg, "The Case for the Pretribulation Rapture Position," in *The Rapture: Pre-, Mid-, or Post-Tribulational,* ed. Archer, Feinberg, and Moo, 62.

9. C. F. Hogg and W. E. Vine, *The Epistles of Paul the Apostle to the Thessalonians* (Fincastle, Va.: Scripture Truth, 1959), 48.

10. Hiebert, *1 & 2 Thessalonians,* 75.

11. Renald Showers, *Maranatha: Our Lord, Come!* (Bellmawr, N.J.: Friends of Israel, 1995), 195.

12. Hiebert, *1 & 2 Thessalonians,* 238.

13. Showers, *Maranatha,* 127.

14. Earl Radmacher, "The Imminent Return of the Lord," in *Issues in Dispensationalism,* ed. Wesley R. Willis and John R. Master (Chicago: Moody, 1994), 254.

15. W. E. Vine, *An Expository Dictionary of New Testament Words* (London: Oliphants, 1963), 4:194.

16. Radmacher, "The Imminent Return of the Lord," 258.

17. Hogg and Vine, *The Epistles of Paul,* 138–40.

18. Showers, *Maranatha,* 130.

19. Ibid., 131.

20. John F. Walvoord, *The Rapture Question,* rev. ed. (Grand Rapids: Zondervan, 1979), 84.

21. Ibid., 86.

22. Ibid., 60.

Chapter 13: The Posttribulational Rapture View

1. Charles C. Ryrie, *Basic Theology* (Wheaton, Ill.: Victor, 1988), 500.

2. John F. Walvoord, *The Blessed Hope and the Tribulation* (Grand Rapids: Zondervan, 1976), 21–69.

3. John F. Walvoord, *The Rapture Question,* rev. ed. (Grand Rapids: Zondervan, 1979), 139.

4. Alexander Reese, *The Approaching Advent of Christ* (London: Marshall, Morgan, Scott, 1932), 18.

5. Dave MacPherson, *The Great Rapture Hoax* (Fletcher, N.C.: New Puritan Library, 1983), 47.

6. Ibid., 67.

7. Douglas J. Moo, "The Case for the Posttribulation Rapture Position," in *The Rapture: Pre-, Mid-, or Post-Tribulational?* ed. Gleason Archer, Paul Feinberg, and Douglas Moo (Grand Rapids: Zondervan, 1984), 172–74.

8. Ibid., 176–77.

9. Ibid., 208.

10. Thomas Ice, "Why the Doctrine of the Pretribulational Rapture Did Not Begin with Margaret MacDonald," *Bibliotheca Sacra* 147 (April–June 1990): 155–68.

11. Walvoord, *The Rapture Question,* 150–57.

12. J. Dwight Pentecost, *Things to Come* (Grand Rapids: Dunham, 1964), 166.

13. Dave MacPherson, *The Incredible Cover Up* (Plainfied, N.J.: Logos, 1975), 156.

14. Grant R. Jeffrey, *Apocalypse* (Toronto: Frontier Research, 1992), 313–22.

15. Grant R. Jeffrey, "Was the PreTrib Position of the Rapture Seen Before John Darby?" 2–3. A paper presented to the PretribStudy Group, 15 December 1993, Dallas, Texas.

16. Ibid., 3–9.

17. Timothy Demy and Thomas Ice, "The Rapture and Pseudo-Ephraem: An Early Medieval Citation," *Bibliotheca Sacra* 152 (July–September 1995): 1–13.

18. Walvoord, *The Rapture Question,* 159.

19. Robert Gundry, *The Church and the Tribulation* (Grand Rapids: Zondervan, 1973), 49.

20. William Arndt and F. W. Gingrich, *A Greek-English Lexicon of the New Testament*, 4th rev. ed. (Chicago: Univ. of Chicago Press, 1957), 233.

21. Renald Showers, *Maranatha: Our Lord, Come!* (Bellmawr, N.J.: Friends of Israel: 1995), 194.

22. Paul Feinberg, "The Case for the Pretribulation Rapture Position," in *The Rapture: Pre-, Mid-, or Post-Tribulational?* ed. Archer, Feinberg, and Moo, 224–25.

23. Showers, *Maranatha*, 206.

24. Walvoord, *The Rapture Question*, 22.

25. Moo, "The Case for the Posttribulation Rapture Position," 171.

26. Leon Wood, *The Bible and Future Events* (Grand Rapids: Zondervan, 1973), 83.

27. Moo, "The Case for the Posttribulation Rapture Position," in *The Rapture*, 208.

28. Feinberg, "The Case for the Pretribulation Rapture Position," in *The Rapture*, 225.

Chapter 14: Other Rapture Views

1. Charles Ryrie, *Basic Theology* (Wheaton, Ill.: Victor, 1988), 478.

2. John F. Walvoord, *The Rapture Question*, rev. ed. (Grand Rapids: Zondervan, 1979), 100.

3. Ibid., 112.

4. Zane Hodges, "The Rapture in 1 Thessalonians 5:1–11," in *Walvoord: A Tribute* (Chicago: Moody, 1982), 76.

5. Thomas R. Edgar, "An Exegesis of Rapture Passages," in *Issues in Dispensationalism*, ed. Wesley R. Willis, John R. Master, and Charles Ryrie (Chicago: Moody, 1994), 206.

6. Gerald Stanton, *Kept from the Hour* (London: Marshall, Morgan & Scott, 1964), 173–75.

7. Ryrie, *Basic Theology*, 497.

8. Gleason Archer, "Mid-Seventieth-Week Rapture," in *The Rapture: Pre-, Mid-, or Post-Tribulational?* ed. Gleason Archer, Paul Feinberg, and Douglas Moo (Grand Rapids: Zondervan, 1984), 139.

9. Ibid., 139–42.

10. Norman B. Harrison, *The End* (Minneapolis: Harrison Service, 1941), 119.

11. Ibid., 231–33.

12. Walvoord, *The Rapture Question*, 125.

13. Ryrie, *Basic Theology*, 499.

14. Walvoord, *The Rapture Question*, 126.

15. J. Dwight Pentecost, *Things to Come* (Grand Rapids: Dunham, 1964), 180; and Paul Feinberg, "The Case for the Pretribulation Rapture Position," in *The Rapture*, ed. Archer, Feinberg, and Moo, 151–58.

16. Walvoord, *The Rapture Question*, 119.

17. Renald Showers, *Maranatha: Our Lord, Come!* (Bellmawr, N.J.: Friends of Israel, 1995), 13. See also Paul Karleen, *The Pre-Wrath Rapture: Is It Biblical?* (Langhorne, Pa.: BF Press, 1991), 10.

18. Marvin Rosenthal, *The Pre-Wrath Rapture of the Church* (Nashville: Nelson, 1990), 60–61.

19. Robert Van Kampen, *The Sign* (Wheaton, Ill.: Crossway, 1992), 178.

20. Rosenthal, *The Pre-Wrath Rapture of the Church,* 105.

21. Van Kampen, *The Sign,* 177–90.

22. Ibid., 191–93.

23. Rosenthal, *The Pre-Wrath Rapture of the Church,* 109.

24. Van Kampen, *The Sign,* taken from the chart at the end of this book.

25. Ibid., 208–13.

26. Rosenthal, *The Pre-Wrath Rapture of the Church,* 60–61.

27. Ibid., 103.

28. Showers, *Maranatha,* 16.

29. J. Randall Price, "Old Testament Tribulation Terms: Terminology as an Indication of Timing," unpublished paper given at the Third Annual Conference of the Pre-Trib Study Group, December 1994, 2.

30. Ibid., 16–17.

31. Leon Wood, *The Bible and Future Events* (Grand Rapids: Zondervan, 1973), 54.

32. John A. Mclean, "A Critique of the Pre-Wrath Rapture Theory Proposed by Marvin Rosenthal," an unpublished paper, 1991.

33. Showers, *Maranatha,* 42.

34. Rosenthal, *The Pre-Wrath Rapture of the Church,* 109.

35. Karleen, *The Pre-Wrath Rapture,* 44.

36. H. E. Dana and Julius R. Mantey, *A Manual Grammar of the Greek New Testament* (New York: Macmillan, 1927), 193.

37. John C. Whitcomb, *Daniel* (Chicago: Moody, 1985), 165.

38. Showers, *Maranatha,* 48.

39. Greg A. King, "The Day of the Lord in Zephaniah," *Bibliotheca Sacra* 152 (January–March 1995): 16.

40. Showers, *Maranatha,* 33–34.

41. Ibid., 36.

42. D. Edmond Hiebert, *1 & 2 Thessalonians,* rev. ed. (Chicago: Moody, 1992), 227.

43. Ibid., 228.

44. Rosenthal, *The Pre-Wrath Rapture of the Church,* 142; and Van Kampen, *The Sign,* 180.

45. Karleen, *The Pre-Wrath Rapture,* 46–47.

46. Van Kampen, *The Sign,* 483.

47. Karleen, *The Pre-Wrath Rapture,* 55.

48. Feinberg, "The Case for the Pretribulation Rapture Position," 60.

49. Robert L. Thomas, *Revelation 1–7: An Exegetical Commentary* (Chicago: Moody, 1992), 457–58.

50. Price, "Old Testament Tribulation Terms," 13.

51. Rosenthal, *The Pre-Wrath Rapture of the Church,* 173.

52. Price, "Old Testament Tribulation Terms," 14–15.

53. Showers, *Maranatha,* 62.

Chapter 15: Daniel's Seventieth Week (The Tribulation Period)

1. Arnold Fruchtenbaum, *The Footsteps of the Messiah* (Tustin, Calif.: Ariel Ministries, 1993), 121–22.

2. Arnold Fruchtenbaum, *Israelology: The Missing Link in Systematic Theology* (Tustin, Calif.: Ariel Ministries, 1992), 768.

3. Robert L. Thomas, *Revelation 1–7: An Exegetical Commentary* (Chicago: Moody, 1992), 476.

4. J. Dwight Pentecost, *Things to Come* (Grand Rapids: Dunham, 1964), 212.

5. Leon Wood, *The Bible and Future Events* (Grand Rapids: Zondervan, 1973), 131–32.

6. Gary Cohen, *Understanding Revelation* (Collingswood, N.J.: Christian Beacon, 1968), 142.

7. Pentecost, *Things to Come,* 340.

8. Ibid., 342–58.

9. Fruchtenbaum, *Israelology,* 783.

Chapter 16: The Coming Judgments and Resurrections

1. Charles Hodge, *Systematic Theology,* vol. 1 (Grand Rapids: Eerdmans, 1995), 416.

2. Joe Wall, *Going for the Gold* (Chicago: Moody, 1991), 112.

3. Paul Benware, *The Believers Payday* (Chattanooga: AMG Publishers, 2002).

4. Charles C. Ryrie, *Basic Theology* (Wheaton, Ill.: Victor, 1988), 514.

5. Leon Wood, *The Bible and Future Events* (Grand Rapids: Zondervan, 1973), 153.

6. Ryrie, *Basic Theology,* 515.

Chapter 17: The Future Kingdom of God

1. John F. Walvoord, *The Millennial Kingdom* (Findlay, Ohio: Dunham, 1963), 300–301.

2. Randall Price, *The Coming Last Days Temple* (Eugene, Ore.: Harvest House, 1999), 556–57.

3. J. Dwight Pentecost, *Things to Come* (Grand Rapids: Dunham, 1964), 492–93.

4. Alva McClain, *The Greatness of the Kingdom* (Chicago: Moody, 1959), 513.

5. W. E. Vine, *Expository Dictionary of New Testament Words* (London: Oliphants, 1963), 3:109–10.

6. Arnold Fruchtenbaum, *The Footsteps of the Messiah* (Tustin, Calif.: Ariel Ministries, 1993), 367.

7. Pentecost, *Things to Come,* 580.

Chapter 18: Death and the Intermediate State

1. Louis Berkhof, *Systematic Theology* (London: Banner of Truth, 1949), 668.

2. Anthony Hoekema, *The Four Major Cults* (Grand Rapids: Eerdmans, 1970), 357.

3. Charles Hodge, *Commentary of the Second Epistle to the Corinthians* (Grand Rapids: Eerdmans, n.d.), 110.

4. Walter Martin, *The Truth About Seventh-Day Adventism* (Grand Rapids: Zondervan, 1960), 122.

5. Loraine Boettner, *Immortality* (Philadelphia: Presbyterian and Reformed, 1970), 101.

6. Ibid., 112.

7. Hoekema, *The Four Major Cults,* 358.

Chapter 19: The Final Eternal State

1. Larry Dixon, *The Other Side of the Good News* (Wheaton, Ill.: Victor, 1992), 145.

2. Louis Berkhof, *Systematic Theology* (London: Banner of Truth, 1949), 736.

3. Dixon, *The Other Side of the Good News,* 181.

4. Loraine Boettner, *Immortality* (Philadelphia: Presbyterian and Reformed, 1969), 118.

5. Berkhof, *Systematic Theology,* 691.

6. Joachim Jeremias, "Gehenna," in *Theological Dictionary of the New Testament,* ed. G. Kittel, trans. G. Bromily, vol. 1 (Grand Rapids: Eerdmans, 1965), 658.

7. Charles Hodge, quoted by Loraine Boettner, *Immortality,* 121.

8. D. Edmond Hiebert, *1 & 2 Thessalonians,* rev. ed. (Chicago: Moody, 1992), 229.

9. Dixon, *The Other Side of the Good News,* 69–96. Also see Alan W. Gomes, "Evangelicals and the Annihilation of Hell, Parts One and Two," *Christian Research Journal* (Spring & Summer 1991); Ramesh P. Richard, *The Population of Heaven* (Chicago: Moody, 1994).

Appendices

1. Gary Cohen, *Understanding Revelation* (Chicago: Moody, 1978), 51–52.

2. J. Dwight Pentecost, *Things to Come* (Grand Rapids: Dunham, 1964), 151–55.

3. Cohen, *Understanding Revelation,* 83–125.

4. Merrill C. Tenney, *Interpreting Revelation* (Grand Rapids: Eerdmans, 1957), 74–80.

5. Pentecost, *Things to Come,* 275–80.

6. Charles C. Ryrie, *Revelation* (Chicago: Moody, 1968), 44–48.

INDEX OF Subjects AND Persons

NOTE: Page numbers in italics indicates charts

INDEX OF

Scripture

NOTE: Page numbers in italics indicates charts